DR. RUTH'S
ENCYCLOPEDIA OF SEX

My beloved has gone down to his garden,
To the beds of spices,
To browse in the garden
And to pick lilies.
I am my beloved's
And my beloved is mine;
He browses among the lilies.

Song of Songs 6:2–3

DR. RUTH'S
ENCYCLOPEDIA OF SEX

Ruth K. Westheimer

CONTINUUM • NEW YORK

For Dr. Floyd Haar (1942-1993)
Medical editor of this volume
with deepest gratitude

The Continuum Publishing Company
370 Lexington Avenue
New York, NY 10017

The Jerusalem Publishing House
39 Tchernichovski Street, P.O.B 7147
Jerusalem 91071

Library of Congress Catalog-in-Publication Data

Dr. Ruth's encyclopedia of sex / Ruth Westheimer, editor.
     p.   cm.
    Includes index.
    ISBN 0-8264-0625-4
    1. Sex—Dictionaries.   I. Westheimer, Ruth K. (Ruth Karola),
1928– . II. Title: Doctor Ruth's encyclopedia of sex.
HQ9.D7 1994
306.7'03—dc 20   94-5009
                                              CIP

Printed in Germany

10 9 8 7 6 5 4 3 2 1

INTRODUCTION

I went from being Dr. Ruth Westheimer, college professor, to being "Dr. Ruth," radio host, in 1980. In the intervening years I have been working hard to help eliminate what I call "sexual illiteracy," in other words the lack of knowledge about human sexual functioning. Great strides have been made since those early days, by me and by others, but I also know from the questions I am asked on TV and radio, in letters and at personal appearances, that there are still many people out there, particularly young people, who need to know more. That's why I am so pleased to be able to offer this encyclopedia, which contains almost every answer about human sexuality that anyone may be seeking.

My reason for wanting to teach human sexuality stems from my experience working in the Planned Parenthood organization in the early 1970s. Young people came and asked all sorts of questions, and I discovered that I didn't always know enough to give them the proper answers. In order to learn more, I enrolled in the Human Sexuality program at New York Hospital-Cornell University Medical School, which was led by one of our foremost experts on the subject, Dr. Helen Singer Kaplan, and I became a psychosexual therapist. Now I've had my own private practice for nearly two decades and I've taught human sexuality at several colleges. I still read all of the literature about human sexuality that I can find and I have written ten books on the subject. You would think that by this time I would certainly know the subject backward and forward. But let me tell you a little secret—even I learned some things in the preparation of this encyclopedia.

You see, that is the wonderful thing about the encyclopedic format. I did not write every article. For certain topics I asked the top experts in their fields to share their knowledge with a wide audience. With a subject as complex as human sexuality, there is always something new being discovered, and these authorities provided me with the latest information. And since I am not a medical doctor, I had the articles on the medical aspects of human sexuality written by noted physicians. I've been told that on some topics there is more information in this encyclopedia than you'd find in a medical textbook.

Though I'm the one who asked the doctors, lawyers, and other professionals to contribute to this encyclopedia, it was not written for the benefit of an expert like me, but rather for the general reader, and especially for high school and college students. You, the reader, will already know some of the facts that are in this book, but quite possibly much in this encyclopedia will be new to you. I am particularly eager to clarify some of the myths about human sexuality that many young people have. But even for adults, sometimes one thinks one knows about something, like exactly how a baby is conceived, but it's wonderful to have the correct knowledge at one's fingertips to either make sure that you have the story straight, to refresh your memory, or to teach you a part of the process that you never really understood. And with an encyclopedia you don't have to go through the entire book to find what you want to know, but can turn to the precise article that will answer your particular questions.

While it was certainly a thrill to hold in my hands my first published book, *Dr. Ruth's Guide to Good Sex,* the publication of this encyclopedia pleases me more than that of any of my other books. These pages contain all of the information that anyone might ever need about human sexuality, and the more of these books that I can get into people's hands, either through public or school libraries, or as part of your family's personal library, the greater the impact I will have made in combatting sexual illiteracy. As a sex therapist I have an obligation to help people avoid the dangerous effects of sexual illiteracy, for example unwantedpregnancies and the spread of sexually transmitted diseases, especially that dreadful killer, AIDS.

Human sexuality gives us all great pleasure, but as our bodies develop into adulthood and we begin to share and enjoy the gratifications of sex, we must also learn the responsibilities that come with these new powers. With the enjoyment of sex come some very serious potential consequences, because the human sexual response was not given to us only for pleasure: it is ultimately tied to human reproduction. Bringing a new life into the world is not something that should be done lightly, and the more information a person has about the process, the better the decisions he or she will ultimately make.

So, as you read and use this encyclopedia, I hope that it teaches you a lot, and if what you learn also stimulates you in other ways, that will please me too.

R. K. W.

CONTRIBUTORS

JUNG H. AHN, M.D.,
Clinical Associate Professor of Rehabilitation
Medicine, New York University School of Medicine,
Howard A. Rusk Institute of Rehabilitation, New
York City, New York.

CARMEN ALONSO, M.D.,
Physician-in-Charge, Consultation Liaison Services,
Schneider Children's Hospital, New Hyde Park, New
York.

SALLY ANDREWS, M.D.,
Senior Assistant Resident in Obstetrics and
Gynecology, University of Texas Medical Branch at
Galveston, Galveston, Texas.

SHAWN ARMSTRONG, M.D.,
Chief Resident in Obstetrics and Gynecology,
University of Texas Medical Branch at Galveston,
Galveston, Texas.

H. RANDOLPH BAILEY, M.D.,
Clinical Professor of Surgery, Chief of the Division
of Colon and Rectal Surgery, University of Texas
Health Science Center, Houston, Texas.

INBAR BEN-SHACHAR, M.D.,
Gynecologist, Department of Obstetrics and
Gynecology, Hadassah University Hospital, Ein
Karem, Jerusalem, Israel.

NANCY YAFFE BRATTER,
Research Assistant, University of Southern California
Law Center, Los Angeles, California.

AMNON BRZEZINSKI, M.D.,
Gynecologist, Department of Obstetrics and
Gynecology, Hadassah University Hospital, Ein
Karem, Jerusalem, Israel.

YEHEZKEL G. CAINE, M.D.,
General Surgeon and Mohel (Ritual circumciser) for
adults and children, Hadassah University Hospital,
Ein Karem, Jerusalem, Israel.

RALPH DEUTCHMAN, M.D.,
Senior Attending Physician, Stamford Hospital,
Stamford, Connecticut.

LYNDA S. DOLL, Ph.D.,
Chief, Social and Behavioral Studies Section,
Division of HIV/AIDS, National Center for
Infectious Diseases, Centers for Disease Control,
Atlanta, Georgia.

FRANÇOIS EID, M.D.,
Assistant Professor of Surgery-Urology, The New
York Hospital-Cornell Medical Center, New York
City, New York.

URIEL ELCHALAL, M.D.,
Gynecologist, Department of Obstetrics and
Gynecology, Hadassah University Hospital, Ein
Karem, Jerusalem, Israel.

CYNTHIA FUCHS EPSTEIN, Ph.D.,
Distinguished Professor of Sociology, The Graduate
Center of the City University of New York, New
York City, New York.

LYNDALL FELIZ ERB, Ph.D.,
Andrologist, Lovelace at Journal Center,
Albuquerque, New Mexico.

SUSAN R. ESTRICH, Esq.,
Robert Kingsley Professor of Law and Political
Science at the University of Southern California Law
Center, Los Angeles, California.

PAMELA F. FARRINGTON, M.D.,
Department of Obstetrics and Gynecology, The
University of Utah Medical Center, Salt Lake City,
Utah.

MICHAEL FREEDMAN, M.D.,
The Diane and Arthur Belfer Professor of Geriatric
Medicine; Director, Division of Geriatrics, New York
University/Bellevue Hospital Center, New York City,
New York.

HARVEY GARDNER,
New York City, New York.

DAN GILON, M.D.,
Cardiologist, Cardiology and Internal Medicine,
Department of Cardiology, Hadassah University
Hospital, Ein Karem, Jerusalem, Israel.

MARC GOLDSTEIN, M.D.,
Director, The Male Reproduction and Microsurgical
Unit, James Buchanan Brady Foundation Division of
Urology, The New York Hospital-Cornell Medical
Center, New York City, New York.

AMOS GRÜNEBAUM, M.D.,
Director of Maternal-Fetal Medicine, St. Luke's
Roosevelt Hospital Center; Assistant Professor,
Columbia University College of Physicians and
Surgeons, New York City, New York.

FLOYD L. HAAR, M.D.,
Clinical Professor of Surgery (Neurosurgery),
University of Texas Medical School at Houston;
President, Pituitary Society of Houston, Houston,
Texas.

STEPHANIE ANN HEDSTROM, M.D.,
Senior Assistant Resident in Obstetrics and
Gynecology, University of Texas Medical Branch at
Galveston, Galveston, Texas.

BEREL HELD, M.D.,
Professor and Director, Division of Gynecology,
University of Texas Medical Branch at Galveston,
Galveston, Texas.

STANTON C. HONIG, M.D.,
Staff Urologist, Yale New Haven Hospital, New
Haven, Connecticut.

G. MARC JACKSON, M.D.,
Assistant Professor, Department of Obstetrics and
Gynecology, The University of Utah Medical School,
Salt Lake City, Utah.

VIVIAN KAFANTARIS, M.D.,
Director, Adolescent Depression Service, Schneider
Children's Hospital, New Hyde Park, New York.

HAROLD S. KOPLEWICZ, M.D.,
Associate Professor of Psychiatry, Albert Einstein
College of Medicine; Chief, Division of Child and
Adolescent Psychiatry, Schneider Children's Hospital
and Hillside Hospital of Long Island Jewish Medical
Center, New York.

NEIL K. KOUCHENOUR, M.D.,
Professor, Department of Obstetrics and Gynecology,
University of Utah Medical School, Salt Lake City,
Utah.

ALFRED N. KRAUSS, M.D.,
Department of Pediatrics, The New York Hospital-
Cornell Medical Center, New York City, New York.

LESLIE KURIAN, M.D.,
Attending Psychiatrist, Northern Westchester
Hospital Center, Mount Kisco, New York.

MARSHA J. LEBBY, Writer,
New York City, New York.

WILLIAM LEDGER, M.D.,
Professor and Chairman, Department of Obstetrics
and Gynecology, The New York Hospital-Cornell
Medical Center, New York City, New York.

JOANNE S. LEHU, Esq., Writer,
Attorney, New York City, New York.

PIERRE A. LEHU, M.B.A.,
New York City, New York.

ABY LEWIN, M.D.,
In Vitro Fertilization Unit, Hadassah University
Hospital, Ein Karem, Jerusalem, Israel.

LOUIS LIEBERMAN, Ph.D.,
Professor Emeritus of Sociology, John Jay College of
Criminal Justice, City University of New York, New
York City, New York.

LARRY I. LIPSHULTZ, M.D.,
Professor of Urology, Scott Department of Urology,
Baylor College of Medicine, Houston, Texas.

BERNARD LUSKIN, Ph.D.,
Los Angeles, California.

DOUGLAS J. MARCHANT, M.D.,
Professor of Obstetrics, Gynecology, and Surgery,
Tufts University School of Medicine, Boston,
Massachusetts.

J. MARK McBATH., M.D., F.A.C.S.,
Surgeon, Cancer Liaison Physician, Park Plaza
Hospital, Houston, Texas.

DROR MEIROW, M.D.,
Gynecologist, Department of Obstetrics and
Gynecology, Hadassah University Hospital, Ein
Karem, Jerusalem, Israel.

KEVIN G. NICKELL, M.D.,
Scott Department of Urology, Baylor College of
Medicine, Houston, Texas.

DAVID G. OSTROW, M.D., Ph.D.,
Professor of Psychiatry; Faculty Associate, Institute
for Social Research; Director, Midwest AIDS
Biobehavioral Research Center, Ann Arbor,
Michigan.

ELLEN PARRILL, M.D.,
Senior Resident in Obstetrics and Gynecology,
University of Texas Medical Branch at Galveston,
Galveston, Texas.

PETER L. PERINE, M.D.,
Professor of Tropical Public Health and Medicine,
Uniformed Services University of the Health
Sciences; Clinical Professor of Epidemiology,
University of Washington, Bethesda, Maryland.

AMY E. POLLACK, M.D., M.P.H.,
Medical Director, Association for Voluntary Surgical
Contraception, New York City, New York.

MARTIN M. QUIGLEY, M.D.,
The Fertility Institute of Northwest Florida, Gulf
Breeze Hospital, Gulf Breeze, Florida.

NATHAN ROJANSKY, M.D.,
Gynecologist, Department of Obstetrics and
Gynecology, Hadassah University Hospital, Ein
Karem, Jerusalem, Israel.

BILLIE LAMB ROWLES, M.D.,
Assistant Professor, Department of Obstetrics and
Gynecology, The University of Utah Medical Center,
Salt Lake City, Utah.

IRA M. SACKER, M.D.,
Chief, Division of Adolescent Medicine; Medical
Director, Pediatric Resource Center/Pediatric Care
Center, Brookdale Hospital Medical Center, New
York City, New York.

GEORGE H. SANDS, M.D.,
Assistant Professor of Neurology, Albert Einstein
College of Medicine; Director of Neurology, Queens
Hospital Center, New York City, New York.

ALBERT J. SBORDONE, Ph.D.,
Practicing Psychologist; Member Psychology Department, AIDS Unit, Terence Cardinal Cooke Health Care Center, New York City, New York.

JOSEPH G. SCHENKER, M.D., Ph.D.,
Professor and Chairman of the Department of Obstetrics and Gynecology, Hadassah University Hospital, Ein Karem, Jerusalem, Israel.

PETER N. SCHLEGEL, M.D.,
Assistant Professor of Urology, James Buchanan Brady Foundation, Department of Surgery, The New York Hospital-Cornell Medical Center, New York City, New York.

HILARY SCHLINGER,
Practicing Midwife in New York State; Member, Board of Directors, The Midwives Alliance of North America, LaFayette, New York.

JAMES R. SCOTT, M.D.,
Professor and Chairman, Department of Obstetrics and Gynecology, University of Utah Medical School, Salt Lake City, Utah.

MARLON S. SELIGER, M.D.,
Assistant Professor of Neurology, Albert Einstein College of Medicine; Department of Neurology, Long Island College Hospital, New York City, New York.

SHMUEL C. SHAPIRA, M.D.,
Attending Obstetrician, Anesthesia and Pain Relief Unit, Hadassah University Hospital, Ein Karem, Jerusalem, Israel.

CHARLES SILVERSTEIN, Ph.D.,
Practicing Psychologist, Founder, *Journal of Homosexuality,* Identity House and Institute for Human Identity Counseling Centers, New York City, New York.

MARY SOLANTO, Ph.D.,
Senior Psychologist, Eating Disorder Center, Schneider Children's Hospital, New Hyde Park, New York.

ARTHUR I. SNYDER, M.D.,
Assistant Clinical Professor of Medicine, Columbia University College of Physicians and Surgeons; Attending Physician, Columbia Presbyterian Medical Center, New York City, New York.

ROBERT STEWART, M.A. (Oxon.),
Editor of *The Diary of Sigmund Freud.*

WILLIAM J. SWEENEY III, M.D.,
Professor of Obstetrics and Gynecology, Cornell University Medical College; Attending Gynecologist, The New York Hospital-Cornell Medical Center, New York City, New York.

LOUISE TYRER, M.D. F.A.C.O.G.,
Medical Director, The Association of Reproductive Health Professionals, Washington, D.C.

SARAH WEDDINGTON, Esq.,
Attorney, Austin, Texas.

GERSON WEISS, M.D.,
Professor and Chairman, Department of Obstetrics and Gynecology, University of Medicine and Dentistry of New Jersey, New Jersey Medical School, Newark, New Jersey.

RUTH K. WESTHEIMER, Ed.D.,
Adjunct Associate Professor, New York University; Fellow, New York Academy of Medicine, New York City, New York.

ROBERT W. WOOD, M.D.,
Director, AIDS Control Program, Seattle/King County Department of Public Health; Associate Professor of Medicine and Health Services, University of Washington, Seattle, Washington.

BEN YAGODA, M.A.,
Assistant Professor of English, University of Delaware, Newark, Delaware.

ACKNOWLEDGMENTS

I am especially grateful to my general editor Howard Epstein, to Yosh Gafni, Rachel Gilon, and Danny Wool of The Jerusalem Publishing House, Jerusalem, to Werner Mark Linz and Cynthia Eller of Continuum Publishing Group, New York, and of course, as always, to my family, many friends, and the loyal Pierre Lehu.

R.K.W

The publishers also acknowledge and wish to express special thanks to Ms. Gale Adina Dorembus R.N. B.S.N. N.N.P., Clinical Instructor N.I.C.U., Shaare Zedek Medical Center, Jerusalem, and to Eli Tzfoni M.D., Dermatologist, Jerusalem.

Illustrations: Amnon Brzezinski M.D. pp. 216, 217; Carnegie Embryological Collection, University of California, Davis p. 99; Liz Green and The Jerusalem Publishing House pp. 13, 14, 22, 45, 47, 48 (bottom), 77, 81, 111 (bottom), 179, 180, 201, 202, 255; Dror Meirow M.D. of the Department of Obstetrics and Gynecology, Hadassah University Hospital, Ein Karem, Jerusalem pp. 43, 44, 48 (upper right), 59, 80 (bottom right), 90, 98, 100, 127, 165, 171, 177, 186, 210; The Jerusalem Publishing House pp. 37, 49, 58, 80 (bottom right), 103, 111 (upper right), 196, 209; Aby Lewin M.D. p. 153; Marina Lifshitz pp. 23, 49, 61, 62, 73, 83, 102, 104, 203, 260; Lennart Nilsson p. 80 (top); Reprinted by permission of The Putnam Publishing Group from *The Potent Male* by Irwin Goldstein and Larry Rothstein. Copyright (c) 1990 by Price Stern Sloan, Inc. and Irwin Goldstein and Larry Rothstein, pp. 148, 149; Baruch Rimon p. 170; Nathan Rojansky M.D. pp. 33, 34, 35.

The Publishers have attempted to observe the legal requirements with respect to copyright. However, in view of the large number of illustrations included in this volume, the Publishers wish to apologize in advance for any involuntary omission or error and invite persons or bodies concerned to write to the Publishers.

Typesetting and Pagination: Devorah Sowalsky Meyer–The Jerusalem Publishing House
Graphics: Margalit Bassan, Techiya Rosenthal
Secretary: Shoshana Lewis
Films: Printone Media Ltd., Jerusalem
Printing and Binding: Mohndruck Graphische Betriebe GmbH, Gütersloh, Germany

A

ABORTION   The termination of pregnancy by loss or destruction of the fetus before it has reached viability. An abortion may be spontaneous or induced. It may further be divided into early or late abortion depending on whether it has occurred before or after the twelfth week of pregnancy (in the first or second trimester). In-

Abortion techniques: (Top) In the suction method a tube is inserted into the uterus. The embryo is then sucked into a bottle. (Bottom) In the saline injection method a thick needle is inserted into the uterus. Amniotic fluid is removed and replaced with a saline solution, killing the fetus. Uterine contractions then expel the fetus.

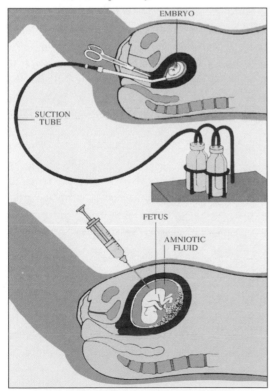

duced abortion is associated with many legal and ethical considerations.

Spontaneous Abortion. This occurs when the embryo ceases to develop and when there is complete or incomplete expulsion of the products of conception—the fetus and placenta—prior to twenty weeks of gestation. As many as one-third of early pregnancies are spontaneously aborted. Most occur before they can be clinically diagnosed and may only be detected by a very sensitive pregnancy test that has only recently become available. After some delay, the woman may experience bleeding and cramping similar to that of a normal menstrual period. With more advanced gestation, however, heavier cramping and blood loss occur as the fetus and placenta are expelled.

In early, first trimester abortions, chromosomal aberrations have been found in about two-thirds of aborted fetuses. Infection, hormonal and environmental factors, and maternal diseases have also been suggested as possible causes. In late, second trimester abortions, where a normally-developed fetus is usually found, anatomic changes of the uterus and uterine cervix can frequently be demonstrated (see also MISCARRIAGE).

ABORTION PROCEDURES.

Induced Abortion. A procedure intended to interrupt a pregnancy by evacuation of the nonviable fetus and placenta from the uterine cavity. Although discouraged by most major religions, induced abortion has been practiced in every culture since ancient times. To date, abortion is legalized and regulated in most developed countries, where it is available on request. Restrictive policies are found in Ireland, fundamentalist Islamic countries, sub-Saharan Africa, and Latin America. Illegal abortions performed in

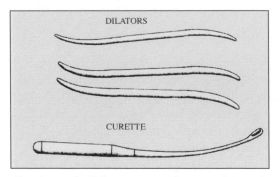

Abortion tools: Dilators are used to open the cervix during an abortion. The curette is used to scrape the embryo and placenta from the uterine wall.

these countries are associated with high morbidity and maternal mortality rates. Although legally induced abortion has been made available in most states of the United States since the early 1970s, abortion remains a hotly debated issue on religious and ethical grounds. In the 1980s, it was estimated that about 40 to 60 million induced abortions occurred yearly around the world; about 33 million of these were legal.

Most induced abortions are performed in the first trimester—during the first twelve weeks of gestation. The technique most commonly used for first trimester pregnancy termination utilizes a procedure called vacuum aspiration, or vacuum curettage. After dilation of the uterine cervix, a hollow plastic tube with a hole near its end is inserted into the uterus. The embryo or fetus and placenta are drawn into the tube through vacuum pressure. This procedure is usually completed by cleaning the remains of conception with a curette—a metal rod with a sharp ring at its end. This instrument has been used for centuries to empty the uterine cavity following spontaneous and induced abortions.

Second Trimester (Late) Abortions. This involves several more complicated procedures, since dilation and curettage are too hazardous after twelve weeks of pregnancy. The most complicated procedure is the injection of a saline solution or hormones (prostaglandins) into the amniotic sac. To avoid an inadvertent injection of these substances outside the amniotic cavity, the procedure is usually performed after the sixteenth week of gestation. Prostaglandins, which

cause efficient uterine contractions, may also be administered by inserting a catheter into the uterus, but not penetrating the amniotic sac. Regular uterine contractions develop promptly and the fetus and placenta are usually expelled after several hours in a process that is very similar to normal delivery. Following abortion, the remains of conception are removed with a sharp curette. When expulsion of the fetus fails or is delayed, a high dose of oxytocin—a hormone that causes labor contractions—may be added intravenously; when this method fails, hysterotomy—surgical incision of the uterus to remove the fetus—may be performed.

In France in the 1980s, an abortion-inducing drug called RU–486 was developed. This antiprogesterone was proved 85 percent effective in inducing abortion during the first six weeks of pregnancy, especially when used with prostaglandins. The drug is taken orally and is so far licensed only in France, China, and England.

Studies of long-term health consequences of abortion indicate that risks of future spontaneous abortion, preterm delivery, and low birth weight are not significantly increased if the procedure is performed early in the first trimester by vacuum aspiration. Late abortion and, especially, illegal termination at any pregnancy stage are associated with a significantly higher rate of morbidity, long-term aftereffects, and maternal mortality.

Religious, Ethical, and Moral Issues. In 1973 the United States Supreme Court ruled in the case known as *Roe v. Wade* that a woman's right to privacy also gave her the right to have an abortion. Her decision could not be overruled by the state or any of its authorities, or by any other individual. With that court ruling, the legality of abortion in the United States was established. The question of abortion, however, is still steeped in intense controversy. Moral and ethical issues continue to infuse it, with emotionalism on the subject often running high.

On a personal level, women contemplating abortion often confront feelings of sadness and loss. A woman may also feel guilt or social shame. However, the overwhelming psychological response from women is relief. For most women, abortion is not approached casually. If a woman decides to terminate her pregnancy, there are usually very compelling reasons.

Perhaps the greatest controversy surrounding abortion stems from the fact that opinions differ widely on the point at which life truly begins. For those in our society who strongly believe that life begins at the instant of conception, abortion may be regarded as murder. This is the position of the Catholic Church as well as of other religious groups, both Jewish and Christian. But this position is not universally held by Christian or Jewish theologians. The Bible itself does not directly address the issue and is open to a variety of interpretations. In principle, most Christians and Jews accept a woman's right to have an abortion; they view the end of the second trimester of pregnancy as the point at which a fetus becomes a distinct and individual human being, or life, capable of sustaining itself outside the womb.

The "pro-life" movement, which believes abortion is immoral and should not be legal, is often in collision with the "pro-choice" movement, which believes abortion must be legal because women have the absolute right to make decisions about their own bodies. The question remains: since there is no standard scientific definition of when life begins, should the religious or moral beliefs of one segment of society, however strongly held, be imposed on the society as a whole?

The moral and ethical issues surrounding abortion are very complex. For example, there is controversy about the rights of fathers; debate about parental consent in the case of pregnant minors seeking abortions; and questions, even in the minds of those who are in principle opposed to abortion, about cases of rape, incest, and the mother's health.

While some American states have laws requiring parental consent for a minor's abortion, the issue of parental consent remains ethically problematic. While most people agree that, ideally, a girl who is under eighteen years of age and finds herself pregnant should discuss the matter with her parents, in the real world teens who do not talk to their parents usually have very good reasons for not doing so. Most pregnant teenagers

turn to one or both parents for guidance. However, many parents are not the right people to turn to for support and advice when it comes to an issue as explosive as abortion. If a teenager's pregnancy is the result of incest, this is almost certainly the case. Some teens know they face punishment for becoming pregnant. While it is argued that minors are not legally, morally, or ethically equipped to make a decision about abortion without parental consent, others believe that every woman's privacy in this matter is a right and needs to be respected whatever her age.

Since *Roe v. Wade* ruled that only a woman has the right to resolve how her pregnancy will end, a number of lovers, fiancés, and husbands have sought injunctions to delay or prevent abortion. At issue is more than the law. It is the mother's versus the father's moral biological right to make the decision. Most people agree that, ideally, the decision to terminate a pregnancy should be shared by both partners. But what if there is no marriage or true relationship? What if a married woman is abused and fears her husband's response? A woman's ethical obligation to involve her partner in her decision is clearly not a cut-and-dried matter (see also BIRTH CONTROL).

The Legal Aspects. The legal aspects of abortion in the United States changed dramatically in 1973. However, they have continued to be an issue in the courts and in legislative bodies—both in the United States Congress and the legislatures of many of the fifty states—since that time. Key issues today include government funding of abortion, restrictions on when abortions are permitted, attempts by abortion opponents to block access to abortion clinics, and the methods of abortion that are considered to be legal.

Prior to 1973, abortion was seldom legally available in the United States. Most states, like Texas, had laws which prohibited abortion except to save the life of the woman, a phrase which was not well defined as to its meaning. Sixteen or so states allowed abortion for the additional reasons of rape or incest and sometimes to protect the woman's health, but often restrictions (such as review of the case by a hospital committee) were imposed. The legislatures in a few states (such as California and New York) had passed laws generally allowing abortion.

Before 1973 women in states in which abortion was illegal traveled to those few states where it was legal if they had the money. Other women traveled out of the country, a few to Europe and many to Mexico, where abortion was illegal but readily available. Some visited places operating illegally in the United States—places which were often ill-equipped medically and therefore dangerous. A few women attempted self-abortion. Women who had undergone abortions in such conditions were often seen in hospital emergency rooms; a few died and others suffered long-lasting medical conditions.

On 22 January 1973, the Supreme Court, in the case called *Roe v. Wade*, declared the Texas anti-abortion law—and by implication the laws of other states—to be unconstitutional. The court's opinion declared that women's constitutional right of privacy applied to the decision of whether to continue or terminate a pregnancy.

The springboard for the decision was a 1965 Supreme Court case, *Griswold v. Connecticut*. That case struck down a Connecticut statute that prohibited the use of contraceptives, a law equally applicable to married and unmarried persons. The Court relied on the right of privacy for individuals to decide whether "to bear a child."

The abortion case was filed by an unmarried pregnant woman, Jane Roe (not her real name), against the District Attorney of Dallas County, Henry Wade, an official responsible for enforcing the Texas law. The Supreme Court voted 7 to 2 in her favor. The opinion was written by Justice Harry A. Blackmun; the dissenting Justices were now-Chief Justice William Rehnquist and now-retired Justice Byron White.

The legal status of abortion issues must be examined in light of the makeup of the Supreme Court, the body that sets the constitutionality of laws for the nation and each of the states. That decision turned out to be the beginning of a stream of litigation on abortion issues that has continued until the present time. The zigzag pattern of abortion litigation after *Roe v. Wade* followed the changing membership of the Supreme Court. In fact, by 1992, forces seeking to overturn or reverse *Roe v. Wade* were only one Supreme Court vote away from victory.

As Justices retired during the 1980s, they were replaced by appointments made first by President Ronald Reagan and then by President George Bush. Each of those presidents opposed the *Roe v. Wade* decision and the legality of abortion. In late 1991, four Justices seemed to be ready to overturn *Roe*: Rehnquist, White, Justice Antonin Scalia, and Justice Clarence Thomas. Other Justices named to the court in the 1980s, such as Justice Sandra Day O'Connor, Justice Donald Souter and Justice Anthony Kennedy, were prepared to modify *Roe* by allowing states to restrict abortion. Only two Justices remained who fully supported *Roe v. Wade*: Justice Blackmun and Justice John Paul Stevens.

When Bill Clinton was sworn in as president in January 1993, the chances of *Roe* being overturned were almost extinguished. Clinton was elected on a platform of supporting the principles of *Roe*, and his first appointee, Justice Ruth Bader Ginsburg, who replaced Justice White, also supported those principles.

While it is now clear that abortion will continue to be legal, at least for the foreseeable future, there are many issues about accessibility to the procedure. One issue is whether the poorest American women, those eligible for medical services paid for by Medicaid, will have access to abortion. Congress, which controls federal funding for those services, in general has refused to pay for abortion services except in very narrow cases of medical necessity. It has, however, sometimes permitted payment for women who are pregnant as a result of rape or incest. Although state governments could choose to provide abortion services to those women, less than a quarter of the states have chosen to do so.

Another issue is whether the youngest women will have access to abortion. A variety of state laws have been passed requiring minors either to have the consent of both parents or of one parent, or to notify them. Supreme Court cases have basically ruled that the states may require involvement of parents, but only if there is a "judicial by-pass" in the legislation. "Judicial by-pass" refers to a speedy procedure that can be used by a minor if mature and if she has an important reason why she feels she cannot talk to her parents. In such cases she can ask a judge for permission to proceed with an abortion.

Another issue is whether the health care proposals now being debated in the United States will include abortion services. The legislation introduced in Congress in 1993 at the urging of the Clinton administration to provide payment for medical services for all Americans would allow coverage of abortion services; members of Congress opposed to abortion have vowed to prevent inclusion of those services when the bill eventually is considered.

Some abortion opponents have used tactics that include picketing clinics and the homes of abortion providers; seeking to prevent entry into abortion clinics by physical blockades; attempting to close clinics via arson or throwing acid and other substances; and in two cases, shooting doctors providing abortion services. One doctor was wounded, and another, Dr. David Gunn, was killed in 1992 by an anti-abortion assailants.

Legal responses have included city ordinances limiting picketing of private homes and setting parameters for picketing activities at businesses (including abortion clinics), and state laws making related offenses felonies instead of misdemeanors. In 1994 it is likely that Congress will pass the Freedom of Access to Clinical Entrances Act, which will make some of the tactics of abortion opponents federal crimes and will result in greater enforcement of those laws.

Other opponents have sought to enact laws to make it more difficult for women to have an abortion. These laws as passed by various states contain a variety of provisions. In general, however, the Supreme Court has approved state laws which: require a waiting period of twenty-four hours between the time a woman goes to or contacts an abortion clinic and the time she has a procedure; require that a woman be told prescribed information about fetal development and alternatives to abortion; and require record-keeping and state oversight of the medical aspects of abortion.

One method of abortion which has not been available in the United States is a drug called RU–486, used for non-surgical abortions in France and a few other European countries for several years. During the 1980s, the Food and Drug Administration refused to allow the drug into the United States and the Supreme Court refused to intervene when a pregnant American woman sought to bring RU–486 in from England for her own use. The Clinton administration has caused the FDA to look more favorably on the drug, and a process is now underway that could well result in RU-486 being available in the United States in the 1990s.

Another issue has been the time frame in pregnancy when states could severely restrict availability of abortion. *Roe v. Wade* said that the states could do so at "viability," the point at which the fetus could live on its own. Medical science has moved back the time of viability from usually twenty-eight weeks in 1973 to usually twenty-four weeks in 1993; some say that point could be pushed back still further. Justice O'Connor commented that "*Roe v. Wade* is on a collision course with medical science."

Others contend that 96 percent of all women who have abortions have them in the first twelve weeks of pregnancy and that the few who have later abortions do so for compelling reasons. Some states allow abortion after viability to save the life of the woman or for severe, irreversible fetal deformity. Medical science has also improved the medical tools for diagnosing fetal deformity at an earlier stage of pregnancy.

Also at issue is the involvement of the man who helped create a pregnancy. For example, the Supreme Court considered a Pennsylvania statute requiring that a woman notify her husband of her intent to have an abortion (except in cases where he was not the father, in cases where he could not be located, and in situations involving domestic violence). It ruled that provision unconstitutional. Boyfriends have sought to prevent abortions, but a legal right to do so has not been established.

In general, if the fertilized ovum or fetus is in a woman's body, she is considered the person legally entitled to make the decision about it. However, in one case in which a pregnant wife was in a coma and therefore could not legally give consent to surgery, her husband was legally recognized to have the right to consent to abortion. In another case involving a fertilized ovum produced by IN VITRO FERTILIZATION, where the ovum was preserved in a frozen solution, the prior husband, whose sperm were involved, was recognized as having a right equal to that of his former wife who wanted to give the ovum to a childless couple, and the transfer was blocked.

Abortion Laws in Other Countries. The laws governing abortion differ in other countries like a patchwork quilt. Abortion is illegal in Mexico and most Latin American countries (abortion is also the leading cause of death of women of childbearing age in many of those countries). Abortion laws are in flux in countries that have recently left the Soviet political sphere. Previously, in Eastern Europe contraception was less available and abortion laws were generally liberal. However, in 1993 Poland passed stricter abortion laws; doctors who violate the law are subject to up to two years in prison. The former East Germany had liberal abortion laws, but in 1993 unified Germany's Constitutional Court overturned a year-old abortion law and replaced it with tougher restrictions. Conversely, in Romania abortion was illegal under the former dictator Nicolae Ceascescu, but is now permitted. As of March 1993, three pregnancies are reported aborted for each live birth. In Ireland, abortion remains illegal but voters in late 1992 overwhelmingly approved permitting women to travel abroad for abortions and obtain information about how to do so, both of which were once illegal.

Abortion is generally legal and available in Western Europe; the same is true in Asia and the Far East, particularly for countries struggling with fast-expanding populations. In Japan, there are half a million legal abortions annually. In India, abortion is legal until the twentieth week of pregnancy. China has encouraged— some believe it has coerced—couples to have only one child. The birth rate for girls has decreased and some suggest a correlation with the modern availability of ultrasound scanners and their use to identify the sex of fetuses. It is reported that many female fetuses are aborted in China solely because of their sex.

ABSTINENCE   There are many different reasons why people today desist from sexual activity for various lengths of time. Some, raised in religions with stern attitudes toward sexual behavior, avoid partnered sex until marriage; officially, they also avoid masturbation, a claim that is generally not disputed by therapists. In fact, some girls have no recollection of gratifying themselves sexually and the same is probably true for some boys.

It is possible to remain a virgin until one's honeymoon, and with good information, love, and patience, a couple can make their honeymoon a very happy experience, fulfilling all their expectations. Abstinence before marriage, even long past adolescence, does not harm a person's sexual health or capacity, either physically or emotionally. Moreover, when a young person is certain that premarital chastity is right and good, commanded and encouraged, it can be a confidence-builder for the lovemaking to come.

A debate now rages over whether to provide school children and youths with CONDOMS or with strong advice to stay   away from partnered sex. Perhaps the best solution is a combination of the two. A well-educated youth can carry a condom without feeling forced to use it. Certainly, youngsters should be told that abstinence is not harmful, and that it is the one sure way to avoid pregnancy and SEXUALLY TRANSMITTED DISEASES: this is absolutely true and should be clarified to every teenager. Nevertheless, a condom can be kept in a pocket or schoolbag, in case of some rare contingency.

While no SEX EDUCATION program or moral instruction will eradicate teenage pregnancy or sex-related disease among adolescents, better sex education, by definition, will produce better results than the ineffectual programs currently provided by so many schools. No sex education program should omit moral teachings or instruction in prudence until a good and stable relationship is possible (see also BIRTH CONTROL, CHASTITY; NATURAL FAMILY PLANNING).

ACNE   A dermatological (skin) disorder that develops to some extent in almost 90 percent of male and female adolescents. Since adolescents can feel anxious about their appearance under the best of circumstances, many boys and girls consider acne to be a serious social and personal matter. It is important that adults treat the adolescent with sensitivity and concern, recognizing that acne is generally at its worst from sixteen to nineteen years of age in males and from fourteen to sixteen years of age in females.

While males and females may continue to experience acne-related conditions for ten to fifteen years after the first episode, the frequency, duration, and intensity of episodes generally decline in the late teens and early twenties. Males tend to have more serious acne for a shorter period of time, and females tend to have less serious acne for a longer period of time.

Biological Causes of Pimples, Acne, and Other Skin Eruptions. Pilosebaceous units, or oil glands, are a type of sebaceous gland with extremely tiny hairs. As might be expected, they are most heavily distributed in the face, neck, and upper body, where most acne occurs.

These glands are present throughout childhood and early adolescence, but they do not become the sites for acne until the adrenal and gonadal glands (testicles and ovaries) begin to secrete androgenic (male) hormones. Sebaceous glands are sensitive to stimulation from the androgen-sensitive hair follicles, and secrete lipids (fats) to lubricate the skin. They also secrete sebum, an oily semi-liquid substance, which is then excreted through a duct to a pore, or opening, in the skin. When there is an increase in the production of

Acne can often leave disfiguring scars

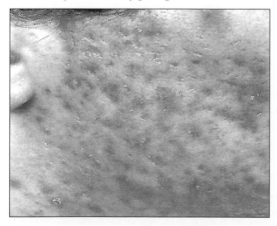

androgenic hormones, the content and volume of the sebum secreted through the pore can change.

This change can facilitate the entry and colonization of the sebum by bacteria. Additional yeast development can result in thickening and inflammation of the skin, and the development of blackheads. Blackheads develop because the sebum turns black when it comes into contact with oxygen. Whiteheads develop when the sebum gets trapped below the thin surface of the skin and rises to form light-colored bumps.

Blackheads and whiteheads can become infected if the sebum stays blocked in the pore. This happens because sebum accumulates there, causing pressure and irritation, a process more likely to result in pimples—bumps on the skin that develop when bacteria and yeast grow in whiteheads or blackheads. Bacteria can also cause pus to develop, and this, in turn, causes pressure and inflammation around the pimple. The infected area can be tender and painful to touch, but the nature and severity of these episodes vary widely from person to person.

It is true that acne can "run in families," but it is equally true that each person is unique and has his or her own genetic make-up. A parent's experience with acne will not necessarily help an adolescent predict whether he or she will share a similar experience.

Acne can develop in a variety of ways, and it affects males and females somewhat differently. Since it does affect almost 90 percent of both males and females, it is usually considered a normal sign of adolescence.

Treatment of Acne. Most adolescents use over-the-counter medications to treat episodes of acne. It is extremely important that the directions be followed precisely and a doctor be consulted when necessary. Many adolescents use medications recommended by friends, but these may not be appropriate for their skin type, skin color, or specific acne condition.

In general it is recommended that the adolescent wash his or her face with a mild soap no more than three times a day. Excessive face-washing can cause skin inflammation. The individual should wash with hot water to open the pores, and rinse with colder water to close the pores. It also helps to use only a clean pillow-case and sheets and to avoid skin moisturizers that clog the pores and contribute to the outbreak of acne. Washing oily hair and keeping hair off the face is another method of preventing some outbreaks of acne.

There is absolutely no evidence that any particular foods cause people to experience acne, so diet management to control it is generally unsuccessful. Some individuals may have specific skin reactions to particular foods, but there is no relationship between acne episodes and the intake of chocolate, soda, oily, or other foods.

There is strong evidence that the usual emotional stresses associated with adolescence can affect outbreaks of acne. This explains why people apparently develop pimples, blackheads, and whiteheads before important examinations, social events, and in other exciting or anxiety-producing times. Stress-management techniques, including biofeedback and relaxation, can be helpful to adolescents who experience stress-related episodes of acne.

Other treatments are available through physicians who specialize in dermatology. Dermatologists may prescribe antibiotics or topical ointments with retinoic acid.

The overwhelming majority of adolescents experience some degree of acne at some time. Parents can make these episodes easier for their sons and daughters by treating adolescent concerns with respect and understanding. If it seems that the acne is unusually troublesome or may result in scarring that threatens to disfigure the young man or woman, medical care should be sought.

ACQUAINTANCE RAPE see CONSENT: DATE RAPE; RAPE LAWS.

ACQUIRED IMMUNE DEFICIENCY SYNDROME see AIDS.

ADOLESCENCE For many young men and women in our society, adolescence is a turbulent period, not only because of bodily changes but also because of the need to move toward breaking dependence on their parents. These years are usually from about the age of eleven, or the onset of puberty, until about the age of sixteen or seventeen. Although adolescents may be physically capable of procreation, they suffer from the inconsistencies that exist between nature and the realities of the social world. Despite adolescents' physical and emotional development during these years, the long period of socialization and education required in modern societies to adequately perform adult roles has extended the concept of childhood to later years; boys and girls many years past the age of puberty are still regarded as "children" without, for example, the competence to vote or buy a glass of beer.

This contradiction between the adolescent's self-awareness as a viable sexual being supported by peer group values, and society's rules and expectations, is the source of much frustration and anger between parents and adolescents. Although it is not feasible for an adolescent to support a family, strong and frequent bodily urges experienced during this period impel most young men and women to violate parental, religious, and social rules on sexual conduct. Adolescents are often forced to choose between what their parents tell them (usually abstinence) and what their bodies, friends, movies, rock and rap groups, and others are saying ("listen to your body"). Adolescent boys usually receive support from other boys (through jokes, bull sessions, and reading and watching pornography together) about the legitimacy of their sexual feelings and how to act on them through intercourse or masturbation. Adolescent girls, however, are given many contradictory messages, even during childhood. For example, little girls see other little girls flirting with little boys in television commercials and shows; they see and hear an emphasis on sexy hair, makeup, and clothes—some of it geared to the very young preadolescent—all with the contradictory message: "Be sexy, but don't have sex." Despite the erotic stimulation directed at adolescents of both sexes, our society's gender-based norms are much more controlling of girls.

Adolescents may also be confused by changes in touching after a certain age. While among some groups in our society, fathers may continue to greet their sons by hugging them, many fathers begin shaking their adolescent sons' hands rather than hugging and kissing them as they did in earlier years. This is often justified by the belief that "real men don't hug." Similarly, in many families the affection once expressed by a father for his daughter through touching, hugging, and kissing may suddenly turn into a more distant and formal relationship as she begins to mature. Generally, a father does not shake his daughter's hand; rather, he may, with some awkwardness, avoid physical closeness without his daughter understanding why. That this growing distance may support the incest taboo is very likely, but in many families it seems to apply more to daughters than sons and is a source of confusion for many adolescents.

The growing sexual feelings of the adolescent girl and her bodily urges, as well as menstrual periods, all tell her that she is becoming a woman and can enjoy her body. However, in Western culture, parents and society want adolescent girls to contain their sexuality until marriage or, at least, until adulthood. On the other hand, this is sharply contradicted by the popular media, in particular in a growing number of television shows that describe a world very different from parents' teachings. Furthermore, rental videos provide contemporary adolescents with a private viewing of the most vivid depictions of every aspect of sexuality and sensual pleasure, often involving sexuality among teenagers. Attempts to prevent or discourage intercourse between teenagers in recent years have not proven successful, and in many communities teenagers are denied effective sex education. For many, this has led to personally unfortunate situations and a serious social problem: according to the Alan Guttmacher Institute, one million teenage American girls become pregnant each year, a figure that has remained constant for the last seven years. In 1984 alone there were 470,000 babies born to young women between the ages of fifteen and nineteen, while an additional ten thousand babies were born to girls aged fourteen or younger.

It appears that our society does not do enough to prepare a young person psychologically for responsible adulthood. Older rules emphasizing "No Sex!" until adulthood appear to be inconsistent with modern values, and there is little preparation or training of the young for responsible nonmarital sex or parenting for high school students. We seem to be inept as a society in preventing children from having children and inept at teaching them responsible parenthood when they do. Adolescence is a learning stage between childhood and adult independence, but there is a scarcity of programming and education to facilitate this growth. At present, adolescence seems to be defined as a holding pattern, one in which teenagers are supposed to avoid adult behavior while learning skills needed to enter career training or college. There seem to be few opportunities during this crucial period for a person to learn the human relations skills of adulthood. To some it appears that we want to shelter our children during adolescence and then let them out on their own after age eighteen without adequate preparation. The consequences of this poor social planning are undoubtedly an important element in perpetuating such social problems as poverty and dysfunctional families (see also CHILDREN'S SEXUALITY; FLIRTATION; SEX EDUCATION; TEENAGERS AND SEX).

Biological Aspects. Adolescence is the stage of human physical and psychosomatic development that generally takes place during the second decade of life. Throughout adolescence, chemical substances called HORMONES increase in level and activity, causing males and females to experience a wide variety of physical and emotional changes. Hormones can also influence how males and females think and feel about themselves, their friends, and their family members.

Although these changes of adolescence help each boy and girl mature, the particular order and extent of change vary from one person to another, even within the same family and gender. Two adolescents of the same age and gender may be in completely different stages of development. One may be more or less physically mature than another, so it is comforting to keep in mind that people follow their own biological clocks of development, yet still reach the same basic milestones on the way to adulthood.

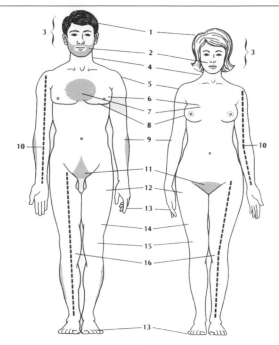

BIOLOGICAL ASPECTS OF ADOLESCENCE

The Male: On average, taller and heavier than the female.   1. Head hair: may fall out with age. 2. Facial hair: grows throughout adult life. 3. Features: more pronounced, face longer, head (front to back) longer. 4. Neck: thicker, longer, larynx one-third larger. 5. Shoulders: broader, squarer. 6. Chest: larger in every dimension. 7. Body hair: more evident, especially on chest and arms. 8. Breasts: rudimentary in size. 9. Muscles: bigger, more obvious. 10. Arms: longer, thicker, "carrying angle" straight. 11. Pubic hair: growing up to a point, forming a triangle. 12. Hips: narrower. 13. Hands and feet: larger; fingers and toes: stronger and blunter. 14. Thighs: more cylindrical, with bulge of muscles. 15. Legs: longer, bulging calves. 16. Angle of thigh and leg: as with "carrying angle" of arm, forming straight line from the thigh to the ankle.
The Female: On average, shorter and lighter than the male.   1. Head hair: more lasting. 2. Facial hair: very faint, usually noticeable only in later years. 3. Features: more delicate, face rounder, head smaller, rounder (from top). 4. Neck: shorter, more rounded, larynx smaller. 5. Shoulders: more rounded, sloping. 6. Chest: smaller, narrower. 7. Body hair: very light and faint. 8. Breasts: prominent, also well-developed nipples with large surrounding rings. 9. Muscles: largely hidden under layers of fat. 10. Arms: "carrying angle" bent. 11. Pubic hair: forming straight line across at top. 12. Hips: wider, more rounded. 13. Hands and feet: smaller, narrower. 14. Thighs: wider at top and shorter in length. 15. Legs: shorter with smoother contours. 16. Angle of thigh and leg: as with "carrying angle" of arm, slightly bent, forming an angle at the knee.

Adolescents are often curious and concerned about the biological changes they experience. Many of the feelings, physical developments, and behavior patterns that accompany adolescence begin with physical changes that happen internally, making it physically possible for young people to create a child. This stage of development is referred to as puberty.

Adolescent males and females generally develop the physical capacity to create children long before they are completely ready to accept the adult responsibility of parenting children, just as infants can physically walk before they are sufficiently mature to judge the safety of certain situations. Since puberty can begin late in the first decade of life (but generally starts in the second decade), it is clear that males and females become capable of reproduction early in the developmental process. This section helps clarify the physical changes a person can expect during puberty, and explains the biological and chemical reasons for these changes.

Physical Changes in Puberty. The first physical signs of puberty include increased height and weight, growth of underarm and pubic hair, increased perspiration, increased hair on arms and legs, and elevated levels of oil in the skin (one of the causes of acne). In females, breasts become larger and more pronounced, nipples stand out more clearly, and the genitals get a little darker and fleshier. In males, the pitch of the voice lowers, facial hair might appear, shoulders get broader, the muscles in the arms, legs, and torso become more defined, and the penis and testicles grow and become a little darker.

How Puberty Progresses for Males and Females. The changes that make puberty possible actually begin before birth. Hormones begin to interact in the fetus. These hormones stimulate

fetal sexual development and result in the forming of primary sexual characteristics. In males the primary sex characteristics are the penis, scrotum, and testicles. In females they are the vagina, uterus, and ovaries. Once these characteristics are developed, the central nervous system of the fetus, infant, and child keeps these hormones at a very low level of activity for approximately the first decade of life.

At some point during the second decade of a person's life, the brain begins to stimulate enough production of these hormones to start the changes of puberty. It is not known exactly what causes the brain to produce these hormones.

The human body has many different kinds of hormones, which are chemicals produced by endocrine glands. Endocrine glands are clusters of cells that are physically attached to certain blood vessels. This connection to the blood vessels makes it easy for endocrine glands to release the hormones through the blood vessels and into the blood stream, so the blood can carry the hormones throughout the body.

During this particular period of growth, a person is getting taller at a faster rate than he or she has experienced since the age of two. Females tend to have their growth spurts earlier than

The development of the adolescent's sex organs

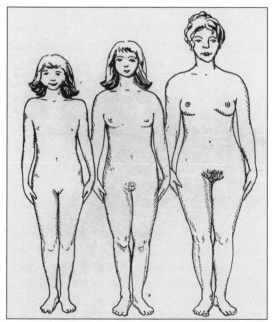
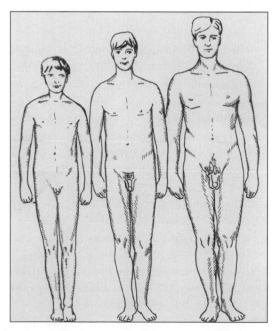

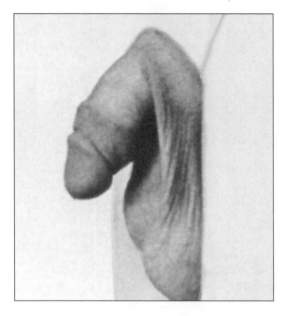 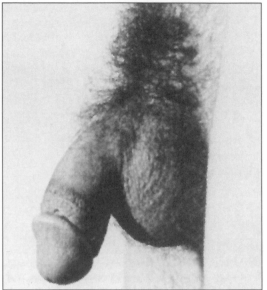

The male sex organs before and after puberty

males, and males tend to keep growing for a longer period of time than females.

Since the entire body has to grow, growth may occur in one part of the skeleton first, and in another part later. Feet and hands might grow bigger, then arms and legs, and then the rest of the torso and even the head and neck. Final height for boys is generally reached by the later teens or early twenties. Final height for girls is generally reached during the middle of adolescence, although variations are normal.

While the skeleton is growing taller and heavier, the shape of the body continues to change. Girls' pelvic bones get wider, so they can eventually accommodate a fetus during a pregnancy. This growth gives girls greater lower body width and strength. Males' shoulders start to get wider, giving them more upper body strength.

Dramatic changes occur in the skeletal structure of the face. Compare the round face of a child with the longer, more defined lower jaw, hairline, and cheekbones of an adult. It becomes easy to see how many changes females and males must undergo before they achieve their final facial structure. In addition to dramatic skeletal changes, females and males increase their muscle mass and weight growth, all as a result of the release of hormones.

At or near the second decade of life, the part of the brain identified as the hypothalamus matures enough to produce hormones called "releasing factors." These releasing factors trigger another part of the brain, called the pituitary gland, to begin releasing higher levels of two hormones: follicle stimulating hormone (FSH) and luteinizing hormone (LH). FSH and LH make ova (eggs) develop in the female ovaries and make sperm develop in the male testes.

Stimulated by the FSH and LH, the ovaries and testes begin to release high levels of sex hormones. The most important female sex hormones are ESTROGEN and PROGESTERONE. The most important male sex hormone is called TESTOSTERONE. Ovaries do produce low levels of testosterone, and testes do produce low levels of estrogen and progesterone.

While these sex hormones help the ovaries and testes continue to mature throughout adolescence, they are also responsible for the more visible changes described above, called "secondary sex characteristics." Estrogen and progesterone stimulate the growth of breasts in girls. Testosterone stimulates the growth of beards in boys, and pubic and underarm hair in boys and girls. Testosterone also stimulates oil glands to be more productive in males and females. In males

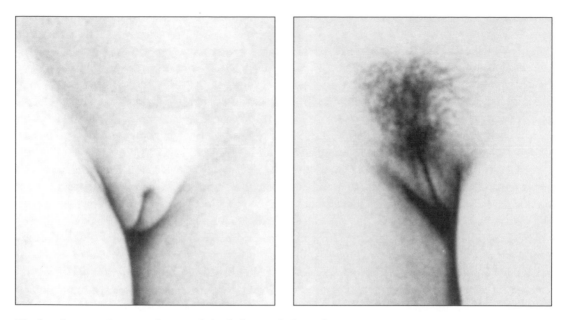

The female secondary sex characteristics before and after puberty

testosterone stimulates the larynx to grow, causing the voice to change and become deeper.

Physical Sexual Maturity in Males. Male sexual maturity takes place in a series of stages. First, the testicles and then the penis become larger. As spermarche, or the capacity for sperm emission, begins to take place, erection and ejaculation can happen in response to sexual excitement. Spontaneous nocturnal ejaculation of semen can happen during sleep. Some amount of sperm will be present in the fluid that is ejaculated. Frequent, spontaneous erections and nocturnal emissions, normal during this stage of development, will diminish over time.

Physical Sexual Maturity in Females. As noted earlier, the first indication of puberty in females can be breast development. This is followed by growth and development of the external sex organs: the vagina, labia, and clitoris. Inside, the uterus and ovaries grow.

At some point during this process, menarche, or the first episode of MENSTRUATION, takes place. However, it may take another one to one and a half years for regular menses and ovulation, the production of eggs, to occur. Menarche is stimulated by FSH, estrogen, and progesterone.

Psycho-social Aspects of Adolescence. Because it is the crucial phase of human development immediately preceding adulthood, adolescence and the turbulence that often marks it have been studied intensively by psychologists and other social scientists. Although not all adolescents experience the "storm and stress" stereotypical of the period, psychologists have suggested that such difficulties are the result of stress placed on the individual adolescent by five development tasks required during this phase of life:

- The physical and physiological changes of puberty;
- Separation from parents or caretakers;
- The development of intimate friendships and a social network;
- The development of vocational and educational goals;
- Initial clarification of sexual orientation.

These developmental milestones can be accomplished by some individuals with relatively few problems but others find these tasks overwhelming or even impossible. In addition to all of these developmental tasks, the adolescent also must adopt a set of ethics and values to guide his or her future life.

Adolescence has been divided into early, middle, and late stages. Early adolescence ranges from approximately eleven and a half to thirteen years of age, middle adolescence from fourteen to seventeen, and late adolescence from eighteen to twenty-two.

Early adolescents are very focused on physical changes and adjustments to puberty. Their peer group becomes stronger at this time, and the development of friendships is very important. The cognitive style of the early adolescent is still childlike in that concrete thinking predominates. For example, if asked the meaning of the proverb "people in glass houses shouldn't throw stones," an early adolescent will give a literal interpretation such as, "if they throw stones, the walls will break."

Middle adolescence is the stage at which separation from one's parents and caretakers is the main developmental task. The beginning of vocational or educational planning as well as experimentation with sexual interaction occur during this stage. Abstract thinking begins to develop during this period but remnants of the concrete thinking of early adolescence remain.

Late adolescence is the stage at which further separation from parents is accomplished and increased intimacy in friendships is developed. Solidification of vocational and educational goals occurs during this stage. Abstract and complex thinking become the predominant cognitive styles for late adolescents.

Adjusting to the physical changes of puberty requires the adolescent to accept his or her rapidly changing appearance, and this is often problematic. As they grow, hormonal changes occur, causing menstruation in girls, nocturnal emissions in boys, and frequently ACNE and bodily odors.

While the peer group increases in importance as adolescence progresses, studies have shown that parents still remain the most influential force in adolescents' lives. It is common, however, for adolescents to feel the need to "test the waters" and prove their independence from their parents. Adopting philosophical or political ideas that may be repugnant to parents is not uncommon, as demonstrated in choice of music, clothes, and even peers. The healthy adolescent is able to maintain a position, point of view, or opinion that is different from his or her parents without experiencing guilt or anxiety. At the same time, the healthy adolescent can hold a point of view that concurs with a parent's without feeling coerced, dependent, or weak because of this agreement. The third developmental task of adolescence—developing intimate friendships and a social network—changes as adolescence progresses. During the early phase the peer group may be exclusionary or inclusionary—a type of clique quite common with girls and boys. Individuals may form friendships with specific others in the group or there can be a group relationship. During middle adolescence individual friendships may become more important, while the peer group continues to exert significant influence. Sexual interest may begin during this time, and the importance of a girlfriend or boyfriend, who is both a romantic figure as well as a best friend, often develops. During late adolescence friendships become more intimate and more intense, with an increased ability to openly share differences of opinion or thought. These differences are tolerated, permitting the relationship to endure.

The fourth developmental task of formulating vocational and educational goals is different during each of the three phases, and it is only during late adolescence, with the development of complex thinking, that adolescents are able to formulate new ideas and concepts. They begin to solidify career goals and develop paths to reach them.

Finally, clarification of sexual identification seems to be complete for most, though not all individuals by the end of puberty and adolescence, although it may occur later (there are some exceptions: see for example, LESBIAN SEXUAL TECHNIQUES.) During the early stage of adolescence, with the onset of puberty, intense crushes and infatuations frequently occur among members of the same sex. Sometimes these are mistaken by the adolescent to mean that he or she may be homosexual. The developmental task of solidifying sexual orientation is quite complex. A recent survey found that 25.9 percent of twelve-year-olds were "unsure" of their sexual orientation. During middle or late adolescence, when sexual activity becomes more common, sexual orientation becomes solidified. It is not only the individual's sexual behavior that is of importance but his or her fantasy life as well. The individual who has not had sexual intercourse by the age of twenty-one but who masturbates exclusively to heterosexual or homosexual fantasies and images has a solidified sexual orientation, in spite of their virginity. By age eighteen only 5 percent of adolescents describe themselves as still unsure of their sexual orientation.

Adolescence, thought it may feel chaotic at times with all the bodily, social, cognitive, and family changes involved, can be an exciting period. It must be emphasized that there is tremendous variability among adolescents in the ease with which all these developmental tasks are accomplished and in the number of years it may take to complete them (see also EATING DISORDERS AND SEXUAL DYSFUNCTION).

A Summary for Adolescent Females, Males, and Their Families. It is normal for adolescents to become concerned with their sexual development. Adolescents may be preoccupied with the variety of ways in which people within their own age group appear to develop. It is normal for the growing adolescent to experience anxiety about whether or not their own development is or is not "right" for their age and what the emotional changes gripping them mean. Adolescents require adults to listen to their questions, and respond with sensitivity, patience, and much emotional guidance. Adolescents deserve support so they can appreciate and celebrate their differences and similarities as they experience the miraculous process of sexual maturation.

ADULTERY In common usage, adultery means sexual intercourse by a married person with someone other that their spouse. From biblical times to the present, societies in the Western Jewish and Christian tradition have meted out punishments—often severe—for adultery, while permitting certain sexual relationships outside marriage. Of all the possible variations of sexual behaviors, adultery is the only one specifically forbidden by the Ten Commandments: "Thou shalt not commit adultery." Another commandment, "Thou shalt not covet thy neighbor's wife," bans similar behavior indirectly.

According to biblical Jewish laws (based on Leviticus 20:10), adultery was defined specifically as sexual intercourse by a married woman with a man other than her husband. It did not apply to a married man who had sex with an unmarried woman. Thus, according to the law, a woman would not be granted a divorce if she caught her husband having sex with an unmarried woman. A similar DOUBLE STANDARD existed in both ancient Greece and Rome and until the rise of early Christianity, when for the first time the prohibitions and punishments specified in laws concerning adultery were applied equally to men and to women. However, according to psychologist Bernard Murstein, the purpose of the change was not to right a wrong for women but to discourage sexual activity by both men and women. Though in principle the laws punished men and women equally, in practice church officials generally urged the wife to forgive her adulterous husband but heaped much condemnation on the adulterous wife, who was often rejected and expelled from the household by her husband.

After centuries of alternating leniency and repressiveness, by the seventeenth century moral standards had again become somewhat lenient and, as the English legal commentator William Blackstone noted, "the temporal courts, therefore, take no cognizance of the crime of adultery, otherwise than as a private injury." The historian Vern Bullough commented:

In surveying the history of royalty from the last part of the seventeenth until almost the end of the eighteenth century, it seems as if kings had to have mistresses as part of the mark of their royalty. Henry IV ... was alleged to have had some fifty-six mistresses. The most famous [mistress of Louis XIV] was ... Madame de Pompadour.

Among the European nobility of the time, there was no secret that many women kept two "husbands," one in name and one for sex.

In the American colonies the influence of the Puritans was increasingly felt. Although PURITANISM arose as a Calvinist reaction to what was seen as Roman Catholic tendencies in the Church of England, in America the Puritans (who did not belong to any particular religion) included Presbyterians, Congregationalists, Quakers, and others dissatisfied with traditional religious groups and hierarchies. They were very concerned with sexual morality and found adultery particularly repugnant. Some Puritan colonies passed statutes making it punishable by death, as were RAPE, sodomy, and bestiality. Gradually, these rarely-invoked penalties were replaced by lesser ones involving public humiliation: flogging, branding, and the infamous "scarlet letter A," and later by a fine or short imprisonment. In spite of these stated prohibitions, many famous Americans, including Benjamin Franklin, Thomas Jefferson, and Alexander Hamilton, had known adulterous liaisons without much damage to their reputations.

During the nineteenth and twentieth centuries, punishment for adultery seemed less and less a social concern; by the middle of the twentieth century it was reduced to become merely one of the grounds for divorce. The frequency of adultery in the United States appeared to be growing and its extent was made apparent when the Kinsey data became available. *The Kinsey Report on Male Sexual Behavior*, published in 1948, said:

On the basis of these active data, and allowing for the cover-up that has been involved, it is probably safe to suggest that about half of all the married males have intercourse with women other than their wives, at some time while they are married.

The Kinsey Report on Female Sexual Behavior, published in 1953, said that by the age of forty, 26 percent of married women interviewed had reported sexual encounters involving intercourse with men other than their husbands.

It seems that we have always had adultery, and observers of the American sexual scene today might say that if we were to repeat Kinsey's study, we would probably find adultery rates to be much higher. For many persons, what had formerly been secretive and marriage-threatening—cheating on one's spouse—has apparently become permissible. How did this attitudinal and value change come about?

The issue of adultery and the moral principles related to it are both simple and complex. From religious and moral perspectives it is always a violation of marital vows, sacraments, or contractual agreements. It is complex because changes have taken place in our modern world that psychologically tempt or pull marital partners away from each other. Observers of contemporary sexual behavior have noted some of the factors placing strain on marital fidelity:

- Little fear of unwanted pregnancy due to effective contraceptives;
- A longer, more vigorous, and healthy life;
- An increasing number of wives entering the labor force, creating a greater number of sexual opportunities in the workplace;
- Greater amounts of leisure time for both husbands and wives;
- A cultural obsession with and emphasis on youthful activities;
- A decline of religious control and influence;
- A decline in social controls with a concomitant rise of peer influence;
- Increased urbanization, resulting in a decrease in general community scrutiny;
- A general questioning of traditional religious sexual values, even by the religiously observant;
- Increasing affluence for all classes, giving them more to spend on "fun";
- More media-generated sexual stimulation;
- A cultural emphasis upon personal satisfaction and happiness.

Some of these factors that contribute to adultery appear to be desirable; others represent increasing strains and dangers to stable marital and family life. However, it is unlikely that Western culture will revert to the mores of a simpler time (see also PROMISCUITY).

AFFAIRS   Love affairs—erotic or loving relationships between men and women outside marriage or between people of the same sex—have been the centerpieces of literature, from the Old Testament and Ovid's *Art of Love* to the modern Western novel. Affairs are distinctive and diverse, both in literature and in life, but they do share some qualities.

It is usually assumed that an affair will involve a sexual relationship (though some may, in time, reveal their essentially platonic nature), but affairs are more than sexual encounters. They are usually rooted in love or erotic attachments of some strength and duration. If an affair lasts only a few weeks or a month it might be called a "brief" affair, but a weekend dalliance should be called a "fling," not an affair, and a "one-night stand" is just that.

Men and women involved in affairs may be married or not, have long term lovers or be totally free. A pair involved in an affair may promise and practice sexual exclusivity or they may be involved with others at the same time. Often, lengthy affairs will culminate in the couple choosing to live together, but at this point their relationship implies continuity and exclusivity, neither necessarily part of an affair. Yet the author George Sand lived with the composer Frederic Chopin for many years, and their stormy relationship has never been defined as anything other than an affair. In rare instances affairs will lead to marriage.

Today the word affair implies that either partner has the freedom to end it, even if one partner or the other dominates the relationship. In previous generations, however, the women in such relationships tended to have less power than the men and often were defined as mistresses, common-law wives, or even as "gold-diggers," all terms with somewhat pejorative connotations that implied dependence on the men in the relationships. (Of course, sometimes women had the upper hand, especially if they had financial independence or other opportunities.) Yet while men may have had more power, they also suffered social disapproval as seducers and exploiters. If either or both partners were married (at a time when, for religious or social reasons, it was not always possible to divorce), there often was the additional social scorn reserved for adulterers.

It is probably true that many of today's affairs fit the old categories, but many do not. Increasing equality between men and women has had a strong impact on their social and sexual relationships (see also DOUBLE STANDARD; LOVE).

AFTERGLOW Just as a sexual episode does not begin with ORGASM—it requires foreplay leading up to climax—it should not end abruptly. The period following orgasm is called the afterglow. Both partners feel relaxed and it is a good time to share feelings and emotions.

Some men develop the habit of falling asleep immediately after they experience their orgasm, particularly at night. While there is nothing wrong with this from time to time, they must realize that in doing so they are leaving the woman by herself, and without afterplay many women feel that they are not needed or appreciated. Their lovers would be better advised to remain awake and share in the afterglow; the positive effects of doing so will remain and will often carry over into the next sexual episode as well.

The afterglow period can include many activities, from hugging or caressing (which some people find even more pleasurable and intimate than sex itself), to conversation (listening is a very important aspect of this), and sometimes can lead to a new sexual episode. But the afterglow activities do not have to be limited to the bedroom and can also extend to taking a shower together, sharing a snack, or going for a stroll. The important thing is that whatever it is, it should by done together, even if it is falling asleep.

AGE OF CONSENT see CONSENT.

AGING AND SEX There are two common misconceptions about sexual activity later in life: both are harmful to individuals who accept them. The first—that sexual interest and activity dwindles and eventually ceases between ages sixty and seventy—should seem a misconception to any energetic person of this age, but coming amid other messages of decline, it can subtly undermine an individual's determination to continue a full life. It can be even more destructive for those living with younger persons, who find their elders' sexual interests inappropriate, or for older people living in group or nursing facilities, where their personal freedoms and activities are restricted. The second misconception—that all older people can have active and wonderful sex lives well into their nineties—is harmful because it does not account for the physical, social, and psychological problems that increase with age and impair sexual activity in many older people.

What then is the reality of sex for most people as they age? Most people with an available partner and reasonable personal health can continue to enjoy sexual relations into their eighties and some even into their nineties. The single most important factor in their sex lives is then the availability of sex partners, within or outside marriage. About half of men over sixty-five are married, but differences in men's and women's life expectancies means that many married women will face eight to ten years of widowhood. The reluctance of many older widows and widowers to begin new marriages has led them to cohabit or begin affairs the way the young do today. But the demographic facts are cruel for women: the ratio of men to women aged sixty-five to seventy-four is 100 to 131; for those aged seventy-five to eighty-four it drops to 100 to 180; and for those over age eighty-five it falls to 100 men to 229 women.

The question of general health also has an impact on older people's sexual lives. Although it is estimated that 80 percent of Americans over the age of sixty-five have some chronic health problem that can potentially affect their sexual functioning, most report having a healthy interest in sex. The single most sexually debilitating disease in older people is diabetes; half of diabetics experience some loss of sexual function—erection difficulties among the men and loss of vaginal responsiveness among the women. In addition, many medications taken by the elderly, especially tranquilizers, sedatives, antidepressants, and blood pressure medicines, have a negative effect on sex functions (indeed, for older men, the use of medications is the most frequent cause of difficulty with erections). Finally, the "substances" that some individuals may have used when they were younger—among them tobacco, excessive alcohol or caffeine, marijuana, and cocaine—can be extremely debilitating to sexual activity as one ages.

Aging does bring changes in sexual activity—as it does to other life activities—even when men and women are in good health and have sexual partners. By the age of fifty most men will notice a slower and reduced intensity of sexual responses. According to a survey known as the Duke Longitudinal Study, 75 percent of all men interviewed in their sixties still engaged in sexual intercourse at least monthly. Over the age of eighty, 50 percent of men were interested in sex, but only 10 percent still engaged in sexual intercourse. The Duke study reported that 39 percent of women between the ages of sixty-one and sixty-five were sexually active, as were 27 percent of those aged sixty-six to seventy-one. Only 10 percent of the men between sixty-six and seventy-one, but 50 percent of the women over sixty-five, expressed no desire or interest in sex. It is clear from this that there is a wide range of sexuality in people as they age.

In a recent study of healthy upper middle class people between the ages of 80 and 102 in a residential retirement facility, the most common sexual activities reported were touching and caressing. MASTURBATION and SEXUAL INTERCOURSE occurred less frequently. Eighty-eight percent of the men and 71 percent of the women interviewed fantasized about sex, but the frequency of sexual activity did not change significantly after the age of eighty.

In men the LIBIDO, or sex drive, is largely due to the male hormone TESTOSTERONE. This hormone reaches its highest level at approximately age nineteen and men will experience a gradual decline in the level of testosterone for the rest of their lives. Testosterone, as well as intact blood vessels and nerves, is a factor in the ability to obtain an erection. Beyond the ages sixty to seventy, as many as one-third of all men have testosterone levels low enough to lose the ability to achieve and maintain an erection. Furthermore, the time needed to achieve orgasm lengthens with age, the orgasm itself decreases in intensity, and there is less ejaculate. Finally, the refractory period (the interval required between erections) increases. In very elderly men, particularly those over ninety, it may be weeks before the man is able to ejaculate again.

In women similar changes occur with age. Their libido is also controlled by the male hormone testosterone but the lubrication of the vagina is partially controlled by the female hormones, mainly ESTROGEN (and also by intact blood vessels and nerves). Therefore, as women age, it becomes more difficult to lubricate the vagina, the plateau period increases, and orgasm becomes less intense. Because of the increase in the refractory period, multiple orgasms also decrease with age in women.

Complaints by older people about their sexuality can be explained in part by changes in their bodies. In women, the most common complaints are vaginal dryness and atrophy, coital pain, a less tight yet constricted vagina, and sagging breasts. These changes have an adverse effect on both sexual performance and self-image. In men, the most common complaints include delayed and partial erection; prolonged plateau; reduced ejaculatory time, fluid force, and contraction; a decreased ejaculatory inevitability sensation; ejaculation with a flaccid penis; rapid penile softening; and longer refractory periods.

Many elderly people of both sexes suffer from psychological causes of sexual dysfunction. They may expect to perform sexually at age seventy as they did at age twenty, which is clearly impossible. Common psychological causes for sexual dysfunction in later life also include a loss of positive body image (exacerbated by physical disease); emotional stresses, tensions, and conflicts; interpersonal conflicts; and cumulative losses of a financial or personal nature.

Treating Sexual Problems of Older People.
Very few patients of any age actually volunteer sexual information to their physicians and very few physicians ask. Clearly, if people want to discuss problems of sexuality, it is necessary to initiate communication with their physicians.

Almost any physical illness, especially those likely to be encountered by older people, can be associated with sexual dysfunction. With any change in sexual function, therefore, the first rule is to be sure that it is not a symptom of some illness. It is also important to be sure that medication is not causing the sexual dysfunction, since some of the most commonly used drugs, both prescribed and over-the-counter, can cause sexual dysfunction. Only by discussing the problem with a physician can the patient potentially be switched to another drug. In addition,

over-the-counter medications such as nonsteroidal and anti-inflammatory agents and substances such as cigarettes or coffee are often unsuspected and not reported to the physician.

Some older men with erectile dysfunction may need injections of testosterone. Others will benefit from negative-pressure devices that pump up the penis to achieve an erection. Rarely is a penile implant necessary (see IMPOTENCE).

Estrogen replacement therapy for women will often help to achieve lubrication of the vagina. It is important to realize that hormone therapy may take up to two years to be effective, but the use of water-based lubricants can also be helpful. For women with depressed libido, treatment with testosterone is useful.

Other recommendations for both men and women encountering sexual difficulties due to normal aging include rest prior to sexual activity, improved nutrition, improved personal appearance, and the use of sexually provocative clothing. The couple should discuss changes in their sexual function such as the longer time needed to achieve orgasm. Many older couples have been having sexual relations in the exact same way for forty or more years and may benefit from changes in sexual position and techniques: oral-genital love-making may awaken sexual interest.

If physical illness is causing sexual dysfunction, it must certainly be treated. Not all illnesses are curable, however, and sometimes medication cannot be stopped. In theses instances it is very important to introduce changes in sexual practices. For example, for people with arthritis, a side-to-side position may be more comfortable: if the leg is in pain, a pillow placed under it may relieve discomfort. A hot bath prior to intercourse can help relax muscles and joints. If the man has had a heart attack, the woman can straddle him in the superior position or with rear entry to make sex easier for him. If there has been surgery, any pressure on painful areas must be avoided. With any illness, there must be an emphasis on sensual, affectionate, and nongenital foreplay. The key to continued sexual activity is for the couple to discuss with each other what is most pleasurable.

Psychological problems can cause sexual difficulties at any age. Depression is common in the elderly and must always be considered. Body image can be improved by exercise, recreation, and relaxation. Social contacts must be encouraged, particularly if one wants to meet people.

While counseling can help older people, all too often they are denied psychological help because of their age. This is "ageism," because studies have shown repeatedly that psychotherapy and counseling are effective at any age.

As people age, they all too often forget the role of ROMANCE in their relationships. The courtship aspects of sexuality are important at any age, but probably more so with advancing age. Typical counseling techniques include the awareness of fantasy; reduction of guilt and anxiety; acceptance of direct stimulation of the genitals (including masturbatory techniques and mechanical aids); techniques to enhance self-esteem regarding one's sexual attractiveness; and acceptance of age-related changes in function (see also SEXUAL DYSFUNCTIONS, FEMALE; SEXUAL DYSFUNCTIONS, MALE).

AIDS (Acquired Immune Deficiency Syndrome) The magnitude of human suffering and death caused by AIDS has made it the plague of the last decades of the twentieth century. By the beginning of 1992 the two known AIDS viruses had infected more than an estimated 13 million individuals worldwide: 1 to 1.5 million in the United States, 10 million in Africa, and 2 million in Asia, and the viruses are still spreading. At present there is no vaccine or cure for AIDS.

AIDS is caused by one of two human immunodeficiency-deficiency viruses (HIV). These viruses, identified by the abbreviations HIV–1 and HIV–2, cause disease by infecting and destroying blood cells called lymphocytes that protect the body against infection by a variety of bacterial, viral, and parasitic microorganisms (microbes), many of which are encountered daily during the normal course of living.

History of the Disease. The origin of the HIV viruses is unknown, but much scientific information suggests that they originated in Central Africa. Tests for the HIV–1 virus done on blood specimens collected in northern Zaire in 1976 established that this virus was present in a small number of persons who had spent most or all of their lives in a remote, rural area there. Tests of blood taken from African green monkeys from the same geographic region led to the isolation of a virus (SIV–1 or simian immunodeficiency virus) closely related to the human HIV–2 virus. A mutation of SIV–1 or related viruses is the probable origin of HIV–1. This conjectural evidence does not, however, prove the African origin of HIV–1.

In 1981 the first cases of AIDS in the United States were recognized by physicians in Los Angeles. They found among homosexual men an unusual type of pneumonia caused by the microbe *Pneumocystis carinii*. This microbe causes illness only when the immune system has been severely weakened by drugs or disease, and is known as an "opportunistic" pathogen. Investigations of these and subsequent cases determined that HIV could be transmitted during sexual contact or through blood, either by transfusion of blood or blood products containing the virus, or by sharing injection needles and syringes contaminated with HIV-infected blood. Most AIDS cases in North America, Europe, and Africa are caused by the HIV–1 virus. HIV–2 occurs mainly in West Africa and destroys lymphocytes at a slower rate than HIV–1.

The United States Centers for Disease Control and Prevention (CDC) reported in March 1994 that as of 30 September 1993, there were 339,250 reported cases of AIDS and 204,290 deaths from the disease in the United States. In 1993 103,500 new cases of AIDS were reported, although 46 percent of this increase can be attributed to a broader definition of the disease, adopted by the CDC in 1993. The report is the first in four years to contain information on heterosexual infection with AIDS. Of the new cases reported, 6,056 women and 3,232 men were infected. About half of these cases were attributed to sexual intercourse with an HIV-infected partner; 42 percent resulted from intercourse with an infected intravenous drug user.

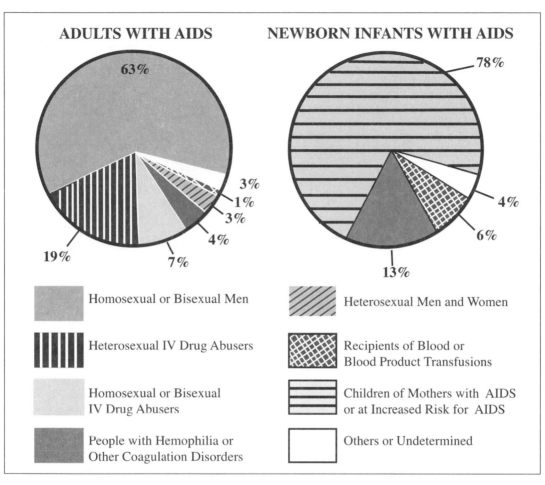

ADULTS WITH AIDS

63%

3%
1%
3%
4%
19%
7%

NEWBORN INFANTS WITH AIDS

78%

4%
6%
13%

Homosexual or Bisexual Men

Heterosexual IV Drug Abusers

Homosexual or Bisexual
IV Drug Abusers

People with Hemophilia or
Other Coagulation Disorders

Heterosexual Men and Women

Recipients of Blood or
Blood Product Transfusions

Children of Mothers with AIDS
or at Increased Risk for AIDS

Others or Undetermined

Breakdown of the AIDS population: adults (left) and newborn infants (right)

Diagnosis of Infection. The HIV–1 virus was first isolated from AIDS patients in a laboratory culture in 1983 by research laboratories in the United States and France. Because culturing the virus is so expensive and time consuming, HIV infection is diagnosed with tests to detect HIV antibodies in the blood. These antibodies usually appear in the bloodstream three to eight weeks after infection and remain positive throughout the course of the infection. Other tests can detect the HIV virus in the blood a few days after infection but these are impractical for routine use. Thus, there is a "window" of time after becoming infected with an HIV virus when a person can have a negative antibody blood test but be able to pass the virus to their partner(s) and to those sharing injection syringes and needles.

What the Virus Does. The mechanisms by which the HIV viruses infect and attack the body are similar: they circulate in the bloodstream within infected cells and plasma. The amount of virus present in the body increases with the destruction of HIV-infected lymphocytes, especially those known as CD4 lymphocytes, which play a critical role in the recognition and destruction of invading microbes. The course of HIV infection is divided into an early viremic stage; a middle stage, where there are few symptoms or signs of disease; and a late symptomatic stage, when other viral, bacterial, and parasitic infections occur.

In the early stage following infection, HIV may produce symptoms resembling those of infectious mononucleosis. This is followed by a variable period of several years, during which few symptoms are present except for persistently enlarged lymph glands. Infected persons usually develop illnesses from microbes they have previously been infected with and from which they have recovered. These "opportunistic" microbes may be normally present on the skin, in the air, or in food. When these opportunistic infections occur, the diagnosis of AIDS is made. Most frequent in the West is *Pneumocystis carinii*, a protozoan parasite that causes an incapacitating and frequently fatal pneumonia in the later stages of HIV infection. Other common opportunists are *Toxoplasma gondii*, that invades the brain, and herpes and cytomegaloviruses, that infect the brain, eyes, and lungs. In Africa and Asia the most frequent opportunistic microbe is *Mycobacterium tuberculosis*. Several of these infections can generally be prevented if certain drugs are taken prophylactically.

Spreading AIDS. Although AIDS can be acquired by transfusion or injection of blood or blood products contaminated with the HIV virus, the vast majority of AIDS cases in North America, Africa, and Europe have been acquired by homosexual or heterosexual intercourse or by sharing injection needles and syringes among drug addicts. Blood and semen are likely to be infectious at any time after infection, but other body fluids such as saliva and breast milk are also infectious, especially in the very early and late stages of the infection. Sexual transmission of HIV–1 may be facilitated by the presence of

AIDS Virus: 1) Reverse Transcriptase; 2) Lapid Bilayer; 3) RNA Molecula

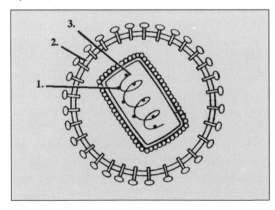

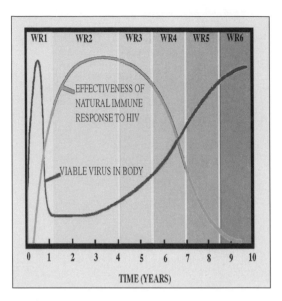

Bodily responses to AIDS

genital lesions caused by syphilis, herpes, chlamydia, and trichomoniasis. Lesions on the genitals provide an opening in the skin or genital membranes by which HIV–1 escapes from the infected person and enters the uninfected partner during sexual contact. Injury to the lining membranes of the rectum during anal intercourse can also provide an opening for the HIV virus.

Course of Illness. In the United States the median life expectancy after being infected by HIV–1 is about twelve years. It is shorter in those infected by transfusions of blood or blood products and in persons who lack access to good medical care. Treatment with the antiviral drugs zidovudine, also called azidothimidine (AZT), dideoxyinosine (DDI), or dideoxycytodine (DDC), together with drugs to prevent infection by *Pneumocystis carinii* and herpes viruses improves the quality of life and may extend it.

The rate of progression of HIV is directly related to the rate at which the virus destroys the blood lymphocytes that defend the body against infection by microbes. The rate of HIV–2 disease progression is slower than HIV–1. It appears that a good mental and physical state of health may affect both longevity and the quality of life after the diagnosis of HIV infection. It is important to avoid emotional stress and strenuous physical exercises, eat a well-balanced diet,

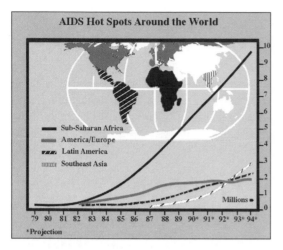

AIDS Hot Spots Around the World

- Sub-Saharan Africa
- America/Europe
- Latin America
- Southeast Asia

79 80 81 82 83 84 85 86 87 88 89 90* 91* 92* 93* 94*

*Projection

PHYSICAL FINDINGS THAT SUGGEST HIV INFECTION

- Unexplained night sweats, fever, weight loss.
- Persistent sore throat or "monospot negative" mononucleosis.
- Possible lymphoma.
- Recurrent seborrheic dermatitis or unusual skin rashes.
- Unexplained persistent headaches.
- Visual changes, symptoms of retinitis.
- Oral hairy leukoplakia.
- Oral candidiasis, especially in a young person.
- Chronic persistent diarrhea.
- Symptoms of PCP, cough, dysphea, constricting chest pain.
- Kaposi's sarcoma
  - Persistent vaginitis or vaginal candidiasis in women.

---

abstain from illicit drug use, and be seen at regular intervals by medical personnel experienced in the care of HIV-infected persons. Most urban centers in North America have support groups for persons with HIV infection and AIDS. Studies of HIV-infected American soldiers and sailors have shown that many have been able to continue working even when most of their CD4 lymphocytes have been destroyed.

Newborn Infants with AIDS. According to the CDC, between 6,000 and 7,000 HIV-infected women give birth each year. Between 25 and 30 percent of their children will be infected, about 25 percent of HIV-babies will develop AIDS in their first year of life, and 50 percent will develop AIDS by the age of three. In February 1994 American health officials announced that treating pregnant women with AZT drastically reduces the chances of their passing the disease to their children.

Prevention of the Disease. In the absence of curative therapy or a vaccine, the only way to avoid becoming infected is to avoid risk behavior. The only certain way to avoid contracting the HIV virus sexually is to be celibate or monogamous with an uninfected partner. The use of male condoms provides considerable, but not absolute, protection, as may female condoms. The latter may provide added protection when used together with male condoms but, when used alone, they are not sufficient to prevent HIV infection. Condoms must be put on the penis before beginning any oral or insertive sexual contact and should be withdrawn from an erect penis after ejaculation to prevent leakage of semen. Oil-based lubricants should not be applied to condoms as they may cause them to break open. Condoms may be coated with spermatocidal substances also used for birth control and that contain the chemical nonoxyl 9. This compound also kills HIV–1 and HIV–2, but its effectiveness as the only protection against HIV viruses has not been determined. Experience has shown that a high percentage of HIV-infected persons will, over time, infect their sexual partner(s) if they continue to have unprotected sexual intercourse.

Treatment. At the present time, there is no vaccine that protects against AIDS, nor is there a cure. Several vaccines for AIDS are under development. One, containing a genetically engineered protein (gp160) present on the surface of HIV–1, has been injected into persons already infected with the virus. This form of immune therapy slowed the rate of destruction of lymphocytes by HIV–1 and may soon be tested as a vaccine for uninfected persons.

AZT has been used to treat health care personnel who have stuck or cut themselves with needles or instruments that were contaminated by blood from HIV–1 patients. It is not clear whether this prophylactic treatment prevents infection. There is some evidence that AZT, given early in the course of the infection, may prolong the life of a patient (see also BISEXUALITY; CONTRACEPTIVE FOAMS, CREAMS, AND GELS; HERPES; HOMOPHOBIA; SAFER SEX).

ALCOHOL   see APHRODISIACS; FETAL AND INFANT SUBSTANCE ABUSE SYNDROMES.

ALTERNATIVE LIFE-STYLES   During the 1960s and 1970s frequent references to alternative life-styles were made in the popular media and on American college campuses. The term was used very loosely to refer to a wide range of living arrangements, ranging from living alone as a single person by choice to large communes, where as many as hundreds of individuals lived as one family, sharing all income and child rearing responsibilities. In a few extreme communes sexual sharing of members by the leaders or by all members was practiced. For some groups of people, the merging of two or three families into a "corporate family" was attempted, and in some of these families the sexual sharing of spouses, by choice, may also have been a facet.

This experimentation with alternative sexual and familial living arrangements and relationships was seen as a reaction to an idealized but often unrealistic portrayal of the American family during the 1950s and early 1960s. It was in keeping with the ideologies of many antiauthority and liberation movements in the late 1960s, especially the antiwar movement, the hippie and drug cultures, the feminist movement, sexual liberation, and the civil right movements.

While there are still small pockets of persons who cling to the 1960s versions of alternative life-styles, today the term generally refers to the reality, not the social experiments, of family life in America. Therefore, it is applied mainly to single parent families, single motherhood by choice, childless (by choice) couples, gay and lesbian couples and parents—in short, stable couple and family relationship structures other than the traditional model of a heterosexual mother, father, and two or more children occupying a single family dwelling.

AMENORRHEA   Women's menstrual cycles involve an extremely complex and interrelated series of physiological mechanisms; the failure of any of these can cause amenorrhea, the cessation of MENSTRUATION. The principal organs involved in menstruation—the brain, ovaries, uterus, and fallopian tubes—are activated by various chemical messengers, or HORMONES: follicle stimulating hormone, ESTROGEN, luteinizing hormone, and PROGESTERONE.

Two types of amenorrhea are clinically recognized: primary amenorrhea, or the failure to begin menstruating when the woman has reached the level of maturity at which it can otherwise be expected; and secondary amenorrhea, or the loss of menstruation after a woman's menstrual cycles have begun. There are three fundamental causes of amenorrhea: first, of course, is the possibility that the woman may be pregnant; second, there is a possibility that one of the organs involved in the cycle is missing or not functioning properly, causing primary amenorrhea; the third, and by far the most common cause, is the absence of specific hormones or the failure of the proper hormones to function properly. Hormonal problems generally stem from the failure of the ovaries to produce the required estrogen and progesterone. In some cases an excess of male hormones is produced instead of the proper amount of female hormones. Amenorrhea and a certain degree of masculinization results, and symptoms may include excess facial hair, acne, and a deepening of the voice.

Other causes of amenorrhea include cysts or tumors, stress, disease, and occasionally the emotional problems of adolescence. Anorexics and women who exercise rigorously—runners in training, for example—can also experience a loss of menstruation. Finally, amenorrhea appears at the onset of MENOPAUSE, the cessation of menstruation in women whose childbearing years have ended.

The treatment of amenorrhea is determined by the precise cause of the individual case. X-rays and blood tests are often useful in determining the cause. As mentioned above, the most common cause of primary amenorrhea is the absence or failure of hormones. Hormone treatment is, therefore, generally successful in initiating menstruation, and is given in the form of oral medication, often in a similar formula to that of the oral contraceptive pill. On the rare occasion of finding an imperforate hymen or other anatomical abnormalities, surgical intervention will be necessary.

The most common cause of secondary amenorrhea among adolescents is stress and a change in life circumstances. It is often found in students, who leave home to live in dorms. In most cases, reassurances and sometimes a simple change in life-style may be all that is needed to relieve stress and resume menstruation

AMNIOCENTESIS A developing baby floats in the uterus within a sac filled with a salty amniotic fluid. At sixteen to eighteen weeks of pregnancy a small amount of this fluid can be removed by inserting a needle through the abdominal wall and into the amniotic sac. (To avoid damage to the fetus, a sonogram is employed, by means of which sound beams penetrate the uterine wall and outline the fetus, placenta, and amniotic fluid.) This procedure is called amniocentesis. Amniocentesis has certain risks to the woman, the pregnancy, and the baby. The risk of interrupting a pregnancy when amniocentesis is used is 1 in 200.

Fluid removed by the needle can be analyzed for certain chemical compounds, enzymes, chromosomes, etc., to help in the prebirth diagnosis of such conditions as mongolism, Tay-Sachs disease in Western European Jews, sickle cell anemia in blacks, B thalassemia in Greeks and Italians, A thalassemia in Southeast Asians, neural tube defects (openings in the spinal column and cranium) that result in such conditions as spina bifida and anencephaly, cystic fibrosis, hemophilia, polycystic kidney disease, and muscular dystrophy. This is just a partial list of the diseases and conditions that the medical profession can now detect in the unborn child.

Amniocentesis is most commonly performed when the mother will be over age thirty-five

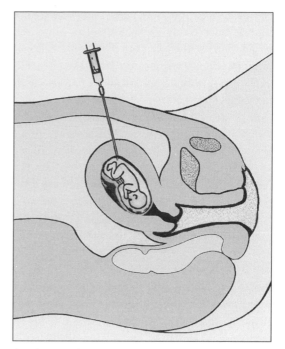

Amniocentesis

when her child is born. It must be noted that this is an arbitrary age, and parents may opt for this procedure at any age. Certainly, all women who have already had a chromosomal-defective child should be tested by amniocentesis, as they should if there is a parental chromosome abnormality. Before the advent of amniocentesis, these abnormalities were only detected after the baby's birth; now these can be detected at a much earlier stage. If gross defects in the fetus are detected, an ABORTION is usually recommended and performed, although some parents will choose to bring the pregnancy to term and raise the child (see also BIRTH DEFECTS).

ANAL INTERCOURSE Anal intercourse takes place when the penis is inserted through the anus into the rectum of a partner. While many heterosexual couples try it occasionally, it appears to be more frequent among homosexual males. Regardless of a partner's sex, the penetration may be painful unless the recipient is very relaxed and a water-based lubricant is used (not Vaseline). Also, because the anus is normally quite small and not designed for heavy thrusting, injury may result from tearing of the anal sphincter or surrounding tissue. While engaging in anal intercourse, the penis, when removed, should not be placed in the partner's vagina or mouth before being thoroughly washed because of the possibility of carrying infectious bacteria from the anus to other parts of the body.

AIDS researchers believe that anal sex is the single most dangerous practice in terms of spreading HIV, the virus that causes AIDS (especially for the recipient). Therefore, unless the partners are absolutely sure that they are both free of HIV, they should always use a new latex condom with generous water-based lubrication (see also AIDS; SAFER SEX).

ANDROGYNY When traits that are commonly regarded as male or female are mingled in one person, he or she is said to be androgynous. (The word androgyny comes from the Greek words *andros*, for male, and *gyne*, for female.) In literature the term has been applied to characters who seemed to move back and forth between male and female sex or roles. One famous example is Orlando in Virginia Woolf's novel of the same name, about an individual who moves through history changing sex with reappearances in successive generations. It might also apply to Scarlett O'Hara's secret love, Ashley Wilkes, in the novel *Gone With the Wind*, seemingly a romantic and sensitive man in a society in which men were expected to be arrogant and macho.

Psychologists once thought they could measure masculinity and femininity using scales based on attributes that were believed to encompass male and female SEX ROLES. Traits commonly defined as male included ambition, self-reliance, independence, and assertivenesss. Those regarded as feminine included affection, gentleness, sympathy, and sensitivity to others' needs. Recognizing that many men and women do not define themselves according to the popular conventions and that many display a mixture of these traits, psychologist Sandra Bem introduced an androgyny scale in the early 1970s that reflects self-descriptions of people who equally endorse masculine and feminine attributes.

In recent years Americans have seen a growth of androgyny in their daily lives, as the distinc-

tions and separations between the sexes seem to dissipate in many ways. Professions such as television announcing, reporting, and the law, once nearly entirely male, and airline cabin attendants, once almost entirely female, have become more androgynous. Beauty salons and barbershops have given way in many areas to androgynous unisex haircutters. Androgynous clothing too, such as blue jeans and sweat suits, are worn by both sexes (see also SEXUAL STEREOTYPES).

ANORGASMIA The inability of women to experience ORGASM in the course of MASTURBATION or sexual activity with a partner; the term can also apply to men. Before the development of modern sex therapy, the term "frigid" was often applied to women who did not achieve orgasms through the efforts of their husbands (it was almost unthinkable for grown women to attempt masturbation). As a pejorative term it was meant to portray the image of a woman totally unresponsive to male sexual activity. Although it was not a clinical term, it appeared in textbooks on human sexuality as late as the 1970s and was incorrectly considered to be a female counterpart to male IMPOTENCE. The word frigid then masked what we now consider to be two separate sexual dysfunctions: an inability to achieve orgasm even when sexually aroused, and a general lack of sexual desire. Sigmund Freud suggested that this problem is rooted in the unsuccessful transition to the "genital stage," resulting in female "immaturity." Sex therapists now find that the problem is more likely due to sexual illiteracy on the part of both the woman and her lover, or to religious and social prohibitions that have precluded learning orgasmic responses through masturbation.

An alternative term for anorgasmia is preorgasmia, implying an expectation that almost any woman who desires it can become orgasmic through techniques suggested by sex therapists—first by masturbation and then, often, by transferring this skill to successful orgasm in coitus (see FAKING ORGASM; SEX THERAPY).

ANTICIPATORY ANXIETY Some individuals have sexual problems because of their worries that they may have sexual problems. If a man worries that he might not obtain or maintain an erection, that concern, or anticipatory anxiety (sometimes called "performance anxiety") about not being able to perform the expected sexual act might actually result in what he fears will happen. Anticipatory anxiety must be relieved to achieve success in sexual acts involving erections. The sex therapist seeks to replace his anxiety by teaching him how to fantasize: with sexual fantasies and MASTURBATION it is often easier to obtain and maintain an erection until climax, without the fear of having to perform successfully for a partner.

A woman who believes that she will not be able to have an orgasm with a partner will probably not have one. As with males, anxiety is reduced by successful performance with fantasy and masturbation. After some success with fantasy, the client may be instructed to create images in which she achieves orgasm with a partner while actually bringing herself to orgasm through masturbation. Sex therapists find that this helps many women to become orgasmic when stimulated by the partner about whom they had formerly fantasized.

ANUS   The point at the lower end of the intestinal tract joining the rectum (which stores feces) with the skin of the buttocks, It is surrounded by the anal sphincter muscles, which contract to allow a person to postpone defecation until a convenient and socially acceptable time and location. The anus also contains sensory nerve endings and, like many other parts of the body, has also been used for sexual stimulation.

Sexual practices involving the anus include ANAL INTERCOURSE, between both heterosexual and homosexual couples, and the insertion of a variety of objects such as DILDOS and fingers. Heterosexual anal intercourse may be used to prevent pregnancy or to allow the female to remain a "virgin." Homosexual intercourse is practiced by gay men and in some other cultures as a diversion from heterosexual intercourse. While there is some stimulation of the prostate gland during homosexual anal intercourse, ejaculation usually occurs as a result of masturba-

tion. Anal intercourse is considered by many gay men as signifying a committed relationship, as contrasted with oral sex or mutual masturbation, which may occur in more casual relationships.

Multiple dangers are associated with anal sexual practices. The anal sphincters do not readily dilate to admit the penis or a dildo. Overstretching of the anus can result in the tearing of the anus (anal fissures) or disruption of the anal sphincter muscles. The insertion of foreign objects into the anus carries risk of perforation of the rectum, laceration of the rectal lining, or loss of the object in the rectum, requiring the services of a surgeon for its removal.

The rectum also contains a huge number and variety of bacteria that can enter the urethra or abraded skin of the penis and cause serious infection. In addition, sexually transmitted infections such as syphilis, herpes, and venereal warts have a predilection for growth in the warm, moist environment of the anus. Of even greater concern today is the fear of infection with the AIDS virus, present in both semen and blood. The use of a condom is mandatory if one practices anal intercourse, but it still may not prevent the spread of infection. Furthermore, persons who practice anal receptive intercourse are at a significantly increased risk of developing cancer of the anal canal.

APHRODISIACS   Any food, drink, drug, scent, or device believed to stimulate sexual interest and increase sexual vigor. For centuries, people have searched for substances that would heighten sexual arousal. Men especially have looked to aphrodisiacs to improve their sexual performance by strengthening their erections.

One of the earliest known potions—goat testicles boiled in milk—came from India. In China and Japan shark liver and powdered rhinoceros horn have been considered popular sexual stimulants for over one thousand years. Oysters, monkey glands, ginseng, and even peanuts have all been prescribed as aphrodisiacs. Perhaps the most legendary aphrodisiac is Spanish fly. It probably originated in Africa, but has been used all over the world. Spanish fly is actually a bright green beetle ground into a fine, dried powder. When consumed, it irritates the bladder and urethra and the resultant tingling is said to be sexually exciting. In fact, Spanish fly is very dangerous. Its continued consumption can be poisonous, leading to genito-urinary infection and urethral scarring.

The most widely used aphrodisiac is alcohol. In fact, a mixed drink or a glass of wine or beer can have a pleasant, disinhibiting effect, creating a feeling of warmth and relaxing a person's sexual anxieties. But too much drink makes it obvious that alcohol is actually a depressant. A woman may find her arousal waning and a man may find himself unable to achieve an erection.

Many illegal drugs, such as marijuana, amyl nitrates (poppers), cocaine, and "ecstasy" have been hailed by their supporters as sexual enhancers. But as with alcohol, misuse or overuse can have the opposite effect, destroying sexual ability. Amyl nitrates and cocaine have even caused death. There have also been many legal, over-the-counter aphrodisiacs available but none has ever been proved effective and many have, in fact, been proven unsafe.

The use of aphrodisiacs has survived for centuries because practically no one wants to see their sexual desire and capacity diminish. Whether or not they actually work, however, is not a simple matter. Certainly, if a person has a real physiologically-based problem, nothing— whether oysters, Vitamin E, ginseng, or rhinoceros horn—will work. At the same time, it has been said that the most important sex organ lies between the ears. A relaxed and confident state of mind plays a major role in sexual satisfaction.

ARTHRITIS AND SEX   Many diseases are included under the general term of arthritis and rheumatism. They may all have similar symptoms—possibly a recurrent fever which can be symptomatic of internal organ involvement. To varying degrees, patients may have joint and muscularskeletal symptoms, resulting in pain and limitation of joint movement.

If someone is not feeling well, he or she will not have much interest in sex. Desire usually increases proportionately to the lessening of a person's discomfort. No study has suggested that sexual activity has any effect on an arthritic or rheumatic patient's medical situation. It is important to reassure patients that if they do feel desire, sexual activity will have no adverse effects on their physical condition.

The key to a satisfying sex life for an arthritic/rheumatic individual lies in flexibility of attitude, approach, and schedule. It is important to remember that the situation varies from person to person. Therefore, the patient should not be made to feel that there is a right or wrong way to approach sex or that they must be like the next person. For instance, patients may have periods during which they are relatively free of symptoms and discomfort. This may vary with time of day, and it may be necessary to adjust sexual activity to the afternoon or midday if that is when they feel best.

The joints involved with arthritis may influence the positions and activities that persons find most comfortable. Obviously, any sexual activity that causes more pain should be avoided. At times, sexual gratification may be achieved more readily by methods other than intercourse— mutual MASTURBATION, CUNNILINGUS, or FELLATIO. An understanding partner open to experimentation is most helpful in terms of sparing discomfort and maximizing pleasure. Frank, open discussion should be encouraged between the patient and his or her partner about which activities are most pleasurable and cause the least discomfort. Since it is extremely difficult for the partner to guess the intensity of the patient's pain, the patient should describe what he or she feels and suggest appropriate sexual activities. The patient can also take a mild, short-acting analgesic or anti-inflammatory medication, such as aspirin or ibuprofen, an hour before sexual activity. In some cases, this will be sufficient to avoid potential discomfort during love-making.

If arthritic/rheumatic patients can manage some satisfying sexual activity, their mood will generally be better and their outlook more positive. The attitude with which they cope with their disability is most likely to improve as well. There is no reason why, with flexibility on the part of both patient and partner, the pair cannot achieve a mutually satisfying sexual relationship, even with severe arthritis or rheumatism (see also HANDICAPPED PERSONS AND SEX).

ARTIFICIAL INSEMINATION BY DONOR (AID)

There are a number of reasons why artificial insemination by donor has become quite common in recent years: it has become more socially acceptable; it is more difficult to find children for adoption; older people and a growing number of unmarried women want to have children. The artificial insemination by donor (AID) procedure was first performed in 1884, but did not become an acceptable option until this century. In the 1950s it was discovered that sperm could be frozen and used later. In the following years the legal and moral aspects of the procedure were studied and criteria for donors were established. Only in 1979 were directives established by which the possibility of hereditary and sexual diseases among donors could be discounted. These criteria were reevaluated in 1986, and an AIDS test was included.

Today the most common reasons to use artificial insemination by donor is male infertility and the prevention of hereditary diseases such as cystic fibrosis, hemophilia, Rh disease, muscular dystrophy, and Tay-Sachs disease. The criteria for male infertility according to which the use of artificial insemination by donor would be justified are: irreversible lack of sperm from childhood or as a result of disease, radiation, chemotherapy, or sterilization; insufficient quantities of sperm or severe sperm malformation; or other forms of incorrectable impotence.

For most couples, impotence is often accompanied by feelings of anger, frustration, and guilt. Even when artificial insemination is offered as a possible solution, the husband may have difficulties facing his sense of failure and a crisis may emerge that can lead to the break-up of the marriage. Therefore, when tests show that there is no alternative, the doctor must present these findings with considerable caution. Treatment should not begin immediately. The couple needs time to confront their problem and deal with it. Women too may sometimes feel disgusted by the injection of foreign sperm into

their bodies, Some women even develop physical problems expressed in menstrual and ovulation disorders and even cessation of ovulation. Obviously, not all couples can be considered suitable candidates for artificial insemination. Any couple that applies for it must be carefully studied and it must be ascertained that no other solution to their problem is available. Both partners must agree in writing to receiving sperm from a donor and the man must also sign that he undertakes to recognize the resultant child as his own. So as to prevent any regrets, the husband should participate in all parts of the process, from the determination of ovulation until the completion of the AID process. Another way of reducing tension is to provide a thorough explanation to both partners about all stages of the procedure, including how donors are chosen and the tests they undergo so that their sperm is considered suitable, the chances of impregnation, possible complications of pregnancy, and the chance of birth defects.

Donors are chosen with great caution so as to avoid those with faulty health, hereditary diseases, and poor potential for fertility. Sperm counts must show a volume of over 1.5 milliliters, a concentration of 20 million sperm per milliliter, motility of over 40 percent, and proper morphology in at least 50 percent of the sperm. Donors are generally chosen from quality populations (many are students); they undergo considerable physical and mental evaluation. A comprehensive interview is made to determine whether there are any problems in the donor's past or family history, with particular emphasis placed on hereditary diseases and the mental health of the donor's family. Comprehensive testing is done to determine if the sperm carry sexually transmitted diseases, particularly AIDS. These tests are repeated every six months: the sperm sample is then frozen until similar responses six months later indicate that the sperm may be used.

A listing of physical factors (blood type, Rh factor, body structure, and color of skin, eyes, and hair) is made. The psychological and social backgrounds of the donor are also recorded to facilitate the child's absorption by the family and surroundings. At the same time the couple must be informed that although every effort will be made, there is no way to ensure that the donor will be similar in every way to the father. The identities of the donor and couple receiving AID treatment remain anonymous in most countries. The information is kept in a hospital safe and is not handed to anyone.

The AID procedure includes tracking ovulation by various methods, including measuring the basal body temperature and ultrasound tracking of the follicle's development. Sperm is injected around the time of ovulation. Prior to the injection a speculum is inserted into the vagina to expose the cervix, and a sperm sample is placed inside by means of a narrow tube. In some cases, sperm is also injected directly into the uterus. The patients lies down for several minutes but can then get up and go home. When an injection is made, it is considered that the ovum is ready in the fallopian tube up to three days after ovulation, but sperm remains functional in the female sex organs for seven days.

One injection is usually sufficient during ovulation, but often two or more injections are given, particularly when the precise time of ovulation is uncertain. When the time of ovulation is certain, especially when ovulation has been brought about by drugs, there is no advantage to additional injections. Because of the sperm's lifespan, it is preferable to inject it before the follicle is shed. When multiple injections are used, it is best that they all be from the same donor to ascertain the father's identity.

If no other problems are involved, the chances for pregnancy are good—about 90 percent after a year of intensive treatment. Pregnancy and birth are no different from other pregnancies and births. In fact, children born from artificial insemination by donor have been found to have a higher intelligence than average (see also CONCEPTION; IN VITRO FERTILIZATION; SPERM BANKS).

AUTOEROTICISM   Self-induced sexual activities and stimulations. These activities consist mainly of two types: MASTURBATION and sexual fantasies. Masturbation may include the use of mechanical devices, and fantasies may either be created solely in one's mind or be the product of reading or looking at erotica or pornographic movies or photographs. Autoerotic arousal may be carried out by persons when they are alone or when they are in the presence of sexual partners. The object of autoerotic activity may be arousal alone, arousal and stimulation carried to the point of ORGASM, arousal during FOREPLAY before physical contact with another person, or a variant of two-person sex with each partner engaging in autoerotic masturbation until orgasm. This latter form is increasingly popular, especially among gay men, who want the intimacy of a sexual experience but are very much concerned about the transmission of AIDS or other diseases (see also VIBRATORS).

B

BESTIALITY see ZOOPHILIA.

BIBLE AND SEX see ABORTION; ADULTERY; DOUBLE STANDARD; MASTURBATION.

BIRTH The birth of a baby begins with the on-set of labor—the rhythmic uterine contractions that force the baby out of the womb and into the birth canal toward delivery and its first moment of life outside its mother. One of the remaining mysteries of life is the precise biological mecha-nisms that signal a pregnancy is complete and the birth process should begin. It is assumed that they are hormonal.

The first uterine contractions felt at the begin-ning of labor may be fifteen to twenty minutes apart and can last up to one minute. There is, however, great variation in their patterns and some women experience no more than isolated early contractions or cramping. Contractions usually become more frequent. Early contrac-tions may be accompanied by other symptoms, most commonly a discharge of bloody mucus or a sudden release of amniotic fluid through the

A mother holding her child for the first time

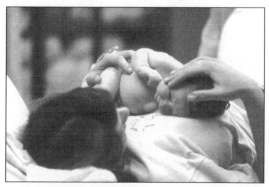

woman's vagina. The mucus is from a plug that seals the cervix during pregnancy and prevents infections from entering the uterus. The amniotic fluid is the fluid in which the fetus is suspended, protecting it in the course of pregnancy. One out of ten women experiences an early rupture of the membranes surrounding it, releasing the fluid. This is commonly called the "breaking of the bag of waters." If it occurs before contractions begin, labor will usually commence within twenty-four hours.

Labor contractions are the major force that pushes the baby out of the womb. Most women experience these as "labor pains." They can be moderate or extremely severe, but they can also be controlled with medication and the use of special breathing and other techniques.

When contractions have established a definite frequency of one every five or six minutes for women having their first child, they should call their physician. (Those who already had children are often advised to call earlier.) Women who have chosen to have their babies in a hospital are generally advised to come to the maternity sec-tion when their contractions are coming at regu-lar intervals of four to five minutes apart.

Many hospitals and other labor and delivery facilities have a "birthing room," where both parents may participate in the birth experience together. They have immediate access to all the hospital equipment that may be needed during labor and delivery—especially if there is an emergency—but birthing rooms are designed to be much less formal or intimidating than mater-nity facilities of the past. Their surroundings provide a nonmedical setting for childbirth in a hospital (see HOME BIRTH; HOSPITAL BIRTH).

On arrival at the hospital, the woman is usually seen by a nurse or other member of the hospital staff responsible for the conduct of her labor and delivery. A brief general physical examination is done, as is a vaginal examination to determine the thickness and dilation of the cervix and the position the baby will present at birth. Many physicians will order the fitting of an external monitoring system to record the fetal heart rate and patterns, as well as the time, duration, and intensity of the woman's contractions. The monitor is followed closely by the attending obstetrician and nursing staff throughout labor. Fastened to the woman's abdomen, it provides both visual and auditory readings, so the medical staff can both see and hear how the labor is progressing. An internal monitoring system can also be employed when necessary. An electrode and a pressure catheter are passed through the dilating cervix. The electrode is attached directly to the baby and the catheter lies within the uterine cavity. This is a more accurate monitoring system, but it is invasive and entails a certain risk.

The duration of labor varies widely from one woman to another and from one birth to another in the same woman. It generally takes longer for the births of first babies. Labor may take as little as a few hours but it may also last twenty-four hours or more. It averages about fifteen hours for the birth of a first baby and under ten hours for successive births.

Medical terminology divides labor into three stages. First-stage labor is preparation for the delivery to follow. It begins with the first contractions felt by the woman even before she has

Fetal heart monitoring at birth

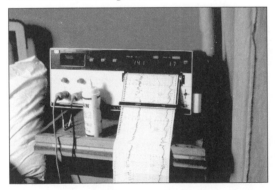

come to the medical facility. In this early first-stage period the cervix begins to thin and dilate to enable the baby to pass from the uterus into the upper end of the birth canal. As labor progresses, contractions are stronger and more frequent and the cervical opening dilates to two inches or more. It is at the end of the first stage, during a period called the transition stage, that contractions become most intense and painful and the cervix dilates to four inches or more.

Second-stage labor is the process of delivery. It starts when the baby begins to emerge from the womb into the upper end of the birth canal, propelled by the force of the mother's contractions. These contractions are regular and stronger, and the baby descends deeply into the pelvis. It sometimes happens that the baby is not in the proper head-down position when the birth process begins and may move through the birth canal bottom or feet first. This called a "breech birth"; although it is more difficult, physicians are trained to cope with it. In some cases potentially difficult births may be accomplished by CE-SAREAN SECTION.

The climax of the delivery nears when the baby's head "crowns" and becomes visible at the vaginal opening. The mother's vagina can stretch to permit the baby's head and body to pass, but usually the attending physician will (with the mother's permission) perform an EPISIOTOMY, an incision in the tissue just behind the vagina, to prevent tearing that may be more damaging and difficult to stitch. The new baby is then eased from its mother's body, and any mucus is cleared from its mouth to clear the way for its first breaths. When the baby's breathing has been established, the umbilical cord attaching it to the mother is tied and cut, separating them. Usually, the baby's first cries have already been heard.

A brief third-stage of labor follows the birth of the new infant. The placenta detaches from the uterus and, together with the fetal membranes, is expelled from the woman's body. These are known as the "afterbirth." Finally, the attending physician sutures the woman's episiotomy and any tears that may have occurred.

Pain Control During Labor and Delivery. Since the nineteenth century it has been possible

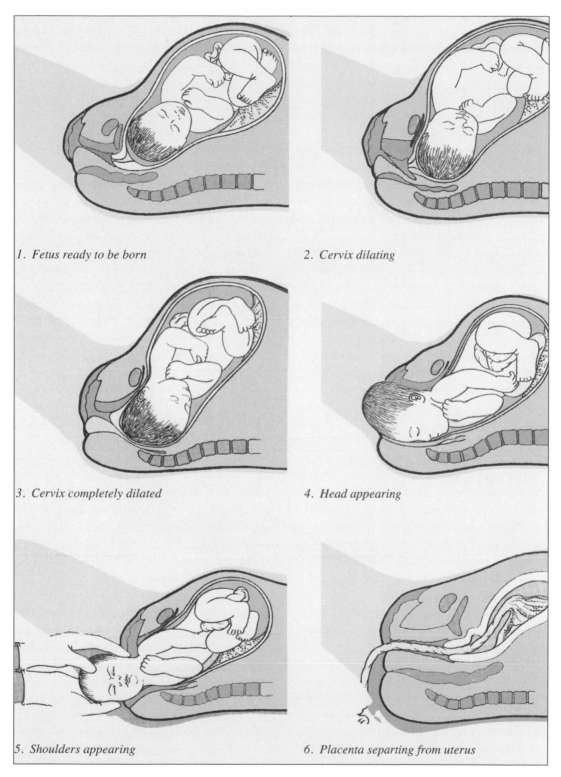

1. Fetus ready to be born

2. Cervix dilating

3. Cervix completely dilated

4. Head appearing

5. Shoulders appearing

6. Placenta separating from uterus

The stages of labor: The cervix dilates and the baby passes out of the womb and into the birth canal. The vagina stretches to enable the baby to pass through. The baby is eased from its mother's body. Finally, the placenta and fetal membranes are expelled from the mother's body.

to control or eliminate the pain of childbirth with the use of drugs or anesthetics. Since the 1920s most women in the West who delivered their babies in hospitals were using some form of pain control, and in some cases were almost totally anesthetized during labor and delivery. However, in the past thirty years opposition to the use of drugs has grown, especially among groups of women who assert that they have been used excessively, depriving women of an important life experience and posing a risk to the baby: most drugs can cross the placental barrier and enter the baby's bloodstream. Another view asserts that pain control need not be excessive if it is carefully tuned to the individual woman's needs, that there is no genuine risk to the baby, and that proper medication can prevent childbirth from becoming a negative or traumatic experience. Although in the past many physicians routinely administered drugs without permission, today they discuss the pain control options available to women giving birth before the process begins.

Whether or not they decide to use pain control medication, prospective mothers can play an important part in helping to control the pain most will encounter in childbirth. This can be begun by following a prudent diet in pregnancy and coming to childbirth in the best possible physical condition. They can prepare for childbirth with exercises and training recommended by any of the prepared or NATURAL CHILDBIRTH methods, especially the relaxation and breathing techniques taught by the LAMAZE METHOD. Prospective fathers can also play a key role in childbirth by training themselves to assist women in carrying out breathing and other exercises before and during labor and supporting them psychologically during the process.

There will still be some pain from contractions and many women will want medication to deal with it. Most physicians will employ pain medication when labor is well established and there is evidence of progressive dilation of the cervix and the baby's descent toward the birth canal. Many doctors use Demerol, given intravenously, and Phenergan, given intramuscularly, during the active phase of first-stage labor. Others use Valium or other tranquilizers.

Other methods of relieving pain can also be used during labor and delivery. One, the pudenal block, controls feelings in the woman's external genitalia (see also EPIDURAL PAIN RELIEF DURING LABOR; INDUCED LABOR; MIDWIVES; NEWBORN INFANT; PLACENTA; POSTPARTUM DEPRESSION; UTERUS).

BIRTH CONTROL   Throughout most of human history, the concept of limiting births would never have occurred to anyone; most children did not live past their fifth birthdays and the only certain way a couple could pass on their genes was to have as many children as possible. In addition, in agricultural societies the more potential farmhands, the better.

It was certainly the desire to prevent out-of-wedlock pregnancies that generated early demand for birth control, but as society began to change, other factors came into play. The Industrial Revolution signaled the end of agrarian societies and the need for very large families. As women became more educated, they developed the desire to control their own fertility. During the two world wars, as more and more women joined the work force—at first temporarily to fill in for men who had gone to war and later permanently—large families became incompatible with women's new life-styles. Now, with overpopulation threatening the existence of the planet, things have turned totally around: it seems that birth control has now become a necessity for the survival of our species.

There are two basic methods of birth control—the prevention of pregnancy and the prevention of birth through ABORTION. Abortion was probably the first avenue tried by women, who may not have understood how they could prevent pregnancy but certainly knew they wanted to end their pregnancies before they resulted in births. Most of the abortion potions cooked up by witch doctors and medicine women probably did nothing more than make women sick, but certainly the desire was there, if not the means.

In preventing pregnancy, douching became the first line of defense. The first historical evidence we have for such potions is from graves dated as far back as 1850 B.C.E., in which recipes for "spermicides" were buried with the dead. These spermicides included such ingredients as honey, carbonate of soda, and crocodile dung.

Other birth control methods used by women included the DIAPHRAGM, the CERVICAL CAP and the female CONDOM. The first "diaphragm" may well have been used by the noted lover, Giovanni Casanova, who is said to have placed the hollowed halves of lemons over the cervixes of his partners. By 1864 the British medical association had compiled a list of 123 kinds of vaginal barrier methods, or "pessaries," being used in the British Empire.

During the 1870s, with the passage of what were known as the Comstock Laws, it became illegal to send birth control devices or information about birth control through the United States mail. In 1916 Margaret Sanger, the founder of the Planned Parenthood Federation of America, began campaigning to reverse such laws. She believed that women's rights to control their own fertility should not be limited by government regulations. Her battle continued until 1965, when the United States Supreme Court, in *Griswold v. Connecticut*, struck down state laws prohibiting birth control.

Today CONDOMS have become the leading barrier method of birth control. They are sold and used not so much because of their ability to pre-

Diaphragm: a & b) application of spermicide; c) insertion of diaphragm; d) diaphragm in place

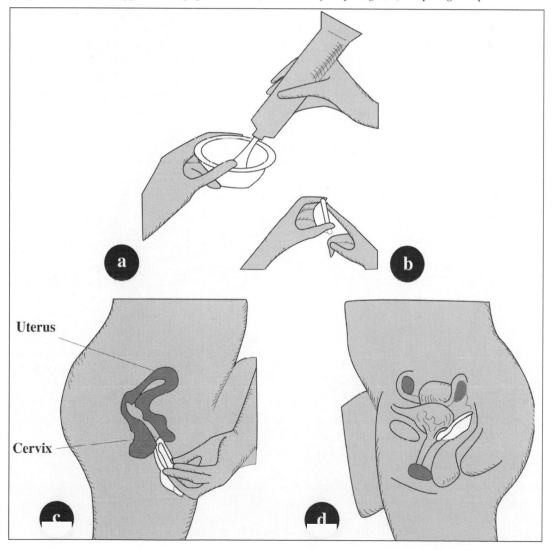

Uterus

Cervix

vent births as because of their effectiveness against SEXUALLY TRANSMITTED DISEASES. Most condoms are made out of latex, hence the nickname "rubbers."

Because some men stubbornly resist using a condom, a female condom was developed so that a woman could benefit from the condom's dual role as a protector against disease and pregnancy. It has only recently become available and research is still scanty. Some women who have used it complain that it is difficult to insert, but many women, once they get the hang of it, like it. The female condom's ability to prevent pregnancy and the spread of sexually transmitted disease should approximate that of the male condom.

Two other popular barrier methods of birth control are the diaphragm and the cervical cap. Both are inserted into the vagina in order to block the cervix, the entrance from the vagina into the uterus, through which sperm pass to

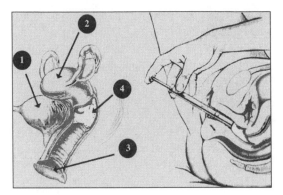

Insertion of spermicide:
1) Bladder; 2) Uterus; 3) Vagina; 4; Spermicide

reach the eggs. The diaphragm is slightly larger and easier for a clinician to fit and for the woman to put into place, but the cervical cap can be left in place for up to forty-eight hours, while the diaphragm can only be inserted six hours in advance of intercourse and left in place for twenty-four hours. Both of these devices are

IUD: 1) IUD inserter & IUD; 2 & 4) Sleeved copper devices; 3 & 5) Copper-bearing IUDs

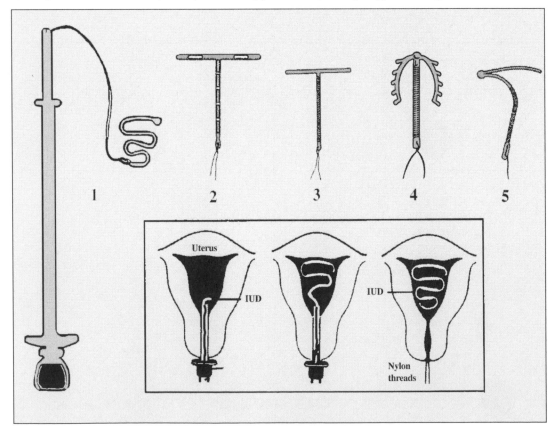

used in combination with a spermicide (a gel or foam that kills the sperm, which can normally live up to seven days). In typical use, each is rated at 18 (that is, 18 possible pregnancies per 100 women for each year of use), but with perfect use the rating increases to a 6. All of these barrier methods of birth control are reversible—that is, women can stop using them if they wish, and immediately become pregnant.

The contraceptive sponge is another barrier method of birth control. Like the diaphragm and cervical cap, it is inserted into the vagina in order to block the opening of the cervix and access to the woman's eggs. The sponge also contains a spermicide. The sponge is not quite as effective as the diaphragm and cervical cap for women who already have a child. The numbers are 28 and 9 pregnancies per 100 women per year of use, respectively. (For women who have not had a child, the sponge's effectiveness is the same as the other two methods.) With use of the sponge

there is also a slight risk of a woman developing TOXIC SHOCK syndrome.

The sponge is available without a prescription, as are many foams, gels, creams, films, and suppositories (see CONTRACEPTIVE CREAMS, FOAMS, AND GELS) that work by creating a barrier over the cervix and killing the sperm with a spermicide. These products are very easy to use, which is why many women like them, and their rates of effectiveness are in a similar range as the other products, 21 per 100 per year for typical use and 3 per 100 for perfect use. Side effects are minimal (some women are allergic to them, as are some men) but they only offer limited protection against sexually transmitted diseases.

The next group of contraceptives are the reversible prescription methods. These must be prescribed by a doctor and work either by keeping the woman from releasing her eggs or by preventing a fertilized egg from implanting itself in the uterus.

Oral contraceptive pills

The most famous of these, and the one credited with initiating the sexual revolution, is simply called "The Pill." Composed of female hormones, the pill keeps the ovaries from releasing eggs. The pill must be taken once a day. Women who use the pill perfectly, taking it every day, have less than a 1 percent chance of becoming pregnant. Even the typical rate—allowing for mistakes in use—is only 3 percent. The side effects from using the pill are minimal, especially with the new mini-pills that contain lower doses of hormones. Women over thirty-five years of age who smoke should not use the pill and it must be remembered that the pill provides no protection against sexually transmitted diseases (see ORAL CONTRACEPTIVES).

Because women sometimes forget to take the pill, other methods of delivering the same hormones have been developed. One, DEPO-PROVERA, consist of an injection which lasts for twelve weeks. Another, called NORPLANT, consists of six soft capsules that are inserted under the skin of the upper arm and release hormones continually for five years. Norplant is the most effective of all these methods, with only 4 women in 10,000 becoming pregnant during one year of use: there is no possibility of the woman making a mistake. Because these hormones do cause side effects, they are not recommended for use by every woman, and again, they do not prevent sexually transmitted diseases.

Another type of reversible prescription method of birth control is the IUD, or INTRAUTERINE DEVICE. IUDs are small plastic devices that contain either copper or a hormone and are inserted into the woman's uterus by a clinician. They work by preventing either the fertilization of the egg or by preventing implantation of a fertilized egg in the uterine wall. In typical use, only 3 women in 100 per year will become pregnant with an IUD in place. The string extending from the IUD must be checked regularly to ensure that the IUD remains in place. Most women adjust to an IUD easily, but there are potential side effects, some of which, while rare, are life-threatening. A clinician will usually ask a patient to sign a consent form saying that all the risks were explained to her before the IUD's insertion.

The next group of methods are the permanent ones—tubal sterilization (see STERILIZATION) for women and vasectomy (see VASECTOMY AND THE MALE PILL) for men. Both require surgery and both are very effective (though, surprisingly, not 100 percent, even though the fallopian tubes in women and the vas deferens in men are permanently blocked). These are both very safe procedures, though complications can arise, and while the initial cost is higher than for other methods, they are one-time expenses. These methods are not effective against sexually transmitted diseases, and it is very important to remember that they are rarely reversible, so if at a later time the desire develops to have another child, that option may be closed.

The final group of methods falls under the category of NATURAL FAMILY PLANNING. With these methods there are no artificial devices or procedures used. Many of these methods can also be used to help a woman become pregnant, particularly if she is having difficulty doing so, by letting her know when the best time to conceive is in the calendar of her menstrual cycle.

The first of these methods is called ABSTINENCE, which means not engaging in sexual intercourse. When two people are sexually involved, for abstinence to be 100 percent effective, care must be taken not to bring semen into contact with the vagina, even without intercourse. If a man ejaculates close to the vagina, or if either partner touches the semen and then touches the women's vagina, sperm could be introduced into it and impregnate the woman.

The other methods are based on partial abstinence (or the use of a contraceptive device only at certain times). These methods rely on the woman knowing when she will ovulate and refraining from intercourse or by using a contraceptive during those times. Because sperm can live up to seven days and the egg as long as three days, the period of abstinence must be long enough to take these factors into consideration. When used perfectly, these methods can be very effective, but in typical use their rate of failure is 20 percent per year of use.

The most common method of partial abstinence is called the calendar, or "rhythm," method. The woman keeps a chart of her menstrual cycles and tries to predict when she will next be fertile. The more regular a woman's periods are, the more reliable this method will be, though even with perfect use the failure rate is 9 percent per year of use. The woman must abstain from intercourse or must use a contraceptive at least eight days before she thinks she will ovulate and for three days afterward.

With the basal body temperature method, the woman takes her temperature every morning before rising. Assuming there is no other cause for her temperature to fluctuate (such as an infection from a cold or flu) she will notice a slight rise in her temperature on the day of ovulation.

Another way of testing for ovulation is by the cervical mucus method. Normally cloudy, the mucus will become clear and slippery in the few days before ovulation. It can then be stretched between the fingertips. (One way that some women can confirm that they have, in fact, ovulated is to be aware of *mittleschmerz*, a slight pain in the lower abdomen that signals ovulation has occurred. But many women never experience the signal.)

Of course, to optimize the effectiveness of these methods, they should be used in conjunction with the calendar method so that the woman can refrain from intercourse (or use a contraceptive) eight days prior to ovulation and three days afterward. When all are used together, it is called the symptothermal method.

There is one last method which some people use as an intended means of birth control — the withdrawal method. In the withdrawal method, the man withdraws his penis from the woman's vagina just before he ejaculates. The basic flaw to this method is that before a man ejaculates, the Cowper's gland releases fluid which serves as a lubricant to help the sperm make their way up the urethra. This fluid can also contain thousands of sperm which can be on their way to fertilize the egg long before the man actually ejaculates. The other danger is that if the man does not withdraw fast enough, he may end up ejaculating inside the vagina. The withdrawal method has a typical failure rate of 18 per 100 and a perfect rate of 4 per 100 per year.

Finally, there are those people who take no precautions, but play "Russian roulette," even though they do not want to become parents. Out of 100 such women, over the course of a year 85 will become pregnant. That is why we have so many unwanted pregnancies, but it also why our species continues to populate our planet (see also RU–486; BIRTH CONTROL MYTHS; PLANNED PARENTHOOD AND MARGARET SANGER.)

BIRTH CONTROL MYTHS Myths can be evocative stories that teach valuable lessons or they can be fabulous tales that delight little children, or in the case of some sexual myths, they can lead to very dangerous practices that result in unwanted pregnancies. Despite the wealth of sex information available and the coverage sex receives in the media and mandatory SEX EDUCATION classes, there are still far too many people who believe some of these sexual myths, many of which have been debunked long ago.

DOUCHING as a method of birth control is a good example of a myth that will not go away. Archeologists have found detailed drawings of douching techniques used in ancient Egypt. In more recent times vinegar was the method of choice, and many people would keep a bottle on the bathroom sink for douching after intercourse. As times changed, so did the mythical douches: word soon spread that Coca Cola was an effective douche. The truth is that douching is not an effective method of birth control — by the time a woman has douched, many of the sperm that were deposited during intercourse have had more than enough time to start their journey toward an awaiting egg.

Another long-standing myth is that a woman cannot get pregnant from her first experience of sexual intercourse or if she does not have an orgasm. While it is true that the orgasmic response can help pregnancy occur (vaginal contractions that occur with orgasm cause the cervix to dip into the pool of semen in the vagina), a woman can still get pregnant without having an orgasm.

Another myth is that women cannot get pregnant from having sex while standing up. While a physician may recommend certain prone positions to a woman who is having difficulty becoming pregnant, most women do not need to be lying down for sperm to meet the egg.

Another myth is that intercourse during menstruation is safe. Unprotected sexual intercourse during menstruation is relatively safer than at other times, but not all women are so regular that they cannot release an egg when they are menstruating. That is why using every possible method of NATURAL BIRTH CONTROL (methods based on the timing of women's infertility periods) simultaneously does not guarantee that a woman will not get pregnant.

The most dangerous sexual myth says that a woman cannot get pregnant if the man withdraws before he ejaculates. This myth continues to be propagated by many men, who are desperate to have sex with a woman even when methods of birth control are not available. Since some men will say almost anything in that situation, it is left to the woman to be sensible. The fact is that before a man ejaculates, the Cowper's gland gives off a few droplets of fluid that appear at the tip of the erect penis. This fluid acts as a lubricant for the millions of sperm that follow during ejaculation, but it too contains thousands of spermatozoa, and only one is needed to fertilize an egg. Whether or not the man is able to pull out and ejaculate outside the vagina is irrelevant. *Coitus interruptus*, as the withdrawal method is called in scientific terms, is not a reliable method of birth control.

BIRTH DEFECTS   While most babies are born healthy and do not suffer from any obvious genetic or other developmental defects, in about 3 percent of cases the infant is born with a major abnormality. These defects may result from genetic or environmental causes, or from the interaction of both.

Genetic factors are involved in all reproductive processes. Indeed, genetic and chromosomal irregularities are responsible for most known causes of birth defects, and some people run a higher risk of having abnormal children. These include couples who have already produced a child with a genetic disease or birth defect, women over thirty-five years of age and women who have had several miscarriages or stillbirths

(babies born dead). A higher risk of birth defects is also associated with race-specific genetic disorders such as sickle-cell anemia in blacks, thalassemia (a form of anemia) in people from Mediterranean areas, or Tay-Sachs disease in Eastern European Jews. Couples in a category of increased risk should seek genetic counseling.

Pregnant women over thirty-five years of age have an increased risk of having a baby suffering from a chromosomal disorder, the most common form of which is mongolism. The risk of this abnormality increases with maternal age, and older women are counseled to seek a prenatal diagnosis through AMNIOCENTESIS or chorionic villi sampling. Amniocentesis involves the drawing of a small amount of fluid for genetic analysis at fourteen to sixteen weeks of pregnancy. A small needle is inserted through the abdominal wall into the uterus to obtain the amniotic fluid, containing cells from the fetus. Chromosomal and other genetic or metabolic evaluation can be performed on these cells to determine if there is an abnormality. Chorionic villi sampling of placental tissue, done through a catheter, allows prenatal diagnosis in the first three months of pregnancy.

During pregnancy, several drugs and other substances can cross the placental barriers and adversely influence the developing fetus. Caution with regard to drug use during pregnancy is recommended, since several drugs may cause developmental defects. Therefore, all pregnant women should consult a physician before using a drug; the potential of a drug to cause malformations of a developing fetus and possible alternative treatments should be discussed. Pregnant women should also be warned about the risk of using "social" drugs—tobacco and alcohol—during pregnancy, since all are associated with birth complications and fetal and infant abnormalities (see FETAL AND INFANT SUBSTANCE ABUSE SYNDROMES; PREGNANCY AND COMMON MEDICATIONS AND SUBSTANCES).

Infections are common and potentially dangerous to both the pregnant woman and her fetus. Fetal infections may result in miscarriage, fetal abnormalities, fetal growth retardation, fetal death, or congenital infection. Primary maternal infection with rubella (German measles) during the first three months of pregnancy is a well-known cause of fetal abnormalities, but infections with other viruses such as herpes simplex may cause fetal anomalies as well. Systemic maternal diseases may also cause birth defects. For example, certain forms of diabetes and lupus may cause heart anomalies in the fetus. Women who suffer from such diseases should be carefully screened during pregnancy (see also PREGNANCY RELATED DISEASES; PRENATAL CARE).

BISEXUALITY Human sexual behavior has traditionally been divided into two categories—heterosexuality and homosexuality. Individuals who identify themselves as heterosexual are assumed to have sexual relationships only with persons of the opposite sex; persons who identify themselves as homosexual are assumed to have sexual relationships only with persons of the same sex. These patterns are frequently believed to be fixed during childhood and to remain constant throughout a person's lifetime.

Although research into bisexual behavior has lagged behind that of heterosexual and homosexual behavior, we now know that the sexual lives of many individuals do not fall easily into either of these categories. Many individuals will be sexually attracted to, or have sexual relationships with, both men and women at some time during their lives. We also know that there are many different patterns of bisexual behavior and that people engage in such behavior for a variety of reasons.

To date, researchers have not identified specific biological, psychological, or sociological determinants of sexual attraction. The determinants, as well as the development of bisexual behavior, may differ from person to person.

The Definition of Bisexuality. The term bisexual may be used to describe an individual's sexual behavior or sexual identity. Bisexual behavior usually refers to sexual contact with both men and women. The timing of these sexual contacts may vary considerably, depending on the individual. Some persons have sexual relationships with men and women at the same time, while others alternate with male and female partners, one after the other. Some individuals engage in bisexual behavior for relatively short periods of their lives, while for others it is a more stable behavior pattern, beginning in adolescence and lasting throughout adulthood.

While persons who engage in bisexual behavior may describe themselves as bisexual, many identify themselves as heterosexual or homosexual. The limited research we have suggests this may be particularly true of African-American and Latino bisexual men and African-American women.

Prevalence and Patterns of Bisexuality. There is relatively little information available on the prevalence of either male or female bisexual behavior in the United States. Estimates from national samples of sexual behavior during 1970–1990, reported in the *Journal of Sex Research* in 1991, suggest that approximately 20 percent of men report some sexual contact with men during their lifetime and approximately 6 to 7 percent during adulthood. Male sex relationships with males during adulthood tend to be episodic or sporadic and most of these men also have sexual relationships with women. Comparable data on bisexual behavior in women have not been published; however, it has been estimated that approximately one-third as many women as men have ever had a sexual relationship with both men and women.

Several studies have suggested that there may be cultural differences in bisexual behavior, and that African-American and Latino men are more likely than white men to have sex with both men and women. African-American and Latino bisexual men are more likely than white bisexual men to identify themselves as heterosexual, to be married, and to not tell their female partners about their same-sex contacts. African-American lesbian and bisexual women report more extensive heterosexual experiences than do white lesbian or bisexual women. The reasons for these cultural patterns are unclear.

Many different patterns of bisexual behavior have been identified among men. Examples include youths exploring their sexuality, men who have sex with other men for money or drugs, men in prisons or other all-male institutional settings, men in primary relationships with women, and men who identify themselves as bisexual. Most men engaging in bisexual behavior do not even fall into one of these identifiable groups; men who identify themselves as bisexual may represent the smallest of all groups. However, these patterns suggest that not all bisexuality may be described as a transitional period in an individual's life, or a form of denial of one's homosexuality. Indeed, most persons who engage in bisexual behavior may do so because they are sexually attracted to both men and women during a prolonged period in their lifetimes.

Very little is understood about patterns of bisexual behavior in women. Like men, they are believed to have very diverse life-styles and sexual histories. The development of a bisexual life-style may be somewhat different between men and women. However, bisexual women report having, on average, earlier opposite-sex sexual experiences but later same-sex attraction and sexual experiences. Unlike male bisexuals, who may marry women despite an awareness of same-sex attraction, female bisexuals' awareness of sexual attraction to other women typically occurs after marriage. Bisexual experimentation may begin with intense, affectionate friendships among women.

Sexual Behaviors. The range of sexual behaviors reported by bisexual men and women mirrors those of their homosexual and heterosexual counterparts. Estimates of the frequency of specific sexual practices with male and female partners are available primarily from recent AIDS-related research, which targets high-risk populations and focuses on specific AIDS-related behaviors. Thus, they are probably not representative of the larger population of bisexual men and women. However, such studies suggest that bisexual men may engage in more sexual risk behaviors than exclusively heterosexual men, but fewer than exclusively homosexual men. In general, studies have shown that bisexual men report greater numbers of sex partners and engage in more oral and anal intercourse than heterosexual men, but less than homosexual men. While married bisexual men report high numbers of sex partners, they report engaging in

anal intercourse less frequently. Bisexual men who identify themselves as gay may engage in less frequent sexual risk behaviors, perhaps because of exposure to HIV educational programs in gay communities. Only a small minority (perhaps 20 percent) of bisexual men in primary relationships tell their wives or other female partners about their same-sex sexual contacts.

To date, very few studies have examined the sexual practices of bisexual women. In a recent AIDS-related study, 88 percent of women who had engaged in sex with a man since 1980 but currently identified themselves as lesbians reported engaging in vaginal or anal intercourse with men without condoms. Nearly 32 percent of these women reported having a sexual relationship with a bisexual man. Indeed, these bisexual women were more likely to engage in sexual risk behaviors, such as anal intercourse, with a bisexual male partner than were bisexual women having sexual intercourse with exclusively heterosexual men. The frequency of bisexual women having a sexual relationship with bisexual men is unclear, but such contact may increase the woman's risk for HIV.

It is important to note that most gay men and lesbian women have engaged in sex at least once with a person of the opposite sex. In fact, between 15 and 26 percent of gay men and 20 and 35 percent of lesbian women have been married.

Health Risks of Bisexuality. Concern with HIV transmission has prompted an examination of the rates of SEXUALLY TRANSMITTED DISEASES (STDs), including AIDS, among bisexual men and women. In general, bisexual men report lower rates of STDs than exclusively homosexual men and higher rates than exclusively heterosexual men. Of the 65,389 men who have had sex with men and whose AIDS diagnosis was reported to the United States Centers for Disease Control and Prevention through June 1990, 74 percent reported having sex only with men and 26 percent with both men and women since 1977. Given the large number of infected gay men in the United States and the greater ease of HIV infection from man to man than from woman to man, it is probable that most bisexual men were infected through same-sex sexual contact.

Data on STDs among bisexual women are strikingly different from those for bisexual men. Bisexual women are more likely than lesbian women to report abnormal Pap smears, cystitis, genital herpes, gonorrhea, and vaginal infections. Through 1989, 103 cases of AIDS in bisexual women had been reported, compared to 79 cases in lesbian women. Nearly all (79 percent) of these women reported injection drug use as their primary risk factor for HIV; the remainder reported sex with a male partner at risk for, or infected with, HIV (16 percent), or a history of blood transfusion (4 percent). While there is potential for transmission of HIV and other diseases through woman to woman sexual contact, the risk for bisexual women is related primarily to the frequency of intercourse with a male partner. Additional studies have reported that bisexual men are more likely to have injected drugs and to have received money or drugs in exchange for sex. However, because of the sampling procedures used for these studies, the ability to make generalizations based on these data with regard to the larger population of bisexual men is unknown.

Bisexuality has not been systematically studied in the United States and knowledge of bisexuals' behavior is tentative at best. Given the numbers of persons who are bisexual or whose lives are touched by those who are, it is important that we develop greater sensitivity and scientific understanding of how individuals manage life-styles that include sexual relationships with both men and women.

BOREDOM, SEXUAL One of the most frequent complaints reported to sex therapists comes from people who have good emotional relations with a sexual partner but have developed a lack of sexual interest that they may interpret as a low sex drive. When this decrease in sexual desire is not the result of organic difficulties or the effects of medication, it very likely results from boredom with sexual activity due to long-term repetition of time, place, and techniques for sexual episodes. This results in a loss of excitement about and anticipation of sexual activity. Routinization may lead to predictability

and, for many others, it will result in sexual boredom.

The treatment of sexual boredom depends upon the participants recognizing that routinization is probably the cause of the problem and that all five senses are usually involved in a successful sexual act. Participants should also recognize that solutions depend on altering as many of the sensory components surrounding the sexual act as possible: the senses of smell, touch, taste, sight, and hearing. Scented body oils, massages, syrups to be licked from the skin, erotic movies, and verbalized fantasies are only a small sample of the wide variety of new inputs into a sexual relationship to help overcome boredom.

BREAST CANCER Breast cancer is the most common malignancy encountered in women and is one of the leading causes of all deaths from cancer in women. The incidence of breast cancer has steadily risen in the West, and is the number one cause of death for women in their forties. One in nine American women develops carcinoma (the medical term for cancer) of the breast during her lifetime.

Mortality from breast cancer has not changed noticeably over the past fifty years. The American Cancer Society estimates that 182,000 women and 1,000 men—will be diagnosed with it in the United States in 1994 and 46,000 women and 300 men will die of the disease.

There is no known method of preventing the disease. Survival rates vary depending on the size of the tumor, whether it is localized in the breast or has spread to other areas at the time of diagnosis, and on the microscopic character of the tumor cells. Therefore, the major opportunity to alter the natural course of the disease lies in early detection and diagnosis.

It should be remembered that breast cancer is an eminently curable disease. Five-year survival rates for early and localized forms of the disease are 93 percent, compared to 18 percent for the most advanced stage of the disease. A woman's fear of possible breast cancer may lead to denial of an obvious lump. Whatever a woman's fears, she should not hesitate to see her doctor when she discovers a lump or other changes in one of

RISK FACTORS FOR BREAST CANCER IN WOMEN

- Advancing age
- Upper socioeconomic status
- Family history of breast cancer
- History of cancer in one breast
- Late childbearing
- Obesity
- Early menarche
- Late menopause

her breasts. The chances of early detection and cure are in her hands.

The risk factors for the development of breast cancer are poorly understood. Epidemiologists have documented some factors that appear to increase or decrease the likelihood that breast cancer will occur. Caucasian women are at higher risk than Latin, Mediterranean, and especially black women. Women born in the West are at higher risk compared to women born in Asia or Africa. The frequency of breast carcinoma increases directly with the patient's age. Breast cancer is almost non-existent before puberty; the incidence gradually increases during women's reproductive years and peaks after age forty. Eighty-five percent of breast cancers occur after age forty-two.

A genetic predisposition to develop breast carcinoma has been recognized in some families. No specific genetic pattern has been identified, but first-degree relations of cancer patients, their daughters and sisters, are at two to three times a higher risk of developing breast carcinoma than others in the general population. The highest genetic risk, six to nine times, occurs in first degree relatives of a premenopausal woman who develops cancer in both breasts.

Women with fibrocystic breast disease (a benign condition), previous cancer of the other breast, or ovarian, endometrial, or colon carcinoma are at a greater risk of developing breast cancer. Women who experience early first menstruation or late menopause are also at increased

risk. The age of delivery of a first child is important. If a woman's first birth occurs before age twenty, she has a lower risk of developing breast cancer than a woman who has never given birth or who had her first term pregnancy after age thirty-five. Obese women are also at higher risk; studies have demonstrated that differences in incidences of breast cancer are directly related to the amount of fat in the diet. Women of upper socioeconomic classes are at increased risk. It is known that large doses of radiation to the breast constitute a definite risk factor.

Many risk factors are additive, but these identify only 25 percent of the women who eventually develop breast carcinoma. Studies are nonconclusive in relating the use of oral contraceptive pills to the likelihood of developing breast cancer. Some recent studies, have suggested that long term use and early use of the pill may increase the risk of breast cancer, but further investigations will be needed. The United States Food and Drug Administration takes the position that no change in oral contraceptive use is currently warranted.

Much concern has been expressed that postmenopausal estrogen replacement, used by many women, may encourage the development of breast cancer. The issue is not settled. It is, therefore, mandatory to examine the breasts and to perform a mammogram before initiating estrogen therapy in postmenopausal women and to repeat these examinations regularly.

Screening and Early Diagnosis. Detection of breast cancer is defined as the use of screening tests in symptomatic women at periodic intervals to discover breast malignancy. Women should be taught the technique of BREAST SELF-EXAMINATION. Clinical examination of the breast is recommended at annual check-ups. Radiological screening (see also MAMMOGRAPHY) can detect breast cancer at an early stage and is recommended, where available, on an annual basis for women over the age of 40. Various studies have shown that screening programs effectively reduce mortality rates related to breast cancer. However, the frequency of screening and the degree of compliance are key factors affecting the success of breast cancer screening.

Biopsy and Surgical Procedures. If screening procedures discover a suspicious lump or thickening in a breast, action must be taken to determine whether it is malignant and to perform the recommended surgery. There are several ways to obtain cells from a lump that has been detected for diagnosis at the pathology laboratory. If the lump contains fluid, a fine needle can be inserted into it and a little fluid is drawn in an almost painless procedure. When the tumor is solid, a wide biopsy needle can be inserted. In some cases, the whole lump or some part of it is removed in an operating room.

If there is concern that the breast malignancy may have already spread to other tissues, further testing procedures, including x-ray evaluations and a bone scan, are necessary. The extent of preoperative investigation procedures should be decided by an experienced specialist.

A woman confronting these tests should be aware of all options available to her and discuss them with a specialist. The different operations performed today for breast cancer, the extent of the operation proposed and the postoperative consequences should be discussed in detail ahead of time. Treatment for breast cancer may involve the expertise not only of a surgeon, but of a radiotherapist and an oncologist as well. At present, the major surgical alternatives available to women suffering from breast cancer can be classified as follows (all involve removal of the breast to insure excision of all cancerous tissue):

Radical Mastectomy. This operation was first described in 1891. All breast tissue, pectoral muscles (the muscles beneath the breast), and axillary lymph nodes are removed.

Extended Radical Mastectomy. Though rarely done, in this operation the internal mammary lymph-nodes are removed in addition to all of the other procedures performed in a radical mastectomy. To do so it is sometimes necessary to remove a section of the ribs.

Modified Radical Mastectomy. The entire breast and the axillary lymph nodes are removed.

Total Simple Mastectomy. The whole breast is removed. The axillary (armpit) area and pectoral muscles are left intact.

Recently there has been increasing support for conservative surgery—surgery that does not require removal of the breast—combined with radiotherapy for women with early breast cancer. Conservative surgery implies removal of just the tumor and some surrounding normal breast tissue. Quadrantectomy implies removal of the tumor plus the whole quadrant of internal breast tissue surrounding it. The terms lumpectomy and segmental mastectomy, sometimes used for these procedures, are imprecise. These operations are combined with axillary lymph node dissection and radiotherapy. The principal advantage of the conservative treatment is cosmetic. Thus, the major criterion for the patient is the ability to adequately remove the primary tumor with controlled cosmetic deformity.

Early diagnosis is the major factor influencing mortality from breast cancer. When cancer is diagnosed in its early stages, curability rates are higher than 90 percent for five years. If the lesions are one centimeter or less and lymph nodes are not infected, the twenty-year survival rate is also about 90 percent. In advanced breast cancer, which now constitutes only a minority of cases, the prognosis is much worse—about 20 percent survival at five years. Therefore, patients who regularly practice self-examination and have annual breast examinations by a physician detect lesions far smaller than those found in women who examine themselves infrequently or not at all. The risk of death among women who are screened is much lower than the risk among women who are not screened (see also BREAST SELF-EXAMINATION; MAMMOGRAPHY).

BREAST-FEEDING The female breast is a mammary gland, or milk-producing organ. Each mature mammary gland is composed of fifteen to twenty-five separate lobes, that are arranged radially and further subdivided. The alveoli, or milk producing units, are provided with small ducts that join others to form a single large duct for each lobe. These ducts make their way to the nipple and open separately to its surface.

The hormonal and neural mechanisms involved in lactation (milk production) are complex. Prolactin, a hormone secreted from the

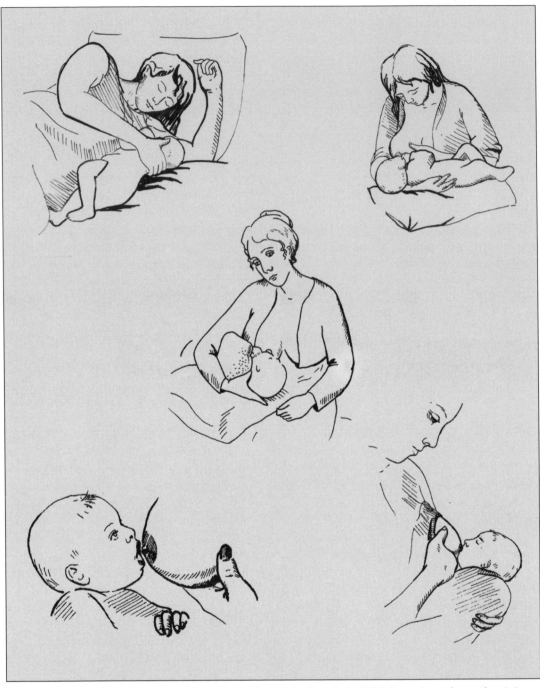

Women can adopt many different positions when breast-feeding their child. Sometimes the mother initates breast-feeding by carefully placing her nipple into the baby's mouth.

protutan gland, is essential for lactation. Other hormones, such as PROGESTERONE, ESTROGEN, cortisol, and insulin, act in concert with prolactin and are important as well. Regular sucking by the infant causes contractions within the ducts, which eject milk through the nipple and stimulate further milk production. In this way the amount of milk production is regulated by the infant's needs.

Most women and infants are physically capa-

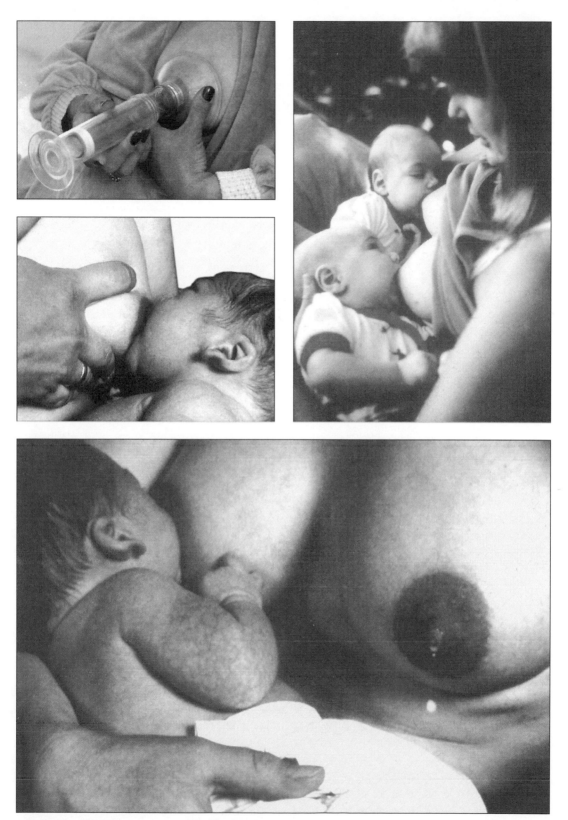

More and more American women are choosing to breast-feed their children

ble of breast-feeding provided they receive sufficient encouragement. Breast-feeding should begin as soon after delivery as the conditions of the mother and baby permit, preferably within several hours. The mother's diet should contain enough calories and vitamins to compensate for those secreted in her milk or those required for its production. Weight reduction diets should be avoided by nursing mothers.

Breast-feeding has four main benefits for the infant:

- The composition of breast milk is ideally suited for the nutritional requirements of the infant. Recently, hormones and enzymes have been identified in breast milk and these are also thought to promote the infant's growth;
- Breast milk contains antibodies that provide protection against common causes of infant infections. The first milk (colostrum) has anti-inflammatory properties;
- Breast milk diminishes the likelihood of the infant devloping allergies by reducing his or her exposure to foreign, nonhuman proteins such as those found in cow's milk;
- Breast-feeding promotes a passive psychological interaction and bond between the mother and the infant.

Breast-feeding declined in most industrialized countries from the 1940s to the early 1970s, when less than 30 percent of mothers breast-fed their infants at one week of age. The main reasons were the difficulties faced by working mothers and the relative convenience offered by infant "formulas" that substituted for breast milk. In the 1970s, when the benefits of breast-feeding were emphasized, a marked reversal of the trend was observed, and about 60 percent of mothers were breast-feeding their infants at one week of age.

Most studies suggest that lactating women have additional energy requirements. It is generally recommended that a breast-feeding woman eat about a quarter more than is recommended for a non-pregnant woman. This is especially true for women who did not gain adequate weight during pregnancy. Increased consumption of milk products is not necessary during lactation. In fact, a woman's body can make milk out of any food, provided it contains the essential nutrients.

Infant sucking can initiate milk flow within ant hour after delivery, although in most cases milk will not flow heavily. Sucking during these first hours also reinforces uterine contractions, which reduce uterine bleeding. Subsequently, frequent sucking is necessary to maintain milk flow, and no restriction on feeding times should be imposed. If the baby is fed on demand, its hunger regulates the amount of milk production.

The size of a woman's breasts does not affect the ability to breast-feed, but depressed or inverted nipples may cause lactation problems that require medical attention. At each feeding both breasts should be offered, each for five to fifteen minutes, and the baby should start on a different side each time. If the mother is nursing from only one breast, the other breast will become engorged and milk production will decrease. Breast engorgement is normal for three to seven days after delivery and can be a source of some discomfort. Gentle milk expression and a nursing brassiere for support are helpful. Tender nipples are common when the baby begins sucking. Sore nipples can be avoided by proper positioning and short sucking episodes. In some cases, nipple creams can be used and manual milk expression and infant feeding with a spoon can be used alternatively. In rare instances, inflammation of the breast occurs and medical attention becomes necessary.

Infant weighing before and after each breast-feeding may provide an indirect measurement of milk intake.

BREAST SELF-EXAMINATION Early detection of BREAST CANCER is possible through the use of periodic screening tests of women who display no symptoms of the disease. Women should be taught the technique of self-examination, and the clinical examination of the breasts is recommended at annual check-ups. Breast x-rays (see MAMMOGRAPHY) can detect breast cancer at an early stage and is recommended on an annual basis for women over the age of forty. Various studies have shown that early diagnosis

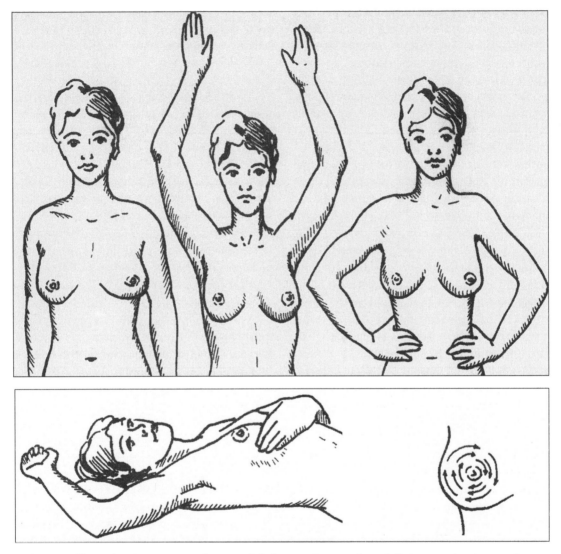

In breast self-examination a woman first stands before a mirror and carefully inspects her breasts for any lumps or growths. She then lies down and palpates each breast in a circular motion, moving outward from the nipple.

through screening programs effectively reduces the mortality rate related to breast cancer. However, the frequency of screening and the degree of attention and responsibility taken by the individual woman are key factors affecting the success of screening.

Self-examination of the breast can be done by every woman and it remains one of the most important screening procedures for breast cancer. The majority of breast cancers are first discovered by the patient. Furthermore, tumors discovered by women who regularly practice self-examination are usually smaller and more curable than those discovered in women who do not take the responsibility. Women who practice breast self-examination should focus on three points: timing, visual inspection, and palpation (feeling the breast).

Timing. The few days immediately after a menstrual period are the best time to detect changes in the breasts. Postmenopausal women or women who do not menstruate for other reasons should perform breast examination on the same calendar day each month.

Inspection. The woman should inspect her breasts in front of a mirror, looking for changes in shape, contour, skin or nipples of each breast—in color, retractions, or lumps.

Palpation. The woman should lie down, initially with one arm at her side and subsequently with the same arm beneath her head. A massaging motion with slight pressure should be applied over the entire breast in a systematic fashion, using the flat part of the fingers (not the fingertips). One of the easier techniques is palpation of the breast in circles, beginning at the nipple and then gradually in larger circles. Many women prefer palpation in the shower, since they have increased tactile sensitivity when the breast is wet.

Any lump should trigger immediate consultation with a physician, even though most lumps in the breast are not malignant. Finally, during self-examination, the woman should gently squeeze both nipples and look for any discharge.

While mammography and other technological approaches to screening can be effective in addition to regular self examination of the breast, an annual breast examination by an experienced physician remains essential.

BREASTS   Women's breasts contain mammary glands capable of secreting milk, marking humans as members of a mammalian species. This milk provides nourishment for the suckling infant from birth to weaning. Although they are not sex organs, breasts also have an unusual erotic significance in Western societies (see BREASTS AS SEX OBJECTS).

The breasts are two rounded organs. They consist largely of soft, fatty, and fibrous tissue on both sides of the female chest. Each breast contains fifteen or more groups of mammary glands, each with ducts that lead to the nipple at the tip of the breast. The nipples are cylindrical in shape and are usually flattened, but they easily become erect in response to the stimulation of touch or cold. The hormonal changes of pregnancy and childbirth usually cause enlargement of the breasts and nipples, as well as enlargement and darkening of the areolae, the circular areas immediately surrounding the nipples. When a woman delivers a baby, her body's hormonal changes activate the mammary glands to begin the secretion of, first, colostrum, and then milk for nursing (see BREAST-FEEDING).

The development of the breasts begins as girls approach puberty, usually at nine to thirteen years of age, although it can begin earlier. Changes in the levels of sex hormones stimulate the growth of the fatty tissue of the breast, and the girl's breast buds and nipples gradually become more prominent. There is a great variety in the size and shape of women's breasts; popular stereotypes about "ideal" sizes and shapes have led many women to seek surgical changes in their appearance, usually to enlarge their breasts but in some cases to reduce their size. The size and appearance of the breasts does not seem to bear any relationship to a woman's ability to nurse an infant.

The nipples are made up largely of smooth muscle fibers. They are sensitive because of their concentration of nerve endings. Breasts and nipples play an important role in the erotic play of some women; others report only mild erotic stimulation when partners caress and kiss them. Whatever is felt by a particular individual, erotic play with breasts and nipples is part of the usual sexual interaction in Western societies.

BREASTS AS SEX OBJECTS   In the United States and, to some degree, in other countries sharing Western culture, women's breasts have become an object of sexual attraction and desire. In recent years, this has reached an extreme, motivating increasing numbers of women to become recipients of surgical breast augmentation

Breast anatomy

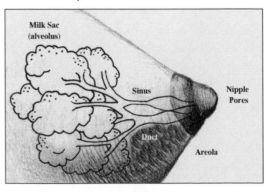

procedures to enhance their sexual desirability. The emphasis placed upon the breast as a sexually exciting object rather than an organ for nurturing appears to be culturally derived and a product of socialization: in most cultures the breast is regarded mainly as a source of nourishment for babies.

While there is no definite explanation for the emphasis placed on the breast as a sexual object in Western countries, one possible explanation relates it to the suppression of visibility of all parts of the anatomy that distinguished males from females during the Victorian era. Consequently, the breast became "forbidden fruit," as did the genitalia. Since it was essentially size that distinguished the female breast from the male breast, size itself became associated with sexuality, and "flat-chested women" became a demeaning term during most of the twentieth century (the period of the desirability of the deliberately flat-breasted "flapper" of the 1920s appears to have been an aberration).

Until the late 1930s many local ordinances made it illegal for both males and females to bathe in public places with the breasts or torso exposed. As males challenged this, their bathing attire eventually became a one-piece topless garment. While topless sunbathing (and in many places, complete nudity) is not uncommon for women throughout Europe, it is still a rarity on American beaches. Although the reasons for greater modesty in America regarding women's breasts are not clear, the banning of topless sunbathing is consistent with the DOUBLE STANDARD that allowing for greater freedom for the male than the female.

BROTHEL   A place—it can be a house, a trailer, or an apartment—where prostitutes and their customers meet to engage in sexual activities. Brothels are also known as "houses of ill repute," "bordellos," "cat houses," and "whorehouses." They are usually managed and presided over by a madam, who sometimes arranges for customers to come and meet her prostitutes. She also pays the house bills, provides protection, and serves as hostess. In return, she receives a large percentage of the money paid to her prostitutes—often as much as half. Some of these madams are highly intelligent and competent in business matters. Perhaps the best known was Xaviera Hollander, who managed a brothel in New York in the 1970s and wrote *The Happy Hooker*.

Brothels may vary from seedy establishments where customers ("Johns") may be victimized by being beaten and having their money stolen, to very elaborate establishments. They are illegal in all American states except Nevada, but nevertheless continue to flourish in most big cities. They are no longer as common today as they once were.

C

CALL GIRLS see PROSTITUTION.

CANCER see specific forms of cancer: BREAST CANCER; CERVICAL CANCER; OVARIAN CANCER; PROSTATE CANCER; TESTICULAR CANCER; UTERINE CANCER; also ANUS; CASTRATION; MAMMOGRAPHY.

CASTRATION The surgical procedure removing the testicles in men or the ovaries in women. In both men and women it often results in hot flashes and flushing episodes. Castration is only very rarely recommended for women because it tends to lead to osteoporosis (thinning of the bones), as well as the menopausal symptoms of hot flashes and changes in secondary sexual characteristics, such as breast size. Among men castration may be indicated for the treatment of PROSTATE CANCER. In such cases, the testicles are usually removed in a simple surgical procedure through an incision in the scrotum.

Often the patient will have the procedure performed and go home the same day. For men who are concerned about the cosmetic effects of castration, prostheses with an external appearance almost identical to testicles are available to place in the scrotum. Since drugs can provide the same effects as castration, many patients choose to have medical treatment rather than surgical castration. However, surgical castration is a simple, one-step procedure that provides definitive treatment for men requiring it, mainly victims of prostate cancer that has spread elsewhere.

Surgical castration can provide an almost immediate resolution of bone pain and a subsequent improvement in the obstruction of the urinary passage from advanced prostate cancer. However, medical and surgical castration both result in a decrease in sex drive, or libido, in both men and women, and changes in erections in many men (see also TESTICULAR CANCER).

CELIBACY Throughout history there have been groups of men and women who have adopted celibacy—agreeing not to marry, and by implication, not to have sexual intercourse. The Roman Catholic priesthood is made up of men who are forbidden to marry. There are also, within the Catholic religion, orders of monks and nuns devoted to a life of worship without priestly status or function, who live under rules of celibacy.

In the Anglican Church, although priestly celibacy is not the rule, some individual priests impose it on themselves; there are also celibate orders of Anglican monks and nuns. In the Greek Orthodox and other Eastern churches, priests may marry—except for those looking to being raised to the rank of bishop, since bishops in those churches may not be married. At times the Catholic Church has found reasons to tolerate married clergy. Among the Roman Catholic clergy are a few married priests, among them members of the Protestant clergy who have been converted and who, though married, wanted to be ordained as Catholic priests. This dispensation has also been given to Eastern rite clergy in certain circumstances.

Catholic canon law regarding priestly celibacy has a stormy history. Many early Christians, laymen as well as priests, believed that marrying was pointless because the end of the world was at hand. Soon there would be the final judgment, and after that, no more marriage. Not everyone was of this mind, however, and there were also

Christians who got married, among them many priests. In one area it would be the custom for priests to marry, elsewhere various rules about priestly celibacy were enforced. Some men became priests after marriage, and were not told to put their wives aside. Others were permitted to stay married but were not supposed to have sex. In the fourth century stronger rules were put into effect but they did not remain in force. Finally, in the twelfth century, the Church outlawed married priests and the rules now in effect were established—but they, too, were much flouted during the Renaissance. In response to the Protestant Reformation the embattled Church tightened its rules; they have remained much the same since that time.

Celibacy is a practice that can be traced back to ancient pre-Christian religions. The priests of certain deities were required to be totally devoted to their religious roles; no interest in sex or in any mortal human being could come between them and their gods. This was especially true for the priests of female deities such as the Egyptian Great Mother Isis. A priest stood apart from other believers and mediated between them and the deity. Similarly, the modern Catholic priest stands at the altar between God and God's children. To perform the priestly offices he must be qualified and ritually pure, and his celibacy is believed to contribute to these conditions.

In pre-Christian times, related types of celibacy were practiced. Philosophers such as Epictetus advocated celibacy as helpful on the way to wisdom and serenity. Through celibacy, he held, one learns to ignore the promptings of appetite and avoids responsibilities to spouse and children. Celibacy has also been practiced by ascetics seeking to prevent sensual contamination of the ideas they espouse.

In popular imagination, cerebral brilliance is often linked with celibacy—as with Sherlock Holmes and Hercule Poirot, the perennially popular fictional detectives. In real life, people commonly practice celibacy while enmeshed in work, in pursuit of higher education or professional training, or while establishing a business or a career. This kind of celibacy may mean abstinence from marriage rather than from sexual gratification (for example, masturbation may still be practiced)—but individual celibacy combined with CHASTITY is not unknown.

Jewish tradition has no celibate priesthood. Traditional Jews certainly discourage celibacy and encourage marrying and having children. Rabbis especially are expected to be models as husbands and fathers.

Eastern religions have some celibate traditions. The first Buddhists were a celibate male order. As the faith spread, its celibate aspect dwindled away. In many of the monasteries young men joined for short terms, usually a year. Some solitary holy men still practice celibacy, along with other self-deprivations. Taoism and Shintoism have disposed of celibacy in their monastic orders.

CERVICAL CANCER After UTERINE CANCER and OVARIAN CANCER, cancer of the cervix is the most common type of cancer of the reproductive tract. It commonly appears in women after age forty-five, but it also appears in women of reproductive age: in 1 percent of cases it is detected during pregnancy. The incidence of cervical cancer has declined during the last decade. Nevertheless, the incidence of precancerous lesions (called carcinoma in situ) of the cervix is rising abruptly. Some precancerous change of the cervix usually precedes the development of invasive cancer by ten to fifteen years.

Factors contributing to the development of cervical cancer include sexual activity and multiple sexual partners; race—the disease is rare among Jewish women, but twice as prevalent among African-American than among white women; low socioeconomic situation; and previous SEXUALLY TRANSMITTED DISEASES.

Symptoms. Carcinoma in situ is usually asymptomatic. Symptoms of the invasive cancer include postcoital bleeding (bleeding that occurs after intercourse); vaginal discharge; and, in some instances, pelvic pain. Only during the invasive stage are there symptoms of malignancy such as weight loss, weakness, and anemia, and clinical features related to the spread of the tumor, such as a pelvic mass and obstruction of the urinary tract.

Diagnosis. When there is only carcinoma in situ, diagnosis can be made through a PAP TEST, colposcopy (observing the cervix with a magnifying glass), and cervical biopsy. In the invasive stages there are physical findings in the cervix that can be observed using a speculum. During the clinical stage, diagnosis is based on a PELVIC EXAMINATION. It is important to determine if the lesion is localized only in the cervix or if it has spread. In progressive stages of the disease the cancer spreads mainly through the lymphatic tracts and may appear later in the lungs, brain, bones, and other organs. CT scans and MRA (magnetic resonance imaging) are used to diagnose the spread of the disease to the lymph nodes and other organs.

Treatment. In its earliest stages cervical cancer can be completely cured by destroying the growth with heat coagulation or laser. In premenopausal and menopausal women hysterectomy is recommended. In later stages of the disease radical hysterectomy is the best treatment: this includes removal of the uterus, ovaries, fallopian tubes, and the upper part of the vagina. Dissection of the pelvic and sometimes of the abdominal lymph nodes is performed. In the more advanced stages the primary treatment should be by radiation. Chemotherapy is sometimes applied in advanced cases. At present, experiments are being made with different combined treatments.

The outlook for patients with cervical cancer is favorable if it is caught at the early, in situ stage. The prognosis is less hopeful for more advanced lesions and depends mainly on the clinical stage of the disease. The earlier the lesion is diagnosed and treated, the better prospects are for cure. In the early stage of the invasive disease the cure rate is 85 percent, while in the more progressive stage of the disease, only 4 to10 percent of patients are cured.

CERVICAL CAP A barrier method of BIRTH CONTROL, the cervical cap is a flexible rubber cap that fits over the woman's cervix and blocks the opening to her uterus. It requires a prescription and is reversible. Thimble-shaped, it must be fitted by a clinician so that it fits snugly over the cervix, assuring that no sperm can enter and fertilize an egg. A spermicide is also used to kill any sperm that can otherwise survive for up to seven days.

The cap is coated with spermicide and can be put in place by a woman up to six hours before intercourse; it may be left in place for up to forty-eight hours. The use of additional spermicide for subsequent episodes of intercourse is optional. The spermicides used with the cap offer some protection against SEXUALLY TRANSMITTED DISEASES.

Of 100 women who use the cervical cap, 18 will become pregnant during a year of typical use. If the cap is used properly, only 6 out of 100 would become pregnant. The cap cannot be used during menstruation or if there is any other kind of vaginal bleeding.

The cap is similar to the DIAPHRAGM, but it is harder for the professional to fit and more time-consuming for the woman to learn how to insert and remove it. The cap is preferred to the diaphragm for women whose pelvic muscles are too relaxed to hold a diaphragm in place.

Caps are inserted deep into the vagina before intercourse and are put into place to cover the cervix. The woman should also check before and after intercourse to make sure the cap has not shifted. Because the cap requires an insertion and removal process, it is not favored by women who feel uncomfortable touching their genitals, though the placement of the cap can be done by the man as well as by the woman, so that insertion can be made part of foreplay. The cervical cap is much more popular in Europe than in the United States.

In general there are no side effects to the cervical cap, though an unpleasant odor may develop if a cap is left in place for several days. Some women have a mild allergic reaction to either the rubber used in the cap or the spermicides used with them.

CERVIX The lowest portion of the uterus. Normally, the cervix is about one inch long. At birth, a female infant's cervix is relatively large in comparison with the rest of the uterus, however, with the hormonal changes of puberty, the cervix grows proportionally smaller than the rest of the uterus. The cervix forms a short transitional zone between the uterus body and the vagina. A portion of it lies above the level of the vaginal vault (supravaginal cervix) and a portion lies exposed within the vagina. The cervix is made up of connective tissue with a small amount of elastic tissue and smooth muscle fibers. It is lined with mucus-producing cells.

Being the lowest portion of the uterus, the cervix plays an important part in pregnancy. It acts as a stopper, holding the pregnancy intact until term. The term "incompetent cervix" is applied to a painless dilatation of the cervix during the midtrimester of pregnancy, followed by rupture of the membranes and subsequent expulsion of the fetus (miscarriage). The causes of cervical incompetence are obscure, but they apparently include a variety of causative factors. Previous trauma to the cervix due to a D & C (dilation and curettage), amputation, conization, cauterization, or traumatic delivery appear to be factors in some cases. There are also instances of congenital structural defects, uterine anomalies, and abnormal cervical development associated with in utero diethylstilbestrol (DES) exposure. After diagnosis of cervical incompetence, the generally accepted treatment is surgical. A purse-string is sutured around the cervix at 12–14 weeks gestation and removed when fetal maturity is achieved—usually after thirty-seven weeks of gestation.

Inflammation of the cervix (cervicitis) is quite common. The cervix is constantly exposed to trauma, for example, childbirth and coitus. The abundant mucus secretion in conjunction with the bacterial flow of the vagina bathe the cervix, creating a situation conducive to infection. However, only an occasional woman will be symptomatic and require treatment.

Cancer of the cervix has been studied in great detail, and several studies have shown that the disease is found more often in women of low socioeconomic status, women who first experienced coitus at an early age, female prostitutes, women having coitus with many partners, and possibly women who are infected with herpes 2 (see also CERVICAL CANCER).

Since most lesions appear without symptoms and are not easily detectable on examination, the Pap smear—a routine screening of cervical cells—is very important. The Pap smear is a simple clinical test which is easy for the physician to administer and free of discomfort to the patient. It is a screening measure and enables tissue documentation of the earliest development of cervical cancer. The Pap smear has a high detection efficiency, which permits treatment at an early stage, when cure is almost certain (see also FEMALE SEX ORGANS; HIGH RISK PREGNANCY; HYSTERECTOMY; UTERUS).

CESAREAN SECTION   The removal of the fetus from the uterus through an abdominal incision in lieu of a vaginal delivery. Cesarean section is indicated when labor is considered unsafe for either mother or fetus, when delivery is necessary but labor cannot be induced, when dystocia or fetal characteristics present significant risks for vaginal delivery, and when an emergency mandates immediate delivery and the vaginal route is not possible or suitable.

The origin of the term cesarean section is not certain. There is a popular explanation that Julius Caesar was born this way, but this is surely a myth since his mother lived on for many years after his birth—a virtual impossibility considering the crude surgical techniques of that era. A more plausible explanation is that cesarean section takes its name from the Roman code of law, the *lex cesara*, which required an unborn fetus to be removed from its dead mother. The first modern operation was said to have been performed in 1610. Successful cesarean sections took another two centuries to develop.

Cesarean section is one of the most important operations performed in obstetrics and gynecology. Its lifesaving value to both mother and fetus has increased over the decades, although specific indications for its use have changed. The initial purposes of preserving the life of a mother with obstructed labor and delivering a viable infant from a dying mother have gradually expanded to include the rescue of the fetus from more subtle dangers. Four major forces have reduced maternal risk from cesarean section: improvement in surgical techniques, improvement in anesthetic techniques, the development of safe blood transfusions, and the discovery of antibiotics.

There has been a progressive increase in the incidence of cesarean section in relation to total deliveries. Because maternal risk is acceptably low, cesarean section can be chosen in preference to those vaginal deliveries known to be associated with increased prenatal morbidity and mortality, including unfavorable breech presentations. Cesarean section is also preferred should the fetus become compromised during labor, as evidenced by an abnormal heart rate, monitor tracing, or scalp sampling, and when fetal distress in labor can be predicted on the basis of prenatal testing. Finally, a cesarean section is now indicated for a larger number of premature or compromised infants because of their increased chances for survival with intensive neonatal care (see also BIRTH).

CHANCROID   Chancroid is a sexually transmitted disease causing painful genital ulcers, which are often accompanied by swelling of the lymph glands draining the ulcer. Chancroid is caused by the bacterium *Haemophylus ducreyi*. It usually starts as a small pimple on the penis of men or on the labia, cervix, or walls of the vagina in women. Fever is usually present, and walking upright may be difficult if the groin lymph nodes are greatly swollen and have formed a tense pocket of pus called a "bulbo." Treatment with one of the new cephalosporin antibiotics is rapidly effective, and there is usually no residual tissue damage, although women may develop a fistula between the posterior vaginal wall and the rectum. If left untreated, rapid enlargement of a chancroid ulcer can occasionally result in amputation of the penis.

CHASTITY   To be chaste, or to practice chastity, generally means to live a life-style in which one refrains from sexual intercourse. In youth, chastity implies virginity.

There are many reasons why a person—especially a young person—may decide to practice chastity. For some, religious or family values may proscribe sex prior to marriage. For others,

the question of when and with whom to first have sex is guided by highly personal values.

Today, it is estimated that eight out of ten people have experienced sexual intercourse by the age of twenty. Chastity is clearly *not* the prevailing trend for young people today. Yet, despite the tremendous pressure within our society for young people to be sexually active, many teenagers choose to follow their own very personal sexual timetable—to wait until they feel they are ready, married, or with the right person to first experience sexual intercourse. There is even an informal chastity movement among young people today, who are choosing at this time in their lives to say "no" to sex.

Advocates of chastity for young people make many good arguments against teenagers rushing into sexual intercourse. In the heat of passion it is easy to forget that sex has consequences—potentially bad as well as good—and, in fact, needs to be handled responsibly. If young people are not quite ready to take on sex and all that goes with it, ABSTINENCE makes a lot of sense.

For example, sex requires a decision to use contraception and an understanding that contraceptives sometimes fail. Pregnancy can occur even when a couple is using contraception. Abstention is, in fact, the only sure method of birth control. SEXUALLY TRANSMITTED DISEASES, including AIDS, can also be the consequence of sexual intercourse. A condom must be used every time one has sex, and even then accidents do happen. Again, abstention is the best protection. There are also emotional consequences of sex—the INTIMACY it brings can open one up to hurt as well as joy. Sex with the wrong person—one who tricks you, pressures you, or uses you—can be very hurtful, especially during adolescence.

Advocates of chastity for young people make the point that teenagers have an entire lifetime ahead of them in which to enjoy sexual relationships. While sex may seem like an urgent matter for teenagers, in fact, it is always better for a young person to wait until he or she feels truly ready to engage in it. Sex at the right time and with the right person is better sex and well worth waiting for (see also CELIBACY; TEENAGERS AND SEX; VIRGINITY).

CHILD ABUSE   The mistreatment of children, including all kinds of cruelty apart from specifically sexual mistreatment, is not a new phenomenon. Crimes against children fill news columns and TV time, and fiction and drama make much use of incest and child rape, all to the public's interest. Beyond our initial horror at the images of what is done to these helpless children, more disturbing is the betrayal of trust by those responsible for their welfare. People wonder how to begin to make life safer for children, not knowing who can be trusted.

With so much fear and distrust in the air, the atmosphere is ripe for a witch hunt. Communities have turned against day care workers who seem to have done no wrong. There is no doubt that some overly zealous social workers and therapists have encouraged children to remember horrors that never actually happened. Good sense must prevail. Parents, police, courts, and the public must realize that while often a child will recall what has actually happened, in other cases children are led in various ways to invent stories. The sexual abuse of children is real, but not everyone accused by a child is guilty.

Children must be protected and the best way to do that is by preventing child abuse before it happens, rather than by attempting to punish those responsible for it. Money must be invested in child-safety programs if we are to be considered a responsible, caring society (see also CHILD MOLESTATION LAWS; EATING DISORDERS AND SEXUAL DYSFUNCTION; INCEST; POST-TRAUMATIC STRESS DISORDER; RAPE).

CHILD MOLESTATION LAWS   American laws fixing the minimum age of legal CONSENT for sexual activity vary greatly from state to state and range from eleven to eighteen years of age; in Delaware in the 1950s children as young as seven were considered legally able to consent to sex. Furthermore, the legal definitions of the acts constituting child molestation vary widely: a nineteen-year-old male having sex with a seventeen-year-old female is committing a crime in some states but not in others.

The "age of consent" has varied throughout history. In thirteenth-century England, for example, the age below which it was prohibited for females to have intercourse was twelve. This was lowered to ten in the sixteenth century, and remained that for about three hundred years. At that time the minimum age was progressively raised until in 1879 it settled at the current age of sixteen. (For a fifty year period, until 1929, the age at which a female could marry was 12, four years younger than the age of consent for intercourse.)

Some argue that laws setting a minimum age of consent should be abolished altogether. These include pedophiles, who have their own agenda, but also those who believe that there should be prosecution only in cases of force or pressure, in which case there already are laws prohibiting such activity. Nevertheless, the vast majority of experts, both legal and psychological, concur with the concept of protecting children from having sex with adults.

Child molestation can be broken down into two different sorts: that involving members of the same family, called INCEST, and that between strangers. Incest has been acceptable in some cultures, including that of the ancient Egyptians (witness Cleopatra's marriage to her brother). Because the permanent breakup of a family, even an incestuous family, might cause more harm to a child than other means of handling such cases, courts have used various methods to deal with incest, including relatively short prison sentences and family therapy.

Today CHILD ABUSE is recognized as a growing problem—either because it is on the increase or because more people are now willing to admit that they have been abused—and state governments have taken steps to protect children suspected of being victims. Anyone in an official capacity, such as a teacher or physician, who comes in contact with a child whom they suspect has been abused in some way, is mandated by law to report such suspicions. However, because of concerns about breaking up families, it is estimated that many incidents are not yet reported.

Another difficulty with enforcing laws against child abuse is that often the only witness is the child, so that proving a case can be difficult. Under the Sixth Amendment of the Constitution, a criminal defendant has the right to confront an adversarial witness. Though the Supreme Court has ruled that a child of any age can be considered a competent witness, the courts have also tried to shield children from the trauma of cross-examination in a courtroom by allowing their testimony to be videotaped beforehand, although in some cases such evidence has been ruled a violation of the defendant's rights. It has also been shown that children can be manipulated into saying that abuse occurred in order to please the person asking the question, and some cases have been rejected by juries that refused to find the children's testimony credible.

CHILDREN'S SEXUALITY   Women and men living in the 1990s, whatever their moral or religious beliefs, know and accept that a healthy sexuality is one of the centerpieces of a full and satisfying personal life. But many have difficulty accepting the idea that a healthy sexuality begins long before adulthood, in the teenage years and, indeed, in childhood and infancy.

We accept that boys and young men experience powerful sexual urges as they mature. We have also come a long way from the days—not too long ago—when most people believed that the female was born without sexual urges and that she remained so (unless corrupted by a seducing male) until marriage, when she would be taught and sexually "awakened" by her loving husband. So much harm was wrought in the name of this sexual purity in the past, when young girls and women believed that they were abnormal because of their sexual feelings. We know now that sexual feelings and pleasures begin—for both boys and girls—soon after birth and for some, even in utero. These feelings, and the desire to satisfy them through sexual pleasure, continue for most persons throughout childhood, into adolescence, adulthood, and old age.

From observations of parents and baby-sitters (and this is confirmed by studies) we know that infants play with and explore their own bodies, as well as the limited world of the crib. Female babies will often rub their genital area when unencumbered by a diaper. Male infants often have erections that they rub and play with in obvious pleasure (some even had erections before they were born). Orgasms can also occur among infants: they may even be fairly common during the first few years of life for both boys and girls. Infants and toddlers of both sexes may deliberately induce pleasurable sexual sensations by rubbing against clothing and toys—and later blankets and pillows—as well as rubbing their legs together. It is not long before they discover that their hands and fingers can be used in very creative ways to achieve sexual pleasure.

Despite (or perhaps because of) the pleasure that their infant may be having, many parents are bothered by this behavior (sometimes because they erroneously believe it is harmful, sometimes for religious reasons, and sometimes merely because they are embarrassed about expressions of sexual pleasure) and they try to make the baby stop. Some parents will slap the infant's hand and firmly say "No! That's bad for you!" (as if he or she were capable of understanding). Others will try to divert the infant or child's attention to something else by offering a toy or food. There are even parents who carry this to an extreme by bundling their child under the blankets and fastening the blankets with diaper pins so that he or she cannot touch this source of pleasure. There are even some who threaten to "cut it off" should they notice their three- or four-year-old son masturbating. While we may not want children masturbating on public streets, it does seem that many, if not most, parents are overly concerned about their children masturbating.

Many therapists believe that impressions made on even a very young child can have a lasting effect on his or her emotional development, and may carry through to the adult years. Imagine what must go through the innocent mind of a child who is giving himself or herself pleasure, only to learn that such pleasure is bad, dirty, wrong, and forbidden. Fortunately, some children have parents who, instead of over-reacting, wait until the child is old enough to understand that genital touching may feel good, but it should be done in private.

Many parents are so uncomfortable about discussions of sex with, or in the presence of, their children, that they impart a message, however unintentional, that sex is so forbidden one should not even know about it, let alone discuss it. In a sense, some of these parents may even believe that the prohibition of both sexual behavior and knowledge marks the extent of the moral teachings required in raising a "good" child. These parents should think how they are helping to reinforce the idea that sex is a "forbidden fruit" that is unreasonably mysterious and irresistibly attractive to their young children. Parents who shy away from talking about sex because they do not want to give their children "ideas" are advised by Dr. John E. Schowalter, chief of child psychiatry at the Yale Child Studies Center "not to worry about putting sex in their child's head" because "it's there already." Many parents abrogate their responsibility in the area of sex education by assuming that the schools will teach all their child has to know and that all *they* have to preach is abstinence. This is usually not enough. There are more facets to sex than merely reproductive mechanisms and "Just say 'No.'" Discussion in classrooms and with parents should stress the complexities and responsibilities involved in sexual behavior as an activity involving human values, not merely a physiological exercise that provides self-satisfaction.

Children get many messages about sex from sources other than their parents and their schools: from their peers (the main source of misinformation); from religious leaders, more likely to stress ABSTINENCE that facts; and especially from the media. Unfortunately, mixed messages concerning sex and sexual values are prevalent in American culture.

The onset of puberty is a very troublesome time for boys and especially girls. While boys will usually receive support from other boys (concerning not only the legitimacy of sexual feelings but also of acting upon them through masturbation and sometimes through intercourse), contradictory messages not only continue for girls but may become even more troublesome. Often, the affection formerly expressed by her father through touching, hugging, and kissing her may suddenly turn into a more distant and formal relationship. That this growing distance may support the incest taboo is very

likely, but it seems to apply much more so, in many families, to daughters rather than sons.

The growing sexual feelings of adolescent girls become a source of concern for them since the message from most of adult society seems to be CHASTITY until marriage and then a passionate—with fireworks exploding— orgasmic life with a loving husband. This scenario has been compared to the image of girl carrying a sexual time bomb between her legs that is not permitted to go off until marriage. This model not only violates the bodily urges of adolescent women but is sharply contrasted by the media, in particular contemporary rock groups, that describe a vastly different world from the preachings and teachings of parents. Rental movies provide today's adolescents with private viewings of the most vivid depictions of every aspect of sexuality and sensual pleasure, often in the most desirable terms, even for the young.

Attempts at prohibition of interpersonal sex by teenagers (and some parents would still not allow even masturbation if they could stop it) have not proven successful in recent years, as they probably did not for their parents when they were young. But, unlike earlier generations, today's teenagers have "a sense that they alone call the shots of their sexual behavior," according to Dr. Lillian Rubin, a sociologist and psychologist at the Institute for the Study of Social Change at the University of California in Berkeley. Specialists agree that young people everywhere in the United States feel that it is their "right" to engage in sexual activity. A partial explanation for this is undoubtedly the widespread availability of effective means of contraception and, for some, the relative acceptability of having a child out of wedlock.

Fear of disease had been a factor limiting teenage sex in previous generations, and one might think that today's AIDS epidemic would result in very little teenage sex, but the evidence shows that other than modifying their behavior slightly by reducing the number of partners and taking some precautions, adolescents are not eager to give up their newly proclaimed "right" to have sex. According to the Alan Guttmacher Institute, 1 million teenage American girls become pregnant each year, a figure that has remained constant for the last seven years.

Two other important changes in our society should be mentioned because of their effect upon teenage sexual activity: "Society doesn't get really uptight about teenage boys being sexual," asserts Dr. Rubin. "What's new among boys is that they're having their first sexual experience at younger ages and don't condemn girls who do likewise." Related to this is the fact that VIRGINITY as a precondition for marriage to a "nice girl" does not seem as important to many young males as it did to males in previous generations. But, perhaps even more important, in many households single parents are dating at the same time they are trying to impose traditional morality on their adolescent offspring. This may easily lead to inconsistencies and hypocrisy that could undermine parental authority. Dr. Hirsch Silverman, a well-known New Jersey family therapist, says that even the best-educated parents no longer "know how to deal with their children's sexual activity."

Another area in early adolescence that is much neglected is the appropriate preparation of a young girl for her menarche—her first menstrual period. Parents often communicate (or, for that matter, do not communicate) some attitudes toward menstruation that have an impact on a young girl's self-image. Such parental messages can also give young boys certain attitudes toward their sisters and other young girls. When a girl has her first menses, it is a sign that she is biologically prepared to create human life. This should be a wonderful time in her life—a time to celebrate. In some cultures, there is a community or tribal party, and gifts are given to mark this rite of passage. In our society, it would be better if we could have a meaningful "coming of age" party, with gifts to the celebrant, who has become a young woman, instead of the vacuous "sweet sixteen" parties that are still given—the closest thing we have to acknowledging that a girl has matured into a young woman. The time spent in anticipation of this—the years before menarche—could be used wisely, not only by parents as an opportunity to provide sexual information to the daughter but also for the neces-

sary discussions of the morality and responsibility related to the act and consequences of intercourse. The same messages can be given to boys as they mature, together with their sisters, forming the nucleus of a new adult generation (see also SEX EDUCATION).

CHLAMYDIA   see GONORRHEA AND CHLAMYDIA.

CHRISTIANITY AND SEX   see ABORTION; ADULTERY; CELIBACY; MASTURBATION; PURITANISM; SEX EDUCATION.

CIRCUMCISION   Circumcision is probably the oldest and most widely practiced surgical procedure. First described in the Bible about 3,000 years ago, ritual circumcision was probably practiced many years prior to that. Controversy still exists over the need for, or advisability of, routine circumcision. Apart from religious reasons, there are several commonly recognized medical grounds to perform circumcision. These include preventing recurring infections of the glans (head of the penis) and prepuce (foreskin); averting the narrowing of the prepuce's opening, obstructing the flow of urine; and preventing a tight prepuce from retracting over the glans. There is also evidence that circumcision reduces the incidence of penile cancer.

The operation is essentially the removal of the prepuce under anesthetic. The area is cleaned and the prepuce is retracted to release adhesions and to clean under it. It is then pulled forward symmetrically, usually with fine clamps. A clamp is placed crosswise on the prepuce to hold the glans back, the prepuce is removed with a scalpel or scissors, and the clamp is removed. The skin of the penile shaft usually retracts and a rim of skin remaining around the glans is sutured to the skin of the penile shaft, completing the procedure. The patient can return home after he has urinated without trouble. In a simplified technique, a bell-shaped cap is placed over the glans, under the prepuce. A suture is tied around its base and the excess prepuce is removed.

Complications involving circumcision are rare, although there is frequently a period of dis-

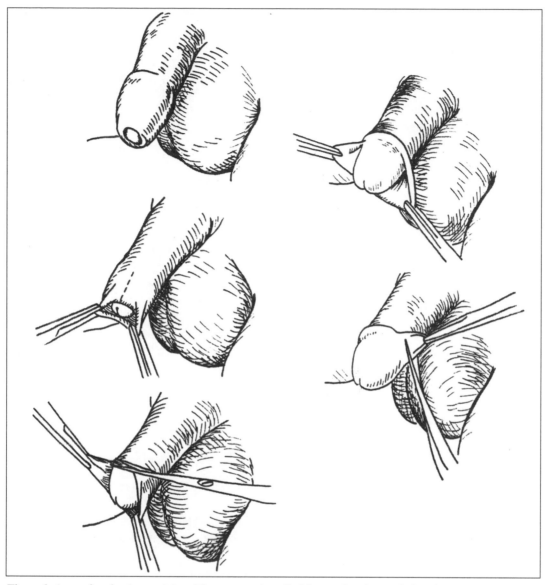

The technique of male circumcision: The prepuce is pulled forward and extended and is then removed sith a scalpel or scissors.

comfort lasting several days. Bleeding, the most common complication, can usually be controlled. Other complications include damage to the glans and infection.

Cultural Aspects. In the United States today, most males are circumcised. Although parents usually cite hygienic reasons for this, medical professionals are in disagreement over the hygienic value of the operation. It can, therefore, be said that circumcision is the most common form of cosmetic surgery in the United States.

Many peoples around the world perform circumcision for divergent ethnic and cultural reasons. It is universal among Jews and Muslims, and among some smaller Christian sects such as the Copts of Egypt. It can also be found among various ethnic groups in Africa, India, and Oceania. In Europe, however, circumcision was rarely practiced—even today it is less common than in the United States.

Sociologists and anthropologists have suggested several reasons for circumcision. It may have been believed to be hygienic, a sign of ethnic belonging, or as attractive to the opposite sex, or it may have been believed to increase sexual pleasure. No single explanation, however, accounts for the prevalence of circumcision among certain groups. For instance, while it may be believed to increase sexual pleasure, this does not explain why so many groups perform circumcision on infants.

In the West circumcision is often associated with Judaism. Traditionally, all Jewish males are circumcised. This is in keeping with the biblical injunction: "This is My covenant between Me and you and your progeny after you; every male child among you shall be circumcised" (Genesis 17:10). Circumcision is performed on the eighth day after the child's birth, unless medical circumstances show that this would be harmful to the child. Circumcision is integral to the Jewish religion: it is the first biblical commandment that Jews are ordered to observe. Circumcisions are generally performed by a *mohel*, an individual who specializes in circumcisions, although in the United States it is not uncommon for the *mohel* to have medical training.

CIRCUMCISION, FEMALE see CLITORIDECTOMY.

CLEANLINESS AND SEXUAL ODORS
There are two main dimensions of cleanliness related to sexuality: physical and psychological. Physically, a certain degree of cleanliness is necessary to prevent diseases. Psychologically, cleanliness may be sexually arousing for some men and women, but it can be a sexual depressant for others.

On the physical and hygienic level, when fingers, penises, or dildos are inserted into the vagina or other body openings, they should be clean so as not to carry any possible infectious matter into the body. For uncircumcised males, failure to adequately clean the head of the penis under the foreskin may result in an unpleasant odor and the possibility of infection from a substance called "smegma," that is produced by small glands under the foreskin.

The musky scent surrounding the male genitalia when it has not been freshly scrubbed may be very arousing for some, while for many the odor is repugnant. Similarly, the natural scent around the vagina (not the strong odors usually due to an infection) excites many, while others are repulsed by it. Some women are attracted to the slightly perfumed odor of the skin just after a man showers, while other women consider this scent as lacking the "smell of a man." Odors usually not associated with sex—such as bad breath odors—are usually responded to negatively by both men and women. Perhaps the most feared of all the sexually-related odors, as judged by television advertisements and products dealing with them, are menstrual odors. Anthropologists have maintained that this is probably due to the very complex set of blood taboos attached to menstruation in most cultures throughout history.

In brief, while most responses to cleanliness and corresponding odors are socially learned or psychological in origin and nature, it is wise for one to understand his or her own likes and dislikes and to be able to communicate them to a sexual partner so that a potentially destructive element of lovemaking is eliminated (see also DOUCHING).

CLIMAX, SEXUAL see ORGASM.

CLITORAL HOOD A fold of tissue that surrounds the CLITORIS, acting as a protection for it. It is actually an extension of the inner lips of the vulva and is comparable to the prepuce, or foreskin, that covers the end of the penis of an uncircumcised male. While in male circumcision only the prepuce is removed, in some cultures where CLITORIDECTOMY is performed, both the clitoris and the clitoral hood are removed.

During sexual arousal, the clitoris begins to enlarge and emerge from the clitoral hood; further stimulation precipitates the retreat of the clitoris back into the folds of the clitoral hood, and in most women it is completely hidden by the time orgasm is reached. To some observers, this is a dramatic sequence, akin to the unfolding of a flower in the morning sunlight and its closing in the evening.

CLITORIDECTOMY A term describing the surgical procedure of removing the CLITORIS, usually in a prepubescent girl around the age of seven. It is sometimes misnamed "female circumcision." While most medical persons and sexologists do not believe that male circumcision has any harmful effects—on the contrary, it has some health benefits—a clitoridectomy will usually deprive a woman of sexual pleasure and may be a permanent source of pain during sexual intercourse.

There are varying degrees of clitoridectomies, ranging from removing the CLITORAL HOOD and parts of the labia minora to removing these, the clitoris, and parts of the labia majora.

In the Middle East and Africa, where the operation is still practiced by certain ethnic groups, clitoridectomy may be accompanied by the closure of the vagina with stitches, except for a small opening to allow urination. When a woman who has had a clitoridectomy marries and is ready for socially-approved intercourse, the opening is enlarged by her husband with a knife or through the forcible entry of his penis. This type of clitoridectomy—called "vaginal infibulation"—is intended to ensure the chastity of young women, especially in societies in which a bride price is paid to the father for his daughter. Clitoridectomies were performed, although rarely, in the West until the early twentieth century, to discourage masturbation in women, which was considered unhealthy.

While the United Nations is on record as being opposed to clitoridectomy, very little success has been achieved in eradicating it since it is deeply rooted in the religious and social practices of many cultures. In these cultures, clitoridectomies have been carried out for centuries and are often used to distinguish women suitable for marriage from those who are not.

CLITORIS The clitoris is the principal organ of female sexual pleasure. Located near the top of the vulva, just beneath the point at which the labia minora (the inner lips on either side of the vagina) meet, the clitoris is usually hidden by a fold of skin called the CLITORAL HOOD. The clitoris is approximately the size of a pea (about one-quarter of an inch in diameter) but there is considerable variation in its size. Its structure is somewhat similar to that of the male's penis and, when stimulated sexually, it fills up with blood and can swell to several times its usual size. It is made up of soft tissues and has many nerve endings, making it extremely sensitive to touch and to erotic stimulation.

The clitoris consists of four parts. The head (glans) is the only visible part of the clitoris and it is sometimes covered by the hood. Below the head and located under the skin is the body (shaft) of the clitoris and below the body spread two wings (crura). The two parts of the clitoris lying under the skin are attached with ligaments to the underside of the pubic bone. The skin covering the clitoris is called the prepuce, or clitoral foreskin. In some women the hood completely covers the clitoris, while in others the clitoris protrudes from the hood.

The clitoris is now believed to be the most important organ involved in female ORGASM. In the past it was believed that there was a superior kind of orgasm, known as "vaginal orgasm." However, this has been proven to be a myth, and all female orgasms are now known to be related to clitoral stimulation directly or indirectly (see FREUD, SIGMUND). Women usually reach the point of orgasm because their clitoris is touched or stimulated. Even female orgasm resulting from vaginal penetration is related to clitoral stimulation. During intercourse the labia minora and vagina are usually stretched. Because they are attached through connective tissue with the clitoris, this stretching leads to pulling and stimulation of the clitoris. This stimulation is responsible for the subsequent female orgasm (see also FEMALE SEX ORGANS; ORGASM; VULVA).

COITAL FREQUENCY Sex therapists frequently find that their clients are concerned that the frequency with which they engage in sexual intercourse may not be "normal": that is, they believe they are having less sex than they should or than is "appropriate" or "healthy." Still others, though satisfied with the frequency of sexual intercourse in their lives, are curious about how often others have sex. This is evidenced by interest in the frequent "sex surveys" in popular magazines.

With respect to marital happiness and sexual satisfaction, there is no normal or correct frequency of intercourse. As long as both partners are happy and satisfied with how often they engage in sex, the frequency of their activity is normal and appropriate for them. Whether they have sex twice a day or twice a month is a matter for their own libidos, desires, and preferences. It is only when one or both or the partners is dissatisfied with the frequency of intercourse that it may be an issue to bring to a sex therapist.

Rates of coital frequency are not easy to compare because they are affected by many factors. The most obvious is the availability of a partner. Therefore, the most useful and reliable statistics are those based on samples of married persons who, presumably, all have partners for sex. Consistently, these studies have shown that the frequency of sexual intercourse, even for married persons, does decline with age. However, for older persons who divorce or become widowed and then remarry, coital frequency may increase for the first few years of their new marriage.

Based on research data collected in 1948 and 1953, Alfred Kinsey reported that the frequency of sexual intercourse for persons aged sixteen to twenty-five was 2.45 times a week, dropping down to .5 per week for those over age fifty-five:

A more recent (1984) study by Consumers Union of sexual behavior and aging among persons aged fifty and older found that among the 4,246 respondents, 28 percent of the 1,016 married women reported having sex with their spouses more than once a week, as did 25 percent of the 1,515 married men. While the median frequencies were not presented, the material presented in this study indicates that changes in social and personal attitudes favor the acceptance of full sexuality among the elderly.

Frequency of sexual intercourse is at its highest during early adulthood for hormonal reasons and because younger persons are in the early stages of the marriage cycle. When comparing single and married individuals, however, the image of "swinging singles" is not borne out by reported frequency of intercourse. In a recent national study, Drs. Janus and Janus report that "…there is consistent confirmation of the fact that, although single and divorced people may have a greater variety of sexual partners, they do not have sex with the frequency that married persons do. Marrieds' easier accessibility to sex partners obviously affects these results." In presenting the frequency of all sexual activity, they report that 64 percent of all singles claim to have sex at least once a week compared with 85 percent of married people.

COITAL POSITIONS   There are two main body positions a couple may use during sexual intercourse: the couple may face each other, or the male may face the female from behind. In each position one or both of the partners might be lying down, sitting up in a bed, sitting in a chair, kneeling on the floor or bed, or standing. There is no one position that is "natural" or "normal," nor is any position abnormal or a sign of perversion or pathology.

Facing Each Other. The most common sexual position appears to be the so-called "missionary position," in which the man is face down, above the woman (male-superior). The term was first used by indigenous people of the South Pacific to describe the preference of missionaries, who considered other positions sinful. The position is anatomically sound and usually pleasurable for both parties; it enables each partner to look at the other during intercourse and facilitates kissing and "love talk" between them. Psychologically, the male is sometimes seen as the aggressor in this position, and the female as the passive partner. This position may preclude sufficient stimulation of the clitoris while the male is thrusting his penis in and out of the vagina. Also, if the male is tired, he may lose his erection or feel uncomfortable supporting himself over the woman, or the woman may feel uncomfortable if the male is unusually heavy. On the other hand, some men find that the male-superior position is too stimulating and they ejaculate before they want to (a condition known as premature ejaculation). In addition, some women may feel more psychologically aggressive or assertive at times and want to remain "in control"

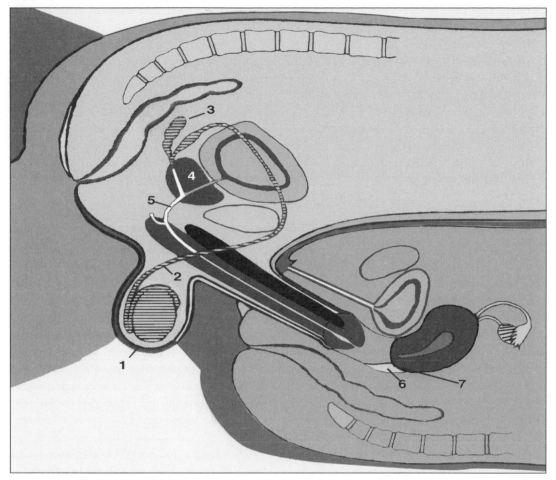

Coitus: 1) Testicles; 2) Vas Deferens; 3) Seminal vesicle; 4) Prostate; 5) Urethra; 6) Seminal pool; 7) Cervix

of the sex act. Thus, many couples who experiment with a female-superior positon—the woman on top—find that it adds a new and preferred dimension to sexual variety.

Sex therapists report that many women who have experienced difficulty obtaining orgasm or who have partners who suffer from premature ejaculation can successfully utilize the female-superior position during treatment of either problem. The female-superior position seems to have most of the benefits of the male-superior position without its problems, and it has the enhanced benefit of making it easier for the male to caress his partner's nipples or clitoris with his hands during intercourse. In addition many women report that it is far easier for them to reach orgasm, since they can move their bodies to maximize

stimulation to the clitoris and continue this stimulation even if the male climaxes first. However, some men may feel uncomfortable having a partner in what they interpret as a dominant role.

Some couples may experiment with a side-to-side position, especially if they are tired. This position does not allow for deep penetration. Some may not find it satisfying, but others may use it during advanced stages of pregnancy or in cases where the length of the man's penis may hurt his partner during deep penetration.

Rear-Entry. The rear-entry position involves penetration of the vagina by the penis while the man is behind the woman. Often the woman will kneel, supporting her body with her hands or elbows. While the rear-entry positon offers a different type of psychological and physical stimulation, it does not have any unique advantages over face-to-face positions except for its novelty. It does, however, provide deep penetration, desirable for some women, although others may find it uncomfortable.

None of the variety of positions that couples might envision should be rejected out of hand. Only after discussion and experimentation can sexual partners decide which positions are suitable and desirable for them (see also PREGNANCY AND SEX; SEXUAL INTERCOURSE).

COITUS   see SEXUAL INTERCOURSE.

COMING OUT   People "come out" when they reveal facts about themselves about which they feel great sensitivity, anxiety, or shame. Most commonly, the term is used when persons reveal that they are bisexual, gay, or lesbian, but it may also be used to describe the revelation that one has AIDS or HIV infection, alcoholism, cancer, or some other medical or physical condition. There are clearly a number of levels at which one may "come out," and it may be an ongoing, lifetime process for many individuals.

A gay man or lesbian may be so terrified of feeling attraction for members of his or her own sex, whether consciously or unconsciously, that the very recognition of these feelings may be blocked. Such a person may be uneasy, confused, flushed, or aroused around members of their sex without knowing what is causing the feelings. This is more likely to occur in an environment that holds strong negative attitudes about homosexual feelings or behaviors or among persons with no sense of the possibility of same-sex feelings. Persons who are more in touch with their feelings or with a broader set of experiences may recognize a same-sex attraction as such but not be able to admit their feelings to anyone.

Feelings and thoughts that are strong and recurrent often need to be expressed to someone. In the first stage of "coming out," they are often told first to the target of affection or a close friend, with a sense of fear proportional to perceptions about the unacceptability of those feelings. Although some persons are truly equally attracted to men and women, an early form of confession about homosexual feelings often takes the form that one is bisexual rather than gay or lesbian, since being attracted to the opposite sex as well might be perceived as more acceptable.

Many gay men and lesbians first come out to a would-be sexual partner. If they are not rejected and have other successful experiences, over time they often gain the courage to tell family and friends about their feelings, loves, and attractions. As a final stage, a small number of homosexuals are courageous enough to openly describe their experiences to the larger community through the media or in college classes, and "come out" to the world.

Even though people may be "out" about their sexual identity, there may still be areas of one's life and experiences that are kept carefully hidden. For example, while homosexuality may be acceptable to family, friends, and coworkers, multiple relationships may remain hidden, even from one's doctor. As another example, FETISHISM or unusual expressions of sexual desire may remain "in the closet" except to a very few people.

HIV infection and AIDS are stigmatized even more than a homosexual life-style. Although there is widespread agreement that it is ethically wrong to expose others to this lethal virus and though there are ways to make sex much safer against HIV transmission, some persons with HIV infection are afraid that the admission of infection may lead to discrimination or loss of relationships.

During the 1990s a new concept of "outing"— revealing another, usually "closeted," person's homosexuality—has developed. For example, although the United States Department of Defense policy prohibits homosexuals from serving in the military, many have nonetheless served, hiding their identities. During the Gulf War, some activist homosexuals asked for recognition of the fact that they had fought in the war without jeopardizing the country's military mission. When recognition was not forthcoming, homosexual organizations "outed" a prominent civilian official with the Department of Defense, who had hidden his homosexuality, pointing out that homosexuals could serve effectively in important military positions.

Should people "come out" about their feelings, behaviors, and conditions? It has been argued that remaining hidden is a heavy psychic burden. Howard Brown's book, *Familiar Faces; Hidden Lives*, speaks eloquently about the difficulty of maintaining dual lives. People who have opened up to their families and friends often report that a huge weight has been lifted from their shoulders; others, however, have found that their worst fears were realized and they could no longer be in touch with family and friends. The decision to "come out" must be carefully weighed, perhaps with trusted friends and professionals (see also HOMOSEXUALITY).

COMMITMENT   In recent decades "commitment" has been a frequently-heard term whenever relationships between the sexes are discussed. All too often, it is the female who complains of a male lack of commitment, while males often seem confused about what is meant. Essentially, commitment means a willingness to continue a relationship indefinitely or to work toward a stable, long-term relationship. For some, a commitment can be similar to MARRIAGE without a formal or legal status, or it may merely mean a commitment not to date others.

In younger persons, making a commitment is a form of play-acting for marital roles in varying degrees, from exclusive DATING and sexual relationships to full-time living together or providing emotional, financial, and social support. In many respects, a commitment is comparable to the older biblical, medieval, and Victorian notion of a "betrothal" or an engagement: it is a promise to act "as if" the couple were going to be married, whether they intend to be or not. Since commitments often imply long-lasting sexual and emotional involvement, they should not be regarded lightly, but as a trial for more permanent relationships in the future (see also LOVE; TEENAGERS AND SEX).

COMPULSIVE SEXUAL BEHAVIOR   see HYPERSEXUALITY.

CONCEPTION   Conception begins when a woman's egg and a man's sperm meet within her body to form the first cells of a new being like its parents. If successful, the meeting of egg and sperm in one of the woman's FALLOPIAN TUBES results in fertilization of the egg and growth of the first cell clusters of the new being's embryo. The fertilized egg then moves through the fallopian tube and implants itself in the woman's UTERUS (womb). When this process is complete, conception is said to have taken place.

The woman's egg is present in the fallopian tube and is fertile for approximately three days after she has ovulated (released the egg from an ovary), usually at about the midpoint of her monthly cycle. The man's sperm, which can remain alive and mobile for up to seven days, is present in the tube because the couple have experienced intercourse during that time. (Although desired, conception often fails to occur for a variety of reasons. However, it can be aided by modern medical techniques, among them artificial insemination and IN VITRO FERTILIZATION, in which important steps of the process occur outside the woman's body.)

When the egg is ovulated (released from a follicle or fluid-filled sac in the ovary), it is surrounded by many cells produced by the ovarian follicle. Within those cells and immediately surrounding the egg is a tough membrane, termed the *zona pellucida*, which represents the major barrier to penetration by the sperm. Fimbria (fringes) at the end of the fallopian tube aid in the transfer of the egg from the surface of the ovary and transportation of the egg to the upper region of the fallopian tube. Simultaneously, sperm have been transported from the vagina to the same region of the fallopian tube.

With normal sexual intercourse, millions of sperm are deposited in the upper vagina. Typically, only a few hundred actually reach the site of normal fertilization. Using a combination of swimming motions and release of chemicals, some sperm are able to penetrate the cells surrounding the egg, but usually only a single sperm is able to penetrate the *zona pellucida* and actually fertilize it. The fertilization process involves fusion of the sperm with the egg itself.

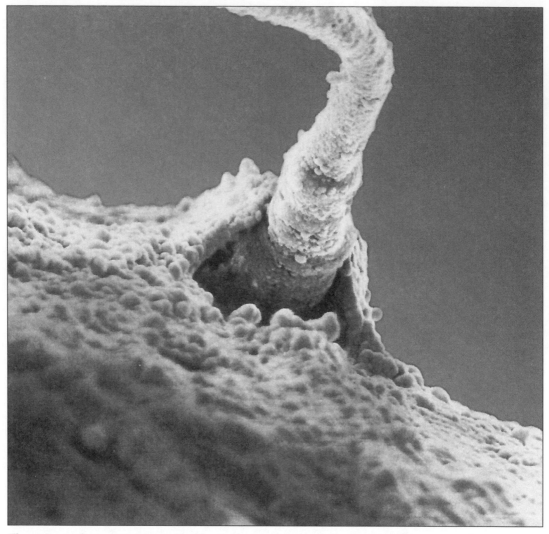

The moment of conception (magnified by an electron microscope)—a sperm cell penetrates the ovum.

Sperm cells approach the egg

Sperm cells approaching, binding with, and penetrating the ovum

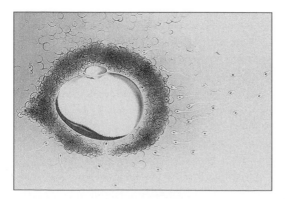

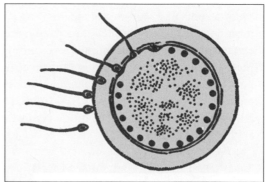

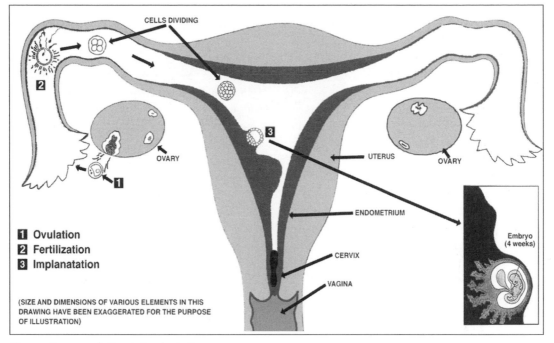

CELLS DIVIDING

1 Ovulation
2 Fertilization
3 Implanatation

OVARY

UTERUS

OVARY

ENDOMETRIUM

Embryo
(4 weeks)

CERVIX

VAGINA

(SIZE AND DIMENSIONS OF VARIOUS ELEMENTS IN THIS
DRAWING HAVE BEEN EXAGGERATED FOR THE PURPOSE
OF ILLUSTRATION)

Conception - ovulation to implantation.

Within the first twenty-four hours after fertilization, the genetic material—chromosomes—carried by the sperm merge with the chromosomes carried by the egg and, approximately thirty hours after fertilization, the fertilized egg divides for the first time. It is now called an embryo. Subsequent cell divisions occur at about twelve hour intervals. Under normal circumstances, fertilization occurs in the outer half of the fallopian tube and the embryo spends about three days floating free in this portion of the fallopian tube. The embryo, now consisting of approximately twelve to sixteen cells, is then rapidly transported into the uterine cavity. It is nourished by uterine secretions and undergoes additional development. Approximately six days after ovulation and fertilization, it "hatches" (emerges from the *zona pellucida*), expands dramatically, and finally burrows into the endometrium—the wall of the uterus. The new embryo produces a hormone (hCG) which, when released into the mother's bloodstream, signals that she is pregnant and causes the *corpus luteum* in the ovary to continue producing the estrogen and progesterone hormones necessary for maintenance of the pregnancy.

The actual process of conception has to be accurately timed. The egg has a very limited lifespan in which it can be fertilized (estimated to be no greater than three days). Sperm, on the other hand, are able to maintain their fertilization ability for a much longer period of time. Actually, sperm are probably able to maintain their motility (ability to swim) as well as fertilizing ability in normal cervical mucus for several days. Thus, even though a couple does not have sexual intercourse exactly at the time of ovulation, pregnancy may occur if the woman has had intercourse any time in the several days before ovulation (see also ARTIFICAL INSEMINATION BY DONOR; FALLOPIAN TUBES; FEMALE SEX ORGANS; HEREDITY; IN VITRO FERTILIZATION; INFERTILITY; ORGASM; SPERM; SPERM BANKS).....

CONDOMS   A condom is a sheath that fits over the penis to block the passage of sperm. It is used as a birth control device and as a means of preventing the transmission of SEXUALLY TRANSMITTED DISEASES during intercourse. The word "condom" is attributed to a Doctor Condom who was supposed to have been a court physician to Charles II of England in the seventeenth century. His condom was made out of sheep's intestines scented with perfume. Actually, the Italian anatomist Fallopius (identifier and namesake of the fallopian tubes) had created a condom out of linen one hundred years earlier. He contended that of the eleven hundred men who used it in his experiment, not one was infected with venereal disease. Among its advantages, he said, was that it could be carried in a trouser pocket.

Another advantage became apparent as condoms (spelled in a variety of ways and also known then as "machines" and later as "rubbers" and "prophylactics") gained wider acceptance in the seventeenth and eighteenth centuries; in addition to protecting against sexually transmitted diseases, they were an effective means of contraception. The man who popularized the use of condoms for their contraceptive value was the eighteenth-century Italian libertine Giovanni Casanova. He was extremely attached to them,

which is evident from the number of affectionate nicknames and descriptions he came up with: "the English riding coat," "the English vestment which puts one's mind at rest," "the preservative sheath," and "assurance caps."

Unfortunately, these early condoms were ineffective. They did not reliably prevent sexually transmitted diseases, because the bacteria that causes gonorrhea and other venereal diseases could pass through the animal intestines from which they were made, and they did not always stay on the penis when in use.

The modern, relatively safe, and effective condom dates back to the middle of the nineteenth century, when vulcanized rubber was developed. The final advance in condom technology came in the early 1930s, when they began to be made of latex, a rubber product that could be made thinner and stronger than before.

In the 1950s and 1960s condom use declined rapidly due to two major developments. First,

When putting on a condom, ensure that about 1/2 inch of space is left at the tip to collect the semen. Pinched the tip so that there will be no air bubbles, and roll the condom down to the base of the penis.

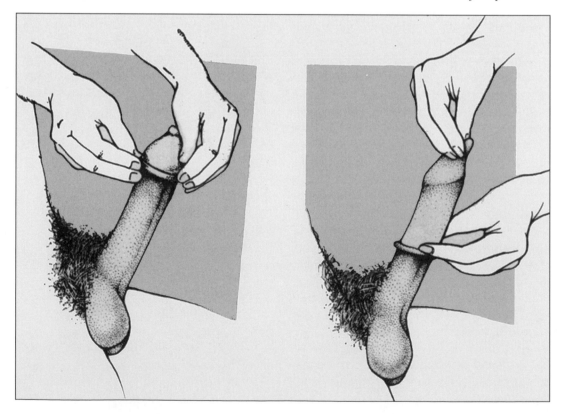

penicillin and other antibiotics were found to be effective in treating syphilis and gonorrhea, and second, the development of a female oral contraceptive—the "pill"—all but took over the main function of the condom: prevention of pregnancy. But, with awareness of the AIDS epidemic in the 1980s, condom use took on new significance as the most effective means of preventing AIDS short of ABSTINENCE or a stable monogamous relationship with a non-infected partner.

Only condoms made out of latex offer protection against sexually transmitted diseases. Condoms made out of lambskin (actually, intestinal tissue) supposedly offer greater sensitivity but they are riddled with microscopic holes. These holes are too small for sperm to pass through, so "lambskins" are effective against pregnancy, but the holes are large enough to allow microorganisms, such as the virus that causes AIDS, to pass through, and they should not be used to prevent the spread of disease.

The condom is placed over the penis so that upon ejaculation the sperm are trapped in the end, called the reservoir. It is important to remember that sperm are present in the pre-ejaculatory fluid released by the Cowper's gland, so the condom must be placed on the penis before any penetration of the vagina.

The condom's effectiveness, as typically used, is rated at 12, based on the number of pregnancies per 100 women during one year of use; if perfectly used, the rating is 2 per 100 women. Condoms can break (though this is rare) and if care is not used when removing them, semen can spill, allowing sperm to penetrate the vagina. One way of increasing the effectiveness of the condom is to use it with a spermicide. Some condoms are already coated with a spermicide, usually nonoxynol-9.

The use of oil-based lubricants can break down the latex and allow seepage of semen. If lubricants are required, they should be water-based. Some condoms are sold prelubricated with safe ingredients.

Both partners should know how to put on a condom, though it is most important for the partner wearing the condom. In their package, condoms come rolled up. Place the rolled condom over the tip of the erect penis, leave a half-inch of space at the tip to collect the semen, and then roll the condom down over the penis right up to the base. Pinch the air out of the tip with one hand: friction against air bubbles is the greatest cause of condom breakage. Do not remove the condom until the penis has been taken out of the vagina, making sure that there is no spillage during that process.

Condoms are easily purchased; they cost as little as 25 or 30 cents apiece (added features such as lubrication, spermicide, and different shapes and colors can raise to $2.50 per condom). All drug stores sell condoms, many displaying them on shelves, and they may also be purchased in some restrooms from dispensers.

Unless a man or his partner is allergic to latex, there are generally no side affects to the use of the condom. Some men complain that condoms reduce feeling; others praise this, saying that it keeps them from climaxing too soon. Whatever its faults, as a protection against the transmission of sexually transmitted diseases, particularly the deadly disease AIDS, it has no competition and should be part of the love-making habits of every sexually-active person not involved in a long-term, monogamous relationship.

The latest development in the long history of the condom is the "female condom," given provisional approval by the United States Food and

The female condom

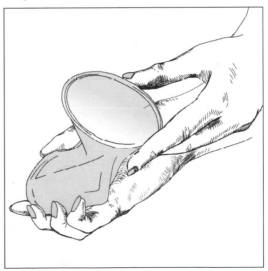

Drug Administration in February 1992. The female condom is a loose-fitting pouch with one closed end that the woman places deep inside the vagina. The open end remains outside the vagina and is entered by the penis. Its potential advantage is in putting safer sex in the hands of women who, in heterosexual intercourse, are most at risk of contracting HIV, as well as removing any excuse a male might give for not using a standard condom (see also BIRTH CONTROL; SAFER SEX).

CONSENT "Between consenting adults" has become one of today's defining terms for acceptable sexual behavior. However, in some situations, the line between what has been consented to and what has not is unclear. In a legal context, to be legitimate, consent must be voluntarily and freely given, without compulsion or duress, by a person who is legally capable of consenting, and it must be obtained without fraud or trickery.

The question of whether, in fact, consent was given may arise in a number of legal contexts including acquaintance rape, in which the victim knows the alleged attacker: statutory rape, in which minors are assumed to be incapable of knowledgeable consent: or rape within a marriage, in which the relationship between husband and wife may imply some degree of consent. The issue of consent is also often involved in allegations of SEXUAL HARASSMENT in the workplace and molestation of children (see also CHILD ABUSE; CHILD MOLESTATION LAWS; DATE RAPE; RAPE).

Rape is generally defined by state statutes as sexual intercourse with someone without that person's effective or reasoned consent. This means that rape is not just intercourse with the use of force. Intercourse with a person who has a mental impairment that makes effective consent impossible is rape. Similarly, minors, usually those under the age of 16 or 18, depending on the state's laws, are also considered to be incapable of giving effective consent to intercourse.

When force is involved in making a woman submit to sexual intercourse, the issue of rape is clear. But some women do not think of themselves as victims of rape if they have been out "partying" and are pressured into sex when in-toxicated or under the influence of drugs and are unable to respond in a fully conscious way to such advances.

At least 1 in every 4 women in America will be the victim of a rape in her lifetime. Studies estimate that over 90 percent of women who have been sexually assaulted do not report it to the police. About 40 percent do not tell anyone.

Although the trend is changing, most rape statutes in the past provided that a husband could not be deemed to have raped his wife. Several states have revised their rape statutes so that a husband can be prosecuted for raping his wife. Prosecution under such statutes, however, presents the problem of proving a lack of consent in a situation that typically occurs in the seclusion of the marital bedroom.

In the absence of clear use of force, the issue of consent in alleged cases of date rape has invariably resulted in controversy. Did one's partner say "no" but mean "yes"? Did one's partner communicate consent through past behavior? Through signals? By the way she dressed? Was one party enticed, so that the result should have been expected?

While some of these questions may confuse the issue, one way to clarify the issue is to remind yourself that you have the right to refuse any type of sexual contact at any time or place and at any stage in a relationship, regardless of the level of arousal that may exist in a would-be partner. There is no such thing as a point of no return, a point at which one no longer has the right to decide what will be done to one's body. "No" means No.

This may be a difficult concept for some to accept, when a woman voluntarily places herself in a situation in which she fears she can be seen to be "asking for it." In such a situation it may be helpful to acknowledge that a partner is entitled to some frustration or even anger at being told "no." One's partner has a right to his or her own feelings. But their rights stop where their partner's personal space begins. While we all have the right to express disappointment, we do not always have a right to impose our will, and sexual intercourse is one of those situations. "No" means No.

Under American law, a person has a right to a work environment free from "unwelcome" sexual communication or solicitation of sexual contact. The employee's acceptance or rejection of such behavior may not be a basis for an employer's refusal to hire or decision to discharge or otherwise discriminate against an individual in the workplace. This means that even if an individual does not lose a job or potential job opportunity, but is forced to endure verbal or physical abuse as a part of their workplace, they would have a claim arising from the hostile environment permitted by the employer. On the job, your job performance should be the sole basis for your evaluation, not your compliance or acceptance of sexually offensive behavior. Some employees hesitate to express their feelings because of fear of retaliation, and sometimes they may tacitly consent through silence. The law shields employees from retaliation in such cases and employees should educate themselves regarding their rights so that they can better exercise their right to say "No."

CONTRACEPTION   see BIRTH CONTROL; BIRTH CONTROL MYTHS; CERVICAL CAP; CONCEPTION; CONDOMS; CONTRACEPTIVE FOAMS, CREAMS, AND GELS; DIAPHRAGMS; INTRAUTERINE DEVICE; NATURAL FAMILY PLANNING; PLANNED PARENTHOOD AND MARGARET SANGER; VASECTOMY AND THE MALE PILL.

CONTRACEPTIVE FOAMS, CREAMS, AND GELS   Over-the-counter methods of BIRTH CONTROL for women include chemical or physical barrier contraceptives, familiar to many people because they are displayed on American supermarket as well as drugstore shelves. (They should not be confused with feminine hygiene methods which cannot prevent either pregnancy or disease.) They are available without prescription and do not have any serious side effects, but they are not as effective as other contraceptives, and several of them are made to be used in combination with other barrier methods.

These products offer a certain amount of protection against SEXUALLY TRANSMITTED DISEASES, including HIV, but because AIDS is a deadly disease, the risks should be considered too high to rely on these methods exclusively when having sex with anyone but a long-term partner who is known to be disease free.

Vaginal contraceptive foam comes out of an aerosol can and is placed into an applicator, which is used to insert the foam into the vagina. (Some brands come prepackaged in one-unit doses inside an applicator.) Because of the bubbling action of the foam when inside the vagina it spreads evenly throughout the vagina, covering the cervix. The foam contains a spermicide which paralyzes sperm, preventing them from entering the uterus and fertilizing an egg. For proper use, the manufacturer's instructions must be followed carefully.

For women who are uncomfortable about touching their genitals, foam offers the convenience of an easy-to-use applicator. Nor does foam have to be removed, as it washes out with the vagina's natural secretions. Some women do find these foams messy and leaky, and since the foams must be inserted prior to each act of intercourse, they do remove some of the spontaneity of love-making, though the application process can also be included as a part of foreplay.

For women who use only foam as a method of contraception, 20 out of 100 will become pregnant at the end of one year of use. By combining foam with other methods of contraception, such as CONDOMS or DIAPHRAGMS, the rate of effectiveness rises significantly.

Suppositories that release a spermicide when inserted into the vagina are less messy to use than foams and do not require applicators, a plus for some women. On the other hand, they must be placed into the vagina at least ten to fifteen minutes before intercourse, and no longer than forty-five minutes before intercourse has been completed, so that they definitely can affect spontaneity, though by integrating their use into foreplay, some of the fun can be restored. If the man has not ejaculated forty-five minutes after the suppository was first placed in the vagina, another suppository must be inserted, and another waiting period gone through.

Spermicides which come in cream and gel form are made to be used in combination with a diaphragm or CERVICAL CAP, though some do come with applicators so that they can be used without these physical barriers. This lowers their effectiveness to about 20 percent. Their low rate of protection against HIV makes them unacceptable for someone who has multiple partners, unless condoms are also used.

Creams and gels are less messy than foams although their application procedure is a bit more complicated because there are no bubbles to evenly spread the spermicide as with the foams. A fresh application of either of these products is required for each act of intercourse, and if intercourse has not occurred within thirty minutes another application is also required.

Like the others, 20 out of 100 women using these products can expect to become pregnant at the end of a year's use, and while there is some protection from sexually transmitted diseases and HIV, it is not very effective, and unless the woman has a steady, monogamous partner, condoms should be used.

The vaginal contraceptive sponge combines both chemical and physical barrier methods of birth control. The sponge itself is round and doughnut-shaped, about two inches long, and made of a soft synthetic substance. It contains the spermicide nonoxynol-9, which it releases when the sponge is moistened prior to insertion. Because the spermicide is released gradually, and also because the sponge itself acts as a barrier, the sponge is effective for repeated acts of intercourse and can be left in place for up to twenty-four hours.

The sponge is less messy than the foams, creams, and gels because it releases its spermicide a little at a time, though it does require more genital manipulation both for the insertion process and for removal.

By itself, the sponge has an effectiveness rating of 18 percent over a year of use, though the sponge is more effective when used in combination with another product or with natural family planning. It is less effective for women who have already had a child.

Sponge users may be at increased risk of TOXIC SHOCK syndrome, especially if they have already had it (in which case the sponge is completely contraindicated). The sponge should not be left in place for longer than twenty-four hours or during any vaginal bleeding. It would be best to check with a physician before opting for this method of over-the-counter contraception.

COURTSHIP   The getting-to-know-you process that takes place between a couple, sometimes leading to marriage. While customs vary according to culture, in every society where would-be lovers woo, courtship functions like a dance, in which both partners can examine their feelings after experiencing and communicating an initial sexual attraction.

In some cultures there is no courtship—only arranged marriages. Modern cultures, however, allow freedom of choice. Men and women must find and select their mates and convince them to love and marry them. This process of romantic persuasion is also the function of courtship.

Although a couple that is dating is not necessarily courting, when that couple gets serious it can be both exhilarating and scary. Courtship allows the couple time to bond and sort out important issues raised by the thought that they may be spending their lives together. Lovers can process the emotions and fears that often seem overwhelming.

Courtship is an active word: one lover actively courts another. Traditionally, the responsibility for courtship fell on the man. He called the woman up for dates, he sent flowers, he wined and dined her, and he convinced her of his ardor and eventually proposed marriage. But even traditionally, it was often the woman who, surreptitiously, did the courting. A common, insightful joke says, "He chased her; she caught him." It is very often the woman who selects the man and then communicates her receptivity through many signals. She laughs at his jokes, lets him buy her a drink, or drops her hand on his knee. The woman has customarily determined how much wooing she requires prior to sex.

All of this maneuvering was part of the courtship dance in the past. However, the rules of the dance have been changing. Many women now feel that they can court a prospective mate openly and assertively. They can ask the man out, pay for dinner, initiate sex, and raise the question of marriage. Courtship is still a dance, where a man and a woman get to explore their feelings and fears; but now a woman can initiate a relationship—as long as she is willing to deal with possible rejection.

For married couples the courtship period is often regarded as having been the best of times. It was the time when they were falling in LOVE, a time of ROMANCE, and a time of intense sexual excitement. This too is an important function of courtship, in that it provides couples with a foundation for romantic and sexual love. With care, that love can last a lifetime of marriage (see also FLIRTATION).

CRABS AND SCABIES   Pubic lice ("crabs") and scabies (itch mites) can be transmitted from one person to another during sexual contact. These parasites cause intense itching, which may chafe the skin of the pubic area. Successful treatment with scabicides requires the decontamination of clothing and bedding.

CUNNILINGUS   A variety of ORAL SEX involving mouth contact with female genitalia. The term comes from the combining of two Latin words: *cunnus*, meaning vulva, and *lingere*, or licking. Cunnilingus is reported by many women to be the most effective means of sexual stimulation; some report that it is the only way they are able to have an ORGASM.

While cunnilingus is not enjoyed by all women, it appears that during the last fifty years there has been growing acceptance of it. For a lesbian couple, it is generally a major source of sexual satisfaction. An indication of the growing acceptance of cunnilingus may be found in comparing data collected by Alfred Kinsey in the 1940s to that of later researchers in the 1970s and 1980s. For example, among married women who have had a college education, the rate of cunnilingus reported in marriage rose from 58 percent to 72 percent.

Many couples find cunnilingus especially valuable for stimulating and satisfying the woman during periods in which the male partner has a temporary problem in achieving erection. In some cases, cunnilingus is favored by women during the period after childbirth until the vaginal area is fully healed.

For most women the main sensation of cunnilingus comes from the stimulation of the CLITORIS by their partner's tongue licking it in slow or rapid motions. For others, however, this stimulation may be too intense and the licking should then focus on the sides of the clitoral shaft and the surrounding area. If a woman's clitoris is reasonably elongated when fully stimulated, her partner may also suck on it. The area surrounding the clitoris, particularly the labia, is often a source of attention during cunnilingus, and it may also be licked and gently pulled by the mouth. Individual variation of sensation is so great among women that it is imperative that sexual partners first discuss which areas provide pleasant or unpleasant sensations to the person receiving cunnilingus.

One irritant reported by women is the stubble of beard that many men have when they engage in sex at the end of the day. This stubble may be a great irritant for some women, but for other women the feel of their partner's heavy beard may actually be stimulating.

For many persons, subtle messages associating the genitals and genital area with dirt have often been communicated to them as children. Most adults appear to have outgrown such associations, but at times odors from the vaginal area may reinforce earlier admonitions. With normal, routine bathing, the vaginal area should not have any unpleasant odor. If one exists, the woman should consult a gynecologist.

Some of the "street" terms for cunnilingus are "eating pussy," "muff-diving," "going down," and "giving head" (see also FELLATIO; SAFER SEX; SIXTY-NINE).

D

D & C   see ABORTION; MISCARRIAGE.

DATE RAPE   Many studies now show that most rapes are, in fact, committed not by strangers, but by someone known to the victim. A recent survey of working women and college students by the University of Arizona Medical School found that more that 80 percent of female rape victims had known the person who raped them and, among college rape victims, more than half had been sexually coerced by dates. While such statistics are never absolutely reliable, there is no question that date rape (or acquaintance rape) is a growing phenomenon and a social issue that has raised a storm of controversy in the United States.

The controversy turns around a central question—in the often nonverbal sex-play between a man and a woman, what constitutes sexual CONSENT? Some cases of acquaintance or date rape, of course, are clearly and unquestionably that— forcible rape of a victim by an acquaintance. But not all cases are so clear-cut. For every clearly violent forced RAPE, there are instances of what might best be called "coerced sex"—times when a man who is dating a woman, or is even in bed with a woman, feels that for a variety of reasons he can ignore her "No" to the question of intercourse and assert his manhood over her objections. Such coercion, if aggressive and physical, may become acquaintance rape. But the lines between seduction, coercion, and rape are blurred.

Men and women often have different perceptions of what constitutes agreement to have sex. When a woman shows interest in kissing and fondling, for example, a man may misinterpret her behavior to mean that she is interested in sexual intercourse. When a woman says "No," it is very often assumed by a man to mean "maybe" and to be the beginning of a bargaining process. Similarly, if a woman agrees to go to a man's apartment or bedroom, some men assume that it means she is willing to have sex. In reality, the woman may not be thinking this at all.

Much of today's confusion between men and women on this issue is deeply rooted in seduction games the two sexes have played for millennia. Traditionally, men and women have not been explicit about sex. They have developed a very rich language of FLIRTATION, sending signals to each other which are sometimes very subtle. It is not surprising that such signals often get crossed, especially when one is sexually excited and predisposed to see willingness in a potential sex partner. Many men sincerely believe that women expect them to overcome their protests—that a woman's refusals are an essential part of a "mating game" that dictates that women must resist. A recent study corroborates this. Men and women had difficulty in agreeing as to what "No" really meant. When the woman said the man was to stop his sexual advance or she would call the police, both sexes agreed this was a strong "No." But when the woman said, "Stop, I'm not in the mood," men often tended to see this as "yes." They often read it as a request to continue their advances to try to arouse her. If a woman's "No" is interpreted as "yes, go further, turn me on," it is easy to see how a man's advances may become more and more physically insistent—even rough—and cross the line from persuasion to actual rape. There is, in fact, wide agreement among researchers that men and women involved in instances of forced or coerced sex often do not realize that they have crossed the line and their encounter has met the legal definition of rape. In one revealing study, men were asked if they would force a woman to have sex if they could get away with it: nearly half said, "yes." But when asked if they would rape a woman if they knew they could get away with it, only about 15 percent said they would.

Such problems of perception are greatly compounded when drinking or drugs are involved. Legally there is a question as to whether a woman can give consent if she is drunk. Yet, we know that many people—both men and women—deliberately use alcohol to reduce their inhibitions and routinely engage in sex while intoxicated. For sex to be truly consensual, both parties must be aware of what they are doing, and responsible for their actions. Heavy drinking can make this impossible. This is especially a dilemma on college campuses, where alarm has been expressed at the prevalence of date rape. The "fraternity house rape" is a very special college problem. The house party, with its drinking, sexual teasing, and competitiveness, may provide a social context that encourages aggressive sexual behavior. Girls who get drunk at fraternity parties may not feel they are asking for sex. Nevertheless, they should be aware that such behavior puts them in a very vulnerable position.

The biggest factors in unduly coerced sex or acquaintance rape are lack of understanding between the sexes, failure to respect the person one is with, and unwillingness to accept responsibility for one's actions. Men must finally accept that women are not always sending out sex signals. The fact that a woman wears sexy clothes, enters a man's room, or allows a man to kiss her does not automatically mean she is interested in intercourse. Men must understand and accept that "No" means "No" and that sex is a privilege, not an entitlement. For their part, women must understand that men cannot read their minds. A woman should know what her sexual limits are and make them very clear to the man she is with. She must also accept that it is her responsibility to take control of her own sexual safety. In real terms that means using good judgment. It is unwise for a woman to get drunk when out with a relative stranger, or to change her mind about sex in the middle of foreplay while nude in bed with a date. Yes, she has a right to change her mind. But in the heat of such a moment a man may be understood for not believing that a woman really means "No." It is unlikely that coercive sex will ever be eliminated from our society. In a very real sense, seduction is a kind of game and the language of sex is not precise. Still, men and women can do a great deal to increase their mutual understanding and respect for one another. When sex is viewed as a shared pleasure and not a selfish act, undue coercion is unthinkable.

DATING Dating appears to be a relatively new phenomenon in Western culture. Sociologists have attributed its growth and popularity to the waning of arranged marriage, coinciding with the development of the automobile and mass transit, both of which gave young people mobility. It contrasts with more traditional forms of socializing with the opposite sex carried out under the watchful eyes of adults, who acted as chaperones. Dating and the later stage of "going steady"—dating only one person of the opposite sex—provide the means for mate selection in lieu of the decline of parentally arranged marriages. Although it is widely believed that most dating begins about the age of puberty, increasing numbers of preadolescent boys and girls are not only dating but "going steady."

Dating during ADOLESCENCE is considered by most professionals to be a normal and healthy stage for learning and practicing the psychosexual skills necessary for a successful transition to more intensive emotional involvements. However, the social exclusivity inherent in going steady may cause some problems for adolescents, who, by limiting this important social experience to one person, may not fully develop other facets of their personality or interests that appear to be boring to their partner.

DELIVERY see BIRTH.

DEPO-PROVERA A reversible, prescription method of BIRTH CONTROL. Depo-Provera comes in the form of an injection and must, therefore, be administered by a clinician. The injection contains a hormone that prevents the ovaries from releasing eggs and thickens the cervical mucus so that sperm cannot join with any eggs that might be released. The effects of the injection last twelve weeks. For women using it who later want to get pregnant, it takes an average of ten months, and as long as eighteen months, to become pregnant after the last injection.

Depo-Provera is a very effective method of birth control: only 3 women in 1,000 will become pregnant after a year of use. Since the woman does not do anything after the injection is given, there is no chance of her making a mistake. Of course, she must go back to her clinician every twelve weeks for another injection.

There are, however, possible side effects, and because Depo-Provera injections last for twelve weeks, there is no way to stop them until the shot has worn off (it often last longer than twelve weeks). These side effects may include irregular intervals between periods, longer menstrual flow, spotting between periods, and long periods without menstruation. The longer a woman uses Depo-Provera, the more likely it is that she will stop having menstrual periods; more than one-half of Depo-Provera users have no periods after one year of use. Other side effects, such as change in appetite, weight gain, headaches, sore breasts, nausea, and increased or decreased sex drive, may also be experienced. As with the pill, women over thirty-five years of age who smoke should not take Depo-Provera.

The cost for Depo-Provera usually includes an initial visit to a physician, which, for a private physician in the United States, might cost between $35 and $125 (it costs less at a clinic). Injections cost from $22 to $30 each. Subsequent visits should cost from $20 to $40, plus the cost of the injection.

DEPRESSION   see EMPTY NEST SYNDROME; POST-PARTUM DEPRESSION; POST-TRAUMATIC STRESS DISORDER.

DIABETES   see HIGH RISK PREGNANCY; PREGNANCY RELATED DISEASES.

DIAPHRAGM   A barrier method of BIRTH CONTROL made of rubber. When in place it covers the cervix, preventing sperm from reaching the woman's eggs. It is shallow and dome-shaped with a flexible rim. It requires a clinical examination and fitting, and cessation of use immediately restores a woman's fertility. The diaphragm is always used with a contraceptive cream, foam, or gel, which is applied to the outer surface of the diaphragm to kill sperm, which otherwise would live up to seven days. The diaphragm must be removed from the vagina after twenty-four hours.

The diaphragm must be of the correct size, which is why a clinician is required for the initial fitting. The clinician will also provide instructions on how to insert and remove the diaphragm and the conditions of its use.

The diaphragm is not suitable for all women. Among the conditions that would preclude the use of the diaphragm are: poor vaginal muscle tone, a tipped or sagging uterus, and recurrent urinary tract infections. The diaphragm should not be used during menstruation.

A diaphragm may be inserted up to six hours before intercourse. It is folded in two and, after insertion into the vagina, pushed up so that it covers the cervix. It must stay in place for at least eight hours after intercourse, and if intercourse occurs again, additional spermicide should be applied while the diaphragm stays in place. In typical use, the diaphragm has an 18 percent failure rate for a year of use, which is reduced to 6 percent with perfect use. Some

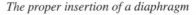

The proper insertion of a diaphragm

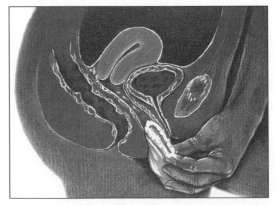

women are allergic to the rubber of the diaphragm, and some can develop bladder infections from its use. More rarely seen are cases of TOXIC SHOCK syndrome. Diaphragms offer some protection against SEXUALLY TRANSMITTED DISEASES, but in these days of AIDS, it is not enough. They are convenient and relatively inexpensive. The examination and fitting will cost about $50 to $85 and the diaphragm itself from $13 to $25.

Some women are uncomfortable placing something inside their vagina, while other women have fingers that are too short to comfortably use diaphragms. However diaphragms do not interrupt sex play if inserted in advance, nor can they be felt by either partner. They may, however, become dislodged during the female superior position of sexual intercourse.

DIET IN PREGNANCY   see PREGNANCY AND DIET; PRENATAL CARE.

DILDOS   Dildos are artificial penises that come in varying lengths and circumferences to provide different sensations of fullness to the VAGINA or ANUS. While there is no reliable data on who uses them and where, sex educators and sexologists believe that they are mostly used by women, who insert them into the vagina to assist in MASTURBATION. They are also used by women to have simulated coitus with another woman or to perform anal intercourse by entering a male partner with a dildo. In these two instances, the woman uses a specially designed harness that holds the dildo securely in place.

Historically, dildos have been made of a variety of substances including gold, silver, and ivory, or less expensively, of wax and wood. They were already mentioned as far back as the plays of Aristophanes in ancient Greece, among them *Lysistrata*. In one old Chinese painting, three women intently examine the wares of a dildo salesman.

Some older dildos were hollow and allowed the passage of a warm liquid to simulate ejaculation. Some modern dildos are battery powered and are known as VIBRATORS. The most common, and claimed to be the best dildos available today, are made of silicone rubber and are available in

shops specializing in sex toys for women. Many women find these silicone dildos to be erotically satisfying because of their smooth and supple texture. They retain heat well and can be easily cleaned or sterilized in boiling water. In her book *Sex For One*, Betty Dodson, an authority on female masturbation, suggests that an effective dildo can be carved from a cucumber and provides the reader with instructions.

Some sex therapists have recommended the use of smaller dildos as dilators in cases involving vaginismus or painful intercourse. Another medical use of dildos was as a prosthetic device for men with penile injuries. These were strapped on to the man's body with a harness and permitted him to simulate coitus by entering his partner with the dildo instead of his penis. Recently, the dildo as a penile prosthesis has been replaced by the penile implant.

Although dildos have a long history throughout the world, they are mostly used as an adjunct to other types of sexual excitement such as a vibrator or digital masturbation. In the words of one catalog from a women's specialty shop: "...we don't think of dildos as imitation penises. We designed them to be tactually and aesthetically pleasing. They're sexual accessories, not substitutes." In general, apart from their use as prosthetics, dildos are treated more as a novelty than as a major source of sexual satisfaction (see also LESBIAN SEX TECHNIQUES).

DISABLED PERSONS   see HANDICAPPED PERSONS AND SEX.

DISEASES OF PREGNANCY   see PREGNANCY RELATED DISEASES.

DIVORCE   From 1850 onward history has recorded more and more divorce in Western countries. This is commonly thought to be a sign of social disintegration in countries otherwise among the most advanced in the world. But there is an argument in favor of the ever more liberal divorce laws of the West. Both men and women can now escape from unworkable partnerships entered into when they were most likely to choose unwisely—when they were young, inexperienced, and in love. Easier divorce laws and the frequency with which they are used have come into being with the growing complexity of modern society and the mobility that individuals have in it. The modern person is more often free of the familial strictures and control that once kept so many unhappy people locked in marital prisons. Women, who now have effective contraception with which to avoid early pregnancy, and jobs or careers to make them independent of incompatible husbands, are especially benefiting from the escape offered by divorce.

It is probably true that most people want lasting, stable relationships with members of the opposite sex and will seek them again and again, not always finding what they are looking for. It is also true that improvement of stable relationships (including MARRIAGE) is a goal of the new art of psychosexual therapy, and that psychosexual therapy works best with people who are in livable, mutually helpful relationships. But there is scant evidence that first marriages are the most successful. At present, about half of all first marriages prove to be lasting. It is an open question as to how many are workable, happy, and mutually rewarding.

Divorce is an ancient institution and is often found in primitive cultures. Divorce was permitted in ancient China and Japan and among the ancient Greeks, Romans, and Hebrews. The Jews have always permitted divorce, although family pressure has leaned heavily against it. But divorce in these traditional cultures was tipped in favor of the man: it was usually the husband who would divorce a wife. A weighty reason was usually needed and there were penalties for divorcing a wife in certain circumstances. For example, among the ancient Chinese, if a man grew wealthy during the marriage, under certain circumstances the wife could sue for divorce or start a legal process that would earn her a divorce. Nevertheless, she was less likely to be able to get out of a hateful marriage than a man was.

From the woman's point of view, today's more easily obtainable divorces are a benefit, even when they lead to the break-up of marriages that have produced children. The modern woman who earns a living is less likely to stay married "for the sake of the children," since there is less social stigma attached to single motherhood and little or none attached to divorce in today's world. It is true, however, that divorce is an extremely painful experience for people going through it, and many people prefer to remain in unhappy marriages rather than face the uncertainties of personal freedom. Furthermore, divorce is often traumatic for children, who may see mothers and fathers transformed into enemies. Despite all this, divorce is usually considered preferable to remaining in a marriage whose unhappiness can ultimately affect the emotional lives of all members of the family.

Divorce Laws. We hear a great deal about messy divorces involving the rich and famous, but it is the everyday divorce that ends almost half of all marriages in the United States that has so changed the world we live in. If current trends in divorce prevalence and procedures continue, courts will have less and less of a role to play as people turn to mediation and other no-frill types of divorce settlements. Yet, with the trauma associated with divorce considered by experts to rank just under trauma from death of a close relative, there will always be a need for regulation of such a volatile end to marriages.

Divorce laws basically originate from three sources in the United States. Because each state has its own set of divorce laws, the statutes enacted by each state constitute the bulk of divorce law. Because these laws must conform to both the American Constitution and the constitutions of each state, these documents also have a role to play. And finally there is case law, the rulings of judges in individual cases, in which statutory law is applied and interpreted and which other judges look to when making their own decisions.

Because divorce has become much more common—in 1990 there were more than 1,200,000 divorces in the United States—most divorces never go to trial but are decided among the participants with the guidance of their lawyers. The courts must approve each divorce and, therefore, the terms of each settlement must coincide with the laws of each state. It is becoming more and more common for people to finalize their own divorces, so that in Arizona, for example, a couple can "divorce-by-mail." The simpler the circumstances (if they have no children, little common property, and both parties are working to support themselves) the less need there is for the courts to intervene. This is sometimes called a "no-fault" divorce, which means that neither party expressly faults the other for causing the end of the marriage. The parties can document that the marriage is over and the courts will adjudge the parties divorced if the documents confirm to state and local court standards. Exactly how this is done varies from state to state.

Of course there are other circumstances, especially when one party has hurt the other in some way—for example by committing ADULTERY, abandonment, or acting in a cruel and inhuman manner—and the injured partner wants a divorce while the other does not. In that case one party must "sue" for divorce. Even after one side brings a court action against the other, the partners may decide on a settlement of their differences and a property division. If no settlement is possible there may be a full trial and a judge will decide the merits of the case. Often there is also an issue of money, and one party (historically the woman, because women did not work in the numbers that they do now) will demand either short or long term spousal support or a payment from the other spouse in lieu of the support she (or he) was given during the marriage. In cases where one of the parties brings considerable wealth to the marriage, he or she may ask the other to sign a prenuptial agreement which expressly limits any possible future divorce settlement to a division of assets acquired during the marriage, though generally courts define marital property divisible upon divorce to be assets earned or acquired as a result of the efforts of both a husband and wife during the marriage.

The other important issue usually resolved by a divorce is the custody of children and their financial support. A mother or father who works is expected to continue to pay for the financial support of their children until they reach adulthood. Sadly, many if not most divorced fathers do not keep up their payments, leaving the mothers to take care of the children both physi-

cally and financially—a heavy burden. More and more states, and possibly soon the federal government, are taking steps to force parents to pay for child support, by requiring employers to deduct the payments from an employee's salary, as is now done with people who withhold taxes, or by attaching property against which outstanding support obligations can be satisfied.

DOMINANCE AND SUBMISSION As individuals develop and enlarge their sexual experiences, some find that unusual sexual practices excite them more than more ordinary acts of sexual intercourse. For some, the sexual activity that may be most satisfying involves a form of sexual dominance or sexual humiliation of their partner. In the broadest sense, these sexual practices are considered a form of paraphilia, meaning a love of unusual sexual practices. More specifically, sexual dominance is often considered by psychotherapists to be a form of SADO-MASOCHISM. While some individuals may have enough of an obsession with these behaviors to warrant a clinical diagnosis of psychopathology, for many, particularly married couples, sexual dominance may only be manifested in consenting "games" involving bondage and discipline or other forms of dominance and submission. In a recent national study, 11 percent of men and women claimed personal experience with dominance and/or bondage.

In these relationships one of the partners behaves in a dominant manner, while the other is submissive during the "game." Behavior during these episodes, for those not considered clinically sadomasochistic, does not usually reflect the relationship of the couple in their everyday activity. On the contrary, some researchers have reported that persons who exert much authority and control over others in their business or profession may enjoy the submissive role during these games while, conversely, the stereotypical "Casper Milquetoast" may desire extreme dominant activities during sex. The distinction between a psyopathogical obsession with such games and their use as diversionary play is a clinical decision and should be made only by a qualified professional. If the submissive partner is not a consenting adult, this behavior is criminal as well.

In its simplest form dominance may involve simple bondage, in which a husband or wife tie their partner to the bed while having sex with them. While many couples may consider this harmless, a recent bestseller by Stephen King explores the horror of such a game gone awry. In more elaborate games, submissive partners may be spanked or whipped for imaginary wrong-doings, as if they were children being punished by a parent. In the most elaborate games individuals may be placed in chains, leather masks, handcuffs, etc.

Some persons (usually males) may prefer to go to a professional dominatrix to help carry out these games in elaborate play-acting involving costumes and settings worthy of a stage play. Rarely do these activities involve sexual performances by the dominatrix. In the United States and other countries there are clubs and bars that cater to dominants and submissives. Some of these bars are called "leather bars" because of the frequent use of leather clothing and paraphernalia by participants.

DOUBLE STANDARD   A term used to describe society's different societal expectations of appropriateness and acceptability of sexual behaviors for males and females. This standard for sexual conduct does not only apply to possible DATING and casual relationships but extends through courtship and MARRIAGE, where cultural norms still appear to be more tolerant of male than female ADULTERY. While most often the double standard suggests that males will be far less condemned than females for engaging in extramarital sex, an increasingly more subtle form allows women to engage in sex without disapproval if they are in a stable love relationship, while the male is still permitted casual sex.

Historians have suggested that the roots of the double standard go back to biblical times, when women were considered the property of men—first their fathers and then their husbands. According to Deuteronomy (22:14–21), if a man found that his wife was not a virgin at the time of marriage and the parents could not prove otherwise, the woman could be stoned. In the case of adultery, a married man who had intercourse with an unmarried woman would be fined, while a married woman who had intercourse with an unmarried man could be stoned to death.

Many social critics believe that the double standard lingers on and reflects female as well as male thinking. Parents often show little or no concern about their teenaged sons having sex but preach ABSTINENCE to their daughters. Some rationalize this by thinking that it is their daughter who could become pregnant, not their son, and selectively overlook the fact that their son could make someone else's daughter pregnant.

DOUCHING   The act of irrigating and washing the interior of the vagina using homemade or commercial preparations. The intention is to maintain cleanliness. However, unless recommended by your physician, douching is usually not necessary. The vagina has a natural acid/base balance which keeps the growth of both yeast and bacteria in check. Douching can change this balance and predispose the vagina to infection. Many ingredients in douches are cosmetics, perfumes, or local anesthetics, and these may cause allergic reactions.(see BIRTH CONTROL MYTHS; CLEANLINESS AND SEXUAL ODORS).

DRINKING IN PREGNANCY   see FETAL AND INFANT SUBSTANCE ABUSE SYNDROMES.

DRUGS AND DRUG ABUSE   see APHRODISIACS; FETAL AND INFANT SUBSTANCE ABUSE SYNDROMES; PREGNANCY AND COMMON MEDICATIONS AND SUBSTANCES.

E

**EATING DISORDERS AND SEXUAL DYS-
FUNCTION** Intimacy, trust, and control—all
factors that are central to healthy sexual relationships—are also bound up with the problems that
lead to severe eating disorders. People who have
healthful attitudes toward food and eating often
have healthful and positive attitudes toward
themselves, their bodies, and their sexual feelings. Those who suffer from eating disorders often reject their physical and sexual selves so
completely that it can become impossible for
them to allow anyone else to accept them sexually or in any other way requiring physical or
emotional intimacy.

Studies have shown that more than 60 percent
of females with eating disorders have been
abused sexually, an overwhelming majority of
them as children. A growing number of case
studies indicates that among male adolescents
and adults with eating disorders there is a strong
correlation with gender identity conflict and
childhood sexual abuse. (There is, of course, a
strong link between childhood sexual abuse and
later sexual dysfunction.) It is evident that individuals with eating disorders use enormous
amounts of energy to conceal their dysfunctional
eating habits. Any of the emotional or physical
intimacy that a healthy sexual relationship requires can compromise the secrecy necessary to
maintain the food and eating rituals involved in
the eating disorder.

In cases involving teenagers—and they form
an especially large proportion of those suffering
from eating disorders—both parents and peers
should be alert to the signs and symptoms of the
disorders and seek a better understanding of how
they can stem from displaced and self-directed
anger growing out of either past or present sexual victimization.

ECTOPIC PREGNANCY A fertilized egg
can become implanted in locations other than the
UTERUS. This is called an ectopic pregnancy and
it can occur in the FALLOPIAN TUBES, CERVIX,
OVARIES, or the abdominal cavity. Over 95 percent of ectopic pregnancies occur in the fallopian
tubes. The incidence of ectopic pregnancy is rising, due to many factors, including SEXUALLY
TRANSMITTED DISEASES, infertility, and various hormonal medications. In the United States there is
one ectopic pregnancy for every eighty births.

Each month, during the mid-portion of the
menstrual cycle, the ovary produces an egg. Normally, the egg is picked up by the fallopian tube
and the tube relaxes and contracts rhythmically
to push the egg toward the uterus. The sperm
usually reach the egg while it is still in the fallopian tube. Once the egg is fertilized it will begin to divide into multiple cells and grow in size.
This collection of dividing cells continues its
course through the fallopian tube and enters the
uterus, where it implants. However, if there has
been constriction of the fallopian tube due to adhesions, prior surgery, or infection, the fertilized
egg can grow too quickly to fit through the tube
and finish the journey into the uterus. At other
times the tube does not contract well and does
not help push the fertilized egg to the uterus. If
either problem occurs, the fertilized egg will develop its placenta in the fallopian tube. The placenta will then nourish the embryo, which
continues to grow.

In a few days the early pregnancy begins to distend (widen) the tube and can cause pain to the mother. The blood supply to the fallopian tube is not as good as that to the uterus. With the distention of the tube and decreased blood supply the tube can tear, causing bleeding into the abdomen. This blood, in turn, may cause irritation of the abdominal lining that, interestingly, can cause right shoulder pain. If there is a lot of bleeding the woman may feel dizzy or light-headed and eventually may go into shock (severe low blood pressure).

Typically, women experience noticeable changes from a tubal pregnancy (ectopic, in the fallopian tubes), five to seven weeks from their last normal menstrual period. Women may have pain on one side of their abdomen associated with irregular vaginal bleeding or may have no bleeding at all. If any symptoms suggesting an ectopic pregnancy are experienced by a woman who has had sexual intercourse during the preceding two months, regardless of the type of birth control being used, a blood pregnancy test should be obtained as soon as possible. If the test is positive, an ultrasound examination can be helpful in locating where the embryo has implanted. If no pregnancy is seen in the uterus, there are three possibilities: the embryo is normal, in the uterus, but too small be to seen; an ectopic pregnancy exists; or the pregnancy has already miscarried spontaneously. If there is a mass to one side of the uterus and blood in the pelvis, an ectopic pregnancy exists.

When a doctor suspects a tubal pregnancy surgery is usually performed. A long narrow tube, like a telescope, may be inserted through the skin of the abdomen. The doctor can look through this tube, called a laparoscope, to identify the pregnancy in the fallopian tube. Once located, an incision can be made in the fallopian tube and the pregnancy washed out of the tube. From 3 to 5 percent of such women need future therapy to treat a small amount of placental tissue left in the tube.

More definitive surgery may be necessary to remove all or part of the injured fallopian tube. If it is removed, sterility can also result if the other fallopian tube is not working well. This surgery can be done either through an incision in the abdominal wall or through the laparoscope.

A new development in the treatment of ectopic pregnancies is the use of a drug called methotrexate. Treatment with methotrexate results in absorption of an ectopic pregnancy over the next one to three months without surgery. However, rupture of the fallopian tube will occur during treatment with methotrexate, and women who select this therapy must be very closely monitored. The advantage is that there is a high likelihood that the tube will be unobstructed after this therapy. With a single injection of methotrexate, side-effects are rare; however, if repeated doses are used, there can be serious side-effects.

If a woman has an ectopic pregnancy, there is increased risk that the next pregnancy will also be ectopic in the same or opposite tube. Therefore, if someone who has already had one ectopic pregnancy develops symptoms of pregnancy, it is important to make sure the pregnancy is in the uterus. The sooner the site of implantation is located, the sooner an ectopic pregnancy can be treated and rupture of the fallopian tube, with possible hemorrhage and death, prevented.

Unfortunately, the chance of having a future normal pregnancy is reduced to 50–55 percent after one ectopic pregnancy and is further reduced if there have been repeated ectopic pregnancies. If both tubes have been severely damaged, IN VITRO FERTILIZATION (test tube pregnancy) can place the embryo in the uterus to allow its normal development.

EGGS see ADOLESCENCE; CONCEPTION; IN VITRO FERTILIZATION; INFERTILITY; MENSTRUATION; UTERUS.

EJACULATION Male ejaculation occurs when fluid is expelled through the opening at the tip of the PENIS during the contractions experienced at the moment of sexual ORGASM. The fluid is called semen (less accurately, "SPERM") and the semen produced during one ejaculation is referred to as the ejaculate. Each ejaculate normally contains hundreds of millions of tiny sperm (reproductive) cells.

The process of ejaculation requires the coordination of several functions. Emission (secretion) of semen occurs into the urethra, the muscular tube through which urine flows. This happens during FOREPLAY, when a man is sexually aroused, and during the penis's thrusting before orgasm. Just before orgasm the neck of the bladder opening closes to prevent the flow of semen back into the bladder. During orgasm, contractions of the urethra and the pelvic musculature result in a forceful ejaculation of semen through the meatus—the opening at the tip of the penis.

Human ejaculate has an average volume of 3 milliliters, though it ranges from 1.5 to 6 milliliters. It is composed of sperm and seminal fluid. The volume of sperm contained in it is insignificant—less than 1 percent of the volume of the total ejaculate. Indeed, postvasectomy men report no change in the volume of their ejaculate.

Semen comes from two glands called the seminal vesicles. Its composition has been studied extensively and contains many components including electrolytes, carbohydrates (fructose), nitrogenous compounds, prostaglandin, enzymes, amino acids, zinc, and cholesterol.

After emission of semen into the back part of the urethra has occurred and the phenomenon of orgasm begins, it is difficult for men to voluntarily contain ejaculation. A refractory period occurs after ejaculation, during which further stimulation will not lead to another orgasm and ejaculation. The duration of this period varies directly with age. It can be as short as a few minutes for an adolescent or a man in his early twenties or several weeks in an elderly male.

Clinical conditions can cause a lack of emission or retrograde ejaculation into the bladder. A total lack of ejaculation during orgasm can occur in men with insulin-dependent diabetes, following spinal cord injury, or after abdominal radical surgery for colon and TESTICULAR CANCER. Men with multiple sclerosis, psychological disorders, or tuberculosis of the vas deferens (the tube that connects the testes to the urethra) also may suffer from a total lack of ejaculation. However, semen for artificial insemination can be obtained from men suffering from lack of ejaculation by a medical procedure called electroejaculation.

Retrograde Ejaculation. Ejaculatory dysfunction is responsible for 2 percent of all cases of male infertility. The most common form is retrograde ejaculation. Retrograde ejaculation is suspected when little or no semen is seen to flow from the penis's opening during orgasm. The diagnosis can be confirmed by the presence of sperm in an analysis of a postejaculatory urine sample. A total lack of emission (anejaculation) is demonstrated by a lack of sperm in postejaculatory urine, provided no obstruction of the vas deferens is noted and the testes are manufacturing sperm. Failure of the bladder neck to close during orgasm results in either partial or total retrograde ejaculation.

Any medical or surgical condition that interferes with the nerves, anatomy, or function of the bladder neck can result in retrograde ejaculation. Over 60 percent of men who are sexually active following transurethral removal of the prostate report no ejaculation during orgasm. In that situation, most of the ejaculate is retrograde and is eliminated by voiding after orgasm.

The phenomenon of retrograde ejaculation may also occur in men with diabetes, multiple sclerosis, and following surgical interruption of the sympathetic nerves. Medications such as alpha-Methyldopa (Aldomet) and phenoxybenzamine (Dibenzyline) may cause a chemical nerve interruption and retrograde ejaculation. Surgical removal of the colon or rectum and deseminated testicular cancer may result in retrograde ejaculation. Abdominal aortic aneurysm repair may also cause both retrograde ejaculation and erectile dysfunction.

Even with no treatment some men with retrograde ejaculation may spontaneously recover normal ejaculation. Although there is no surgical treatment to correct retrograde ejaculation, a number of medications have been used with some benefit. In men who do not respond to medication, an alternative method is available involving sperm retrieval from the bladder for use in artificial insemination (see also IMPOTENCE; INFERTILITY; MOMENT OF INEVITABILITY; ORGASM; PARAPLEGICS AND SEX; RESOLUTION PHASE; SEMEN AND SEMINAL FLUID; SEXUAL DYSFYNCTION, MALE; VASECTOMY AND THE MALE PILL).

ELECTRA COMPLEX   Although less firmly established in traditional psychoanalytic theory than the OEDIPUS COMPLEX, the term Electra complex is used to describe a little girl's intense attachment to her father and rivalry with her mother during the genital stage of development. The girl's response to her "castration anxiety" is to transfer her love of the missing organ, the penis, onto the bearer of that organ, hence her insistence on being "daddy's only loved one." The resolution of the Electra complex normally results in a shift away from the paternal figure to a suitable love object, who can provide a satisfying emotional and sexual life and can join her in bringing children into the world. According to Freudian psychosexual theory, failure to resolve the Electra complex can create serious problems for women, making it difficult for them to abandon their fathers for acceptable partners.

The Electra complex takes its name from the Greek legend of Electra, the sister of Orestes, who helped him kill their mother, the evil Clytemnestra, in retaliation for Clytemnestra's killing of their father Agamemnon. In the modern theater, Eugene O'Neill's *Mourning Becomes Electra* is a famous retelling of this ancient tale (see also FREUD, SIGMUND; PSYCHOSEXUAL STAGES OF DEVELOPMENT).

ELLIS, HAVELOCK (1859–1939),   British physician and author, Havelock Ellis was a groundbreaker in sexual investigation and discussion. Before Masters and Johnson there was Kinsey, before Kinsey there was Freud, and before Freud there was Ellis. By the time of his death he was overshadowed by Freud's more sweeping work, which focused less on physiology and more on the whole sexual human being. Ellis's major work, the seven-volume *The Psychology of Sex*, came out a single volume at a time from 1897 to 1928. The first volume was banned in Britain; the judge called it "filth masquerading as science." Later volumes were published in the United States and issued to the medical profession only—making it a great prize for young readers to get hold of and share! Ellis frightened many people by indicating that various sexual behaviors then considered "freakish"

and "abnormal" were much more widespread than they wanted to believe. Subsequent researchers, facing much less opposition in later times, validated his findings.

EMBRYO/FETUS AND DEVELOPMENT
Once ovulation and fertilization of the ovum has occurred, an embryo forms and implants itself into the endometrium and PLACENTA forms. Four weeks after ovulation the amniotic sac measures 1 inch in diameter, and the embryo about one-quarter of an inch in length. The heart and its enveloping tissues are very prominent, arm and leg buds are present, and the amnios is beginning to envelop the body stalk, which thereafter becomes the umbilical cord.

Six weeks after fertilization the embryo is about one inch in length; the head is quite large compared with the trunk. Fingers and toes are present and the external ears form definitive elevations on either side of the head.

The end of the embryonic period and the beginning of the fetal period are arbitrarily designated by most embryologists to occur eight weeks after fertilization. At this time, the embryo is nearly one and one-half inches long. Few, if any, major new structures are formed thereafter; development during the fetal period of gestation consists of the maturation of structures formed during the embryonic period.

By the end of the twelfth week of pregnancy, the expanded uterus can be felt just above the

A four cell embryo

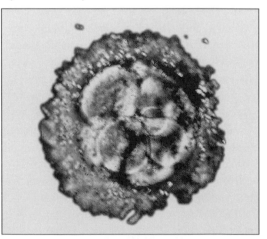

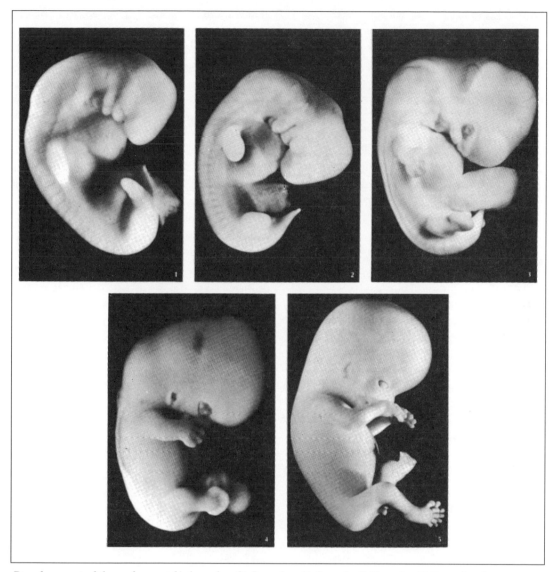

Development of the embryo at 1) 4 weeks , 2) 5 weeks , 3) 6 weeks 4) 7 weeks, 5) 8 weeks of pregnancy. During that time the head, trunk, and limbs develop.

pubic bone. Bone structure is continuing, the fingers and toes have become differentiated and are provided with nails, scattered beginnings of hair appear, and the external genitalia are beginning to show definite signs of male or female sex. By the end of the sixteenth week, the sex of the fetus can be identified.

At the twentieth week, the midpoint of pregnancy or gestation, the fetus now weighs approximately 11 ounces. The skin is less transparent, a downy lanugo (soft hair) covers its entire body, and some scalp hair is present.

By the end of the twenty-fourth week, the fetus weighs about 22 ounces. The skin is characteristically wrinkled and fat is deposited beneath it. The head is still quite large; eyebrows and eyelashes are usually recognizable.

At the end of twenty-eight weeks of gestation, the fetus weighs approximately 39 ounces. The skin is red and covered with *vernix caseosa* (a fatty, cheese-like substance that protects the fetus's skin in the amniotic fluid). The eyes can open. An infant born at this time in gestation moves his or her limbs quite energetically and

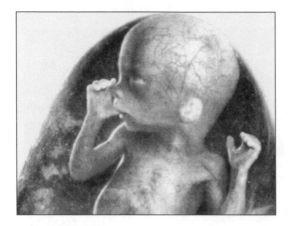

A fetus at 4 1/2 months

cries weakly. The infant of this gestational age, with expert care, most often will survive.

At the end of thirty-six weeks gestation, the body loses its previous red and wrinkled appearance. At forty weeks, or term, the fetus is fully developed, with the characteristic features of a newborn infant.

The average term infant at birth weighs 7–8 pounds, depending upon race, parental economic status, and size of parents. On average, boys weigh slightly more than girls.

The fetus receives oxygen and nutrients from the mother via the placenta. Through the placenta it transfers carbon dioxide and other metabolic wastes to the mother. The placenta and, to a limited extent, the attached membranes, supply all material for fetal growth and energy production while removing all fetal wastes (see also BIRTH DEFECTS; CONCEPTION; FALLOPIAN TUBES; MISCARRIAGE; PREGNANCY; RH DISEASE).

EMPTY NEST SYNDROME The portrayal of women—and to a lesser degree their husbands—as being depressed after the youngest child goes off to college or gets married has been part of the popular literature and media since the early 1970s. The parents' relationship is presumed to have changed—to have been diminished—because many or most couples are thought to have little communication in their marriage except around issues concerning children. There also is the popular belief that unless the marriage is a very good one—usually assumed for only a minority of marriages—the situation precipitates crises and problems, often manifested in a loss of sexual desire due to depression. Proponents of the empty nest syndrome concept sometimes point to its temporal association with MENOPAUSE and note the assumption that menopause also causes depression and anxiety about advancing years.

Researchers have repeatedly contradicted popular assumptions about the empty nest syndrome as well as the psychological consequences of menopause. Studies of women from all socioeconomic classes, who had been mainly homemakers until the youngest child left home, report that these women feel only brief sadness at separation from the child, and that this is generally followed soon after by a sense of relief that they are no longer tied down by their children's needs. In another study of aging, women with children that have grown up and left home are likelier to report happy marriages than women with dependent children at home. This study also reported that the psychosexual life of post–middle-aged persons is far happier than popular myths had assumed.

While depression does not appear to be inevitable at this stage of life, if depression does appear it should be taken as a warning signal that perhaps there is a problem in the marriage or elsewhere in the woman's life. Unless the causes are obvious, depression may be a serious condition that should be addressed by an appropriate physician, counselor, or therapist.

ENDOMETRIUM see MENSTRUATION; UTERUS.

ENDOMETRIOSIS A small number of women—possibly 1 percent—suffer from a condition in which tissue resembling endometrium, the mucus-like internal layer of the UTERUS, which is sloughed off during MENSTRUATION, is found outside the uterus, principally in other parts of the pelvic cavity. (Tissues that occur in places other than where they are normally found are referred to as "ectopic.") Ectopic tissue and lesions common to endometriosis can be found in many locations—the OVARIES, uterine walls or ligaments, VAGINA, appendix, VULVA, and CERVIX.

In rare cases the lesions have been found in the bladder, intestines, and lungs. The condition can lead to pain and abnormalities in menstruation, intercourse, and other sexual functions.

The disease has been diagnosed with increasing frequency during the past three decades. Its exact prevalence is difficult to fix because it has been found that many women have the disease without clinical symptoms and are unaware of it. Endometriosis is most commonly found in women in their thirties, among those of higher social class who have had few children or have deferred having children. In the United States it is more commonly found among Caucasian women, but with increased screening and improved diagnostic procedures, the disease has been found increasingly among African-American women and those of Japanese origin.

The symptoms of endometriosis include:

- Dysmenorrhea (painful menstruation), starting prior to the woman's period and persisting until it is over. The cause of the pain is unknown but is probably related to secretory changes in the ectopic endometrial tissue with subsequent bleeding;
- Dyspareunia (painful intercourse), which can occur when endometrial lesions appear near uterine ligaments or the vagina;
- Premenstrual staining and a reduced volume of menstrual bleeding. In cases of extreme involvement of the ovaries, there may be abnormal menstrual periods;
- Bowel obstruction and blood in stools and in urine, which can be caused by endometrial lesions outside the abdominal cavity.

Infertility is often associated with endometriosis. It is estimated that 15 to 20 percent of women afflicted with infertility suffer from some degree of endometriosis. While women who have the disease may conceive normally, the probability is low and is lower still if the disease is severe; endometrial lesions can result in scarring around the ovaries or FALLOPIAN TUBES and interfere with ovulation.

Pregnancy has been found to be the most curative treatment for endometriosis. Where it is not possible because of a patient's age, infertility, or disinterest in motherhood, hormonal treatment aiming at producing a pseudopregnancy or pseudomenopause is often recommended. Introduction of a state of pseudopregnancy is most effective for the treatment of small lesions and is usually achieved by administration of steroid preparations, androgens, estrogens, and any of the currently used ORAL CONTRACEPTIVES. Surgery is usually recommended only when symptoms are severe and have not been relieved by other means or when the patient is trying to become pregnant. A radical surgical approach is usual only if symptoms are extensive and the woman has completed her family and is near MENOPAUSE.

EPIDURAL PAIN RELIEF DURING LABOR The labor pains experienced by women during delivery ranks among the most severe forms of pain. Their amelioration should be mandatory to avoid suffering by the mother and to reduce pain-related physiological side-effects on the mother and the newborn. Epidural anesthesia for labor has achieved widespread use due to its effective pain relief and safety when properly administered. Its simplicity makes it the technique of choice for rendering the mother insensitive to pain while keeping her fully conscious during labor.

Epidural pain relief is performed by an anesthetist during active labor. The woman lies on her left side, with the medical staff and husband assisting and facing her. The anesthetist stands at her back, scrubs it, and administers a local anesthetic to minimize the discomfort associated with the epidural injection. To assist the anesthetist in locating the proper spot to insert the injection, the woman is asked to curve her back into the "fetal," or "angry cat," position, so as to widen the gap between the vertebrae. The needle is then carefully inserted in the lumbar region. The correct location of the needle tip is confirmed using a minimal dose of local anesthetic. A thin catheter is then inserted through the needle, and secured in the epidural space after removal of the needle. The catheter enables the anesthetist to add an additional drug if labor is prolonged; to use it for full epidural anesthesia if cesarean section is required; and to provide effective analgesia after the operation. The

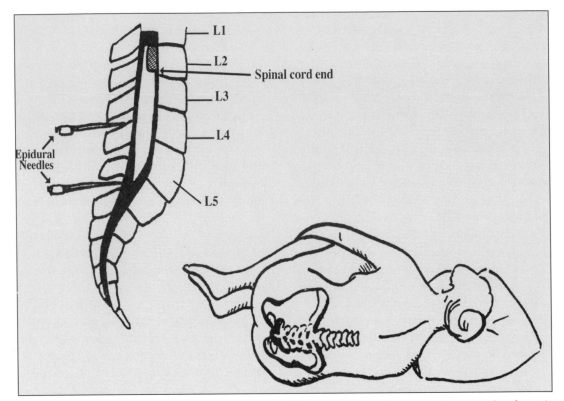

L1

L2

Spinal cord end

L3

L4

Epidural Needles

L5

Epidural anesthia is inserted in the lower portion of the woman's spinal column. To assist the obstetric anestheseologist find the precise location to insert the needle, the woman lies on her side and curves her back in the fetal position.

catheter is easily removed after labor. The usual drugs used for epidural labor pain relief are long-acting local anesthetics. The addition of a small amount of narcotics makes possible reduction of the required dose, while achieving better pain relief with fewer side effects. Recently a new group of drugs has been used: these act on the adrenergic part of the spinal cord, taking a role in pain modulation.

During epidural anesthesia the laboring woman often feels temporary weakness in the legs, a decrease in sensation, and occasional bouts of shivering; nausea is rare. Headaches are rare and usually occur if the dura is unintentionally punctured by the needle. Serious nerve damage is extremely rare. However, epidural injection should not be administered in the case of bleeding or severe local or general infection.

When adequately performed, epidural pain relief can make labor a joyful experience for the mother by keeping her awake and alert during delivery. The relaxed mother is able to assist in advancement of the labor process, while the attenuated stress of labor-induced pain can be physiologically beneficial for both mother and newborn (see also BIRTH).

EPISIOTOMY An incision made in the perineum (the area between the vagina and the anus) in order to enlarge the area of the vaginal outlet and facilitate delivery during childbirth. The most common form of episiotomy is in the midline, from the rear part of the vagina in a direction toward the anus. Occasionally this incision is made at a 45 degree angle and is termed mediolateral, as opposed to a median or midline episiotomy. There is general agreement that an episiotomy is called for in cases in which the fetus's descent is delayed or as an aid to some forceps or vacuum deliveries.

The role of episiotomy as a routine procedure in normal deliveries is debated. Advantages in-

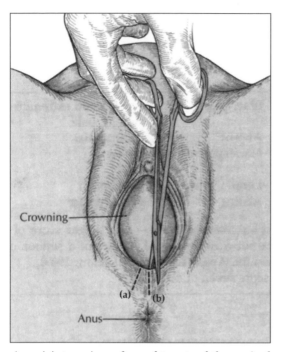

Crowning

(a) (b)

Anus

An episiotomy is performed to extend the vaginal opening and to prevent tearing of the perineum during birth. Incisions are made a) to the side of the vagina, or b) directly underneath the vagina.

clude substitution of a straight surgical incision for a ragged laceration of the mother's tissues and reduction of trauma to the musculature of the pelvic floor. Recent evidence indicates that severe lacerations are more common in patients who have had episiotomies than when episiotomy was not performed. The disadvantages of episiotomy include increased blood loss from the incision and the possibility of an increase in trauma over that which would have occurred spontaneously. The debate is, as yet, unresolved.

ERECTILE DIFFICULTIES see IMPOTENCE; SEXUAL DYSFUNCTION, MALE.

ERECTION A man's PENIS is said to become erect when it increases in size, girth, and firmness, changing from its usually flaccid (soft or yielding) state to one of rigidity. The penis's erection is a complex process that depends on the coordination and integration of psychological, neurological, endocrinal (hormonal), and vascular mechanisms. These mechanisms have

only been understood since the late 1980s and there are still steps in the phenomenon that remain a mystery.

An erection can be caused either by psychogenic stimuli (erotic thoughts) or by reflexes which occur when sensory receptors on the penile skin and glands are activated (touched). However, the penis's *corpora cavernosa* (vessels containing caverns that become engorged with blood during erection) must also be healthy if an erection is to occur and be maintained.

Within the penis a dense fascia, the *tunica albuginea*, surrounds the *corpora cavernosa*. Arteries supplying blood to the penis run deep in the middle of each corpus and lead to tiny caverns. When the penis is flaccid, the arteries are constricted and the caverns they connect with are squeezed by surrounding muscle tissue. When aroused, the arteries dilate and the smooth muscle tissue surrounding the caverns relaxes.

The expansion of these caverns not only serves to store blood and increase the size and girth of the penis, but also compresses the small exit veins (located at the periphery of the *corpus cavernosum*) against the thick and relatively inelastic *tunica albuginea*. This is the mechanism by which blood is trapped within the penis to enlarge and stiffen it. A substance called nitric oxide is released by cells lining the caverns and blood vessels as well as from the nerve endings, and serves as an activator of muscle relaxation.

If muscle relaxation fails to occur, not only is resistance high to blood flowing into the penis, but resistance is low to blood flowing out, because veins draining blood from the penis remain open. It is this nitric oxide-mediated relaxation that is currently thought to be impaired in men suffering from impotence related to diabetes mellitus, arteriosclerosis and high cholesterol levels. More than 80 percent of the men treated obtain a firm erection with a small and painless injection of a vasodilator substance directly into one of the *corpora cavernosa*.

Erectile dysfunction, or IMPOTENCE, is a major problem of adult men in the United States. An estimated 10 million men suffer from erection problems and it is likely that this number will grow as the population ages. Treatment options

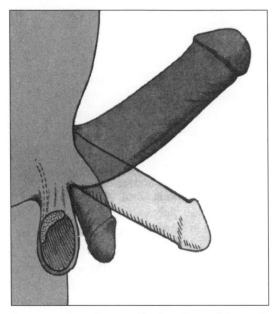

In an erection, the erectile chambers of the penis fill with blood and the penis swells and grows firm.

include the use of an external vacuum tumescence device, self-injections, or penile prostheses. In young patients with a history of pelvic trauma, vascular reconstruction is also performed but with much less success. Currently, painless penile injections with prostaglandin E when erection is desired seem to be the treatment of choice by most men suffering from IMPOTENCE (see also PSYCHOGENIC ERECTION).

EROGENOUS ZONES Many people, particularly younger people, want to know which parts of the body will provide their partner with erotic, arousing sensations. However, it is misleading to talk about "zones" or areas that are common to everyone, other than the obvious genital areas. Practically every part of the body, even the navel, may produce erotic sensations when touched—from the stroking of hair to the touching and sucking of toes. It all depends upon who is doing the touching, how, when, and under what conditions. It is very important to learn one's own preferences and to be able to communicate them. Therefore, one should touch and stimulate one's self in all parts of the body (within practical limits) with bare hands, oils, massagers, and vibrators, for example. Similarly,

one may explore one's partner's body and ask him or her what is most pleasing.

It is important to realize that no two men or women are identical in the erotic intensity of each part of the body. This is because eroticism is not merely a matter of nerve endings; it is also a matter of perception. For example, the nerve endings that produce erotic sensations in the vagina are concentrated only in the outer third of the vaginal entrance. But this is not as important as how a woman perceives sensation in the inner two-thirds if they too are stimulated. If she is equally or even more responsive in the deeper parts of the vagina, then she should relax and enjoy stimuli there. If a man gets turned on when his wife rubs her breasts across his bald head—wonderful. It does not matter if you believe you are the only one in the world who enjoys a certain kind of stimulation. It is your body. Only you know the sensations you feel, so learn as much as you can about that body. Think of your entire body as a map maker thinks of the planet Earth. You, and later your partner, can map the different types and degrees of erotic sensations that you each get from exploring every inch of the other person's body. Just as map makers have kept refining maps over the years, you should keep on exploring your own body, at times with the help of others, to know every inch of the "erotic road"! (See also FOREPLAY; G-SPOT; KISSING; ORAL SEX).

EROTICA Erotica may be best understood by comparing it to PORNOGRAPHY. Although the distinctions are often legal in nature and sometimes confusing to the public, many observers—both lay persons and professionals—agree that the two are very different. Verbal communications (books, song lyrics, telephone messages), pictorial communications (movies, videos, photographs), and live performances that portray a demeaning, humiliating, or exploitative image of sexuality and are without artistic merit can be considered pornographic. Works acknowledged by art critics and other critical viewers or readers to have artistic or literary merit can be judged erotic, as can warm and sensual depictions of individuals in mutually satisfying sexual situations. However, both pornography and erotica are often sexually arousing. Many times the line between the two is blurred by the fact that "community standards" are the main criterion for the distinction, and communities are often divided on this subject. A further complication is added by changes in community standards over time.

Erotic art has existed in most cultures and throughout history. The ancient Greeks, for instance, were intensely interested in the concept of beauty, first symbolized by idealized perfection in naked men and later in naked women. The Greek notion of beauty—it stood as a paragon until the early twentieth century—recognized that the appreciation of beauty is mixed with sexual desire. Statues of Aphrodite, the goddess of love (called Venus by the Romans), almost always showed her clothed or at least partially draped, until the Greek artist Praxiteles created a nude sculpture for a temple on the island of Kos. According to Pliny, the people of Kos rejected the statue because it was nude, but the people of Knidos cheerfully took it instead. It became one of the most celebrated sculptures of antiquity. In contrast to the modest poses prescribed by Greeks and Romans for female nudes, male statuary was shamelessly naked. Even less inhibited were ancient depictions of satyrs: lusty creatures with goatlike ears, horns, and even an occasional tail.

Almost every culture with a strong tradition of visual expression has produced some artistic works that depict positions for sexual intercourse. In Japan, volumes called "pillow books" were placed in the bedclothes of newlyweds to advise them on the delights that awaited them. In Renaissance Italy, Giulio Romano produced a set of engravings called *I Modi* (*The Positions*) that outline some sixteen different variations for coitus. The ancient Greeks displayed diverse positions on wine jars and drinking vessels.

It is thought by scholars that the sexual activity displayed on Indian temples is an aspect of Tantric belief, in which sexual acts are one of five offerings made to the deity. As that society evolved, it is theorized, ritual sex that once took place in magic ceremonies was replaced by sculptures of sexual acts on temple facades and interiors. On these temple walls we find highly detailed carvings of persons involved in twosomes, threesomes, foursomes, and more. In Japan we find beautiful prints of heterosexual and lesbian activities and illustrations of all commonly known variations of the sexual act, as well as the use of DILDOS and other devices. Other forms of erotic art from Europe, Asia, and elsewhere depict MASTURBATION—both male and female—with a variety of imaginative positions and techniques.

Erotica for Today's Women. Historically, erotica was created by men and directed at a male audience. Of course there were exceptions: *Lady Chatterly's Lover* is certainly a story that has excited women ever since it was published, and the diaries of Anaïs Nin are arousing to both sexes. However, since males have constituted the bulk of the consumers of erotica, the field has been dominated by them creatively as well. In the 1990s this is changing. Bookstores now have sections devoted to erotic literature for women alongside shelves filled with mainstream fiction and cookbooks. Erotic books aimed at an audience of women are advertised in popular magazines, and women are not ashamed to display them at home. In fact, these books are not usually found in porn shops catering to men.

To some degree these books are an outgrowth of the romance novel, a literary field that has exploded in recent times. While romance novels follow a fairly established format, the obligatory love scenes have gotten steamier over the years. Under the circumstances, it is not surprising that women readers would want to go one step further and read genuine erotica written for them.

What distinguishes the books written for women, with titles like *Touching Fire*, *Erotic Interludes*, and *Slow Hand*, and standard erotica is that most of these novels and short stories are written by women. A female writer probably has a better understanding of what a woman will find arousing, both in terms of what is going on within the pages of the book and what the reader must feel in order to respond physically to the story. Women are often interested in reading a story with greater emphasis on teasing anticipation and a gradual build-up than two people meeting, tearing their clothes off, and jumping into bed.

Many of these authors also make the effort to describe more than just the physical attributes of the lovers. To a woman, vivid descriptions, such as a garden bursting with flowers, lovers covered in silk and velvet, and the sensory stimuli that fill the air, are all exciting details that must be included for a story to be truly satisfying.

The very fact that such literature exists may begin to change the way women respond to sexual stimulation. It has been scientifically shown that women take longer than men to become fully aroused, but what is not known is whether this is a physical attribute or merely a conditioned reflex. Women have been told that they should hold back their feelings of excitement and that "nice girls don't enjoy sex," but these stories tell women that it is not necessary to wait for anyone's permission to become aroused and enjoy a sexual fantasy.

One positive aspect of erotica penned by women is that these writers do not idealize the female form. Not every woman in these books looks like a *Playboy* centerfold. These books show that women of all shapes and sizes, tall or fat, with small breasts or large thighs, can have fulfilling sexual lives. Another difference from the myths surrounding women's sexuality is that these books' heroines are aroused just by seeing an attractive man. In many stories the women have frank discussions about male anatomy, talking about which parts they find arousing and which they do not, while making it clear that the size of a man's sexual apparatus is not the most important factor to them. Society usually frowns on women who look men up and down the way men look at women, but in these stories women are given the freedom to do just that.

Not all these books paint sexuality in an entirely positive light. Some female characters do give in to the urge for casual sex, which, in this day and age of AIDS and other SEXUALLY TRANSMITTED DISEASES, can only be described as foolish behavior. Another dangerous theme running through some stories is one of women being overpowered by men, either physically or emotionally. In such fantasies the women give up their own sexuality to please others, usually men. Such story lines do women no favor; they should be reclaiming their right to being sexual beings, not ceding them.

How these books are used also differs among the sexes. For men, erotica is often used to enhance self-pleasure; while women who do not have a partner can certainly masturbate while reading such novels, women with a partner often use such literature to lead up to a genuine sexual encounter. Not only can reading such stories make a woman sexually aroused, but by incorporating the story lines into love-making, either by experimenting with some of the activities described in the book or by using them as fantasies, she can make her bedroom a more exciting place for her and her partner (see also AUTOEROTICISM; OBSCENITY; SEX IN THE MEDIA).

ESTROGEN   One of the major female sex HORMONES. It is mainly converted from androgens in the ovaries and, to a lesser degree, in the adipose tissue. Estrogen is linked to other hormones in the body that control the level in the blood at various times. Estrogen is especially important in the menstrual cycle, during ADOLESCENCE, and in PREGNANCY.

In the brain, the hypothalamus sends a message to the pituitary gland which then releases FSH (follicle stimulating hormone) and LH (leutinizing hormone), influencing the ova-containing follicles in the ovary. As a consequence, there is a proliferation of cells that stimulates the synthesis of estrogen. The increase of estrogen in the blood triggers the release of LH, causing a rupture of the follicle and releasing the mature egg. The ruptured follicle becomes the *corpus leuteum*, which responds to regression of LH by a decline in hormone production and endometrial shedding (MENSTRUATION).

Estrogen has other functions in the body besides menstruation. It is part of a coordinated group of hormones responsible for development and maturation of the breasts during puberty. Other changes that are due to estrogen are thickening of the labia minora, color change of the vaginal mucosa from bright red to pink, and the presence of mucoid vaginal secretions.

In the pregnant woman estrogen is part of a group of hormones responsible for breast tissue growth. Throughout life estrogen plays an important role in the balance of calcium in the bones. This becomes more noticeable as estrogen levels fall and bones become calcium deficient (osteoporosis).

As the woman matures and reaches MENOPAUSE, many changes occur as a result of the reduction in estrogen. The most visible event is the cessation of menstruation. Other hormone–deficiency-related symptoms are genitourinary atrophy, vasomotor instability (see HOT FLASHES), and osteoporosis (loss of calcium from bones). Other probable hormone-related symptoms include atherosclerotic cardiovascular disease and psychosocial symptoms of insomnia, fatigue, and possibly depression.

Synthetic estrogen replacement is used to alleviate signs and symptoms of menopause. It has been found most useful for prevention or lessening of osteoporosis and for prevention of cardiovascular disease in women with a strong family history of this disease. Once the decision has been made to prescribe estrogen replacement therapy, the physician must determine which estrogen to use and the dosage, route of administration, and means of monitoring the therapy for each woman.

All patients receiving HORMONE REPLACEMENT THERAPY should have an annual follow-up, including nutritional information, breast and PELVIC EXAMINATION, a Pap smear, and fecal occult blood. There is also a need for MAMMOGRAPHY and blood lipid screening (see also AMENORRHEA).

EXERCISE AND SEX Modern medicine places physical inactivity among the big health risks—others being cigarette smoking and high fat and high cholesterol diets. Physical inactivity is most evident among desk workers, but also among people who tire themselves out doing repetitive and limited physical tasks. Housekeepers, painters, plumbers, and factory toilers may not derive health benefits from the work they do. Everyone needs to learn, plan, and regularly carry out exercise that is known to be good for the body and for the enjoyment of sex.

Moderation is emphasized, especially for the person who has been habitually omitting or resisting exercise much of his or her life. A sudden violent venture into athletic activity is dangerous. People who go abruptly into heroic physical performance are, of course, comic strip material. A heart attack or wrenched back are only two of the serious possibilities.

The saying "No pain, no gain," so widely known in this age of aggressively promoted exercise, is simply a lie, and a health threatening one. You do benefit from mild exercise, which may be very gradually increased. But the first feeling of strain is the signal to stop. It may just mean that you should moderate the exercise, or, if the signal is alarming to any degree, that you should consult your doctor.

An exercise program will produce serious benefits if begun cautiously, increased very gradually, and continued regularly. It will increase blood circulation, strengthen the heart, benefit the lungs, and bring bigger supplies of oxygen to all parts of the body. The danger of heart attack and stroke will be lessened.

All systems of the body will be improved—glands, muscles, bones, nerves, and brain. The most noticeable effect will be a lightened mood and increased capacity for sustained mental work. Chronic fatigue, the couch potato's problem, will be replaced with periods of vigorous wakefulness and restful slumber.

While all of the above is promised in good conscience, direct benefit to sexual performance is another matter. Many other things in a person's life may be impinging on sexual activity—money problems, office worries, relationship difficulties, ingrained negative attitudes—and all can contribute to sexual dysfunctions. A program of exercise will probably enhance your sex life if it is basically healthy anyway. Enhancement is not to be disregarded, but it is not necessarily a cure.

People of very limited physical capacity, including some for whom the only possible exercise is passive exercise with the help of a physical therapist, are still capable of sexual desire and meaningful gratification. This must be remembered.

Some women have complained about partners who are obsessed with conditioning and body-building. Some exercise enthusiasts leave no time for sex, or have no erotic interest in the bodies of others. A physical culturist, like a woman obsessed with her own appearance, can be less than sexually rewarding as a sex partner. But such problems do not originate in sensible, balanced physical activity.

When you hear "moderate exercise," do not suppose that this means never needing to pause for breath or never breaking into a sweat. Moderate means moderate for you in your present physical condition. Moderate exercise can make you feel a lovely sleepiness, and can replace caffeine for waking you up and tranquilizers for calming down. The day after one that includes a brisk walk or a jog will probably find you feeling more cheerful, less irritable, more ready to take on challenges and chores alike, than the day after a day of slothfulness.

Besides the aerobics class, or dance class, or regular swim, or a cycle workout, it is wise to try to include exercise in ordinary activities. Use the stairs when you can, instead of the elevator. Walk to the coffee shop or news stand. At work at your desk, get up now and then to stretch and take a short walk. The work you do at the desk will benefit, and so will your sex life (see ARTHRITIS AND SEX; HEART CONDITIONS AND SEX; HANDICAPPED PERSONS AND SEX).

EXHIBITIONISM While many people believe that an exhibitionist is merely one who displays his or her genitalia in public, the legal and psychiatric definitions include the element of an unwilling audience or person at whom this is directed. Furthermore, psychiatric considerations assume that some form of sexual gratification motivates or follows the act of exhibiting one's sex organs. The term is complicated by the fact that for many decades the stereotype of the exhibitionist has been solely described as male—often the image of a man wearing a raincoat with nothing on underneath—who confronts young women on the street and exposes his penis to them. Research on apprehended exhibitionists indicates that, indeed, most are males, usually under the age of thirty. Writers on sexual deviance have suggested that there may be a cultural bias at work that ignores a female exhibitionism that is both tolerated and even admired, e.g. women who wear very revealing clothing at parties or in public. If a woman wears a very short and revealing skirt in public, is she a tease, an exhibitionist, or just a sexy and fashionable person? Is a stripper at a bachelor party legally an exhibitionist if one of the men present does not approve of public female nudity? Probably not, because she is considered to be a performer and there is the assumption that she is neither motivated by her own sexual gratification nor intends to shock rather than entertain. Motivation, however, is not relevant to persons at a nudist camp since, regardless of motivation, the social norms of the setting do anticipate public nudity there. "Streaking," e.g., running nude through a public auditorium or the streets, may or may not be considered exhibitionism, depending on whether the motivation is sexual in nature or not.

The existence of male exhibitionists alarms many people, particularly women and parents of young children. Although there is little evidence to indicate that exhibitionists follow up on their activity by touching or physically harming their victims, the psychological damage may be great when the victim is a child.

F

FAKING ORGASM Since ORGASM is essentially a subjective experience with physical signs not always clear to a partner, it is possible for a woman—or a man—to moan, gyrate the body, and fake an orgasm. It is assumed that women are more likely to fake orgasms since most men can reach climax more quickly during intercourse. Since traditional sexual role performances called for the male to bring the woman to orgasm, the man's sexual pride is often connected with an ability to bring his wife or lover to orgasm. This has created an undesirable situation in which some women, out of love and consideration for their husbands or partners, pretend that they had an orgasm either during their partner's orgasm or shortly thereafter. Some women do not want it known that they are anorgasmic out of fear that their partner will think them to be less "womanly."

Faking orgasms appears to stem from a lack of sexual literacy. These women have not learned to train their bodies to become orgasmic. In other instances faking an orgasm may result from conscious or unconscious problems in the relationship, while in still others, an inability or reluctance to discuss subjects such as orgasm may result in the wife failing to communicate to her husband the ways in which she can be brought to orgasm. If a person feels the need to fake orgasm, she or he should take this as a sign that something may be wrong in the sexual or emotional relationship and seek the help of a qualified health professional (see also SEXUAL DYSFUNCTION, FEMALE; SEXUAL DYSFUNCTION, MALE).

FALLOPIAN TUBES The fallopian tubes are hollow tubes extending from the upper surface of the UTERUS to the OVARIES on each side of a woman's pelvis. Each tube is about four inches long. The part of the tube closest to the uterus is termed the isthmic portion while the part of the tube closest to the ovary is termed the ampullary portion. The isthmic portion of the fallopian tube connects with a channel, termed the intramural portion of the tube, through the thick wall of the uterus. At the end of the ampullary region, the open end of the fallopian tube is covered with fine finger-like projections termed fimbria. The open end of the fallopian tube generally lies in close proximity to the ovary. The fimbria aid in picking up the egg from the surface of the ovary as it is released (ovulated), and in transporting the egg into the opening at the end of the fallopian tube. It is within the ampullary region of the fallopian tube where fertilization (the meeting of egg and sperm) occurs and where the new embryo spends approximately the first three days after fertilization. During that time, the cells of the embryo typically divide several times before being transported into the uterus.

The largest single cause of INFERTILITY in women is blocked or damaged fallopian tubes. Fallopian tubes generally become damaged through infection. Many fallopian tube infections are sexually transmitted (particularly GONORRHEA AND CHLAMYDIA) but fallopian tubes can be damaged by other infections, such as a ruptured appendix. When fallopian tubes are infected, the fimbria at the end of the tube swell up, stick together, and ultimately result in blockage of the tube, The cells that line the fallopian tube continue to produce secretions, but with an obstructed opening, the fluid builds up within the fallopian tube and ultimately produces what is termed a hydrosalpingx. This is a condition in which the fluid accumulation expands the fallopian tube, giving it the appearance of a water balloon. Fluid pressure on the wall of the tube causes further damage to the tubal function.

Conventional microsurgical techniques, including the use of lasers, have been quite unsuccessful in restoring normal function to fallopian tubes which have been blocked as a result of infection. In fact, the success rate (successful pregnancies) following surgical repair of blocked fallopian tubes is generally no better than 25 to 30 percent. It is for this reason that IN VITRO FERTILIZATION treatments were developed.

At the present time, almost 1 percent of all pregnancies are tubal ectopic pregnancies, in which the fertilized egg implants in the fallopian tube rather than in the uterus. Because the fallopian tube has only a limited ability to contain a growing pregnancy, it will ultimately rupture and produce significant intra-abdominal bleeding. Although surgical removal of the ectopic pregnancy is generally required, current diagnostic tests often permit the tubal pregnancy to be diagnosed early enough so that the fallopian tube can be saved. Ectopic pregnancies are particularly common in individuals who had previous tubal surgery, infections, or other pelvic abnormalities (see also CONCEPTION; ECTOPIC PREGNANCY; FEMALE SEX ORGANS; HYSTERECTOMY).

FELLATIO   A form of ORAL SEX. The term "fellatio" is derived from the Latin verb *fellare*, meaning "to suck." In the vernacular, the terms, "blow job" and "giving head" are synonyms. Fellatio has become much more acceptable today than it was in the nineteenth century, when it was considered a "perversion." In 1983 one research team reported that 90 percent of the couples studied engaged in fellatio at some time during their relationship. *The Janus Report* (based on a national sample) found that 88 percent of men and 87 percent of women reported that oral sex was "very normal" or "all right."

Fellatio involves the sexual stimulation of a penis by a partner's mouth and/or tongue. It may be limited to licking or sucking the glans of the penis or the entire penis may be taken into the mouth. The stimulation is performed by the partner licking the penis or moving the mouth (closed tightly around the penis) up and down the shaft.

Depending on the partner's willingness, the male may ejaculate into his partner's mouth or may withdraw just before ejaculation. Fellatio appears not only to be highly stimulating for the male recipient but often to the person performing it as well. It may be part of the process of FOREPLAY leading to SEXUAL INTERCOURSE or it may be an end in itself, with EJACULATION.

Since the ejaculation of semen into a partner's mouth may pose a risk of AIDS or other SEXUALLY TRANSMITTED DISEASES, it is important to use (non-lubricated) CONDOMS during fellatio unless there is complete confidence in the other person because of a long-term monogamous relationship. Withdrawal of the penis prior to ejaculation is insufficient, since a few pre-ejaculatory drops of semen often appear during stimulation of the penis, and these may also be infected with HIV (see also CUNNILINGUS; SAFER SEX; SIXTY-NINE).

FEMALE CONDOMS   see BIRTH CONTROL; CONDOMS.

FEMALE SEX ORGANS   Women's sex organs are either internal, and can be neither seen nor felt outside the women's bodies, or they are external. Most of the female sex organs—and specifically those involved in reproduction—are part of the internal genitalia.

The External Sex Organs. The external and visible female sex organs are usually referred to collectively as the VULVA. The vulva consists of the mons pubis (or mons veneris), the CLITORIS, the paired labia majora, the paired labia minora, and the HYMEN.

The mons pubis is the uppermost part of the vulva. It is the fatty area overlying the pubic bone and it is covered by coarse pubic hair. Immediately below the mons pubis is the clitoris, an erectile organ analogous to the male PENIS. It is approximately two-thirds of an inch long and less than one-third of an inch wide. The clitoris is exquisitely sensitive, becomes enlarged with sexual excitation, and is the most sexually re-

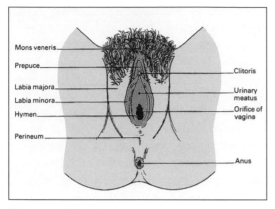

The external female sex organs

sponsive portion of the vulva. It is the primary source of women's sensations of sexual pleasure.

Beginning on either side of the clitoris are the labia minora (minor and inner lips), which surround the vaginal opening, extending from the clitoris to just above the anus (opening of the rectum). Outside the labia minora are the labia majora (major and outer lips), which, like the mons pubis, are covered with thick pubic hair. Between the labia minora is the vaginal opening. In girls and women who have not had sexual relations or used tampons, the opening is partially covered by a thin membrane called the hymen. In rare instances the hymen may completely obstruct the vaginal opening and prevent menstrual periods. Between the vaginal opening and the clitoris is the opening of the urethra, the tube

from the bladder that permits the passage of urine.

The Internal Sex Organs. The internal female sex organs consist of the VAGINA, CERVIX, UTERUS, FALLOPIAN TUBES, and OVARIES.

The tubular-shaped vagina extends from the vulva to the uterine cervix. The vagina is approximately four inches long, although it is enlarged during sexual relations and childbirth. It is located between the rectum and the urethra and bladder. If there is nothing in it, the vagina is collapsed like an empty balloon. The vagina's functions are two-fold: it is the internal female sexual organ, accepting the penis during sexual intercourse and receiving the male's SPERM when he ejaculates, and it also functions as a portion of the birth canal, providing passage for the baby from the uterus to outside the body.

The cervix, or mouth of the uterus, is actually the lowest portion of the uterus. In a nonpregnant woman it is approximately one inch long and protrudes about one-third of an inch into the upper end of the vagina. In the center of the cervix is the opening (or os) of the cervical canal. In women who have never been pregnant, the cervical opening is generally circular, while in women who have had one or more pregnancies it tends to be more elliptical and somewhat irregular in shape.

The uterus is approximately three inches long and is the size and approximate shape of a pear,

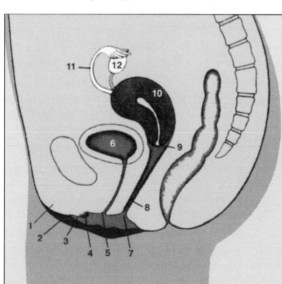

THE FEMALE SEX ORGANS
1. Mons veneris
2. Labia majora (one of a pair)
3. Labia minora (one of a pair)
4. Clitoris
5. Opening of urethra
6. Urinary bladder
7. Vaginal opening
8. Vagina
9. Cervix
10. Uterus
11. Fallopian tube (one of a pair)
12. Ovary (one of a pair)

with the stem of the pear representing the cervical opening. It is a solid, muscular organ that contains a triangular-shaped cavity (the endometrial cavity). As with the vagina, the endometrial cavity is collapsed when empty. The endometrial cavity is lined by a tissue, called the endometrium, which develops and is shed (see MENSTRUATION) in response to ovarian hormones.

The fallopian tubes are paired structures approximately four inches long and one-third of an inch in diameter. They are attached to the uterus at one end, with the other end open and lying adjacent to the ovaries. The open ends of the fallopian tubes (called the fimbriated ends) are covered with a fringe of tiny fingers (fimbria) that assist in picking up the egg from the ovary as it is released (ovulated) and in transporting it into the fallopian tube.

The fallopian tubes have a thick, muscular wall in the part of the tube closest to the uterus and a relatively thin wall in the part of the tube closest to the ovary. The opening of the fallopian tube is relatively large at the ovarian end (the ampullary portion) but narrows abruptly as it reaches the portion of the tube closest to the uterus (the isthmic portion). This narrow portion of the fallopian tube is connected to a similar narrow channel that passes through the muscular wall of the uterus and connects with the endometrial cavity.

The ovaries are paired structures measuring approximately one by one and one-half inches. They are a glistening white and their surface is generally irregular and convoluted. Depending upon the stage of the menstrual cycle, the ovaries may contain one or more developing follicles—the fluid-filled cysts in which an egg is developing—or a *corpus luteum*, the remains of a follicle from which the egg has been released. The *corpus luteum* is responsible for producing hormones to prepare the lining of the uterus for implantation of a fertilized egg and maintenance of the new PREGNANCY.

Physiology and Function. Many of the female reproductive organs exhibit dramatic changes in structure and function as a result of cyclic hormonal activity and pregnancy. The most obvious physiological changes can be observed in

the cervix, endometrium (lining of the uterine cavity), and ovaries.

The cervix contains a tubular opening (the cervical canal) lined by glands that produce a mucus-like secretion. The quantity and quality of the cervical mucus varies in response to the hormones produced by the ovaries. During the first half of the menstrual cycle, particularly as the time of ovulation approaches, the cervical mucus is abundant, clear, and watery. At this point, it is very receptive to sperm penetration and survival. When sperm are deposited in the upper vagina during sexual intercourse, the moving (motile) sperm rapidly swim into the cervical mucus, where they may maintain their motility and fertilizing ability for several days. Once ovulation occurs (at about the fourteenth day of a twenty-eight-day menstrual cycle), the cervical mucus changes dramatically in character. It becomes thick, semi-opaque, and viscous, and is virtually impenetrable to sperm. This change is brought about by the release of PROGESTERONE from the ovaries after ovulation. Similarly, a woman taking birth control pills will have cervical mucus which is impenetrable by sperm. This is one of the ways birth control pills prevent pregnancy.

During labor, as a result of the uterine contractions (labor pains), the cervix expands dramatically, with the diameter of the cervical canal reaching four inches at the end of the first stage of labor. When fully dilated, the cervix forms the upper part of the birth canal, with the vagina forming the lower part.

As noted, the uterine cavity is lined by endometrium, a tissue that grows and is shed in response to ovarian hormones. These changes in the endometrial lining, part of the menstrual cycle, prepare the uterus for the possible establishment of a pregnancy. In the first half of the menstrual cycle (the follicular, or proliferative phase), the lining of the uterus progressively grows and develops. In the second half of the cycle (the luteal, or secretory phase), the endometrium matures as a result of progesterone produced by the *corpus luteum*, and is prepared for implantation of a fertilized egg. As part of this process, the endometrium releases secretions into the uterine cavity that nourish the early embryo before it attaches to the wall of the uterus. If fertilization and implantation do not occur, the developed lining of the uterus is shed and results in menstrual bleeding. The cramps most women experience at this time are a result of the contractions of the muscular uterus, which aid in the expulsion of menstrual blood and endometrium from the uterine cavity. The same type of contractions during labor produces dilatation of the cervix and expulsion of the child through the vagina.

The outer portion of the fallopian tubes is the normal site of fertilization (egg/sperm interaction). The fimbria aid in the process of egg pickup and transportation into the ampullary region of the fallopian tube at the time of ovulation (egg release from the ovary). At the same time, if sperm have been deposited in the upper vagina, they enter the mucus in the cervical canal and make their way to the upper region of the fallopian tube. Although hundreds of millions of sperm may be deposited into the vagina, typically only a few hundred reach the site of fertilization. If fertilization is successful, the early embryo spends about three days in the upper region of the fallopian tube before it is transported into the uterine cavity. It then spends another three days floating in the uterine cavity before it attaches to the wall of the uterus.

The ovaries have two main functions: production of the woman's eggs and of the female hormones ESTROGEN and progesterone. The female hormones are necessary first, for development of the normal secondary sex characteristics (for example, breast development and growth and maturation of the reproductive organs) and second, for the preparation of the uterine lining in each menstrual cycle for possible attachment of a fertilized egg. If a fertilized egg successfully attaches to the uterine wall, the ovaries continue to produce these same hormones in large amounts to sustain the early pregnancy during the first eight to twelve weeks.

The ovaries respond to the PITUITARY hormones, follicle stimulating hormone (FSH), and luteinizing hormone (LH). A woman's ovarian cycle is continuous and is generally thought of

as beginning with the onset of menstrual bleeding. At that time the production of hormones from the ovaries is at its lowest level. In response to the low levels of ovarian hormones, the pituitary releases FSH which stimulates the growth of a follicle—a fluid-filled cyst containing an immature egg. As the follicle grows and develops, the egg matures and the cells surrounding the egg begin to make estrogen. The estrogen thus produced develops the lining of the uterus, results in production of favorable cervical mucus, and causes the pituitary to decrease the amount of FSH produced. When the ovary has produced a critical amount of estrogen for a certain period of time, the pituitary is triggered to release a burst of LH (the LH surge). The LH surge initiates the final maturation of the egg, preparing it for possible fertilization, causes the follicle to rupture and release the egg (ovulation), and finally, changes what had been the follicle into the *corpus luteum*. In addition to producing estrogen, the *corpus luteum* produces progestrone, necessary for the preparation of the lining of the uterus for possible implantation of a fertilized egg. If pregnancy occurs, the hormone human chorionic gonadotropin (hCG) is produced by the early pregnancy and causes the *corpus luteum* to maintain its production of estrogen and progesterone and thus sustains the early pregnancy, If there is no implantation (and hCG secretion) the *corpus luteum* spontaneously stops producing hormones. This leads to a shedding of the lining of the uterus and a menstrual period, beginning the entire cycle anew.

FERTILITY SEE BIRTH CONTROL; CONCEPTION; INFERTILITY; NATURAL FAMILY PLANNING; VASECTOMY AND THE MALE PILL.

FERTILIZATION SEE ARTIFICIAL INSEMINATION BY DONOR; CONCEPTION; FEMALE SEX ORGANS; IN VITRO FERTILIZATION; INFERTILITY; SPERM.

FETAL AND INFANT SUBSTANCE ABUSE SYNDROMES A fetus or newborn infant can be affected in several ways by drugs, alcohol, or other toxic substances taken by the mother during pregnancy. At the time of CONCEPTION and during the first two to three months of PREGNANCY, the formation of body structures can be affected by drugs or other toxic substances, resulting in birth defects. Later in pregnancy, drugs may affect overall growth, with the result that the fetus or newborn infant does not reach its full potential for growth. Finally, drugs may affect the ability of the newly born infant to make a successful transition from fetal life to life outside the uterus (see also PREGNANCY AND COMMON MEDICATIONS AND SUBSTANCES).

Alcohol. The first report of abnormalities in children of alcoholic mothers appeared in France only in 1968, and independently in the United States in 1973. Reported abnormalities include a significant reduction in intelligence to an average IQ of 60 to 70, hyperactivity, poor coordination and muscle strength, growth failure before and after birth, and an abnormal and characteristic facial appearance. By some estimates, as many as 5 percent of all birth defects may be attributable to alcohol exposure through the mother during pregnancy. The effects of alcohol become more apparent as the mother's intake of alcohol increases, with the risk of fetal alcohol syndrome as high as 30 to 50 percent in chronically alcoholic women. An intake as low as two "standard" drinks (one ounce of absolute alcohol) per day has been associated with a reduction in birth weight, and partial expression of the fetal alcohol syndrome in some children may be quite common. Thus there is no "safe" level of alcohol consumption during pregnancy below which the effects of alcohol will not be seen in the newborn infant.

Narcotics. Drug abuse during pregnancy has been associated with a number of severe problems in the fetus. Many of these problems are probably related to the poor social situation of many drug abusers. Women (and men) who abuse narcotics have a high rate of infections, especially with SEXUALLY TRANSMITTED DISEASES. Drugs obtained illegally by abusers are frequently impure and contain chemicals which may have their own damaging effects on a pregnancy. Individuals who abuse narcotics often abuse other substances too, such as tobacco and

alcohol, which also have significant damaging effects on the fetus.

While other factors may contribute to problems in infants of mothers who abuse narcotics, a clearly recognized pattern of fetal and infant risk associated with narcotic abuse during pregnancy has emerged. There is an increased risk of MISCARRIAGE associated with heroin use. Infants of narcotic addicts are often born prematurely, with all the problems associated with low birth weight. Even when born at term, these infants are frequently small for the length of the pregnancy. The most significant problem associated with narcotic use in pregnancy is withdrawal in the newborn after birth. Newborn infants undergoing withdrawal are jittery, tremulous, and cry inconsolably. They eat poorly, and may develop vomiting and diarrhea. In severe cases, restlessness can result in skin abrasions, and in some infants convulsions may appear. These symptoms are classically associated with heroin and methadone withdrawal, and appear because the fetus has become accustomed to receiving these drugs from its mother. While mildly affected infants may be treated by swaddling and comforting, more severely affected infants may require treatment with sedatives or tranquilizers.

Although no definite patterns of birth defects have been associated with maternal narcotic abuse, there are significant long term problems in infants of addicted mothers. These include learning and other developmental disabilities, sleep disturbances, and a greater incidence of crib death (sudden infant death syndrome/SIDS). Unfortunately, drug addiction is also associated with many serious social problems, and the help of community organizations, drug counselors, and social workers is often necessary for an optimal outcome. While withdrawal of a mother from narcotics will obviously avoid the medical complications of narcotic exposure for the infant, the decision to withdraw during pregnancy should be carefully considered by the mother and her medical advisor. Her fetus can also undergo withdrawal, and this may cause serious problems in certain cases.

Cocaine. Exposure to cocaine during pregnancy has many serious effects on the developing fetus. Cocaine use has been associated with a high rate of prematurity, often associated with separation of the placenta, resulting in increased fetal and neonatal distress. Retardation of fetal growth, absence of limbs, and severe defects of the brain and kidneys have also been attributed to cocaine use during pregnancy. These effects may be due to cocaine's ability to interrupt uterine blood flow. While the exact mechanism by which cocaine acts on the fetus is not known, during pregnancy cocaine should be avoided.

Marijuana. The use of marijuana during pregnancy appears to result in infants who are more restless and have more sleep disturbances than infants not exposed to this substance. No definite withdrawal syndrome and no definite patterns of birth defects have been associated with marijuana use during pregnancy. Some reports indicate that infants of marijuana users are lower in birth weight than infants born to non-users, but these results have not been confirmed by all studies (see also BIRTH DEFECTS).

FETISHISM   In sexual terms, fetishism involves endowing a physical object with sexual powers so that the person with the fetish requires the object either to become sexually aroused or to be sexually satisfied. Common objects of fetishes include parts of the body such as the breasts or feet, or physical objects such as women's lingerie, shoes, or rubber clothing, although almost anything can potentially become a sexual fetish.

Fetishists (people with fetishes) are usually male and they can derive pleasure either from looking at or touching the object of their fetish, usually masturbating while they do so, sometimes onto the object. While the exact cause of fetishism is not known, it is linked to conditioning. In other words, if a young boy were to masturbate while holding his mother's or sister's undergarments, this could develop into a fetish in that he might always require a piece of women's lingerie in order to become sexually aroused (as opposed to someone who uses a piece of lingerie as a masturbatory aid from time to time but is also able to be aroused by a person). The objects may provide certain sensa-

tions, such as the feel of leather or the smell of women's underwear. It has been theorized that the fetishist transfers his feelings to the object because he is revolted by his own sexual feelings: the fetish then becomes the sinful object.

Some fetishists have sex only with the object of their fetish, while others use the object as part of having sex with another person. Some men, who cannot get their spouse to go along with their fetish or who are to ashamed to admit having a fetish, will ask prostitutes to have sex with them while using the fetish: for example, while wearing a certain article of clothing. Transvestites, who derive sexual pleasure from wearing the clothing of the opposite sex, are considered to be extreme examples of fetishism (see also HYPERSEXUALITY).

FLIRTATION   Flirtation involves sexual teasing without the immediate necessity for sexual encounter. It means a great deal more to those involved in the sexual game. It is the opening move between a man and woman, indicating an availability and an interest in the possibility of a relationship. Of course, people flirt with others even when they are not available, when spouses or partners are present and they have no interest beyond demonstrating their ability to attract or enjoying an evening's arousal. But flirtation is exciting because it declares that all kinds of possibilities are open—and sometimes it leads to relationships even if the man or woman (or both) really did not think they were available. So while it may be "a playing at courtship," "transitory," and "superficial," often it is more than this. It is a bit like a dance that may (or may not) lead to a successful sexual encounter.

Most people seem to be able to flirt naturally, without a word from a sex therapist. Anyone who has observed high school girls giggling together while the boys strut and stroll past in groups has seen flirtation at work in a way that minimizes risk.

Because risk is an element in all flirtation, the high school boy who shows off his muscles as he walks by the girls, the man who catches a woman's eye across a crowded room—all are taking the risk that there will not be a response or at least the response they want. People with problems of self-esteem or who do not rate themselves as attractive enough (and who does not have these problems at some time in life?) are often reluctant to take the risk implicit in opening a flirtation.

Happily, it is often possible to flirt without seeming to do so. That is, for the high school girl who giggles and glances admiringly at the boy who walks past, or for the man who caught a woman's eye "across a crowded room"—if the response is chilly or rebuking, it is possible to pretend the giggle or glance never happened or were intended for someone else. Because what we fear even more than rejection is the public knowledge that we have been rejected, we can usually pretend it away. In every society there are social rules governing flirtation; they offer guidance and a certain protection too, but the risk-taking remains.

For all these reasons, people, especially young people, often feel anxious when they are trying to decide whether they have the courage to make that first move. Dr. Ruth has told patients that it is a little like being a turtle. If a turtle wants to be safe and not be hurt, then it is not moving forward and nothing ever happens. As soon as a turtle wants to move, it has to stick its neck out. The same with flirtation. If someone wants a new experience, they have to stick their neck out and take the risk of being rebuked. But even if they are hurt it is not going to be fatal and they can try again and in different ways. Sometimes flirtation can be tried in an intellectual conversation; with the right person or people it can be very exciting sexually. I have seen wonderful flirtations take place between people pretending to be looking at paintings in museums. In fact, the possibilities are endless (see also COURTSHIP).

FOREPLAY　In previous generations authors of popular marriage manuals gave a good deal of attention to "foreplay." By this they meant all the sexually stimulating behaviors that prepare a woman to enjoy sex and reach ORGASM. Even today many people use the word in nearly the same sense. However, there are biases and sexist implications in the term that make it unsuitable for a modern approach to sexual behavior.

Women are not passive, chaste innocents, waiting to be awakened by their husbands, as was portrayed in the past. They have an equally strong LIBIDO as men and may come to bed just as ready and desirous of sex as any man. Nor must all sexual activity have orgasm as a goal. Sexual activity that has been termed foreplay—KISSING, hugging, massaging, licking, or stroking—should more correctly be seen as pleasuring one's partner, whether or not intercourse is begun or orgasm is reached. Many of the pleasuring or arousal techniques can be used on one's self to learn more about one's own EROGENOUS ZONES so as to be better able to communicate this to a sex or love partner. Thus, the use of VIBRATORS and other autoerotic devices can play a role in pleasuring one's self or another and bringing excitement and variety to sexual interactions, with or without the goal of orgasm.

FREQUENCY OF INTERCOURSE　see COITAL FREQUENCY.

FREUD, SIGMUND (1856–1939)　The founder of psychoanalysis, which is an extensive body of theories concerning normal and abnormal behavior as well as special techniques for the treatment of persons diagnosed as neurotic. Born in Moravia, Freud grew up in Austria and completed medical school at the University of Vienna, where he concentrated on neuroanatomical research. After serving at the Vienna General Hospital, Freud went to Paris (1885–1886) to study with the French neurologist, Jean-Martin Charcot. After observing the use of hypnosis in the treatment of hysterical disorders, he became interested in the hidden or "unconscious" factors in normal and abnormal behavior. While Freud did not invent or discover the unconscious, he made it the central point of his emerging theories about human behavior and motivation.

Freud returned to Vienna and began a private medical practice specializing in nervous disorders. He became disillusioned with the temporary effects of hypnosis in the treatment of neurosis and developed the basic technique of psychoanalysis: free association, in which the patient relaxes and relates to the therapist whatever comes to mind. These free associations, with their supposedly symbolic meanings, were believed by Freud to be clues to the unconscious processes within the human mind and a path to learning the causes and maintenance of a patient's neurosis.

Freud's work with patients was the basis for his psychoanalytic theories based on a conceptualized framework of the mind: a hypothetical model of the id, ego, and superego, described in *The Ego and the Id* (1923). These are not physical parts of the brain but categories of mental processes and functions. The id constitutes the biological, instinctual drives of LIBIDO (Latin for "lust") and aggression. It is present at birth and operates on a "pleasure principle" that causes the individual to want to discharge sexual and aggressive tensions. Freud described the ego as the repository of rational processes based upon memory, perceptions, and communication. The ego is said to be the source of the "reality principle" controlling and keeping the id from becoming dangerous to the individual. While the ego is partially conscious, it often works in an unconscious manner to protect the person through the use of "defenses." Freud considered the superego to be a kind of mediator between the id and ego by providing moral support (the conscience) to help curb the id and aid the individual in making moral choices of behavior. He also theorized that the id is present at birth while the ego develops in the early stages of childhood, followed by the superego as the child grows and learns the moral norms of the society.

Freud's writings, as well as the work of many of his followers, have led to the formulation of theories and models of the PSYCHOSEXUAL STAGES OF DEVELOPMENT: the oral stage, the anal stage, and the phallic stage. During the phallic stage, which occurs at the age of four or five, children's sexuality focuses on the genital area. It is during this stage that boys become sexually attracted to their mothers (the OEDIPUS COMPLEX) and girls to their fathers (the ELECTRA COMPLEX). By the age of six, most children will have realized that they cannot have their opposite-sex parent as a love partner and move on to the latency stage, during which children are supposed to have virtually no sexual feelings or urges until puberty, when they reappear but are directed toward peers of the opposite sex (the genital stage). Central to Freudian theory is the belief that many adult neuroses are the result of the patient not having successfully moved through each of the stages with a normal resolution of urges appropriate for that stage of development.

One controversial aspect of Freud's thinking was his belief that women have two types of ORGASMS: vaginal and clitoral. He believed that "vaginal orgasm" was an indication that a woman had successfully reached the genital stage, Women who could have only "clitoral orgasms" probably had not successfully resolved the conflicts of the phallic stage. Modern researchers (see MASTERS AND JOHNSON) claim that there is no scientific evidence for such a differentiation of women's orgasms, but merely differences in the techniques that bring on orgasm in women and variations in the intensity of orgasmic responses to different techniques under differing circumstances. Furthermore, the belief that vaginal orgasm exists and is superior to or more mature than clitoral orgasm may itself create conflicts in women, who may need manual stimulation through MASTURBATION during or after intercourse to achieve orgasm. Another of Freud's beliefs that has come under criticism was the notion that all young females go through a period of "penis envy" during the phallic stage. He claimed that this has an impact on the development of female personality and leads to adult feelings of inferiority relative to men.

Freud extended his theories to include the arts, religion, and even society itself. In *Civilization and Its Discontents*, Freud discussed the restriction that society places upon the instinctual drives of people and how these may result in conflicts and neuroses. In *Moses and Monotheism*, he reinterprets the historical Moses. Freud had strong negative feelings toward religion, which he saw as a social device to meet infantile wishes to overcome mortality and existential helplessness by creating and believing in an omnipotent father who will save his children.

While Freud's work, particularly his writings related to female sexuality, has come under criticism, its importance is undiminished. A product of the Victorian era, in which expression and discussion of sexuality were greatly suppressed and denied, Freud wrote and taught that sex is an important part of the developing child and, perhaps even more important, that sex is a legitimate subject for scientific analysis and research.

Freud, a Jew, was driven into exile following Austria's incorporation into Nazi Germany in 1938. He went from Vienna to London, where he continued his work until his death from cancer the following year. His work was continued in London by a core of collaborators, among them his daughter, Dr. Anna Freud (see also HOMOSEXUALITY; PSYCHOSEXUAL STAGES OF DEVELOPMENT; SEX THERAPY).

G

G-SPOT (Grafenberg Spot) Some sex therapists claim there is a spot in a woman's body—about two inches inside and on the upper side of the vagina, between the pubic bone and the cervix—that, if sufficiently stimulated by a finger or some other means of rubbing, will bring on a very intense orgasm and secretion equivalent to EJACULATION from that point. This spot was first identified by the German gynecologist, Ernest Grafenberg. At present, there is no scientific research or consensus supporting this, but writers have noted that different areas of the vagina may be intensely erotic for different women and that urinary secretions, perhaps mistaken for "ejaculate," occasionally accompany orgasmic responses in some women. Certainly, women should not feel that they are inadequate or have a physiological problem because they cannot find such a location in their vaginas.

GAY AND LESBIAN LIFE Before 1969 gay and lesbian life was largely hidden from society and the activities of its members were secretive. Gay people at that time were deeply "in the closet" about their homosexuality, and most people would have claimed never to have known a homosexual. In many cases, gay men and women lived a furtive, secretive life, desperately trying to appear heterosexual to colleagues, family, and friends by day, while seeking gay romantic and sexual relationships by night. During this time, gays collected in places that were safe from prying eyes, and hopefully from entrapment by the police. Lesbians were even more secretive than gay men. They collected in friendship groups, in which they socialized and chose lovers. Like most women in our society,

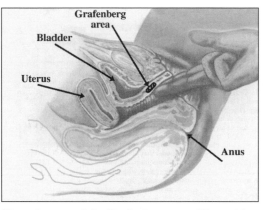

The existence of the Grafenberg spot (G-spot) has not been confirmed by researchers.

they sought out and cherished intimate relationships with other women. Gay men, on the other hand, were more sexually motivated. They met in bars (gay women also had bars, but these were much fewer in number), in bath houses, and while "cruising" the streets. They often did not know the names of their sexual partners—anonymity was the safest policy against exposure as a homosexual, and exposure might mean being discharged from one's job, rejected by one's family and friends, and even arrested and jailed.

There were homosexuals, both men and women, who suffered such low self-esteem that they never permitted themselves to engage in romantic or sexual contacts with members of the same sex. They led overtly heterosexual lives, often marrying and having children, all the while damning themselves for their homosexual desires, which, they were taught, were perverted and sinful. Many suffered serious bouts of depression, and some committed suicide. Self-hating homosexuals are now known to be suffering from internalized homophobia.

In 1969 police raided "The Stonewall," a gay bar in New York City. For the first time, homosexuals fought back and rioted in the streets, beginning the modern gay liberation movement. The gay movement simply followed examples set by the black movement and the women's movement. It insisted that a homosexual lifestyle be treated with the same respect offered to a heterosexual one. It held that all gay men and women should have the same rights as everyone else and rejected laws aimed specifically at gay people, such as laws against congregating, laws punishing consensual homosexual sex in private, and discrimination in employment and housing.

Twenty-five years have passed since the gay liberation movement began, and the lives of gay people have changed materially for the better. Most states have rescinded their sodomy laws and many cities have enacted civil rights legislation to protect gay people from discrimination. The American Psychiatric Association no longer considers homosexuality a mental illness; this encouraged even more people to come out of the closet so that there are now openly gay people in every profession.

More and more homosexual men and women live openly gay lives. They have "come out" to family, friends, and coworkers, and this attitude of self-respect has improved others' attitudes immeasurably. Lesbian and gay couples live together with much less fear of their neighbors (and landlords) than ever before. While marriage between homosexuals is still not legal in any state, many cities allow "domestic partnership" agreements, providing a small measure of recognition to gay employees of those cities. Even more interesting is the fact that some large corporations have recognized gay and lesbian couples by granting spousal rights to fringe benefits. Gay and lesbian couples have even changed the nature of the family: thousands of children have been adopted by these couples; other children have been born to lesbian couples by artificial insemination; and children are often brought into a gay or lesbian relationship from a previous heterosexual marriage.

GAY AND LESBIAN LOVE RELATIONSHIPS Love relationships between men or between women have been documented since ancient Greek times. The Greek poetess Sappho wrote of her lover, "We came together like two drops of water." The Greek philosopher Socrates maintained a relationship with Alcibiades until he was forced to commit suicide for "corrupting youth" (a charge that stemmed from his irreverent ideas, not his homosexuality). Hephaestion was the lover of Alexander the Great and fought at his side. The historical record gets muddled after Jewish and Christian morality condemned same-sex relationships as "unnatural."

There are many documented examples of women living together in close and intimate relationships in the nineteenth and twentieth centuries. It was not at all uncommon for spinsters to live together and even to sleep in the same bed, maintaining the relationship until death. Historians call these relationships "Boston Marriages," suggesting that they were lesbian relationships that may or may not have been sexual. There are also examples of bachelors living together harmoniously. But in all cases, homosexual intimacies were expressed privately, away from the condemning eyes of family, friends, and especially the police.

Today gay and lesbian couples live in every part of the country, in cities and in rural settings. Homosexual couples are found in loving, lifelong relationships with all the ROMANCE and passion found in heterosexual marriage. These couples are an important economic force in many parts of the country. They buy property in common, sign contracts together, and benefit from survivorship. They demand, but have not yet received, full economic parity with heterosexual married couples, e.g., family medical insurance and legal recognition of the union. Nevertheless, for the most part, the lives of gay and lesbian couples are very much like the lives of other people in their communities. Where competition and dynamism are in the air, as in New York City, gay couples compete in that fast-paced society; where time is measured more slowly, as in our rural settings, gay and lesbian couples mirror the pace of their neighbors.

Gay and lesbian love relationships are now quite common, and in many cases couples are open about their homosexuality. What are homosexual relationships like? In some ways they are very similar to heterosexual relationships, yet they differ in other ways. All couples, gay and straight, want to develop lifelong relationships. Gay and lesbian lovers want to live in a secure home, protected from discrimination and legal harassment. They want to socialize as other couples do. They want the opportunity to raise children as heterosexuals do. In short, they want to be integrated into society like any other family.

There are also differences. Not all men and women are the same, but potential trouble spots in both lesbian and gay male love relationships are often based on the following generalizations. Lesbians seem more demanding of INTIMACY than gay men, while at the same time they are less demanding sexually. It is quite the opposite with men in homosexual relationships. They prize sexuality above other concerns. Many men appear to experience discomfort when involved in an emotionally dependent relationship with another person, and especially with another man. These characteristics seem true whether we are speaking about homosexuals or heterosexuals and are probably the result of the different socializations of men and women. Lesbian relationships sometimes have a problem called "merging." In this situation women become too dependent on one another. Gay men, on the other hand, may seek too much independence, especially sexual independence.

Gay and lesbian couples may also have trouble with their respective families, who may be either supportive or destructive of the relationship. Most parents today are at least respectful of their children's choices of lovers, but others have been known to physically or verbally attack them, withdraw financial support from them (for school, for example), and refuse to allow the son or daughter to ever enter the house again. This is just another example of society's HOMOPHOBIA.

GAY AND LESBIAN PARENTING Gay men and lesbians have been parents throughout history, mainly to children raised within the con-

text of heterosexual marriages. While feeling genuine affection for their spouses, they often entered these unions with the hope of hiding or changing their sexuality and in order to provide a traditional context in which to raise children. However, a new phenomenon has emerged: gay men and lesbians are now establishing families and raising children within the context of same-sex relationships or as single parents. This phenomenon began in the lesbian community in the mid–1970s and has become so widespread that it has become known as the "lesbian baby boom." Lesbians can adopt children or become pregnant via artificial insemination. Some utilize SPERM BANKS, but often they arrange for a partner's male relative or for a gay male friend to be a sperm donor. Gay men usually find children through adoption, though they sometimes enter into coparenting arrangements with lesbians for whom they have been the sperm donors. They will occasionally enter into a formal or informal contract with a surrogate mother. This "new breed" of gay fathers has grown dramatically since the late 1980s, and many young gay men today are expressing an interest in fatherhood.

Gay and lesbian parenthood challenges our society's fears and stereotypes about relationships between homosexuals and children. However, all of the scientific research to date suggests that these stereotypes are no more than myths. Studies indicate that there are no observable differences between the children of lesbian and heterosexual mothers in terms of overall psychological development, gender identity, gender role behavior, or sexual orientation. Research about gay fathers indicates that they do not sexually abuse their children nor do they produce a disproportionate number of homosexual offspring. Furthermore, there do not appear to be significant differences in the child-rearing practices of gay and heterosexual fathers. Nevertheless, because they challenge conventional views of what constitutes a healthy family, lesbian- and gay-headed families will often encounter misunderstanding and prejudice.

GAY AND LESBIAN POPULATIONS It is estimated that in the United States roughly one in twenty persons—5 percent of the population—may be attracted primarily to a member of his or her own sex. However, the number of individuals who have engaged in homosexual behavior is a subject of debate, based primarily on objections to the validity of data provided by existing studies.

Homosexuality surveys have not always been based on groups randomly drawn from the population, and questions have been raised about the reliability of self-reported data obtained from such studies and about the biases of their authors. Another issue concerns a lack of consensus on how to define homosexuality. In the 1940s Alfred Kinsey proposed a seven-point scale: A "0" on the Kinsey scale was assigned to persons who denied ever having any physical attraction to a member of their own sex—a "pure heterosexual." Kinsey assigned a "1" to subjects having experienced a physical attraction but who never had sexual contact with a person of their own sex. Kinsey "2," "3," and "4" subjects were persons who reported bisexual activity but with increasing homosexual preponderance, "3"s being persons who were equally excited about and involved with both sexes. "5" was assigned to persons who may have reported heterosexual attractions but who never had sex with the opposite sex, and "6" was assigned to someone who was exclusively homosexually attracted. A final category, "X," was used to rate persons who reported not responding erotically to either heterosexual or homosexual stimuli, nor having physical contacts with persons of either sex. Although few males beyond puberty could be assigned "X," nearly 20 percent of females remained in this category after adulthood.

One of Kinsey's findings of little dispute was that age at the time of the reported sexual activity is a key variable in determining the prevalence of homosexual experiences. For example, about half of the older males (48 percent) and nearly two-thirds (60 percent) of the preadolescent boys interviewed reported homosexual activity in their preadolescent years. Although exhibitionism was the most common behavior reported, two-thirds of the men with such homosexual experience also reported mutual mastur-

bation, and 17 percent reported trying anal penetration. As men reached their late teens and early twenties, the frequency of homosexual contact subsided greatly, especially among the group that went to college. Thus, prevalence depends on age and other social factors.

The earlier (1940s) Kinsey studies have been criticized as not being representative of the entire population: they drew heavily from residents of college and university communities and from delinquent and prison groups. However, as unrepresentative as their subjects may have been of the entire population of the United States, the numbers of Kinsey's subjects (5,300 males; 5,940 females) were forty times greater than the sizes of previous studies of human sexuality, and the data was obtained by a highly trained, nonjudgmental staff, who may have gathered the best in-depth, standardized data to date.

The validity of data obtained by self-report, whether gathered from a questionnaire or by personal interviews, is often considered suspect, unless more "hard" data (e.g., laboratory serologies) or unobtrusive corroborating data provide confirmation. Yet virtually all data on human sexuality (except for studies on sexual physiology or performance, like those obtained by MASTERS AND JOHNSON) are based on self-reports. Nevertheless, one may check the validity of self-reported data using a number of methods, including collecting the same data at a later date (test-retest reliability) and inserting redundant questions with different phrasings to check on key issues. Most confirmatory studies, in fact, show that self-reported data is quite reliable.

Given considerations about levels of homo- and heterosexuality, the effects of age, and doubts about self-reported data, what are the best guesses about the prevalence of male-to-male and female-to-female sex? For males it appears that about 20–30 percent of preadolescent males have some homosexual experience, many to the point of orgasm, and that 6–10 percent may continue to have predominantly homosexual experiences. Less is known about bisexually active men; however, researchers have guessed that there may be an almost equal number of men who are predominately sexually active with women but have some homosexual contact. The earlier Kinsey data and the most recent study reported in the scientific literature (Fay *et al.*, *Science*, 1989), which drew conclusions from a random study done in 1970, gathering data by self-completed questionnaires, came to similar conclusions. Fay reported that at least 20 percent of men have had a sexual experience culminating in orgasm with another man, nearly 7 percent had such an experience after age nineteen, and 2 percent had it within the previous two years. But the authors believed there might have been under-reporting of these behaviors.

Among the females in the large 1940s Kinsey studies, by age forty, 28 percent reported psychological arousal in response to another female, 19 percent reported some physical sexual contact, and 13 percent reported achieving orgasm with another female. The authors comment, however, that because their female samples included "a disproportionate number of females in college and graduate groups, where the incidences of lesbian practices seem to be higher than in the grade school and high school groups, the figures" for their sample population might be higher than might be found in the American population as a whole. For nearly half of the women reporting homosexual activity, this was limited to only a year or less in their lives and roughly the same proportion (51 percent) reported having homosexual relations with only a single partner.

Kinsey's data suggests that females with homosexual experience are distinct from men in regard to the numbers of partners they report. Only 20 percent of these females reported homosexual experiences with two or more partners, 29 percent with three, and 4 percent with more than ten partners, while among men with same-sex experience, a high proportion reported contacts with several different persons and 22 percent with more than ten partners.

In summary, the proportions of the samples of males and females who reported homosexual responses and activities were higher for males than for females. Furthermore, a much smaller proportion of females than of males remained homosexually active as they aged. Nevertheless, many persons have homosexual erotic responses, engage in sexual activity, and achieve orgasm with a member of their own sex, and perhaps one in twenty Americans remains primarily attracted to and sexually active with members of their own sex (see also BISEXUALITY).

GENDER The two fundamental ways in which individuals are defined as male or female are by their biological sex and by the sets of roles and behaviors that society imposes on individuals solely as a result of their sex. Gender refers to both a person's biological sex and to the designations of sex that are made and enforced by the society in which one lives. The designations of gender that exist in different societies are always regarded as "natural," no matter how they may vary.

Thus, a person's female gender would include a whole cluster of psychological traits and social behaviors that are regarded as suitable for a woman, such as nurturance and dependence, while a person's male gender would entail characteristics such as assertiveness and independence. Most social roles—in the family, in the workplace, and in the political structure—are assigned on the basis of gender. Women are encouraged to become housewives and secretaries and men are expected to become breadwinners and have an occupation outside the home.

Roles linked to gender vary in different societies and sometimes in different social classes within a society. For example, in many African societies women are expected to be the farmers, and in some Asian societies they are the small shopkeepers. In American society, even when it was considered appropriate for women to stay at home to care for children, African-American women were expected to work outside the home. Upper-class women in a number of patriarchal societies (e.g. India, Pakistan) have assumed high political office. Despite their seemingly natural links to biological sex, men's and women's gender roles may change over time because people begin to live in ways other than the conventionally approved ones, because of objections raised by social movements, or through changes in the law (see also SEX ROLES).

GENDER DYSPHORIA   There are rare persons who experience an intense feeling of being trapped sexually in the wrong body—men who have a continual craving to physically be a woman, and women whose craving is to physically be a man. Gender dysphoria exists when a person maintains a deep conviction over many years that his or her gender, or inner identity, is incongruous with his or her sexual anatomy. This is distinct from transvestism, which is a form of role-playing in which a person wears the clothing of the opposite gender but finds this sexually exciting as a member of their own sex.

Gender dysphoria and TRANSSEXUALITY, however, overlap in meaning to some degree. A transsexual experiences the deep and uncomfortable feelings of gender dysphoria before seeking medical consultation and sex-change procedures. The transsexual who is now female although born a male (or vice-versa) has undergone the surgical, hormonal, and psychological therapy necessary to actually become a person of the opposite sex (see also ANDROGYNY).

GENDER ROLES   see SEX ROLES.

GENETIC ABNORMALITIES   see BIRTH DEFECTS.

GENITAL WARTS   Warts occurring on the external genitalia, like warts occurring elsewhere on the body, are caused by a virus infection. Genital warts (also called *Condyloma acuminata*, or venereal warts) result from infection with specific subtypes of the human papillomavirus (HPV). This virus inserts its own genetic material (DNA) into the host's human gene code. The viral DNA produces rapid replication of virus particles and cell division, producing warts that are often visible to the naked eye. They are reddish, soft swellings that can grow rapidly. They thrive in a warm, moist environment and are commonly found in the perineal, genital, and anal regions of the male and female. The male foreskin and the female CERVIX and VULVA are common sites.

Genital warts are identified as venereal because the HPV is sexually transmitted. Estimates suggest that 1 million new cases of this infection occur annually in the United States. The medical importance of these infections is in the link that has been demonstrated between HPV infection and cervical dysplasia, a premalignant precursor of cervical cancer.

The treatment of HPV disease is hampered by the fact that most HPV infection does not result in wart formation. The detection of the infection when warts are not visible can be aided by applying diluted acetic acid to the genitalia. Involved areas of skin will turn white and can be biopsied and treated.

The treatment of genital warts is notoriously difficult: recurrences and reinfection are common. Certainly, visible lesions should be removed. Warts can be surgically excised, frozen and removed, or removed with a laser. Medicinal agents have also been used with success. Women with a history of genital warts or sexual partners who have genital warts should have routine gynecological follow-up, including annual Pap smears, to check for cancerous changes of their cervixes. Since the infection is sexually transmitted, CONDOMS are recommended when lesions are present or suspected, to prevent the infection of sexual partners.

GENITO-UROLOGICAL EXAMINATION
A genito-urological examination is usually performed as part of a general medical examination or separately by a urologist, when it seems prudent to check for any abnormality or disease that may affect the genito-urinary system. Urologists generally specialize in genital examinations of men and examinations of urinary systems in both men and women, while gynecologists specialize in genital examinations of women, usually carried out during pelvic examinations. Reproductive or fertility disorders are generally evaluated by urologists for men and by gynecologists for women, sometimes in association with an endocrinologist (hormone specialist). Some urologists and gynecologists are trained in a "couple-oriented" approach to the evaluation of INFERTILITY.

The genito-urological examination usually begins with inspection of the abdomen for abnormal masses or appearance and by stethoscope for abnormal bowel sounds. Then, the examining physician places hands on the abdomen to examine the internal organs. On the upper right side, underneath the rib cage, the kidneys may be examined by placing a hand on the patient's lower back and moving the kidneys forward. The bladder area is similarly inspected and then palpated (felt by the physician's hands). Groin areas are examined for the presence of hernias.

The male's examination continues with visual inspection of the PENIS for sores on the skin and palpation of the penis for any lumps or irregularities on its surface. The scrotum is examined to detect the presence and size of the TESTICLES as well as their consistency. Examination of the testicles is important to detect any hard areas or masses that might suggest the presence of cancer or a tumor in the testicles. The epididymis (area around the testicles) is also examined, as is the vas deferens, which carries sperm from the testicles to the ejaculatory area.

At this point the examining urologist will usually have the patient stand. For men a finger is placed along the cord carrying the blood vessels to the testicles into the region of the groin where hernias may occur. The patient will usually be asked to cough or bear down to detect the presence of hernias. The cord of blood vessels going to the testicles will also be examined to detect the presence of a varicoele (an enlargement of veins within the scrotum) that may affect the function of the testicles and fertility.

The urological examination also includes an examination of the rectum with a lubricated, gloved finger. This allows the physician to gain important information about the size and consistency of the PROSTATE, as well as any other abnormalities in the rectum, such as tumors.

In women the urological examination includes an external examination of the vulva. Usually, the physician will separate the labia to examine the outer portion of the urethra (urine passage). The physician will generally perform an internal pelvic examination (see also GYNECOLOGICAL EXAMINATION; IMPOTENCE; PELVIC EXAMINATION).

GIGOLO   see PROSTITUTION.

GONADS   see OVARIES; TESTICLES.

GONORRHEA AND CHLAMYDIA   In men, the most common sexually transmitted disease is infection of the urethra (urethritis) caused by the microbes *Chlamydia trachomatis* and *Neisseria gonorrhoeae* (gonococcus). Symptoms begin within a few days after sexual exposure, with the onset of painful urination and the discharge of pus from the urethra. These symptoms may be minimal or absent in up to 10 percent of infected men. Left untreated, the gonococcus can travel up the urethra and infect the spermatic cords (epidydimitis) and testicles (orchitis). In rare instances, the gonococcus can also enter the bloodstream and potentially infect most organs and tissues, including the joints, skin, and nervous system. Symptoms of gonococcal bloodstream invasion include fever, acute arthritis, and blister-like sores on the extremities. If not treated in time or appropriately, healing results in scar tissue that may block the urethra and spermatic cord. This may often cause INFERTILITY and the formation of an abnormal opening in the PENIS (fistula) for passing urine.

In women, gonococci and chlamydia infect cells lining the opening into the womb (endocervix). Usually asymptomatic infections occur unless these microbes enter the UTERUS (womb) and ascend into one or both FALLOPIAN TUBES. There they can cause an abscess, which may block one or both fallopian tubes, causing an acute fallopian tube infection (salpingitis) and abdominal pain. If the abscess is in the right fallopian tube, it cannot be easily distinguished from an attack of acute appendicitis. Without treatment, scar tissue will form and possibly block one or both fallopian tubes. This may cause infertility or block the descent of a fertilized egg into the uterus and result in a tubal pregnancy. Male sexual partners of women who are diagnosed with salpingitis often have asymptomatic gonococcal urethral infections.

An infant delivered through an infected birth canal has a good chance of having its eyes contaminated with infected maternal secretions and developing an eyesight-threatening gonococcal eye infection (ophthalmia neonatorum) in the first week of life, or a less serious eye infection and pneumonia if infected with chlamydia. Tetracycline eye ointments are given routinely after birth to prevent these eye infections, but chlamydia pneumonia may still develop within the first three months of life and require additional antibiotic treatment.

Because as many as 50 percent of men and women with gonorrhea are also infected with chlamydia, treatment is routinely given to eliminate both types of microbes. Although penicillin was the treatment of choice for gonorrhea for many years, a large percentage of gonococcal strains have developed resistance to this drug, and the treatment of choice in the United States is now an injection of newer antibiotics such a ceftriaxone or spectinomycin. Gonococcal infections of the back of the throat (pharynx) resulting from ORAL SEX (FELLATIO) are also effectively treated with a single injection of ceftriaxone. For chlamydia, a ten day course of tetracycline is recommended, except for pregnant women who are given oral erythromycin, because tetracycline can permanently damage the teeth of unborn children.

Lymphogranuloma Venerum. Sexually transmitted chlamydia can cause the further venereal disease, lymphogranuloma venerum. This disease involves the lymphatic tissues, causing painful enlargement of the lymph nodes in the groin or the lining of the rectum and colon. Fever accompanies the swelling of lymph nodes and this condition may resemble a blocked hernia. Treatment requires an extended course of tetracycline (see also SAFER SEX; SEXUALLY TRANSMITTED DISEASES).

GROUP SEX   In recent years the term "group sex" has been used to refer to sexual behavior involving four or more persons at the same time. While group sex has diminished considerably, particularly with the spread of HERPES and AIDS, it still exists, especially at "sex clubs" found in many large cities. Despite public health officials' attempts in many cities to close such clubs, they still exist, although they may insist on the use of condoms. These clubs usually cater to couples, but prostitutes may be available as escorts for unattached males. Sexual activities in these clubs may involve as many as fifty or more people at the same time.

Group sex contacts are also made in clubs that arrange parties at members' homes or in resorts rented for an evening or weekend. Some researchers report that large group sex parties tend to have a dehumanizing effect on participants after a short while, resulting in more informal parties approximating social friendship groups of from three to fifteen couples. Because these are unorganized, there is no reliable data on how many couples in the United States are involved in them (see also MATE SWAPPING; SWINGERS).

GUTTMACHER, DR. ALAN   Alan Guttmacher (1898–1974) was a distinguished American gynecologist who began advocating birth control in the 1930s. The son of a rabbi and a social worker, he was one of the early champions of the INTRAUTERINE device (IUD). He was president of Planned Parenthood in the 1960s and established the first Washington branch of the organization, which soon became an autonomous institute, first called the Center for Family Planning Program Development, and, after Guttmacher's death in 1974, The Alan Guttmacher Institute. It continues to publish regular reports on topics related to family planning which are highly respected all over the world.

GYNECOLOGICAL EXAMINATION   Most women are very vocal about the fact that they hate having to get a PELVIC EXAMINATION. In reality, visiting the gynecologist does not have to be traumatic, and there are ways to make the experience better. But it is understandable why so many women do not look forward to getting up on the examining table.

The examination position itself is awkward. In order to be internally examined, a woman must lie down on her back, spread her legs open, and insert her heels into metal stirrups. In this position women often feel exposed and vulnerable, especially on a first visit or with a new doctor. It is important for a woman who is feeling vulnerable to remember that she is the one who chooses which doctor she goes to. A good relationship

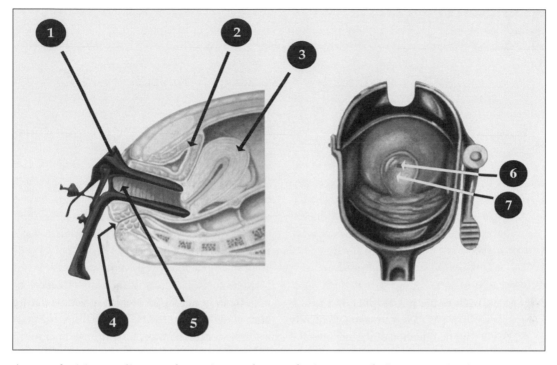

A gynecologicist uses 1) a speculum to inspect the reproductive organs during an examination.
2) Bladder; 3) Uterus; 4) Anus; 5) Vagina; 6) External os; 7) Clear, watery mucus prior to ovulation.

with your gynecologist is crucial. If a doctor does not answer questions or makes the patient feel uncomfortable in any way, she should choose another. In fact, a woman may have to visit two or three gynecologists before finding one she likes and trusts.

Another cause of anxiety is the internal pelvic examination itself. It can be physically uncomfortable. Relaxing the muscles is a great help. In general, it is a good idea to relax as much as possible. Deep breathing can help, as can remembering some pleasant experience.

Many women feel uncomfortable that they cannot see what the doctor is looking at or even what she or he is looking for. The reproductive organs may be a total mystery to the woman. Therefore she should simply ask questions. Whether it is her first time to the gynecologist or her one hundredth, a woman should come with a list of questions. She should tell the doctor any-

thing that is bothering her, and ask her or him to explain what is happening or if there is anything she should know. If the woman is involved in a sexual relationship or even contemplating one, the gynecologist is the person with whom to discuss contraceptive choices.

Confidentiality may be another source of concern. Even if a woman is under eighteen years old, her relationship with her gynecologist must be entirely confidential. For teenagers this may mean choosing a different gynecologist than the one used by their mothers. A woman who shares the same gynecologist as her mother must make sure that her privacy is respected.

The best psychological approach to a gynecological exam is to take responsibility for the experience. Choosing the right doctor, asking the right questions, and relaxing will make the experience a great deal easier (see also GENITO-URO-LOGICAL EXAMINATION; PELVIC EXAMINATION).

H

HANDICAPPED PERSONS AND SEX
Until modern times, persons who were physically challenged due to birth defects, accidents, various diseases, or other reasons, were viewed as "disabled"—to the point of not having or needing sexual activity or intimacy. More recently, many rehabilitation workers, sex educators, and sex therapists have become advocates of the sexual rights of handicapped persons. Not only do physically challenged persons have a need for sexual expression, they often have the ability to participate in sex, although there may be limitations on their sexual activities because of the nature of their individual disability.

While we have become increasingly sensitive to wheelchair accessibility in public buildings, this sensitivity has yet to be extended to include "bedroom accessibility." There have been movies in which paraplegics are portrayed as having sex with partners who are not handicapped, but this marks the extent of the public's education and awareness of the issue. Some believe it is sufficient to teach handicapped persons or their partners innovative acts and positions in which they may potentially engage. For handicapped persons without partners, however, the main difficulties seem to be social—initiating contacts that might lead to sexual involvement. There is still a great deal of prejudice against recognizing the legitimacy of sexual needs in the handicapped. Sometimes even rehabilitation center administrators believe that allowing couples to have sex at these institutions may create problems with those who do not have partners, or that it may be illegal or immoral.

If a couple in which one or both partners are physically handicapped chooses to have a child by natural means or by adoption, their choice should be respected no less than the same decision by any other responsible and adult couple. However, for persons who are intellectually or emotionally handicapped, various ethical considerations come into play. If they are not emotionally capable of raising a child or intellectually able to understand the responsibilities and consequences of parenting, should they be allowed to have children? Should our society encourage or even insist on mandatory birth control of some type for these couples? These are not easy questions to answer because the issues involve many more persons than the couple themselves. Clearly, much sex and parenting counseling is needed for the mentally handicapped since they, no less than the physically challenged and those fortunate enough to have no physical or mental handicaps, may also have very strong sexual feelings and needs (see also ARTHRITIS AND SEX; PARAPLEGICS AND SEX).

HARASSMENT, SEXUAL See SEXUAL HARASSMENT.

HEADACHE AND SEX see SEX AND HEADACHE.

HEART CONDITIONS AND SEX People who have suffered acute myocardial infarction (heart attacks) or with angina pectoris often raise questions concerning sexual activities with respect to their condition. What sexual activities are permitted? When are they permitted? Are there any restrictions on activities? Should special medication be taken to make sex either possible or less dangerous for them? These questions are also raised by patients following invasive cardiac procedures, such as coronary artery bypass operations or "balloon" angioplasty (percutaneous transluminal coronary angioplasty, PTCA).

In fact, sexual function disturbances do exist in many patients with cardiac disease. Difficulties are most common in patients after heart attacks or with angina pectoris. The dysfunction is due to one or more of three major problems: psychological—fear on the part of the patient or the patient's partner that sexual activities might lead to a worsening of the patient's general condition or even sudden death; cardiac dysfunction—mainly angina or dyspnea; and drug-related side effects, especially from beta-blockers and diuretics, on sexual function.

There have been many studies on the problem of sexual activity after heart attack: at least half of all patients interviewed reported changes in their sexual activities. There was a significant reduction in the frequency and duration of intercourse, often because of decreased libido, depression, anxiety, a partner's reluctance, fear of symptom relapse, angina, and IMPOTENCE. Erectile difficulties occurred in almost half the patients: permanent impotence was found in approximately 10 percent, although ejaculatory difficulties were rare. A similar decrease in sexual activity was found in women: ANORGASMIA was a common complaint.

Complaints of cardiac origin, such as angina, shortness of breath, or palpitation, occur at all four stages of sexual response (excitement, plateau, orgasm, and resolution; see SEXUAL RESPONSE CYCLE). They are markedly increased in the resolution phase of these patients.

Therapeutic Approach. Resuming sexual activities, as part of rehabilitation following a cardiac event or cardiac intervention, must be based on four factors:

- Medical assessment of the patient's cardiac condition, particularly heart function (left ventricular function) and residual ischemia. Ventricular function assessment can be achieved by echocardiography (ultrasound of the heart) or nuclear mapping of the heart. Ischemia can be assessed by an exercise test, with or without adjacent nuclear mapping, or by prolonged electrocardiogram (ECG) monitoring;

- Reassurance of the patient by the family physician or a cardiologist, based on the patient's medical condition, and providing more detailed recommendations on what activities are possible. It is important to be aware of recommended positions during intercourse—usually the most familiar to the patient, or side-by-side;

- Reevaluation of the patient's medication and, if possible, attempting to change any medication that might be impairing their sexual function. The list of drugs associated with sexual dysfunction is long, headed by beta-blockers and diuretics. However, no medications should be changed or stopped without first consulting a physician;

- If the above steps have failed to improve the patient's sexual dysfunction status, a sex consultant or therapist should be consulted.

In conclusion, sexual dysfunction in coronary heart disease patients is not unusual, especially in post-myocardial infarction patients. Very often this unpleasant situation is at least partially reversible. Reasonable medical evaluation, treatment and reassurance play a critical role in this aspect of rehabilitation.

HEPATITIS An inflammation or infection of the liver. Infectious hepatitis is usually caused by a virus. There are several different types of acute viral hepatitis, the two most common types being "type A" and "type B." Early symptoms include loss of appetite, nausea, vomiting, fatigue, joint and muscle aches, headache, sore throat, cough, and fever. More severe cases develop jaundice (yellowing of the skin), weight loss, enlargement of the liver, and abdominal discomfort. There is no medication or treatment that cures viral hepatitis although, in most cases, the body repairs itself within several months.

Type A. The hepatitis A virus is generally the less severe of the two. It is most commonly transmitted by eating food or drinking water or milk contaminated by feces containing the virus. It occurs most often in communities with overcrowding and poor sanitation facilities. Although not usually transmitted through sexual contact, type A hepatitis can be acquired by direct contact between the mouth of an uninfected person and the anus of an infected partner. A person infected with type A hepatitis may not develop clear symptoms or know that he or she has it. Almost all patients who are otherwise healthy recover.

Type B. The type B hepatitis virus is usually more severe than type A and is also more likely to be transmitted sexually. The virus is only rarely found in feces, even from an infected individual, but it is commonly found in semen, saliva, and vaginal secretions. Any of these body fluids may transmit hepatitis to another person during genital-genital, genital-oral, oral-oral and genital-anal sex.

The likelihood that a person will transmit the hepatitis B virus to a sexual partner varies, depending on age, sexuality, number of sexual contacts, and whether the person has had other SEXUALLY TRANSMITTED DISEASES. It occurs in .5 per cent of the general population. In a population of people being treated in a sexually transmitted diseases clinic, the virus has been found in as many as 20 percent of heterosexuals who have been with more than fifty sexual partners. In the male homosexual community, more than 4 percent are infected and capable of transmitting the disease. However, female homosexuals have an extremely low likelihood of infection.

Hepatitis B is far more contagious than AIDS. The virus can be transmitted even without direct sexual contact. Approximately 1.2 million Americans are carriers of the virus and can infect other individuals; each year there are an additional 30,000 new carriers.

Most cases of type B hepatitis recover after three to four months but about 10 percent are associated with severe liver damage and the illness can be fatal. In the United States, an average of fourteen people die each day from ailments that occur more frequently following type B hepatitis, including cirrhosis and cancer of the liver. Worldwide, more than five thousand people die daily from the aftereffects of hepatitis B, making this the ninth leading cause of death.

Since there is no cure available once hepatitis has occurred, prevention is of great importance. One should certainly avoid any sexual contact with a known carrier of active viral hepatitis. Within the general population, however, people are often unaware that they are carriers of the virus. The use of a condom during sex may offer protection against transmission of hepatitis B virus but this has not been definitely proven. If a partner has already had a hepatitis B infection, their blood test may show that they are immune to another infection.

Hepatitis B is the only sexually transmitted disease for which there is an effective vaccine available. Those at greater risk of being infected include homosexual men, anyone with multiple sexual partners, passive partners during anal sex, and those having sexual contact with a hepatitis B carrier. Others at greater risk include health care personnel and others who render medical assistance, such as police and fire department personnel, and users of illicit drugs. People in these higher risk groups should consider being vaccinated, but since vaccination is only effective before the virus has already been contracted, it is a preventive measure, and not a treatment, for hepatitis B.

HEREDITY The passing of traits from parents to offspring. When sexual reproduction occurs, both parents contribute to the cells of the new being a copy of a chemical code that controls its development and inherited traits—its heredity. Each new individual resembles its parents in some ways and differs in others.

The SPERM produced in the TESTICLES of the male and the ova, or eggs, stored in the OVARIES of the female contain the chemical blueprint for each new life. This information is contained in the chromosomes, strands of genetic material composed of deoxyribonucleic acid (DNA). Hereditary characteristics such as skin color, hair color, body type, and height are determined by the precise combinations of DNA that we acquire from each parent and from subsequent environmental influences.

All human cells contain forty-six chromosomes, except for the sperm and egg cells (the sex cells), which contain twenty-three chromosomes each. When a sperm joins with an egg during fertilization, the chromosomes of the two sex cells combine to form a zygote with forty-six chromosomes — a complete set of instructions for the formation of a unique individual. Each gene, or piece of DNA strand, accounts for a single trait handed down in reproduction to the new individual.

All eggs produced by a female can potentially join with sperm to create either male or female offspring. The factor that determines a baby's sex is contributed by the sperm cell. All eggs carry a sex chromosome, called the "X" chromosome. When the sperm cell that joins with an egg also contains an "X" chromosome, the new zygote gets two "X's" (XX) and the new individual is a girl. If the chromosome contributed by the sperm cell is a "Y" chromosome, the result is an "XY" individual, or a male.

In some ways all human beings are alike. That is, all of us carry the genes for certain traits. Such traits, like the ability to speak, are called species traits. Individual traits make people different from one another (unless they happen to have an identical twin). Scientists have long debated which of our traits result from heredity and which result from environmental effects, or the outside forces that act upon each individual (see also HETEROSEXUALITY).

HERMAPHRODITE   Hermaphroditism is an extremely rare condition in which an infant is born with the genital or reproductive organs of both sexes. Such an infant exhibits both male and female sexual traits and characteristics.

In Greek mythology, Hermaphroditos was a handsome young man who rejected the love of a nymph. Not willing to take "no" for an answer, the nymph embraced Hermaphroditos so tightly that her body actually merged with his. Man and woman came together in one flesh. The cause of hermaphroditism, however, is not mythological but biological.

As a baby grows inside the mother's womb, its organs form and develop to the point of completion we see at birth. In cases of hermaphroditism, something interferes with this process and the infant is born with its sex organs (and, therefore, its biological sex) not yet completed. A "true hermaphrodite" is born with both testicular and ovarian tissue. Such a child, possessing both a rudimentary penis and a vagina, is certainly bound to experience gender conflict as it grows older.

Fortunately, hormonal and surgical treatment can help "finish" an afflicted child's sexual development. Parents of such a child should seek professional medical and psychological assistance so that, in time, a definite sexual identity can be established and maintained (see GENDER DYPHORIA).

HERPES   There is widespread confusion about genital herpes infections, due to a number of misconceptions that arose in the early 1980s, when the increased number of reported herpes cases began to attract publicity. To the public "herpes" meant the outbreak of painful lesions in the male or female genital region after sexual intercourse with an adult who knew he or she carried the virus. The public was judgmental about both victims and carriers: the former were believed to have acquired the disease through irresponsible sexual behavior; the latter, to have knowingly infected their sexual partners. (It was then widely believed that all carriers who had herpes symptoms knew that they had the virus when they spread it to a partner.) "Herpes is forever" — the virus can never be eliminated from the body — and infected males and females could infect future sexual partners. Carriers became social lepers, for when they revealed their medical history, relationships ended abruptly. For women there was the additional burden of knowing that the virus could be passed to the fetus during labor and delivery, resulting in an infection with potentially serious results to the newborn infant's central nervous system.

Recent studies indicate that this is an extremely narrow and often inaccurate view of the range of herpes infections. Most adults infected with the herpes virus have never had clinical symptoms of the disease and can thus, unknowingly, spread the virus, infecting sexual partners or their babies.

There are two separate and distinct herpes viruses—herpes simplex 1 (HSV–1) and herpes simplex 2 (HSV–2) Different sites of infection show differences in the frequency of HSV–1 and HSV–2 infections. The two most common sites of infection are the mouth (cold sores) and the genital region (genital herpes). Approximately 85 percent of cold sores are caused by HSV–1 and the remainder by HSV–2, while more than 85 percent of genital herpes cases are caused by HSV–2 and the remainder by HSV–1. HSV-1 is not always sexually transmitted (though it may be spread by kissing or oral sex), but HSV-2 is usually transmitted sexually.

The clinical manifestations of HSV–1 and HSV–2 infections are diverse. Most adults with an oral or genital tract infection with HSV–1 or HSV–2 do not know that they have the infection. For example, nearly 90 percent of adults with HSV–2 antibodies have no history or signs of genital herpes. They either had no symptoms or had symptoms so mild that they have not sought medical attention. In contrast, some patients have had recurrent herpes outbreaks, usually at the same sites in the mouth or the genital area. Adults with oral lesions—cold sores—often have outbreaks after excessive exposure to the sun. Victims of genital herpes outbreaks often find a relationship between the eruption of lesions and recurrent stress in their lives.

Many patients have preoutbreak symptoms that follow a pattern: a tingling or burning at the site of the infection, followed by the appearance of small lesions with clear fluid (vesicles), which rupture and heal, usually over five to eight days. The most severe illness due to the herpes virus occurs in immuno-compromised patients, particularly those with HIV infection: life-threatening infections of the central nervous system can be seen in such people. Once acquired, the herpes virus remains in the body and is held in check by the host's immunological defense mechanisms. When the immune system is diminished or absent in a patient with the herpes virus, more serious forms of the disease erupt.

Because of the recent awareness of the diffuse nature of HSV–1 and HSV–2 infections in humans, there has been a change in the approach used to diagnose the disease. Formerly, diagnostic accuracy depended on a laboratory check of herpes cultures from patients with new or repeated genital tract lesions. Today, a positive culture is taken to be a definitive sign that symptoms and lesions are caused by herpes. However, the converse conclusion does not follow a negative culture. Recent studies indicate that many women with mild symptoms and small genital lesions do not produce a positive culture. Because of this, there has been increasing emphasis placed upon detecting the presence of HSV–2 antibodies in the blood.

Antibody screening could have widespread applications in the future. Many couples planning a long term relationship now contemplate HIV screening (for AIDS) before they become sexually intimate. A similar focus upon HSV–2 antibody screening would obviate the possibility of a future herpes infection acquired from a sexual partner with no symptoms but who is, nevertheless, infected and can spread the virus. If she is pregnant, an antibody-negative woman may be advised to either abstain from any sexual contact or require the use of a condom if the male is HSV–2 antibody positive.

Although the herpes virus cannot be eliminated from the body, treatment is available. Prevention is, of course, the primary strategy. Men and women with known oral or genital herpes should inform their partners, recognize their patterns of symptoms when they have outbreaks, and avoid intimate contact at that time. This is particularly true for pregnant women, since active genital lesions at the time of labor require a CESAREAN SECTION to lower the risk of transmitting the herpes infection to the infant. For a pregnant woman, a first genital tract infection near or at the time of delivery is a far greater risk to the fetus than a recurrent infection.

In addition to these preventive measures, new antiviral agents are available for central nervous system herpes infection in the immuno-compromised. There are a number of instances in which the drug acyclovir can be an important treatment. For patients with genital tract herpes infection, the early use of oral acyclovir reduces the duration and degree of symptoms. For patients with frequent genital tract recurrences that prevent any chance of leading normal lives, acyclovir can be taken daily for six months to two years to markedly reduce the frequency of outbreaks. There will probably be a use for acyclovir in the prevention and treatment of newborns exposed to the herpes virus, but studies are not yet available to establish definite treatment guidelines (see also SAFER SEX).

HETEROSEXUALITY The human species has evolved to be heterosexual—that is to reproduce through the mating of males and females. No one knows exactly how two separate sexes evolved, but millions of years ago individuals of two complementary strains appeared, followed by the emergence of two distinct sexes—one carrying eggs, the other, sperm. These were our sexual ancestors, the forbears of human heterosexuality.

While other species have elected alternative methods of reproduction, humans have succeeded through a complex system of male/female bonding. In strictly biological terms, heterosexual reproduction has a number of advantages, the principal one being that it allows for greater variability in the species. While asexual reproduction most often produces offspring that are identical to the parent, sexual reproduction produces individuals that reflect the traits of two distinct parents. Over generations, this constant mixing and re-mixing of the genetic pool produces a species of tremendous adaptability. So humans evolved to be men and women and they must mix their genes or become extinct.

The necessity of coming together sexually in order to reproduce has led to an amazingly complicated system of mating. A woman and man must send off sexual signals to each other, must feel attraction, and must be attractive. Beyond this, they must feel compelling sexual emotions as reasons to invest time not only in sex but in pair-bonding as well. Pair-bonding is a hallmark of the human animal, a clever strategy for the rearing of defenseless young. It is a basic principle in heterosexual culture. When a woman and man fall in love, coupling is a norm. This is the human way, governed by culture, but also determined by our heterosexual biology as the way to best propagate our species.

For all heterosexual animals the reproduction game begins with sexual attraction. Humans are no exception. Accordingly, men and women have evolved very specific anatomies, instincts, and behaviors. Body shape, stature, hair, odors, and sensuously reddened lips function as gender flags, designed to entice a prospective mate. While Charles Darwin was aware that sexual selection could not account for all sexual traits, the eternal struggle of heterosexuality—to decide who will mate and breed with whom—is the most likely explanation for our most seductive and alluring anatomy.

Women's breasts, for example, are uniquely human and their size is completely unnecessary for the sole purpose of nursing. Ethnologist Desmond Morris proposes that they function as sexual bait. Other physical aspects of human sexuality emerged as our ancestors jockeyed for prized mates. As they emerged, behaviors evolved to make the most of our capacities to attract. Why do women, not men, wear lipstick? Why do men expand their chests when they are attracted to a woman? Why is it still a general rule that women flaunt their looks while men impress with money and social status? While there are many men and women who do not follow these patterns, much of our courting behavior may be governed by instincts of which we are not aware.

One of the greatest biological determinants of human heterosexual interaction is the female's continuous state of sexual receptivity. To males and females of almost any other living species, sex is not constantly available. The females of most species have a period of heat, or estrus, and when they are not in heat they generally refuse to accept the male. Human females can, if they wish, copulate at anytime. In practice, this biological imperative has led to an entire matrix of flirting, with complex customs, rules, and protocols both women and men understand and employ. Smiles, gazes, a toss of the head, the arch of the eyebrow—these actions are the grammar of a very rich language, a vocabulary that defines us as sexual beings.

Perhaps the most human quality of sexuality is our capacity to fall in love. Scientists point out that this, too, is rooted in biology; the emotions that encourage and even compel us to bond and to fall in love are physiologically ordered to a surprisingly large extent. What are these emotions which drive us to couple? In love, humans experience a panoply of feelings. But the twin locomotives of human pair-bonding are first, infatuation and then, emotional attachment.

There is evidence to suggest that infatuation is chemically triggered by the limbic system of the human brain. The limbic system governs our most basic, primitive emotions—fear, rage, joy, love, and hate. It is almost certain that the storm of infatuation is similarly jump-started by that part of the brain. The extraordinary euphoria and hyperenergy of attraction are caused by a brain bath of natural amphetamines in the emotional centers of the brain. This may be why our craving for romantic love is so intense; why we risk the emotional roller-coaster of falling in love.

Sexual infatuation seems to have a very natural life expectancy, and its waning enables another emotion to emerge—attachment. This is, perhaps, the most elegant of human feelings, that sense of contentment, of sharing, of oneness with another human being. In the attachment state of love, the brain begins to stimulate production of endorphins, the opiates of the mind. A relationship during the attachment phase is no longer turbulent; it is stable. The man and woman who were driven together by sexual attraction and romantic love stay together because of their strong affectional and loving bonds.

Humans are a heterosexually reproducing species, designed, as all organisms are, to procreate. Sexual union gives them the means to achieve great variety, and the sexual chemistry of their species may provide the incentive (see also BISEXUALITY; LOVE; SEXUAL INTERCOURSE).

HIGH BLOOD PRESSURE   see HIGH RISK PREGNANCY; FLIRTATION; PREGNANCY RELATED DISEASES.

HIGH RISK PREGNANCY   Many problems in PREGNANCY can be prevented by evaluating women for certain risk factors and treating them as soon as their pregnancies are diagnosed. An effective way to pay extra attention to a woman who might need special care in pregnancy is to classify a pregnancy into high risk or low risk categories. This classification can be made either before she becomes pregnant, at the beginning of her pregnancy, or at any time during her pregnancy. Some women already have certain conditions before pregnancy which will make them high risk. It is important for these women to be evaluated and treated well before pregnancy begins so that they can begin their pregnancies expecting the best outcome. Other women may begin their pregnancies as low risk patients, but subsequently be diagnosed as high risk. High risk factors develop either slowly or very quickly during the course of a pregnancy, and it is extremely important to identify them as soon as they occur.

Women who know well beforehand that they will be at high risk during pregnancy should enter their pregnancies in optimal condition to ensure the best outcome for themselves and their babies. It is best for them to have a checkup by a doctor trained in high risk pregnancy before becoming pregnant so as to discuss possible complications and preventive measures. For example, women with diabetes should have their blood sugar levels controlled during the months leading up to their pregnancies. This significantly decreases the major risk to the fetus of developing birth defects.

Women who must take medication should consult their physicians before pregnancy. While most medications are safe for use during pregnancy, there are a few that might present potential problems for the fetus or the mother. Sometimes switching to a safer medication before pregnancy may be better for the mother and the developing fetus. However, no medications should be stopped abruptly because of pregnancy without consulting a physician. Abrupt cessation of medication without consultation with a physician may lead to serious and unexpected problems.

Most women are not aware that they are at risk of developing problems in pregnancy. However, there are several conditions that are indicators that a woman might be in a high-risk category. An adverse outcome in a previous pregnancy places a woman at high risk for future pregnancies. If, for example, the previous pregnancy ended in a MISCARRIAGE, a stillborn infant, or PREMATURE BIRTH, there is an increased possibility that this might happen again. If a previous baby was too small or too big, if the pregnancy went significantly beyond the due date, if there was a diagnosis of a medical condition such as diabetes, hypertension, or bleeding disorders, or if the woman was unable to deliver vaginally due to a small pelvis, had a prior CESAREAN SECTION, or gave birth to a baby with a congenital malformation, she is usually at high risk for another adverse outcome.

High-Risk Factors During Pregnancy. Vaginal bleeding, or spotting, in pregnancy indicates that a patient is at high risk. Whenever a woman experiences bleeding during pregnancy, she should immediately inform her care provider. The first advice given to a pregnant woman who experiences vaginal bleeding is usually to abstain from vaginal intercourse to prevent a potential problem from worsening.

About 20 percent of all women experience minor bleeding during the first few months of pregnancy. While most have a normal baby, vaginal bleeding may also indicate that there is a problem. Reasons for vaginal bleeding during pregnancy are usually classified according to the timing of the occurrence during pregnancy: whether it occurs spontaneously or after sex, whether it is associated with pain, and whether the bleeding is bright or dark red. Pregnancy is divided into three trimesters: the first three months (first trimester), the middle three months (second trimester), and the last three months (third trimester). Bleeding is classified into first-, second-, and third-trimester bleeding. Vaginal bleeding, or spotting, in the first two trimesters of pregnancy is called a threatened abortion or threatened miscarriage. Bleeding in the last three months is simply called third-trimester bleeding.

When a woman complains about vaginal bleeding in pregnancy, the first thing a doctor usually does is to find out whether the bleeding originates outside of the UTERUS, from the VAGINA or CERVIX, or if it comes from inside the uterus. The pregnancy is checked to see whether it is viable and if the fetus is still alive and growing well. If pain accompanies vaginal bleeding early in pregnancy, the doctor will check whether the pregnancy is in the right place within the uterus. A pregnancy outside the uterus is usually located in the FALLOPIAN TUBES and is called an ECTOPIC PREGNANCY. Ectopic pregnancy is very serious; if it is not diagnosed in time, it may lead to severe life-threatening internal bleeding.

Vaginal bleeding during or shortly after intercourse during pregnancy is a potentially serious condition. It may be due to a vaginal or cervical infection, a tumor of the cervix, injury to the vagina or cervix, or an abnormal positioning of the PLACENTA.

Vaginal infections are often indicated when the vagina or cervix are reddened and look inflamed, or when there is an abnormal vaginal discharge. Analysis of the discharge with a microscope helps in identifying the organisms responsible for the infection. Treatment of the infection with antibiotics or other specific medication is common. Usually, the sexual partner must be treated too. (During treatment, the partner should wear a condom during sex to prevent reinfection.) Untreated vaginal infections have been implicated in cases of premature birth, infections of newborn infants, and infections of the uterus after delivery. Vaginal sex may be resumed during pregnancy after the vaginal infection has been successfully treated and both partners have been cured.

A tumor of the cervix (cervical neoplasia) is rarely the cause of vaginal bleeding in pregnancy, but it can be very serious if not diagnosed in time. If a woman has a regular PAP TEST, cervical neoplasia are usually diagnosed very early and treated before vaginal bleeding occurs. The diagnosis of cervical neoplasia is usually made by performing a cervical smear, looking at the cervix directly or with an instrument called a colposcope, or by doing a biopsy, in which a small piece of the cervix is excised. Early diagnosis and treatment of these cervical abnormalities has a nearly 100 percent success rate.

Abnormal placement of the placenta (*placenta previa*) may be another cause of vaginal bleeding associated with sex. It usually occurs during the last part of the pregnancy. Normally the placenta is located in the top portion of the uterus. In cases of *placenta previa*, the placenta is abnormally located in the lower part of the uterus, on top of the cervix and between the fetus and the vagina. Bleeding caused by *placenta previa* is usually painless and bright red in color. The diagnosis of this condition is usually made by ultrasonography (also called ultrasound or a sonogram). If this condition exists, vaginal sex is forbidden for the rest of the pregnancy because it may lead to life-threatening bleeding.

Another reason for bleeding in the last trimester may be the threat of premature birth. Patients with this condition should inform their physician immediately. If there is vaginal bleeding, premature labor with premature contractions of the uterus may also be present. Unfortunately, many women do not feel these contractions, and they may go on for a while before vaginal bleeding is observed. Vaginal spotting, or bleeding, may be the first indicator of premature labor. Doctors usually admit patients with threatened premature birth to the hospital and give them medicine (tocolytics) to stop labor.

Sometime, a woman's cervix opens even without contractions and pain, leading to vaginal bleeding and the possible loss of a pregnancy. This condition is called an incompetent cervix and usually occurs during the fourth or fifth month of pregnancy. If this condition is diagnosed early enough, or if the woman has had the condition in a previous pregnancy, a stitch (sometimes called cerclage) is placed in the cervix during the fourth month of pregnancy. A diagnosis of incompetent cervix places women in the highest risk of pregnancy loss.

SEXUAL INTERCOURSE may lead to a worsening of uterine contractions because semen contains hormones (prostaglandins) that may induce contractions. In addition, if the cervix has already opened, vaginal intercourse may weaken the fetal membranes, possibly leading to premature rupturing of these membranes. Patients with a history of premature labor should be carefully counseled about sex. Using a condom may prevent semen from entering the vagina, preventing the stimulation of uterine contractions.

Another serious cause of vaginal bleeding is the detachment of the placenta from the uterus. This is called *abruptio placentae*. Women with this condition usually complain about severe lower abdominal pain associated with passage of dark red blood from the vagina. *Abruptio placentae* is a potentially life-threatening condition. Immediate admission to the hospital with fetal monitoring and delivery is usually indicated to save both the fetus and the mother.

Diabetes in pregnancy also places the mother and the fetus at high risk. This condition can be diagnosed through special blood tests. A prior big baby or diabetes in a prior pregnancy indicates an increased risk. Pregnancy itself worsens diabetes, but early diagnosis and treatment with diet or insulin injections ensures a good pregnancy outcome in most patients.

High blood pressure during pregnancy constitutes one of the most frequent reasons for defining a woman as being at high risk during pregnancy. Elevated blood pressure may be either long-standing (chronic hypertension), or it may suddenly appear in pregnancy (toxemia or preeclampsia). Toxemia is a condition that usually occurs in women carrying their first pregnancy; it happens in the latter part of the pregnancy. Diagnosis of this condition is usually made by finding an elevated blood pressure (usually over 140/90), diagnosing the appearance of protein in the urine, and sudden weight gain. Woman with toxemia are usually admitted to hospital for bed rest. Possible complications include seizures (eclampsia) and detachment of the placenta (*abruptio placentae*). Delivery of the baby is considered the best treatment in such cases, especially when the condition occurs close to the due date (see also PREGNANCY AND COMMON MEDICATIONS AND SUBSTANCES).

HIRSCHFELD, DR. MAGNUS (1868–1935), A German physician, who specialized in "psychological sexual disorders." Through his research he concluded that the legal persecution, then common, of homosexuals was unjust, irrational, and inhuman, and he took up the fight against Germany's antihomosexual laws. He founded a committee for scientific research into HOMOSEXUALITY in 1897 and coedited a journal that took up the cause, while continuing other work on human sexuality.

In 1921 Hirschfeld organized the International Congress for Sexual Reform in Berlin: this later developed into the World League for Sexual Reform. The League's members included Havelock Ellis, August Forel, and Bertrand Russell. Among his long list of publications, the most important are *The Transvestites* (a term he invented), *Homosexuality in Men and Women*, *Sexual Pathology* (three volumes), and *Sexual Knowledge* (five volumes).

In 1933, when Adolf Hitler came to power, the Nazis raided his institute, destroyed his files, and burned his books. Hirschfeld was away at the time and could not return. He died two years later in France. The Nazis went on to violently persecute homosexuals, killing many in concentration camps. Although such persecution ended with Hitler's defeat, it was not until the late 1960s that Germany's antihomosexual laws were finally repealed.

HIV   see AIDS.

HOME BIRTH. An overwhelming majority of the world's people alive today were born at home despite the nearly universal adoption of HOSPITAL BIRTH in Western societies over the past half century. Yet, even in the United States, hospital birth is a relatively recent practice; at the beginning of the twentieth century, only poor and destitute Americans gave birth in hospitals. At that time, women whose families could afford to provide satisfactory home care and who had access to physicians or MIDWIVES preferred to have their babies at home.

The shift from home to hospital birth was dramatic and practically universal in the West by the 1960s and 1970s, and yet even in the United States home birth was never entirely eradicated. Just when the practice of hospital birth appeared to have become universal, a small but significant group of women again began looking to their homes as the ideal place to give birth. Largely middle class, these women typically were well informed and highly motivated. Some came from a feminist women's health background and others had ideological or religious convictions that supported the idea of home birth. All shared the desire to avoid or minimize the medical interventions in childbirth commonly in use, not be separated from their newborn babies, retain control over decision making in the childbirth process, and respect the private, spiritual, and familial aspects of childbirth. In the past twenty years, the home birth movement has grown to include women and men from all walks of life.

The keys to safe home birth are comprehensive prenatal care to reveal any risk factors and the choice of a skilled and qualified birth attendant. The attendant must be qualified to recognize whether a PREGNANCY and BIRTH are in the range of normal. The mother's and baby's conditions are generally monitored during labor—the fetal heart is checked intermittently, the color of amniotic fluid noted, and the mother's blood pressure taken. Equipment must be available for dealing with emergencies should they arise, and the attendant must be competent to recognize when transfer to a hospital is necessary and be prepared to do so quickly. Although the decision to give birth at home is not the norm in the United States, it can be a safe and appropriate choice for many responsible parents. Home birth confirms that pregnancy is not an illness and birth is not a medical event. Home birth attendants are available in all fifty states although it may take investigation to locate an appropriate and licensed care provider in some communities.

HOMOPHOBIA   Homophobia is defined as a fear of homosexuals, sometimes to an extreme degree so that it becomes pathological. Like many forms of discrimination, such as anti-semitism or racism, homophobia is often displayed by people who are angry at their own lot in life, and rather than blame those in positions of authority, pick on others whom they abhor and who are not as capable of fighting back.

Like all phobias it is often tied to the unknown, so it is most likely to be felt by people who do not really know any homosexuals. Part of their stated fear is their belief that homosexuals try to seduce heterosexuals, although this would pose no threat to someone who is truly heterosexual. However, since homophobia may also be tied to an inner fear of homosexual tendencies that the homophobe is afraid of admitting, even to him- or herself, the threat of such seduction does have the potential to instill terror in the homophobe. Often the homophobic person will go out of his or her way to declare how much they hate homosexuals, really fearing that if they were to act sympathetically toward them, others might think they are homosexual. When pushed to extremes by events in their lives, homophobic people may actually try to physically harm homosexuals.

The AIDS epidemic that has hit the homosexual community with particular severity has given rise to a recent increase in homophobia, in part due to some individuals' fear of AIDS itself, and in part due to their latent homophobia. While sexual contact with anyone who has AIDS could lead to a transference of the disease, AIDS cannot be spread by casual contact and the disease offers no excuse for homophobic inclinations.

HOMOSEXUALITY

Causes and Theories. The causes of male and female homosexuality have been debated for at least two thousand years. While the question of what makes people homosexual may, at first glance, seem simple, the answer is shrouded in controversy. For instance, we have not yet settled the "essentialist versus constructionist" argument. Essentialists say that a homosexual identity (in contrast to homosexual behavior) has always existed, and they ascribe it to a biological origin. Constructionists, on the other hand, believe that the concept of being a homosexual, as someone different from other people, is relatively new, having emerged only in the past few hundred years. Neither of these theories denies that homosexual behavior has always existed and that we have records and paintings of homosexual behavior from thousands of years ago. The question is whether in ancient times those people thought of themselves as being different from their contemporaries—as being "homosexual" in the way we think of it.

The oldest biological theory was proposed by Aristotle, who wrote that men who like to be sodomized have an extra nerve running down the spinal cord and ending in the rectum. Stimulation to the rectum causes pleasure during ANAL INTERCOURSE. It is interesting to note that Aristotle did not find it necessary to explain the behavior of the inserter. The oldest psychological theory was formulated by Persian physicians, who suggested that a man's preference for boys (rather than women) depended upon how he learned to masturbate. Men who held their penises tightly came to like boys, while those who were more gentle preferred women.

As charming as these theories may be, we now know that they are incorrect. But during the past hundred years, other biological and social theories about the causes of homosexuality have been espoused. During the latter half of the nineteenth century, a biological explanation dominated. Homosexuality in both men and women was considered a form of degeneracy that would eventually lead to madness. In this century, especially after World War II, biological explanations waned in popularity, and were replaced by a number of psychoanalytic theories. Recently, biological theories have experienced a resurgence.

Sigmund Freud, the originator of psychoanalysis, believed that homosexuality in a man developed when a boy identified with his mother, rather than his father, at about the age of five or six. In the 1940s other psychoanalysts suggested that a particular family constellation produced homosexuals. They said that gay men were phobic toward women because their mothers were emotionally engulfing, while their fathers were hostile. There is no evidence that either of these psychoanalytic theories is true, and considerable evidence tends to show that they are wrong. Nonetheless, there are people who continue to believe them.

Most research done during the past twenty-five years has focused on the biological origins of homosexual behavior and includes studies on hormones, genes, and anatomy. Hormonal research has studied the differences in androgens (male hormones) and estrogens (female hormones) in homosexuals and heterosexuals. Although results showed no differences between the two groups, clinicians often gave androgen injections to male homosexuals in the belief that a shot of masculinity would change them from gay to straight (heterosexual). It did not succeed.

Genetic studies have focused on the concordance rates of sexual orientation of both monozygotic (formed from the same egg) and dizygotic (formed from separate eggs) twins. Since monozygotic (identical) twins have exactly the same genetic makeup, if sexual orientation is inherited, these twins should have exactly the same sexual orientation (a 100 percent concordance rate). On the other hand, dizygotic twins should have a lower concordance rate. The lowest concordance rate should be between non-twin brothers and sisters. The results of these studies have shown the concordance rate of homosexuality is 50 to 55 percent in monozygotic twins, about 20 percent in dizygotic twins, and only about 8 percent between brothers and sisters. A strong inheritable factor is therefore established, but it does not account for all cases. Something more than heredity must be involved.

Anatomical studies have looked at the brain structures of homosexuals and heterosexuals. In some cases, differences have been found, but the origin of these differences is unknown. It is possible that they began prenatally. One researcher has suggested that brain structure differences between homosexuals and heterosexuals begin at about the fourth or fifth month of gestation, and once set are unalterable. This research is very speculative at this time.

While gay men are mostly comfortable about biological research, many lesbians are not. Some lesbians feel that their homosexuality is a choice, not a condition, and certainly not a biological impulse. Some maintain that they chose lesbianism for political reasons, as a way of rejecting patriarchal society (see also BISEXUALITY; GAY AND LESBIAN LIFE).

Cultural Attitudes. Individual attitudes toward homosexuality grow out of the cultural beliefs of the larger society, and are rooted in ethnicity, tradition, religion, and social class. There may be considerable variation in the degree of acceptance or toleration of homosexuality, within the society or even within a particular cultural group, however, and historians have noted substantial changes in group attitudes over time.

In some countries there is now near complete acceptance of homosexuality. For example, in the late 1980s Denmark passed a law permitting homosexual couples to legally marry. Although Holland, Norway, and Sweden do not legally sanction marriage, homosexual relationships in those countries are generally well respected and are incorporated into the social structure like heterosexual couples. Nevertheless, even in such countries many homosexuals still feel a need to hide their true feelings, while in other countries homosexual behavior is severely punished.

Legal attitudes towards homosexuality in the United States vary by state. Two states—Massachusetts and Minnesota—and many cities have enacted legislation to prohibit discrimination against homosexuals, while in other jurisdictions (e.g., Georgia) homosexual sex is punishable by law. However, laws against homosexual behavior are rarely used, and when tested in courts they are often found to be unenforceable.

Religious attitudes vary by denomination, locale, and time. Episcopalians, for example, have recently voiced support for male and female priests who are openly homosexual, and many parishes have hired them. While most Baptist groups believe homosexuality to be a sin, one Baptist church recently hired an openly homosexual minister. Roman Catholicism currently holds homosexual behavior to be a sin; however, in the early Middle Ages Roman Catholics found little wrong with homosexual behavior (see Boswell's *Christianity, Homosexuality, and Social Tolerance*). Thus, taboos now said by some religious denominations to be based on the Bible were not considered sinful according to earlier interpretations of biblical writings.

Although early professional literature considered homosexual feelings and behavior abnormal and a sign of arrested psychosocial development, in the 1970s many psychiatrists changed their attitude. Rather than judging homosexuality to be an illness, they now came to regard it as a normal (although minority) variation of sexual behavior. This decision resulted from a more scientific appraisal of the biases present in older "studies" of homosexuals (mostly by psychiatrists reporting on homosexual patients understandably troubled by their situation within society) and from growing anthropological and biological evidence of sexual variation in societies and within many mammalian species. The reclassification, however, remains contested by a minority of psychiatrists. Despite the reversal in attitudes, many homosexuals are troubled by their feelings and desired or actual behaviors; given the high prevalence of antihomosexual feelings in the society, they may be diagnosed as suffering from "ego-dystonic homosexuality."

Anthropologists (e.g., Mead's *Coming of Age in Samoa*) and historians (Boswell's *Christianity, Sociology, and Homosexuality*) have described homosexual encounters in other societies as normal and expected. In ancient Greece homosexuality was a common practice; however, male homosexual relationships usually involved older adult men initiating and maintaining active relationships with younger men. For older men to play a passive sexual role was deemed unusual and discouraged.

To the extent that the larger society and culture hold negative attitudes toward them, homosexual persons will be less able or willing to "come out" (see COMING OUT) and may remain "closeted." Strongly negative attitudes about homosexuals may severely limit their ability to recognize, accept, or express internal feelings, creating confusion or even self-loathing. If society's negative attitudes are strongly internalized, they may lead homosexuals to depression or even suicide. The high prevalence of both have, in fact, been documented in homosexual men of the San Francisco Bay area. These prevalences are more likely the result of HOMOPHOBIA (society's fear or negative attitudes to homosexuals) than intrinsic to homosexuality *per se*. (However, these findings may also be the result of biases introduced by the sampling designs of the studies.) Suicidal behavior is even more common among gay adolescents, resulting in calls for better education of youth about the nature of homosexuality and variation of human sexual objectives. Finally, there has long been evidence of overt hostility and violence aimed at homosexuals — gay and lesbian "bashing" has increased in association with the AIDS epidemic.

Since it is possible to change popular cultural attitudes through education, leadership behavior, and the law, and since the preponderance of evidence suggests that many men and women will continue to be sexually attracted to their own sex, it appears to be very much in society's interest to develop healthier attitudes toward homosexuality. Such attitudes would decrease violence towards sexual minority persons, diminish their need to hide feelings and relationships, encourage healthier and longer-lasting relationships, lower the numbers of sexual partners and the sexual transmission of diseases, and reduce the depression and suicide that may result from confusion over sexual identity, lack of self-respect, and feelings of isolation. Negative social attitudes hurt not only homosexuals but all of society.

Male Sex Techniques. Male-to-male sexual practices include a wide array of activities. Some are entirely safe from the standpoint of SEXUALLY TRANSMITTED DISEASES, including infection with the human immunodeficiency virus, HIV, or from the standpoint of physical injury; others, especially without the protection of a condom, are either risky or frankly dangerous.

The spectrum of male homosexual practices begins at the safe end with VOYEURISM — watching another or others having sex. For many gay men this vicarious activity produces extreme pleasure and may be their sole sexual aim, or it may be an accompaniment to their own MASTURBATION, possibly to ORGASM. Although in mainstream society voyeurism is generally considered a rude invasion of privacy, many gay men are willing to be observed, and some are actually excited by being observed having sex.

Another activity frequently practiced by gay men is masturbation in groups of two or more. This may be solo masturbation in the presence of others or mutual masturbation, where one masturbates the other, including "cycle jerks," where one man masturbates the next, who masturbates the next, and so on. In the AIDS era, most major cities in the United States and Europe have developed "J/O Clubs," that provide an environment in which gay men may masturbate together. Most clubs have strict rules that penises may only be touched with the hands and not enter mouths or anuses.

KISSING is as erotic for many gay men as it is for heterosexuals; however, some gay men think kissing is repulsive although they are willing to engage in oral-penile or oral-anal sex. For other gay men kissing may be their only or primary sexual aim.

Frontage is the term used for body rubbing. This is generally considered a safe sexual activity in which two men, often in association with kissing, hold each other tightly and rub their bodies, and especially their penises, against one another, often until climax.

Perhaps the most common form of sex between men is FELLATIO—oral-penile sex. Like most other sexual behaviors, this may be the main sexual aim or it may be a prelude to other forms of sexual activity. A particular form of fellatio is called "SIXTY-NINE" because this position—two bodies head to crotch—looks like the numerals "6" and "9." In this position, two persons may lick, kiss, and suck each other's genitals for pleasure to the point of orgasm. It is generally thought that ejaculation into the partner's mouth makes transmission of sexual diseases, including HIV, more likely, so in recent years partners are more likely to avoid it.

The mouth, lips, and tongue may also be applied to other parts of the male body, including the testicles, anus ("rimming"), nipples, ears, navel, feet, and hands. Such sexual activities are relatively risk free, except for oral-anal contact, which has the potential to spread diseases such as hepatitis A and amoebic dysentery.

Of the more common forms of gay male sex, perhaps the most risky for transmission of HIV is penile-anal sex. This occurs when one man's penis is inserted in his partner's anus and then stimulated with a series of thrusting movements designed to achieve orgasm. This not only provides pleasure to the "top," or inserter of the penis, but most "bottoms" also find it intensely pleasurable to be penetrated and to have their PROSTATE and rectum stimulated in this way. The danger of STDs and HIV in this activity are thought to accrue both from the ejaculate and from the rectal lining, which is easily torn or abraded, permitting easy access to the blood stream. Although many try to ejaculate outside the body, the desire to remain in one's partner's anus may be strong, and there is the possibility that small quantities of fluid before ejaculation may be capable of spreading infection. The use of condoms to block the transmission of HIV and other infections is highly recommended.

A relatively small proportion of gay men engage in what even gay men call "kinky" sexual behaviors: "water sports"—where one either urinates on or is urinated upon by one's partner; "fisting"—where one either inserts or has one's partner insert the hand (or "fist") into the rectum; fetishes; "S & M" (SADISM/MASOCHISM) and/or "B & D," involving spanking, the use of whips, slings, handcuffs, etc. (see also LESBIAN SEXUAL TECHNIQUES).

HOMOSEXUALITY AND SEX THERAPY

Very few sex therapists or psychotherapists still believe that HOMOSEXUALITY can be "treated" with the objective of changing the client's sexual orientation to a heterosexual one. The few therapists that do believe this are usually associated with fundamentalist religious organizations and their approach is mainly intended to help homosexuals who may, out of religious conviction, want to cease homosexual activity and enter a heterosexual relationship instead. Critics of this type of therapy have argued that such therapists are merely helping clients repress their true, homosexual orientation and act "as if" they were heterosexuals.

Most mainstream therapists accept their clients' sexual orientations and treat the emotional and sexual problems of homosexuals in the same ways they treat those of heterosexuals. Thus, when a homosexual couple or individual walk into a sex therapist's office with a relationship problem or a sexual dysfunction, they are treated with the same treatment techniques as heterosexuals. Rather than try and influence homosexual behavior, most reputable sex therapists treat the problem presented.

HORMONE REPLACEMENT THERAPY

HORMONES are chemicals produced by glands in the body. Some regulate metabolism and others, the female hormones, regulate the menstrual cycle. In women, the two main hormones specifically for female functions are ESTROGEN and PROGESTERONE. Estrogen also plays a key role in maintaining the health of a woman's heart, blood vessels, and bones.

MENOPAUSE is the time in a mature woman's life when her OVARIES stop producing estrogen and progesterone and when she stops having menstrual periods. (Some women go through an "artificial" menopause if their ovaries are estrogen removed surgically or rendered inactive.) Estrogen is also produced in the fat cells of the body, so even at menopause the estrogen level never falls to zero. Nonetheless, it is at a very low level, insufficient to protect a woman from osteoporosis and heart disease.

When estrogen levels fall, almost all women experience symptoms of it. The HOT FLASH is the most common. This is a sudden feeling of heat which spreads over the body, and the skin may flush and sweat. These sensations rarely last more than twenty minutes, but may occur many times over a twenty-four-hour period. Often hot flashes occur at night, interrupting sleep.

The lining of the vagina, the vaginal mucosa, also responds to decreased estrogen levels. The cells produce less LUBRICATION and become thinner, and itching, burning, or painful intercourse may result.

Osteoporosis (accelerated loss of bone density) is another consequence of decreased estrogen levels. After menopause, some women are at greater risk of hip, wrist, or spinal bone fractures. This is due to an increased loss of calcium from the bone, making them more prone to fractures. Slender white women are at the greatest risk of getting osteoporosis, but all post-menopausal women are at risk. Smoking and lack of proper exercise aggravate the process, as does inadequate nutrition.

Heart attacks occur only rarely in women prior to menopause. Estrogen has a protective effect on the arteries of the heart and elsewhere. Estrogen helps maintain the HDL or "good" cholesterol level and decreases the LDL or "bad" cholesterol level. After menopause, and without estrogen replacement by pills, heart attacks are more common.

Menopause is usually preceded by irregular menstrual periods. A woman may skip one or two months or may stop menstruating suddenly, or the amount of flow may change. Hormone therapy is started at menopause or earlier if a woman develops the symptoms before menopause actually occurs. If a woman has her ovaries surgically removed, she would start hormone replacement therapy at that time.

Estrogen therapy alone can stimulate the lining of the uterus (the endometrium) and, in fact, it increases the incidence of cancer of this lining. To negate this effect, progesterone is added to the hormone therapy regimen.

There are a variety of methods employed to replace hormones. One can cycle the woman with estrogen twenty-five days of the month, add progesterone the last ten of these days, and then allow a period of five to six days without hormones. Most women will have a menstrual period during the time off hormones. This bleeding is regular and usually light. Another method is to give estrogen and progesterone daily, with no hormone-free interval. Using this method, some women will experience irregular spotting, and others will not have any bleeding. There are estrogen and progesterone pills, as well as a skin patch containing estrogen, or these hormones can be administered by injection.

Any time that a woman has irregular bleeding after menopause an endometrial sampling of the uterine lining should be performed either by endometrial biopsy or "D & C." This is to ensure that the bleeding is not from abnormal cells or from cancer of the uterus (see UTERINE CANCER).

With few exceptions, nearly all women can take hormones in the menopausal years. Estrogen replacement therapy after menopause eliminates hot flashes, helps retard development of osteoporosis, reduces the risk of cardiovascular disease, corrects thinning of vaginal tissue, and also helps to make the menopausal years a more enjoyable and satisfying time in a woman's life.

There have been reports that women using hormone replacement therapy are at a slightly increased risk of breast cancer. However, the relationship has not been scientifically proven and any women who are concerned about this risk should consult their physicians (see also AMENORRHEA; MENSTRUATION).

HORMONES The chemical messengers of the body, called hormones, are secreted by the endocrine glands. The endocrine glands include the pancreas, which secretes insulin regulating sugar use by the cells of the body; the gonads, which secrete the sex hormones regulating reproduction; and the thyroid, which secretes thyroxine to control metabolism. Regulation of body growth, reproduction, and many metabolic functions, such as energy use, is managed by hormone secretion. The hormones are released by the endocrine system at a slow and steady rate and reach their targets through the blood. This is quite different from the other regulatory system, the nervous system, which relays signals from cell to cell electronically in fractions of seconds. The chemical messages take from several minutes to hours to be received and acted upon, and their effects are usually long-lasting.

The endocrine glands themselves are regulated by a complex mechanism called "feedback." When the activity of the responding tissue reaches a critical level, the information is relayed back to the regulating endocrine gland, reducing the activity of the gland. Endocrine glands can respond to increases in activity of the target tissue by decreasing their own activity and can respond to decreases in target activity with subsequent increases.

There are many classes of chemical structures that are defined as hormones. The most common hormones are either small peptides, steroid molecules, or complex proteins. In evolutionary terms, steroids are possibly the oldest of the hormones used by the body. They are constant throughout the vertebrate world, functioning in fish as they do in mammals. The steroid struc-

ture is simple and easily recognized by the cell that will react to the hormone.

Hormones interact with cells of the body through cellular structures called receptors. Receptors are shaped so that only a specific hormone will bind on a specific receptor, like a lock and key. If a cell does not have the specific hormone receptor, it will not respond to the hormone. Receptors are found both in the cell plasma membrane and within the cell. Steroids pass through the plasma membrane, binding to receptors inside the cell. Receptors in the plasma membrane bind hormones that do not enter the cell. Once the hormone has bound to the receptor, it changes the shape of the receptor, thereby activating it. The activated receptor transfers the stimulus from outside the cell wall to chemical mechanisms within the cell and causes a response. Often, the response will be an increase in protein production or the production of a particular metabolite. The response can also affect the amount of enzymes found in a particular cellular reaction, increasing the rate of reaction. The end product may be a protein that will increase or decrease metabolism, or it could even be another hormone.

Hormonal control is found at many levels of reproductive function. Hormones stimulate gonadal development, sperm and oocyte (egg) production, and secondary sexual characteristics. They also play a role in regulating sexual behavior and LIBIDO (see also AMENORRHEA; ESTROGEN; HORMONE REPLACEMENT THERAPY; IMPOTENCE; PITUITARY GLAND AND HORMONE SECRETION; PLACENTA; PROGESTERONE; TESTICLES; TESTOSTERONE; VASECTOMY AND THE MALE PILL).

HOSPITAL BIRTH In the early part of the century most babies were delivered at home by MIDWIVES or birth attendants. Only a small percentage of babies was delivered by a doctor. By 1935, however, 35 percent of births in the United States occurred in hospitals. The proportion of hospital deliveries increased to 88 percent in 1950 and peaked at over 99 percent in the early 1970s. Today, most women deliver their babies in a traditional hospital labor and delivery unit. However, alternative choices for childbirth have evolved in recent years with respect to facility, birth attendant, and degree of technology used. In traditional units, women are in labor rooms while in labor, and then move for the actual birth to a delivery room, closely resembling an operating room. Alternatives include in-hospital birthing rooms, also known as labor/delivery rooms (LDR). These rooms are usually located within the traditional labor and delivery unit, but constitute a compromise between the traditional hospital facility and an out-of-hospital birthing center. Rooms in LDR units are usually equipped with furniture, providing a home-like setting. When delivery is close, they can be changed to resemble traditional delivery rooms. For normal deliveries, mothers deliver in the same LDRs in which they labor, and the babies usually stay with the mother afterward. Mothers and babies are then transferred to postpartum units. Most recently, labor and delivery/postpartum units have been developed in which the mother stays with the baby overnight, and is then discharged from the same room. Other options for childbirth include hospital-based birthing centers, directly connected to a hospital but separate from the labor and delivery unit, and free-standing birthing centers, that are not physically connected to a hospital. Only a few women still choose to deliver at home (see HOME BIRTH).

The primary advantage of delivering a baby in a hospital, compared to home birth, is that equipment is available for ensuring the best potential outcome for the mother and her baby. This includes electronic fetal monitoring equipment and equipment for cesarean sections. If the mother develops a complication, trained professionals are available for her care. If CESAREAN SECTION is needed, an operating room is available and no time is lost. In addition, if the baby has a problem, other doctors, including pediatricians, may be called on for help.

HOT FLASHES An acute and common symptom of MENOPAUSE. Also known as flushes, they are characterized by a sudden feeling of intense heat, followed by a flushing of the upper body, profuse sweating, and often heart palpitations. A sensation of pressure in the head may mark the beginning of a flash. The actual feeling of warmth or burning is centered in the face, neck, upper chest, and back; it is sometimes accompanied by patchy flushing of the skin and an outburst of sweating follows immediately. Both the feeling of heat and sweating subsequently spread all over the body. Vertigo, lightheadedness, fatigue, nausea, and headache are some of the less frequent symptoms accompanying flashes. The flash typically ends in a cold shiver.

Hot flashes are disturbing and uncomfortable; the feeling of heat forces most women to fan themselves, move off bed covers, shed clothing, or open the window. Since flushes are more common at night, they are commonly known as "night sweats." Women usually wake up from the discomfort, and consequently may suffer from insomnia, drowsiness, or inattentiveness.

The average length of a flush is about four minutes, although it varies from a few seconds to ten minutes. Some women experience a flush as often as once or twice an hour, whereas others have it once or twice a week. During the year after their last menstrual period, 75 percent of women experience hot flashes. Among these women, 82 percent will have symptoms for more than a year, and 25 to 85 percent will continue to have repeated episodes of flushes for more than five years. Few women complain about this ten years after menopause.

The subjective feeling of hot flashes is associated with physiological changes, such as an increase of skin temperature and a decrease of the body's core temperature. These changes occur just before the actual hot flash and disappear several minutes afterwards.

Since both women in natural menopause and women who have had their ovaries removed (surgical menopause) suffer from hot flashes, scientists believe that lowered female sex hormones are responsible for their occurrence. Body temperature is controlled by regulatory centers in the brain that operate like a thermostat with a certain temperature set point. Both natural and surgical menopause lead to a reduction of estrogen, which triggers a severe drop of the thermoregulatory set point. Mechanisms that induce heat loss, such as sweating and flushing, bring the core temperature to the level of the new set point.

Since hot flashes are most likely the result of estrogen withdrawal, the most common and effective treatment is estrogen replacement. This reduces hot flashes and generally improves sleep. However, although estrogen provides temporary relief, it is not a cure, and symptoms will return without continued treatment.

Other drugs have also been used to relieve the symptoms of hot flashes. Progestins such as de-pomedroxyprogesterone acetate (DEPO-PROVERA), the second most commonly used therapy, are prescribed for patients who cannot take estrogens. Clonidine (Catapres), an antihypertension drug, is relatively effective in relieving the symptoms. It is often used in hypertensive women, since they have a better tolerance of its side effects. Other agents, such as tranquilizers, sedatives, and antidepressants, along with vitamins E and K, belladonna alkaloids, and mineral supplements have been tried; their efficiency is not clearly known. Because of the potential for addiction and drug-related side effects, they are not usually prescribed for the treatment of hot flashes (see also HORMONE REPLACEMENT THERAPY).

HUMAN IMMUNODEFICIENCY VIRUS
see AIDS.

HYMEN A thin membrane situated at the opening of a woman's vagina. Its structure is extremely variable; it may be almost entirely absent, form an opening that admits one or two fingers to the vagina, or occasionally form a barrier across the lower edge of the vaginal opening. Despite this variation, the presence of an intact hymen (often called "the maidenhead" in past literature, or "the cherry" in the vernacular) has been taken to be proof of a woman's virginity in the many traditional cultures that value it. Indeed, "proof" of an intact hymen—sometimes bedsheets stained with chicken blood—is still required of girls and women in some traditional cultures when they marry.

In America and other Western countries it is widely accepted that the hymen may be virtually absent when a woman first experiences intercourse; it may have been stretched or torn as a result of vigorous sports or the insertion of fingers into the vagina, or it may (rarely) have been surgically cut. When a woman's hymen is intact at the time she first experiences intercourse it will usually be stretched or torn as the male's penis enters her vagina, possibly causing some pain and minor bleeding. If a woman is worried about this possibility, she can usually stretch the hymen with her fingers or have a physician cut the membrane.

In rare cases, a hymen may actually block the vagina's opening either totally or nearly so. When girls with such a hymen begin to experience menstruation, the monthly flow of blood from the vagina will be prevented, causing progressive pelvic pain. The problem is usually solved by a surgical incision through the membrane (see also FEMALE SEX ORGANS; VIRGINITY).

HYPERSEXUALITY The term "hypersexuality" is used to describe the entire range of conditions more familiarly described as PROMISCUITY, SATYRIASIS, NYMPHOMANIA, sexual addiction, and erotomania. Today it is more often referred to as compulsive sexual behavior (CSB).

The driving force behind compulsive sexual behavior is the person's need to reduce anxiety; the specific sexual behavior involved is less important. It may be considered paraphiliac (an addiction to unusual sexual practices) or nonparaphiliac. Although nonparaphiliac behavior is generally accepted as "normal" sexual behavior, individuals suffering from CSB often carry it to pathological extremes. An example might be MASTURBATION, generally accepted to be a normal behavior except if carried out compulsively, non-stop past orgasm, or until physical injury or pain occurs.

However, some forms of nonparaphiliac behavior, even when taken to extremes, might actually be normal when they occur within the framework of appropriate psychosexual development. For example, adolescents may be obsessively occupied with sexual matters for months at a time, and such behavior may recur in episodic form later in life. Here, the distinguishing factor is that the behavior exists for a limited time only and the individual eventually returns to a normal behavior pattern.

The most commonly know examples of CSB are those pathologies that fit into the group of behaviors classified as paraphiliac. These behaviors have both conscious and unconscious elements. They are characterized by intense sexual fantasies, are distressing to the person, and are overwhelmingly compelling in intensity. These behaviors are devoid of any feelings of love; their only objective is the elimination of anxiety.

Paraphiliac behaviors include:

EXHIBITIONISM: exposing one's genitals to unsuspecting strangers;

FETISHISM: sexual fantasies involving material objects such as women's shoes;

PEDOPHILIA: sexual activities involving an adult (the pedophile) and a child;

SEXUAL SADISM: achieving sexual excitement by imposing on others acts which cause them psychological or physical pain;

SEXUAL MASOCHISM: receiving abuse, punishment, torture, or humiliation to obtain sexual excitement;

VOYEURISM: surreptitiously observing unsuspecting persons disrobing or engaging in sexual activity;

ZOOPHILIA: using an animal for sex.

Hypersexuality is a response to anxiety caused by a psychiatric condition. It is an attempt by the mind to defend itself against tremendous emotional discomfort, which may be temporarily relieved by the sexual activity. Hypersexuality is a form of obsessive-compulsive disorder; it is not the result of a hormonal imbalance nor do such individuals have a high level of sexual desire.

Treatments for hypersexuality are still evolving. As yet there are no precise or preferred therapies. Treatments currently in use may include behavior therapy, individual or group therapies, and/or various medications. The newest class of serotonergic antidepressants seems to be emerging as particularly helpful because they seem to have antilibidinal properties that lower the intensity of sexual drives. Antiandrogens—drugs that lower the level of male sex hormones—have had limited success in treating these disorders (see also EXHIBITIONISM; FETISHISM; SADISM/MASOCHISM; VOYEURISM; ZOOPHILIA).

HYSTERECTOMY The operation performed to remove a woman's UTERUS (womb). The uterus contains two parts, the body (or corpus) and the CERVIX (or neck). A total hysterectomy involves removal of the entire uterus—the body and the cervix. A subtotal hysterectomy is an operation in which only the body of the uterus is removed but the cervix is left in place. Sometimes, at the time of a hysterectomy, the woman's FALLOPIAN TUBES and OVARIES are also removed. If this is done, the procedure has the medical designation "hysterectomy with bilateral salpingo-oophorectomy," meaning removal of the fallopian tubes and ovaries from both sides. Salpingo-oophorectomy (removal of tubes and ovaries) can be performed with either a total hysterectomy or a subtotal hysterectomy. In common parlance this nomenclature is confused so that the term total hysterectomy is erroneously used to mean a total hysterectomy and bilateral salpingo-oophorectomy, and partial hysterectomy is used to mean total hysterectomy without removal of the tubes and ovaries. This is an inaccurate and confusing usage of the terms.

A radical hysterectomy is the procedure performed for some types of UTERINE CANCER. This operation involves not only a total hysterectomy, but removal of the ligaments and connective tissue surrounding the uterus as well as the lymph vessels that drain the uterus and the lymph nodes into which they drain. Usually both tubes and ovaries are also removed during a radical hysterectomy. The purpose of a radical hysterectomy is to treat cancer limited to the pelvis. When cancer cells spread from the cervix, they spread to adjacent tissues and, through lymphatic vessels, into the lymph nodes, the first line of the body's defense. The theory of a radical hysterectomy is that it removes the cancer together with its primary area of spread so that all the cancer cells have been removed.

There are several methods of performing a hysterectomy. Vaginal hysterectomies can be performed with the assistance of a laparoscopic procedure to help remove tissues not readily accessible through the vagina. In addition, a subtotal hysterectomy can be performed through a laparoscopic procedure, without the need for a vaginal incision. An abdominal hysterectomy is performed through a surgical incision in the lower part of the belly. This incision can either be vertical (up and down) or transverse (side-to-side). There are many reasons for performing an abdominal hysterectomy, including the removal of large tumors and, if there is a possibility that cancer is present, the ability to evaluate and examine the entire abdomen for spread of the cancer. In patients whose conditions have been complicated by factors that resulted in the uterus being scarred or adherent to other structures in the abdomen, such as the colon or small intestines, the transabdominal approach is necessary to allow the physician to perform more delicate surgery. The major advantage to the abdominal approach is that it provides the surgeon with a larger field of view and better access to structures inside the abdomen. The obvious disadvantage is that it leaves a visible scar on the lower abdomen. The recovery period is slightly longer for abdominal than for vaginal surgery.

If the uterus is not adherent to other structures in the abdomen and it is not too large to safely remove through the vagina, a vaginal hysterectomy can be performed. In this operation a circular incision is made around the cervix, separating it from the vagina and adjacent tissues. The operation is then extended into the abdomen through the vagina, removing the uterus. The advantage of a vaginal hysterectomy is that there are generally fewer complications, no visible scars on the abdomen, and a shorter recovery period.

Hysterectomies are performed to save the woman's life or to correct serious problems that interfere with the woman's normal activities and thus improve her quality of life. One example of the life-saving potential of hysterectomy is in cases of severe uterine bleeding that cannot be stopped by medicines or more simple operative procedures; the bleeding will respond to hysterectomy. An example of the second reason is the relief of incapacitating pelvic pain that may be due to severe infections, symptomatic EN-DOMETRIOSIS, or fibroid-related pain. A woman's quality of life may be measurably improved by a hysterectomy done to remove a prolapsed uterus that has lost its support within the abdomen and sags so that the cervix protrudes through the vagina.

Perhaps the most common reason for hysterectomy is in the treatment of uterine fibroids (myomas), benign (non-cancerous) tumors of the uterus. These fibroids may grow large enough to interfere with the function of other structures in the abdomen and produce discomfort or pressure on the bladder and/or rectum. Occasionally fibroids produce pain severe enough to require removal. Fibroids also are associated with prolonged and heavy bleeding, and this may also be an indication of the need for a hysterectomy.

Endometriosis is a non-cancerous condition in which the lining of the uterus develops in areas outside the cavity of the uterus. This can produce scarring and pain that may occasionally require a hysterectomy. Other causes of pelvic pain include chronic infections of the ovaries and fallopian tubes. These infections cause scars (adhesions) that hold together structures not normally connected. This can produce fairly severe discomfort and may require a hysterectomy as a definitive treatment.

If the woman has not yet gone through MENOPAUSE and her ovaries are removed, this will result in a surgical menopause. This may produce unpleasant symptoms, such as HOT FLASHES, sweats, fatigue, and vaginal dryness. HORMONE REPLACEMENT THERAPY may be necessary to reduce the risk of osteoporosis (thinning of the bones) and heart disease.

Major surgery is clearly a traumatic event; many patients experience an emotional depression several weeks after. A hysterectomy clearly indicates a final removal of all childbearing potential. Since to many women childbearing, possession of a uterus, and menstrual periods are indicative of normal female functions, the removal of a uterus may be associated with a sense of defeminization.

Hysterectomy may affect a woman's enjoyment of sex, but if it removes a painful condition, it may also improve a woman's sex life.

I

IDENTITY, SEXUAL see ADOLESCENCE; BISEXUALITY; GENDER DYSPHORIA; HOMOSEXUALITY; TRANSSEXUALITY.

IMPOTENCE In recent years our understanding of how men's erections develop has improved tremendously and has helped physicians to understand how the process can fail. We now recognize that most cases of impotence are a result of physical problems, and the condition is no longer a taboo topic. There are many reasonable options of treatment, allowing people to regain a more satisfying sex life.

An erection develops in the following way. Normal levels of the male sex hormone TESTOSTERONE create the LIBIDO, or sex drive, that encourages sexual stimulation. Stimulation, whether by touch, vision, or thought, causes the blood vessels leading to the erectile chambers of the penis (*corpus cavernosum*) to dilate, thus increasing the flow of blood to the penis. This increased blood flow causes the erectile chambers to fill with blood. Subsequently, there is a natural and normal release of chemical substances

that causes the muscle tissue within the penis to relax. This increases the space in the erectile chambers that can fill with blood. When the penis is not erect, blood flows in and out of it quite freely. However, during an erection the increased blood flow causes the erectile chambers

Hydraulic penile implant

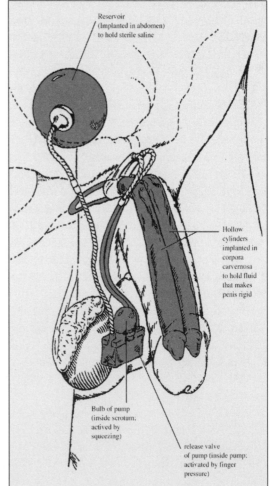

Penile self-injection therapy

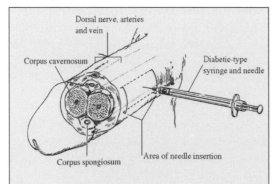

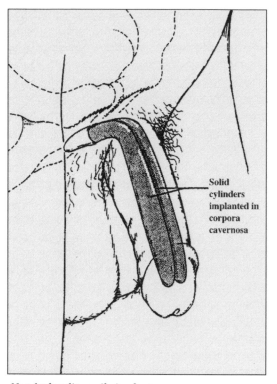

Non-hydraulic penile implant

Vacuum constriction device

Rubber ring

Flexible tube

Solid cylinders implanted in corpora cavernosa

Plastic cylinder

Hand-held pump

to swell. The normal swelling or expansion of these chambers prevents the usual flow of blood out of the penis, creating a sustained erection. When sexual stimulation stops, the blood flow to the penis decreases, the muscles in the penis contract, and blood flows out of the erectile chambers through the "holes or veins" (called subtunical venules) leading out of these chambers and that were compressed by the increased blood flow.

Any abnormality in this process can cause problems with erections. There can be vascular problems, such as decreased blood flow into the penis, abnormal relaxation of the muscles within the penis, and/or increased blood flow out of the penis. Conditions that increase the likelihood of such problems are similar to the factors affecting circulation to other parts of the body: high blood pressure, heart disease, smoking, high cholesterol, diabetes, trauma (to the penis or pelvis), and radiation injury.

Injuries of the nerves leading to the penis can also cause problems with erections. Conditions such as spinal cord injury, multiple sclerosis, di-

abetes, severe alcoholism, or surgery in the penile or pelvic area (such as radical prostate, bladder, rectal, or colon surgery) can cause nerve-related impotence.

Male hormones are responsible for creating the normal male libido, or sex drive. The absence or low levels of these hormones can be caused by medications or by high levels of other circulating hormones, such as prolactin from a tumor of the pituitary gland. Certain medical conditions can lower hormone levels, too. If an erection problem is the result of a hormone imbalance, it is usually associated with a decreased sex drive and can be treated with replacement hormones.

Treatments for Impotence. Urologists are well-trained in the diagnosis and treatment of impotence. At present, the two most successful treatments for impotence are injection therapy and the implantation of a penile prosthesis. However, these treatments are reserved for patients whose cause of impotence cannot be reversed by, for example, treating high blood pressure or a hormone imbalance.

A major breakthrough in the treatment of erection problems occurred in the 1970s with the development of a functionally reliable penile prosthesis. The idea of using a substitute for the erectile chambers was first described in 1936, when cartilage was used for this purpose. Penile prostheses are now made of inert materials.

Penile prostheses or implants are either hydraulic or non-hydraulic. Non-hydraulic prostheses were developed first and are rigid or semi-rigid rods that are surgically placed within the erectile chambers. These are easy to insert, have few mechanical failures, a low complication rate, and a high degree of patient satisfaction. However, although the implanted penis can be positioned downward when sex is not occurring, it stays rigid at all times, and this can be embarrassing.

Hydraulic penile prostheses were developed to produce a more natural appearing penis in both the flaccid and erect states. This implant has three parts: cylinders placed inside the erectile chambers; a pump placed in the scrotum; and the reservoir placed behind the abdominal muscles. When the penis is in the flaccid (non-erect) state, fluid sits in the reservoir and the cylinders are empty, giving the penis a relatively normal appearance. When an erection is desired, fluid is transferred from the reservoir into the cylinders. The patient can do this manually by activating the pump mechanism that has been surgically implanted in the scrotum. Patient satisfaction is highest with this type of implant but the mechanical failure rate is higher.

The penile prosthesis is a very effective form of treating otherwise intractable impotence. Advantages include its relative simplicity, a minimal loss of spontaneity, and overall reliability. However, placement of a penile implant does involve surgery which usually requires a hospital stay. If infection occurs, the device is almost always removed as part of the treatment of the infection. Despite overall satisfaction, penile length and girth with a prosthesis are not always as good as with prior erections. Pre-operative counseling leads to more realistic expectations. Unlike silicon breast implants, no problems have been reported to date with penile implants.

The development of penile self-injection therapy has been the major breakthrough in the treatment of impotence in the 1980s. This involves the injection of medications with a small needle directly through the skin at the base of the penis and into the erectile chambers. The medications relax the muscles within the penis. This treatment works best in patients with injury to the nerves of the penis, but it is also effective in other situations. The medications have been used in the United States for many years, although they are not approved by the government for such use. Nevertheless, self-injection has become a very common and successful treatment of impotence in this country and overseas.

A relatively painless injection results in an erection after about ten to fifteen minutes and lasts from thirty minutes to one hour. Of all the treatment options, this provides the most natural erection. Patients learn the technique of self-injection at a urologist's office, where the correct dose of the medicine is determined. Short-term side effects are relatively few but include rare liver problems, scarring at the injection site, and potentially the most serious: priapistic erections, sustained, painful erections that can only be relieved by medication. Though extremely rare, priapistic erections must be treated promptly.

Another treatment option for patients with erection problems is the vacuum constriction device. To obtain an erection with this device, a hand-held pump is placed over the end of the penis and air is sucked out, creating a vacuum and causing blood to flow into the penis. The vacuum device is removed, but a constriction ring is left in place, impeding the outflow of blood and maintaining the erection. During intercourse, the rubber ring is kept in place. This treatment is noninvasive and does not require surgery, but some find the device difficult to use because of decreased spontaneity, mild bruising, difficulty with ejaculation, and a lower quality erection. These problems have precluded its more widespread use.

Reconstructive bypass blood vessel surgery has also been used to treat impotence, but it is successful only in specific cases. Overall, the diagnosis and treatment of erection problems have improved significantly during the last ten to fifteen years. Almost all erection problems can be successfully treated in some fashion.

Male Sleep Disorders Centers and the Evaluation of Impotence. Sleep disorders centers play a new and innovative role in evaluating patients for medical, neurologic, and psychiatric causes of sexual dysfunction. These centers and their laboratories can provide valuable information to help determine if a patient's sexual response problem is "organic" or "psychological." In this context, "organic" means due to a medical disorder such as diabetes or high blood pressure; "psychological" indicates a cause such as depression or a personality disorder.

A male patient coming to a sleep center with a complaint of impotence (medically, an erectile dysfunction) first undergoes a medical and neurologic evaluation for any physical disease. If no obvious cause of the erectile dysfunction is found, the center will try to determine if the problem is organic or psychological. One way to answer this question is to determine if there are any circumstances under which erection is possible. The key to the center's work is a phenomenon called "nocturnal penile tumescence" (NPT). Sleep occurs in several stages, and the last, called REM (Rapid Eye Movement) sleep, is the stage during which most dreams occur. During this stage, normal men and boys have penile erections. These erections occur reliably during REM sleep, whether the man is dreaming or not and whether the dream is sexual or otherwise in content.

When NPT was first discovered, it was thought it would be a perfect way to evaluate impotence. If a man could have an erection while he slept, researchers theorized, he was physically capable of erections and any problem was psychological. If he did not have erections when he slept, then the problem was physical or organic. Unfortunately, things are not so simple. Medical, psychiatric, and technical problems may prevent erections in a man with a primarily psychiatric problem and allow erections to occur in one with a primarily physical one. However, if the manifestations of NPT are interpreted by a qualified physician or therapist in the context of

an appropriate evaluation, NPT can still be valuable in determining the cause of impotence.

There are several means of evaluating NPT. The simplest is to ask the patient if he ever wakes up with an erection. Since we frequently wake up from REM sleep, most men, at least occasionally, will wake with an erection. It is important for the physician to ask this specific question because many men do not associate these erections with sex and may not recall waking up with them.

One of the oldest methods is the STAMP TEST. In this simple test, the patient goes to sleep with a ring of postage stamps around the penis. In theory, if the ring of stamps is broken in the morning, then NPT has occurred, but this test is fraught with problems. The stamps used will vary in the strength of attachment, glue, perforation, and size, and all these factors will affect the size of the erection needed to snap them. Furthermore, movement by the patient at night can break the ring in a man who did not experience NPT or cause it to slide off intact in a man who did experience NPT.

One way to avoid these problems is a device called the snap gauge. This consists of three plastic layers and Velcro connectors that attach around the penis. The bands are designed to break at 10, 15, and 20 ounces of pressure. Thus an attempt to quantitatively measure the pressure of the erection is made. If all the bands are broken during the night, it is likely that a full, firm erection has occurred. If no bands are broken, the capacity for erection is impaired. However, this method still has major limitations. Unless the patient's sleep is professionally monitored, there is no way to know if the crucial stage of REM sleep occurred during the night.

While there is no "gold standard" for measuring NPT, the best is probably sleep laboratory evaluation. This provides a fairly uniform and objective environment for the study. The disadvantage is that the environment is unfamiliar to the patient and the studies can be expensive. The exact procedures of each sleep laboratory vary, but almost all incorporate the following features: the patient sleeps in the laboratory with monitoring devices called electrodes pasted to the head and legs to measure brain wave and sleep stage activity; elastic belts are placed around the chest to monitor breathing; and strain gauges are fitted around the penis at the base and under the glans (the dome) of the penis to monitor its circumference. The entire procedure is carefully explained to the patient before the study begins. The patient then sleeps in the laboratory for one or more nights and various characteristics of the erections that might occur, such as size and duration, are measured.

An alternative means of measuring rigidity is with a device called the rigiscan. This instrument places loops around the penis that automatically tighten at fixed intervals of time and monitor characteristics of the erections similar to those described above. The rigiscan can be irritating and uncomfortable to wear but it has the advantage of adaptability for home use. The patient is instructed in the use of the device and places it on the penis at home at bedtime. This is an inexpensive and convenient way of doing the test, but great caution must be taken in interpreting the results, because it relies on the technical skills of the patient and because there is no means of determining whether sleep, especially REM sleep, was adequate.

A device called the plethysmograph, which can monitor blood flow, and a technique called ultrasound doppler scanning, which measures blood velocity in the blood vessels, have also been used to measure penile erectile function. More research and clinical experience is needed to determine the role of these methods.

The evaluation of sexual function in women has lagged behind that in men. This is partly due to social and cultural factors, but it is also due to the mechanical difficulties of studying physiological sexual responses in women. Nevertheless, it is known that vaginal and clitoral blood flow and temperature changes do occur as part of a sexual response. Several devices have been developed to measure these variables. One of the more promising instruments is the "light reflectance vaginal photoplethysmograph." This device measures vaginal pulse amplitude and contraction pressure. One type is constructed of clear plastic with a head and base separated by a

steel rod, which forms a central space enclosed by a flexible, clear, rubber membrane. Although the device can be placed in the vagina by the woman herself, the wires and attachments must be placed by an experienced technician. This device should be able to measure the sexual response of women in the same way that the NPT procedure does in men. However, much more experience is needed in this area and clinical sleep laboratories do not generally offer such testing at this time.

Sleep disorders centers can serve as a valuable adjunct in the evaluation of sexual dysfunction in both men and women. Some of the equipment can also be adapted for home use, but the tests must still be supervised and interpreted by qualified professionals (see also ERECTION; PENIS; SEXUAL DYSFUNCTION, MALE).

IN VITRO FERTILIZATION   A baby girl born to Louise Brown in Britain in July 1978 was the first child ever born that was not conceived within her mother's body. In the United States today approximately one in six couples are unable to have a child at a time of their choosing. The largest single reason for a woman's inability to become pregnant is that her fallopian tubes have become blocked or damaged. Without normally functioning FALLOPIAN TUBES, the egg and the sperm are not able to meet normally and PREGNANCY will not result. Conventional INFERTILITY treatments such as microsurgery and laser surgery often have very poor success rates when used to try to repair damaged or blocked fallopian tubes.

In an attempt to better treat this form of infertility, the *in vitro*—"in glass," in a laboratory—fertilization process was developed. Simply stated, in vitro fertilization involves removal of one or more eggs from the woman's body, addition of the husband's sperm to the eggs in a laboratory dish, and observation in the laboratory for one to two days to document that the eggs have been fertilized by the sperm and are developing normally. The fertilized and divided eggs, now called embryos, are then placed in the wife's uterus, bypassing the fallopian tubes entirely. Because some of the early experiments

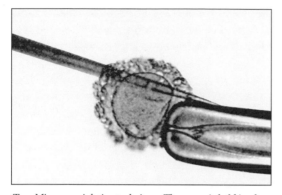

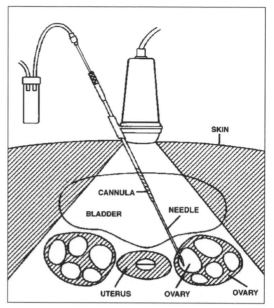

Top: Micro-maniplation technique: The ovum is held in place by a suction device (right) and is punctured by a tiny needle (left), making a hole in the zona pellucida. *Poor sperm can then penetrate and fertilize the ovum.*

Right: An early stage of in vitro fertilization (right). A tiny needle is inserted into the ovary and an egg is removed for fertilization outside the woman's body.

mixed the egg and sperm in test tubes, the in vitro fertilization process is sometimes referred to as the "test tube baby" procedure.

Although initially developed for couples in whom the wife had untreatable tubal disease, the use of in vitro fertilization and related technologies have been expanded to treat conditions such as ENDOMETRIOSIS, low sperm count or motility in the husband, or cases in which an explanation for a couple's infertility is not known.

As practiced today, in vitro fertilization involves several steps. Since the pregnancy success rate is raised by increasing the number of embryos placed in the uterus, the first goal is to increase the number of eggs simultaneously developing in a wife's ovaries. In a normal menstrual cycle, one egg develops within one ovarian follicle (a fluid-filled cyst in which the egg develops). A woman going through in vitro fertilization is treated with drugs normally given to women who do not ovulate. When a normal woman receives these drugs, her ovaries typically overrespond by developing numerous follicles, each containing an egg. The woman's response to these drugs is monitored by measuring the levels of ESTROGEN produced by the growing follicles and by ultrasound imaging of the ovaries to check the size, number, and growth rate of the follicles. It is not unusual for a

woman undergoing in vitro fertilization and receiving these drugs to develop ten, twenty, or even more follicles simultaneously. When it has been determined that the follicles are fully developed, the woman is then given an injection of hCG, a hormone that triggers final maturation of the eggs within the follicles so that they will be able to be fertilized when they are recovered.

Approximately thirty-four hours after the hCG injection, the eggs are removed from the woman's body. Today this is done with an ultrasound guided aspiration procedure, most commonly performed through the vagina. After giving drugs for relaxation and pain relief, the physician places an ultrasound probe in the vagina to locate the ovarian follicles. A needle is attached to the ultrasound probe and passed through the top of the vagina directly into the ovarian follicles, bypassing the fallopian tubes. The contents of the follicles (including the eggs) are then removed by suction and examined in an adjacent laboratory. The recovered eggs are assessed, rinsed in culture media (a nourishing fluid), and placed in an incubator. The husband then collects a sperm sample. The sperm are washed, suspended in culture media, and later-added to the eggs. The following morning the eggs are examined for signs of fertilization and, if normally fertilized, are returned to the incubator. The following morning the eggs have divided one or more times and are typically at the two to four cell stage. At this stage they are termed embryos. The embryos are then placed in the woman's uterus by means of a catheter passed through the cervix. If a pregnancy results, it continues as any normal pregnancy.

At present the success rate of in vitro fertilization is approximately 15 percent. In other words, about one out of seven women who attempt it becomes pregnant. The procedure is expensive, with a cost of $6,000–$8,000 for a single treatment cycle.

The in vitro fertilization process has led to the development of other related treatments. One example is called gamete intra-fallopian transfer (GIFT). This procedure begins in a manner identically with the in vitro fertilization treatment. However, egg recovery is usually done by LAPAROSCOPY rather than ultrasound-guided aspiration. Laparoscopy is a surgical procedure in which a lighted telescope is inserted into a woman's abdomen to allow direct visualization of the tubes and ovaries. After the eggs are removed from the ovaries, they are mixed immediately with sperm. The egg/sperm mixture is immediately placed into the wife's fallopian tubes rather than allowing fertilization to occur in the laboratory. This procedure is most suitable for couples in whom the wife has normal fallopian tubes and there is some other explanation for the couple's infertility.

A similar procedure is zygote intra-fallopian transfer (ZIFT). This is a combination of GIFT and in vitro fertilization in which fertilization is carried out in a laboratory but on the day after insemination the early embryo is placed into the woman's fallopian tube. Again, this requires that the woman have normal fallopian tubes.

In vitro fertilization, coupled with the use of eggs donated by volunteers, can be used to establish a pregnancy in a woman who was born without ovaries or has lost ovarian function at an unusually early age. Finally, micromanipulation procedures such as partial zona (egg membrane) dissection or sperm microinjection can be used where there is a great decrease in the number of sperm or loss of sperm motility. These proce-

dures involve operating on the eggs themselves, making it easier for sperm to penetrate and fertilize them (see also CONCEPTION; INFERTILITY).

INCEST Incest is usually defined as any sexual activity between persons related by "blood" (genetically)—for example, father and daughter, uncle and niece, or brother and sister. It also may extend to relationships based on marriage such as between a stepfather and stepdaughter. The concept becomes less clear and varies by state law in its application to first and second cousins and other somewhat familial relationships such as in-laws. While many people assume that SEXUAL INTERCOURSE is inherent in the definition of incest, this is not true when children are involved. In such cases incest includes not only penetration but fondling of a child's genitals—or the child's fondling of the adult's—or ORAL SEX.

Incest, particularly parent-child sex, has been forbidden in nearly all cultures throughout history. Some exceptions to brother-sister incest were accepted for the nobility in a few cultures—for example, in ancient Egypt, where pharaohs were required to practice it.

Estimates of the frequency of incest in the United States have ranged as high as 30 percent of the population. In a recent national survey by Drs. Sam and Cynthia Janus, 14.9 percent of the women and 4.7 percent of the men studied reported they had been sexually molested by a relative when they were children. Their study also reported that women are more likely than men to view incest as a major problem in American society today, probably because women are more likely than men to be victims of incest as children or young teenagers. Other researchers have reported that women were the victims in 92 percent of reported cases of incest.

The most frequent form of incest is reported to be between a brother and sister—almost five times more frequently than between father and daughter. In one study 13 percent of college students said they had experienced some form of sexual activity with a brother or sister. The most common activities were said to be looking at genitals or touching them, while four percent reportedly involved sexual intercourse. Incest between a mother and son appears to be the least common of all forms of incest; it is reported in less than 1 percent of families. Women who had stepfathers during their childhood years were eight times as likely to have been sexually abused than those whose biological fathers were at home during this period. Little has been reported about homosexual incest, but some researchers studying CHILD ABUSE have indicated that this too may be a serious problem.

While father-daughter incest is considered by most people to be abhorrent, there is little evidence that the male adults in these situations are emotionally disturbed in such a way that they are incapable of restraint. Even researchers who believe just the opposite—that most are mentally disturbed—believe, nevertheless, that they should be prosecuted. However, evidence shows that adults accused of incest are rarely prosecuted unless there is concomitant physical abuse.

Anecdotal reporting of father-daughter incest indicates that a fairly common scenario involves a father involved in a sexually frustrating relationship with the mother. Researchers report that many mothers are somewhat aware of incestuous relationships but choose—out of passivity, dependency, fear of public exposure, or other reasons—to deny it until confronted. Often, the mother will blame the child for the situation, creating even more psychological damage after the relationship is ended. In most instances the child is coerced into the incestuous relationship through fear and even force—the equivalent of familial rape. There is agreement among many writers in this field that parent-child incest does not occur in stable, loving families.

Incest is not usually a one time sexual act: it tends to continue for many years. The average duration of an incestuous relationship between a parent and child is approximately five years. It is evident that incest is very likely to have a profound, emotionally traumatic impact on the child, that may carry over to later adult emotional and sexual relationships (see also CHILD ABUSE; CHILD MOLESTATION LAWS; RAPE).

INDUCED LABOR The initiation of labor by medical means rather than the spontaneous onset of labor. A number of choices are available to induce, or stimulate, labor. The most common method is the infusion of a dilute solution of oxytocin, a hormone produced in the pituitary gland, into a maternal vein, causing uterine contractions. One stimulus for the release of oxytocin is breast stimulation, resulting in the very common occurrence of uterine contractions following nipple stimulation or nursing.

A second method for the induction of labor is rupture of the fetal membranes. This can be done with either a needle or a small sharp instrument designed especially for that purpose. The cervix must be partially dilated and the presenting part of the fetus (the body part that will emerge first at delivery) should be well engaged in the pelvis so that when the membranes rupture, the umbilical cord does not descend into the vagina with the escaping amniotic fluid. In a patient with a thinned and dilated cervix, rupture of the membranes is an effective method of inducing labor and the use of oxytocin is usually not required.

A third way to induce labor is placing prostaglandin, a potent uterine contractor, into either the cervix or the vagina to induce uterine contractions. The action of prostaglandin is much more difficult to control than the intravenous infusion of oxytocin and is, therefore, less common, but it is sometimes used to help in the dilation of the cervix (see also BIRTH).

INFANT HEALTH see PREGNANCY AND DIET; PRENATAL CARE.

INFERTILITY An inability to achieve CONCEPTION after a year of unprotected intercourse, or an inability to carry a PREGNANCY through its full term to a live birth. Of the estimated 28 million couples of reproductive age, at least 15 percent will experience some aspect of infertility. About 4 million couples wanting children will experience the emotional frustration of having their child-bearing plans go awry.

The cause or causes of infertility may be difficult to diagnose, since they can be due to a number of factors with either or both partners. Female problems are the cause of infertility in 30 to 40 percent of cases; another 30 to 40 percent are due to male problems; approximately 25 percent are due to a combination of male and female problems, and approximately 5 percent are unexplained.

A diagnosis of infertility once was considered to be final and treatment was not even offered. Today there are many treatments and, while not all causes of infertility can be resolved, some causes have up to a 50 percent treatment success rate. A couple experiencing difficulty in conceiving should seek a physician who specializes in infertility. These doctors are more often aware of the problems that couples with infertility face and are also expert in specific treatments for various types of difficulties. For their part the couple must be prepared to talk freely about their questions and feelings and must realize that infertility is a problem they are experiencing together and not the fault of one or the other.

The most common causes of female infertility are endometriosis, blocked fallopian tubes, lack of ovulation, poor hormonal support of ovulation, and polycystic ovarian disease. Less common causes are uterine or fallopian tube abnormalities. ENDOMETRIOSIS, which is the growth of the uterine lining outside of the uterus, is the single most common cause of female infertility. Endometriosis also can be quite painful. Ovulation disorders, such as anovulation, polycystic ovarian disease, or insufficient luteal phase can be detected with hormone tests, as hormone levels will indicate whether ovulation occurs and if it is well supported. In many cases, if the hormones produced by the ovary are not adequate for successful reproduction, they can be supplemented. Women with menstrual irregularities and anovulation can be given hormones that will simulate the natural process and cause or support ovulation. Surgery may be necessary to remove endometriosis or to clear blocked fallopian tubes before other treatments can be tried.

The most common causes of male infertility are low sperm count, poor sperm motility, abnormal physical structure, low volume of seminal fluid, or sperm that do not function well. Less common causes are azoospermia (lack of any sperm), absence of the *vas deferens*, a lack of hormonal stimulation, or an inability to respond to hormonal stimulation. While the presence of any sperm at all indicates a potential for fertility, it is hard to determine the ability of sperm to perform the functions needed for fertilization. The sperm's ability to fertilize the egg, and the embryo's ability to implant in the uterus and continue growth are the ultimate tests of fertility. Hormonal treatment for male infertility has had only limited success. The most common treatment is to prepare the sperm for artificial insemination directly into the woman's uterus. This procedure gets sperm closer to the site of fertilization and also provides supplemental fluid for their support.

For fertilization to occur sperm must be able to traverse the female reproductive tract and penetrate the oocyte (egg). In addition, the female reproductive tract should be able to assist sperm transport and an oocyte must be in the proper part of the fallopian tube, ready to be fertilized. After fertilization has occurred, the fertilized egg, or zygote, is transported to the uterus, where the uterine lining should be ready for implantation. The hormonal controls are extremely important, since hormones determine the readiness of the oocyte and uterus, as well as preparing sperm for transport. The failure of any part of this complex process can cause infertility.

IN VITRO FERTILIZATION (IVF) and gamete intrafallopian tube transfer (GIFT) are new and difficult techniques that are used when other treatments have failed. The egg can be removed from the ovary, incubated with the sperm out of the body, and then the fertilized egg can be placed back into the mother's uterus or into the uterus of a woman who is not the genetic mother but who is willing to carry the embryo and fetus until natural birth occurs. A woman with blocked tubes or a man with a low sperm count are good candidates for IVF or GIFT. Ultrasound and microsurgical tools and techniques have made these treatments less invasive.

Dealing with infertility can be most difficult time for a couple. It is often a time of crisis and breakdown of communication. Diagnosis may require precise timing of intercourse and treatment may call for the male partner to collect a semen sample in the doctor's office. Infertility can create an atmosphere of tension and stress in a relationship that can disrupt an everyday lifestyle. Normal sexual relations often become frustrated due to lack of spontaneity or to the timing necessary for the meeting of the sperm and egg. Couples often find this difficult to talk about with their doctor, which can add to the frustration and anxiety. Support groups are available and most infertility doctors are open to discussing problems. Taking time to choose the best doctor and to deal with aspects of the problems of infertility can ease many of these tensions (see also CONCEPTION; ENDOMETRIOSIS).

INTERCOURSE, FREQUENCY OF see AGING AND SEX; COITAL FREQUENCY; PROSTATE.

INTIMACY Many persons use the words "intimate" and "intimacy" in everyday parlance to refer only to the sexual act, as in the question "Were you intimate with him last night?" What they should really ask is whether the pair was "sexually intimate," since the word intimacy used alone implies a very high degree of interpersonal closeness — and not necessarily the physical closeness of a sexual encounter. As one dictionary defines intimate: "it is not only marked by close acquaintanceship or familiarity with another person but also involves knowledge of the innermost being of another." Therefore, when two people are intimate with each other, it does not have to involve sexual activity: it should, however, mean that they are able to express their most personal thoughts to each other as well as their experiences and feelings. Other characteristics of intimacy are caring for the well-being of the other person and the ability to communicate openly, without fear of judgment and reprisals. Intimacy should be present not only between lovers but also between best friends and between parents and children. Intimacy is something that develops over time in these relationships.

Perhaps the greatest value of intimacy is the sense of belonging that is engendered and the feeling of security this brings to the persons in an intimate relationship. Often, acts of intimacy convey to the recipient the feelings of being re-

spected and loved. Intimacy, for some, helps them to deal with various anxieties in life, knowing that support will be forthcoming in times of need (see also COMMITMENTS; LOVE).

INTRAUTERINE DEVICE (IUD) Commonly known as IUDs, intrauterine devices are a reversible prescription method of BIRTH CONTROL. They are small shapes of plastic that contain copper or a hormone and are inserted in a woman's uterus. They usually work by preventing fertilization of the egg, but they may also be able to prevent implantation of a fertilized egg.

Insertion of the IUD is usually done by a clinician during menstruation, to insure that the woman is not pregnant. There is some pain during insertion, but it is usually no worse than menstrual cramps. The IUD is effective: only 3 women out of 100 who use it will get pregnant in a year, and it is effective for a whole year.

It does not prevent SEXUALLY TRANSMITTED DISEASES, so it is best used by women who have one partner or who are willing to use a condom in addition to the IUD. There is a string that hangs from the IUD through the cervix, permitting the woman to check to make sure it is still in place. If a woman wants to become pregnant, she can ask her clinician to remove the IUD at any time.

The copper IUD is one of the most effective forms of birth control available and it is the most popular reversible birth control method in the world. Most women adjust to the IUD with few problems, but potential side effects might include cramping for a brief period after insertion, and it is not unusual for women's periods to be heavier and last longer (less so with IUDs containing hormones). In rare cases the IUD can cause complications which could be life-threatening, and one brand of IUDs had to removed from the market because of severe health problems that occurred with it. For that reason a clinician will ask a woman to sign a consent form which states that she is aware of the potential dangers before inserting the device.

The uterus can push the IUD out. This is most likely to occur during the first few months after insertion, and it is also more likely to happen in a woman who has not had a child. Pregnancy could occur during this time, which is why it is necessary to check the string from time to time.

Because the IUD must be inserted by a clinician, the cost ranges for $150 to $300 for private doctors in the United States . For this price, the IUD protects a woman from pregnancy for one year, though again she may want to supplement the device with condoms if she has multiple partners.

Although it happens rarely, it is possible to become pregnant although an IUD is properly in place. If a woman using an IUD misses a menstrual period, she should see her physician immediately. A pregnancy with an IUD in place can lead to serious complications from infection or from implantation of the pregnancy outside the uterus, in the fallopian tubes (see ECTOPIC PREGNANCY).

J-K

JEALOUSY According to one dictionary, jealousy is rooted both in fears of losing what one has—especially LOVE or affection—to another person and in feelings of resentment about a rival's successes or advantages. What both have in common is an individual's inability to control situations involving other people. Jealousy may arise from a real or imagined situation or from an expectation that something will occur. Most people who have experienced jealousy know what it feels like but are generally unable to understand or explain just the emotions they feel—they can only explain what the situations are that precipitate the feelings. Jealousy is clearly a strong emotion with accompanying physiological reactions: a feeling of "gut-wrenching" anxiety, sometimes with a strong sense of depression following an experience or thought involving the sexual or love partner and another person.

In our culture, there is generally social support for jealousy when a spouse or lover displays inappropriate behavior with another person. However, not all people experience jealousy, even in extreme circumstances. This attracted the attention of a number of researchers in the 1960s and 1970s, producing evidence of the important and often destructive role of jealousy in couple relationships. The emphasis in this research is often not on why people do become jealous but rather on why they do not in situations that should call for a jealous response.

What has consistently emerged in this research is that sexual jealousy is most likely to be felt when a person feels that he or she is not in control of the circumstances involving a partner and another person. In the view of one researcher cited in the book *The Sex Researchers*:

What matters is the feeling of being in control rather than the actuality of being in control. It seems to be sufficient (to ward off jealous reactions) that a person feels that he is in control of the situation even though he is not, whereas it is not sufficient for him to actually be in control if he does not feel that he is.

Some common characteristics of people who experience jealousy have been reported in a number of studies: feelings of inadequacy as a lover or sexual partner; strong feelings about the traditional norm of sexual exclusivity; and a lack of self-esteem.

Some researchers have noted that historically and in some traditional cultures jealousy may have played an important role in curtailing infidelity. In some groups jealousy is taken as a sign of a strong love and a spouse might question the strength of the relationship if a partner did not display jealousy in appropriate situations. Some people feel flattered when a lover is jealous, however, in the last few decades these views have been giving way to the idea that jealousy, if unchecked, may be destructive in relationships.

Most people experience jealousy at some point in their sexual, marital, or love relationships. Some writers contend that jealousy can be minimized when a couple agrees on the boundaries of permissible behavior, affection, or display of the body. Thus, communication about what provokes feelings of jealousy and agreed limits on such behavior can curb spontaneous and destructive jealousy.

KAMASUTRA While Hinduism has given rise to ascetic practices among holy men, it has also celebrated sexual pleasure in what is perhaps the most famous sexual manual in history—the *Kamasutra* ("love precepts"). It was written in the second century B.C.E. by the revered Indian sage, Vatsyayana. In it, Vatsyayana treats sexual intercourse as a means of spiritual enrichment and as an art that must be studied in order to bring profound joy. The *Kamasutra* instructs both men and women to give the highest priority to the pleasures of the senses and graphically details an astonishing variety of sexual techniques.

KAPLAN, DR. HELEN SINGER

Born in Vienna in 1929, Helen Singer Kaplan emigrated to the United States in 1940. She was educated at Syracuse University, Columbia University, and New York Medical College. As a psychiatrist she has specialized in human sexuality, and in that field she has been a therapist, teacher and supervisor of therapists. Among her trainees in psychosexual therapy was a teacher of social workers, Dr. Ruth Westheimer.

Dr. Kaplan, a physician with a Ph.D. in psychology, was a pioneer in adapting the laboratory methods of MASTERS AND JOHNSON, the founders of SEX THERAPY, to the needs of busy people who could not take off two weeks for that course of treatment in Saint Louis. Maintaining high standards of treatment, Dr. Kaplan adapted sex therapy techniques so that people could visit the therapist at his or her office for regular instruction and consultation, meanwhile carrying out homework assignments, doing the exercises prescribed in their own bedrooms at home.

Today clients may be in relationships or solitary, they may be wage-earners, top executives, or welfare clients at clinics. Therapy is not just for the rich or leisured but for anyone who needs it. For making sex therapy so available, a large share of the credit goes to Dr. Kaplan and to the Helen S. Kaplan Group for the Evaluation and Treatment of Sexual Disorders, located in New York City.

Sex therapy is not a dry, mechanical business, carrying out rulebook procedures with robotic clients all needing the same advice and instruction. It is an art as well as a science. Dr. Kaplan's own work has enriched it, and her teaching of other therapists has been inspired and inspiring.

KEGEL EXERCISES

In the early 1950s Dr. Arnold H. Kegel, a gynecologist, devised a series of exercises to strengthen bladder control for women suffering from incontinence. Control is enhanced through exercises of the pubococcygeal muscle, sometimes called the "PC" muscle. Sex therapists soon discovered that the same exercises also enable many women to feel more actively involved in the coital process by enabling them to tighten the pubococcygeal muscle during intercourse. They report an increase in stimulation not only to their vaginal areas but also to the penis of their male partners. Many women who have undertaken the Kegel exercises report they are more likely to have orgasms during intercourse.

A quick method for women to identify and learn how to exercise the pubococcygeal muscle is to urinate, stop the flow of urine, and then urinate again. After a few repetitions, most women are able to tighten this muscle without the involvement of urination. In another method for learning the Kegel exercise, the woman places one of her fingers about two inches inside her vagina. The muscles in her vaginal area are then contracted just as if she wanted to stop the flow of urine, and she will feel the pubococcygeal muscle tighten around her finger. She continues to contract the muscle tightly for a few seconds and then to relax it, repeating the exercise many times in a session and as often as possible during the day. Since this is a simple exercise and can be accomplished without the fingers once the muscle is identified, it is an especially effective aid in SEX THERAPY. The toning of the pubococcygeal muscle can be achieved rather quickly, allowing a woman to feel confident about developing control and skills during coitus.

Devices known as "Kegel Exercisers" have been developed. These appear to be little more than DILDOS and there is no evidence that using a resistance-producing device, or even the fingers, as a form of resistance produces better results than the simple squeezing of the pubococcygeal muscle without any insertion once muscular contractions have been learned.

KINSEY AND THE INSTITUTE FOR SEX RESEARCH

Most sex researchers, sex therapists, and sex educators trace the beginning of today's scientific knowledge of human sexual behavior to the work of Alfred C. Kinsey and the organization that he founded: the Institute for Sex Research at Indiana University in Bloomington, Indiana. Kinsey was born in 1894 in Hoboken, New Jersey, into a devoutly religious, middle-class family. He studied mechanical engineering (1912–1914) and then transferred to Bowdoin College in Maine to study biology. In 1916 he began graduate studies at Harvard University, concentrating on entomology, the study of insects; he received his Ph.D. in 1920.

Kinsey was an unlikely person to become the most renowned sex researcher of his generation. He became an instructor in biology at Indiana University in 1920, and built an illustrious academic career specializing in the classification of wasps and other insects. In particular, he became the world's foremost authority on gall wasps. His life changed in 1937 when, as a family man with four children and because of his reputation as a biologist and a person of irreproachable conservatism, he was asked to develop and teach a new course at Indiana University on sex and marriage. While preparing for this course, he quickly learned that research in the area of human sexuality was very weak and that much of the accepted knowledge about the subject was based on outmoded beliefs and speculation rather than on scientific studies. He began to collect his own data through surveys of sexual behavior among his students and gradually expanded this to include the general public.

In a short while he attracted a team of unusually talented social scientists to Indiana University; together they began large-scale interviews of more than 11,000 people for their main research projects. By 1947 Kinsey and his colleagues had founded the Institute for Sex Research at Indiana University. Financing for the Institute first came from the Rockefeller Foundation, but when publications of the Insti-

tute's studies became very much in demand, royalties from their books financed further research.

In the years that Kinsey headed the Institute, over 17,000 people were interviewed by it. The topics studied included: childhood sexual activity (see CHILDREN'S SEXUALITY; TEENAGERS AND SEX); MASTURBATION; petting; the onset of various kinds of sexual activity; frequency of sex before, during, and after MARRIAGE; HOMOSEXUALITY (see also GAY AND LESBIAN POPULATIONS); nocturnal emissions; EXTRAMARITAL SEX; and sex among the elderly (see AGING AND SEX). The two main works produced at the Institute by Kinsey and his colleagues have provided the base line data on human sexual activity to which all subsequent sexual behavior research has been compared. They were: *Sexual Behavior in the Human Male*, using a sample of 5,300 males, and *Sexual Behavior in the Human Female*, using a sample of 5,940 females. When first published, these two 800-page books were considered by the publisher and the Institute to be of interest only to a limited medical and professional market. However, the lack of information about sexual behavior and the public's hunger for knowledge about this virtually taboo topic led to both books becoming national best sellers and to a host of secondary commentaries on them by other science and medical writers.

The main work of the Institute and its publications occurred at a time when the United States was politically and socially very conservative. Extreme right wing groups led by Senator Joseph R. McCarthy of Wisconsin believed that a deterioration of SEXUAL MORALITY was exacerbated by communist teachings and that the Kinsey Institute's work fed, unintentionally, into this plot. Consequently, in a few cities these books were seized and destroyed—justified by federal and state laws, commonly known as the Comstock Laws and dating back to the 1870s, making it a crime to send "erotic material" or sexual matter through the mail. (Almost a century later, in the 1960s, these laws were found to be in violation of the First Amendment.) Pressure on the Rockefeller Foundation to withdraw funding from Kinsey and his colleagues proved successful during the McCarthy period, but by 1957, after Senator McCarthy and "McCarthyism" had been discredited, the attacks on the Institute eased considerably and funding began to increase. Since then it has remained an important research center.

Kinsey died in 1956 at the age of sixty-two. Although there has been some scholarly criticism of some of the sampling techniques of the Kinsey studies, there is no question that the meticulous procedures that Kinsey employed were the best in use at the time and the studies still stand as the best social data ever collected on the sexual behavior of the human male and female. Whenever studies of sexual behavior are reported today, they invariably use the Kinsey data to compare changes in sexual behavior over the past fifty years.

KISSING   An oral activity that is almost universally popular—in nearly all cultures and throughout the ages—is the kiss. While kissing is often used as a friendly greeting, we examine it here within a sexual context.

According to the dictionary, kissing means touching or caressing with the lips, But this definition does not really convey the many and varied joys of kissing. Kissing communicates both love and sexual desire and it is often enjoyed as a foreplay to coitus. But kissing can be highly pleasurable in and of itself. Couples in love have been known to spend hours just kissing. Couples who have been together for a long time should remember that kissing is a wonderful act of intimacy and should remain an important part of their sexual repertoire for life.

The lips are an erogenous zone, highly sensitive to sexual stimulation. Though some cultures do not enjoy mouth to mouth kissing, most societies do—as with other lovemaking practices and techniques, some individuals have raised it to an art form. But kissing is not necessarily limited to two pairs of lips. One can kiss the eyes, neck, earlobe, breast, testicles, armpits, and toes. Exploring a partner's body with your lips can be tremendously exciting, as can deep kissing, the passionate exchange of tongues while kissing.

In modern society's rush to reach quick sexual goals, kissing has often become a neglected art. But the accomplished lover is probably always a good kisser—and with good reason. Human lips were made for kissing. During erotic arousal they grow more sensitive and inviting, infused with color and swelling in size, all the better to attract.

L

LABIA   See FEMALE SEX ORGANS; VULVA.

LABOR   See BIRTH; NATURAL CHILDBIRTH; UTERUS.

LACK OF SEXUAL INTEREST   Letters received by the "Dr. Ruth" radio and TV shows and newspaper columns show that a lack of sexual desire is one of the most frequent complaints of people writing about sexual dysfunction. Almost one quarter (24 percent) of all people reporting a sexual problem mentioned lack of sexual desire—and this was equally divided between men and women.

In the past medical professionals often assumed (erroneously) that all men had a "naturally" strong LIBIDO, or urge to have sex, while women had to be aroused during loving FOREPLAY. Women's lack of desire was thought to be the result of incompetent lovemaking, especially during foreplay, by their male partners.

Modern studies have found, however, that sexual desire is the natural outcome of one's interest in sex. Sexual desire, just like interest, may precede any kind of physical or psychological stimulation. In the vernacular, people use the term "horny" to mean a state of strong and sustained sexual desire. It is that inner sexual feeling that does not need erotic stimulation and upon which further sexual stimulation then builds. Sexual desire can be worked on and acted upon through sensuous stimulation and erotic behavior alone. But, if one neither has nor recognizes this inner urge to have sex, one can usually be stimulated physically to this point—and sometimes one can be stimulated mentally or by a romantic mood.

The sex manuals of yesteryear were well intentioned and romantic in orientation, but not very knowledgeable about the workings of sexual desire. The research of MASTERS AND JOHNSON, and Helen Singer Kaplan revolutionized our thinking about sex. We now know that all too many men and women deprive themselves of the pleasures of a loving sexual relationship, even within marriage, because they are "just not interested" in sex. That is, they prefer not to do anything about sex, or even to think about it.

What is meant by "lack of sexual desire"? Some people think it describes a woman or a man who experiences no ORGASM or even sexual excitement after stimulation from a sexual partner or through MASTURBATION. But that is not what is meant, because lack of desire may be an ordinary condition for many people before sexual interaction and arousal.

Do not confuse a lack of orgasmic response with a lack of sexual desire. When one has no interest in sex at all, one does not put one's self in a position where one has to behave sexually. If persons have some interest, but very little desire, they may act very passively, waiting until their partners take the initiative.

Some researchers suggest that at least for women, a lack of desire is the result of the way they were raised. They were taught to suppress their sexual feelings until "aroused" by a man. The paradox is that some women complain of a lack of sexual desire but are easily able to reach orgasm, while other women with a great deal of sexual interest and desire are nonorgasmic.

Sex therapists frequently see cases in which women have married because it was the right time or because the men they were dating seemed potentially good husbands and fathers.

They knew that they were expected to have intercourse, and though they had no desire for sex, they knew it would create conflict if they did not carry out their part of the marital contract. So they went through the motions without enjoying it. This does not mean that they did not care for or love their husbands, but the element of passion was missing. They did not want to risk ruining their marriages by confronting their feelings.

In some cases, a lack of desire is "situational." This is most often found among those who profess to have no real desire for sex, yet can respond and even have orgasms upon stimulation. If a partner initiates sex, such a person is responsive, but if no sex is initiated they will be just as content. These are "situational," because some outside factor is interfering with the innate desire for sex. If this situation were altered to remove the interfering factor, the client would more readily perceive that he or she does indeed have a desire for sex, perhaps even a very strong desire. One fairly common cause is an unrecognized anger that a person may have for their partner and which they take to bed with them. However, in some cases, a woman's sexual desire may fluctuate with hormonal influences during her menstrual phases.

There are many other situations that may result in lowered or even blocked LIBIDO, sexual desire, or performance. Some of them are: stress in work, family, and money matters; a fear of pregnancy; problems with a partner's appearance or sexual behavior; alcohol and drug use; sexual abuse as a child or adult; a poor self-image; or a general fear of sex or the sexual organs.

Sexual desire is neither present nor absent—it is a matter of degree. Look at it as if it were on a scale of one to ten. There is no way to tell if someone is a ten or an eight or a one. It is only a relative indicator by which you can try to measure how often and how intensely one thinks about sex and acts upon these thoughts. Can one move up the sexual desire quotient from a three to a seven? Most sex therapists believe this can be achieved by developing more erotic attitudes along with healthy self-esteem (see also BORE-DOM, SEXUAL; SEX THERAPY; SEXUAL DYSFUNCTION, FEMALE; SEXUAL DYSFUNCTION, MALE).

LACTATION   see BREAST-FEEDING.

LAMAZE METHOD   One of the methods of "prepared" childbirth. The basic theories behind prepared childbirth are self-awareness, self-control through programmed exercises, and reduction of pain through educational understanding of the labor and delivery process. The Lamaze method prepares mothers and their helpers to deal actively with labor contractions and the emotional, intellectual, and physical aspects of childbirth. A primary goal is to have a healthy and aware mother delivering a healthy baby. Lamaze offers psychological techniques, or tools, to use during labor to make it a more shared, enjoyable, and meaningful experience.

The basis of the Lamaze method originated in Russia, where women were conditioned or trained to respond to their contractions with relaxation. In the 1950s Fernand Lamaze, a French physician, adapted the Russian techniques and introduced this method of prepared childbirth in the metal workers' clinic where he worked. The conditioned, or automatic, response is still the basis for the method but Lamaze added special breathing techniques to the Russian model. In the United States the method has been expanded to include fathers (or others) in a coaching role, allowing couples to share actively in the birth of their child. Today the Lamaze method is a very popular technique for managing labor pains.

LAPAROSCOPY   A medical procedure used to inspect the inside of the abdominal cavity with a telescopic instrument called a laparoscope. The procedure is also called pelviscopy. The operation is frequently done as an out-patient procedure, as it has a much shorter recovery time than an exploratory operation in which the abdomen is cut open. However, as with any procedure in which instruments are placed inside the abdominal cavity, it is considered a major surgical operation. The laparoscope is inserted into the abdominal cavity through a small incision made below the navel. To make viewing easier and decrease the chance of damaging tissue, before the laparoscope is inserted, the abdominal cavity is distended by inflation with a gas, usually carbon dioxide, inserted through a needle puncture into the abdomen. After the laparoscope is in place, additional small incisions can be made to enable other instruments to be utilized for probing, manipulation, or surgery. The laparoscope allows for a complete inspection of the abdomen: all the organs inside the abdominal cavity can be viewed directly.

There are two general reasons for performing laparoscopy: diagnostic and therapeutic. Diagnostic reasons include evaluation of patients suffering pelvic pain or patients with difficulty becoming pregnant. The UTERUS can be seen with the laparoscope and, utilizing an instrument in the VAGINA that manipulates the uterus, it can be elevated so that there is vision around and behind it. Irregularities of the uterus such as uterine fibroids can be seen directly. The FALLOPIAN TUBES, which transport the egg from the ovary to the uterus, can also be observed directly and evaluated for inflammation or blockage. Dye can be introduced through the CERVIX and, if the fallopian tubes are open, it can be seen to exit from the upper ends of the fallopian tubes and enter the abdominal cavity. In this way laparoscopy can be used to determine if tubes are open or closed. The ovaries can also be seen directly, as can the presence of cysts, evidence of ovulation, and other structures in the abdomen.

The most common therapeutic laparoscopy procedure is tubal sterilization to prevent pregnancy. Under direct vision, the fallopian tubes can be blocked by cauterizing a segment of each tube with an electric current or a laser or obstructed by placing bands around their midportion. Through the laparoscope, adhesions (abnormal areas of scar tissue that bind together tissues that are not normally held together) can be cut or cauterized. Similarly, areas of ENDOMETRIOSIS can be surgically destroyed and small cysts can be aspirated (have their contents sucked out) using a laparoscope. Occasionally, fallopian tubes can be repaired through use of this instrument. Another common usage of laparoscopic surgery is the removal of an ECTOPIC PREGNANCY. The fallopian tube can be removed or the pregnancy removed from the fallopian tube using laparoscopic instruments only. Some

A gynecologist uses a laparascope to observe a woman's internal sex organs.

ovarian cysts may be removed through the laparoscope and occasionally ovaries may be removed too. Using the laparoscope, the fallopian tubes and ovaries can be freed from their attachments to the body, enabling vaginal hysterectomies (see HYSTERECTOMY) to be performed in cases when major abdominal surgery would once have been necessary. General surgeons have recently begun using the laparoscope to remove gallbladders.

In recent years the use of the laparoscope has been expanded so that now it is increasingly common to perform major operative procedures with it. This shortens the hospitalization and recovery period. Minor complications of laparoscopy include infection at the site of the abdominal puncture or an ecchymosis (black and blue area) around the puncture site. Serious complications can also occur, including injury to the bowel or major vessels in the abdomen. These complications may require immediate major surgical intervention. As with all operations, there is the possibility of complications from anesthesia as well.

LESBIAN SEXUAL TECHNIQUES A lesbian is generally defined as a woman whose principal sexual attraction is toward other women and who, as a result, engages mainly in homosexual acts with women. The specific form these sexual acts take varies widely, just as it does with heterosexual sexual activity. Lesbian sex is anything sexual that women do together and is, therefore, difficult to generalize about. There are, however, sexual practices and issues that are common across the lesbian community.

Perhaps the greatest distinction of lesbian sex is that it does not involve male genitalia and is, therefore, not centered around SEXUAL INTERCOURSE. Activities that in many heterosexual unions are regarded as "FOREPLAY" take on a greater importance in lesbian sex, and may be engaged in for longer periods of time than is common between men and women. Touching, KISSING, licking, and sucking are the primary techniques of sexual arousal, with lesbians generally regarding the entire body as the sensual field of play. BREASTS are highly erogenous and many lesbians enjoy playing with each other's nipples—rolling them between their fingers, kissing them with their mouth, circling them with their tongue. Because both partners have breasts, lesbians can also enjoy the sensation of pressing their breasts against those of their partner, stimulating their own nipples as they arouse those of their lover.

A sexual technique that is frequent in lesbian sex is body-to-body rubbing. The genital area of one partner is pressed hard and rubbed against the leg or thigh of the other. A common variation is "tribadism," where two women lie face to face, one on top of the other. The genitals are pressed tightly together while the partners move in a grinding motion. Some rub their CLITORIS against their partner's pubic bone. In the nineteenth century lesbians were sometimes referred to as "tribades," and for many years racy French novels depicted tribadism as the main lesbian sexual activity. An advantage of tribadism is that it allows the hands and mouth to be free to stimulate other areas of the body.

Touching and rubbing the clitoris and other genitals with one's fingers is enjoyed by most lesbians. VIBRATORS may also be used to stimulate a partner's genitals. Oral sex, or using one's mouth on a partner's genitalia, is another form of clitoral sex play. During oral sex the tongue, teeth, and lips can all be used to nibble, bite,

lick, or manipulate and to explore the clitoris, labia, and VAGINA. Partners may choose to engage in simultaneous oral sex by aligning themselves face-to-genitals. This is usually accomplished by lying side-by-side or with one woman on top and the other on the bottom. Many women find simultaneous oral sex too distracting and choose, instead, to take turns stimulating each other.

Many lesbians enjoy vaginal penetration by a partner's fingers or tongue. The insertion of foreign objects is also commonplace, but in the case of DILDOS this can be controversial, especially if the dildo is shaped like a PENIS. Some lesbians do use dildos, but others are uncomfortable with what they regard as intercourse with a substitute male organ. The lesbian community takes pride in the fact that lesbian sex is not conventional sex, and that lesbian women are not bound or limited by traditional understandings of sexual roles or rules. This is why some lesbians reject the very idea of sex with dildos, which they feel is male-defined. It also explains why many lesbians refuse to judge any form of lesbian sex, choosing instead to celebrate a woman's right to define and determine her unique sexual self, whatever habits, fantasies, or practices that involves.

Just as heterosexual culture has tended to define sex as intercourse, lesbians may fall into the trap of defining sex as finger-vagina or tongue-clitoris interaction—with ORGASM as an end goal. The lesbian community at large, however, believes that all sex play is valid. The end goal of sex should be pleasure, whether it leads to orgasm or not. Nevertheless, some studies made in the 1980s have found that the reported frequency of orgasm for lesbian partners is higher than that for heterosexual women. Researchers speculate the reason may be that lesbian couples tend to arouse one another more slowly and deliberately and to talk more during sex, often communicating quite explicitly about what is sexually pleasing. What, specifically, is sexually pleasing is as varied as the lesbian community itself.

At times lesbians may stimulate the ANUS for sexual pleasure. The anus can be rimmed (the tongue moved around its edge), stroked with the fingers, or penetrated with the fingers or a dildo. Some lesbians enjoy bondage games or incorporate sadomasochistic fantasies (see SADISM/MASOCHISM) into their sex-play. Others find the possibility of "getting caught" very arousing. It can be very exciting to be doing something that others would find scandalous if they recognized it. Often lesbians touch each other surreptitiously under lap blankets in public places or have sex in the woods or in public bathrooms.

Lesbians may even have sex with a man, although this is controversial within the lesbian community. Some have sex with men occasionally or anonymously for variety. Others have fairly regular sexual encounters with a particular man. For some lesbians, sex with men is a wonderful adjunct to their on-going sexual relating to women, and does not alter their self-identification as lesbians. Lesbianism, for them, is a sexual state of mind. It is an identity that goes much deeper than individual sex acts.

The spectrum of lesbian sexual activity is wide, and depends on the tastes of the individuals involved. Some may assume specific gender roles—dressing "butch" or "femme." So called "lipstick lesbians" are conventionally attractive but many others run away from such traditional models, taking pleasure and pride in what they describe as a full exploration of their sexuality (see also BISEXUALITY; GAY AND LESBIAN LIFE; GAY AND LESBIAN LOVE RELATIONSHIPS; GAY AND LEBIAN POPULATIONS; HOMOSEXUALITY).

LIBIDO   The sex drive or one's sexual appetite is commonly called "libido." It is the first component of Helen Singer Kaplan's triphasic sexual system—desire, arousal, and orgasm (see SEXUAL RESPONSE CYCLE)—and is a complex balance of physical and social factors. Researchers such as Alfred Kinsey and Masters and Johnson have suggested that the libido goes through periodic increases and decreases during one's lifetime. The most frequent complaint about libido is usually heard when it is much decreased in relation to what a person feels is his or her normal level.

The physical factors affecting libido may include pain during intercourse (dyspareunia) from organic disease, illness, and erectile dysfunction.

For example, dyspareunia can be caused by atrophy or thinning of the vaginal tissue after MENOPAUSE (from loss of estrogen production), from infection, and from recent vaginal delivery. Endocrinal diseases such as diabetes mellitus and spinal injuries, as well as certain drugs, can affect a man's ability to have and maintain an ERECTION, and this may, in turn, influence libido.

The relationship between libido and sexual performance is complex and, as noted above, influenced not only by one's physical condition but also by one's emotional situation. Sexual dysfunction in both men and women is exceedingly common; over a lifetime half of all individuals will experience some sexual dysfunction, most often transient and situational in nature rather than indicative of serious underlying organic disease or psychopathology. If alterations in libido or sexual performance persist, appropriate medical evaluation and consultation should be sought (see also BOREDOM, SEXUAL; MENOPAUSE; SEXUAL DYSFUNCTION, FEMALE; SEXUAL DYSFUNCTION, MALE; TESTOSTERONE).

LOVE   Probably more has probably been written about love than any other subject in human experience and history. It has drawn the attention of philosophers and social scientists, poets and playwrights, psychotherapists and theologians, but none of this attention has produced a consensus as to exactly what love is, where it comes from, and what it signifies. In all likelihood, there will never be such a definition, simply because love has so many faces: erotic love, romantic love, love of family, love of God, love of nature, love of humanity, love of art, love of animals, love of friends, self-love, *ad infinitum*.

Among the modern theories of love that have received scholarly attention are those advanced by Sigmund Freud, Erich Fromm, Abraham Maslow, and Robert Sternberg. Freud viewed love as a necessary expression of the basic sexual energy drive that, in his view, motivates all human beings. Whether it is directed at parents, friends, or lovers, Freud contended, love is always a manifestation of sexual tension.

Although trained in psychoanalytic theories, Erich Fromm departed from Freud's somewhat narrow conceptualization of love. Fromm specified five types of love: brotherly, parental, erotic, self-love, and love of God. According to him, a fully developed person is capable of all five. He also stressed that the different types of love are interconnected with one another. For example, individuals who are unable to love themselves will probably not be able to love others. Also, according to Fromm's theory, learning to love in any of the key areas enhances learning the other kinds of love.

Fromm believed that love is active rather than passive: there is no such thing as being "in love." Rather, love is a kind of behavior that helps others enhance their potential for social and emotional growth. One who loves is giving rather than receiving. Therefore, according to Fromm, love involves "care," "responsibility," "respect," and knowledge of the loved one.

The psychologist Abraham Maslow discerned two types of love: one based on selfish need and taking (he called this D-love, that is, "deficiency love") and one based on unselfish giving (Maslow termed this B-love, that is, "being love"). He noted that D-lovers look for and fall in love with persons who can meet their needs for security, self-esteem, social recognition, and sexual gratification. At the same time, they may be (unintentionally) meeting their partners' own D-love needs. If their needs are complementary, the couple may see themselves as happy and the relationship might last. Not surprisingly, Maslow sees the most mature relationship, resulting in a synergistic growth of both parties, in unions between two B-loves.

In his 1988 work, *The Triangle of Love*, psychologist Robert Sternberg isolated three major components—INTIMACY, passion, and commitment, that in combination account for most of the various types of love. He pictured these components as the sides of a triangle. When passion is present without intimacy or commitment, it is infatuation. If there is only a commitment, it is an empty love, as when a married couple stays together for religious reasons but shares no passion or intimacy. Intimacy alone, without passion or commitment, constitutes friendship. Sternberg says that some couples have a com-

panionate love, with both commitment and intimacy but no passion, while others are engaged in romantic love, with intimacy and passion but no commitment (this is found particularly among the young and among persons involved in extramarital AFFAIRS). Love-at-first-sight, married-six-weeks-later relationships, combining passion and commitment but no intimacy, are described by Sternberg as fatuous love. Finally, there is the ideal of consummate love, in which passion, intimacy, and commitment exist in equal proportions.

Sternberg stresses that none of these relationships is written in stone. At any given time, either through choice or inadvertently, a couple may shift from one type to another—or to a nonloving situation, in which none of the components is present.

Implicit in Sternberg's theory is the idea that love relationships cannot be taken for granted or justified solely because they "feel good." Like most other contemporary thinkers on the subject, he believes that a satisfying love relationship is not something that "happens" to a couple; it is something they *make* happen (see also COURTSHIP; FLIRTATION; GAY AND LESBIAN LOVE RELATIONSHIPS; INTIMACY; KISSING; MARRIAGE; ROMANCE; SEXUAL INTERCOURSE).

LOW SEX DRIVE see BOREDOM, SEXUAL; LACK OF SEXUAL INTEREST; SEXUAL DYSFUNCTION, FEMALE; SEXUAL DYSFUNCTION, MALE.

LUBRICATION Lubrication of the VAGINA occurs in response to sexual arousal. The woman's lubrication is not manufactured by a gland, but occurs when fluid filters into the vagina from blood vessels surrounding it. Engorgement of the veins around the vagina at the time of sexual arousal causes increased pressure which, in turn, causes the fluid within the blood serum to be pushed through the tissues of the vaginal wall.

Lubrication acts as a moisturizer for the mucous membrane of the vagina and decreases friction during intercourse. Where lubrication is inadequate, intercourse can be uncomfortable and even painful. Following MENOPAUSE, when the vaginal tissue is no longer stimulated by ES-

TROGEN, and immediately after childbirth are two periods when decreased lubrication can create problems with intercourse. Local vaginal infections can also interfere with the normal process.

Since sexual arousal is dependent upon psychological as well as physical factors, one's libido and mood (setting, time, etc.) may also influence lubrication. If lack of sufficient lubrication is a persistent problem, the specific cause should be diagnosed. For example, if it is due to an estrogen deficiency in the menopausal years, topical as well as oral estrogen replacement (see HORMONE REPLACEMENT THERAPY) may be appropriate; if it is from vaginitis or infection, antibiotics may help. Even if the problem cannot be diagnosed, it can be managed symptomatically. Creams containing glycerin can be used to restore moisture to the vaginal tissue. Various oil-based products are available over the counter and, in fact, many are available with a variety of scents, textures, tastes, and even thermal properties, which may enhance intercourse by acting as more than merely a lubricant.

Care should be taken when using these products in conjunction with a condom. Petroleum-based products can cause a change in the elastic properties of latex used in CONDOMS, resulting in condom failure. Finally, any lubricant can cause an allergic or irritative reaction. If this occurs, the product should be discontinued immediately.

M

MALE PILL see VASECTOMY AND THE MALE PILL.

MAMMARY GLANDS see BREASTS.

MAMMOGRAPHY The American Cancer Society (ACS) estimates that in 1994, 182,000 new cases of breast cancer will be diagnosed and approximately 46,000 women will die of this disease. (The ACS also estimates that 1,000 cases will be diagnosed in men in 1994.)These figures are alarming, especially when one considers that the usual warning signals for breast cancer—a lump, thickening, swelling, changes in the skin—represent late development of this disease. In addition, based upon current medical knowledge, breast cancer cannot be prevented.

What about risk factors? Unfortunately, 80 percent of women with breast cancer do not have any of the well-known risk factors: an age of fifty or over, a personal or family history of breast cancer, no children, or the birth of a first child after age thirty. It is obvious that early detection is the best protection, and today mammographic screening offers the best hope.

Mammography is a reliable method of detecting breast cancer at early stages, which are highly curable. Breast cancer grows slowly for six to eight years before reaching a diameter of about one-third of an inch that can be detected by breast examination. In this early preclinical stage the cancer can be seen and located precisely by mammography.

The mammogram is a special X-ray of both breasts. It was first described more than thirty years ago, and during the intervening decades there have been improvements both in safety of the equipment and the quality of the image produced by it. With modern equipment there is no danger of excessive radiation exposure. In fact, the amount of radiation associated with the current equipment is equivalent to the additional radiation received at increased altitudes, for example, living in Denver as compared to Boston or New York. This examination should never be refused based upon imagined dangers from radiation.

Mammography has reduced the death rate from breast cancer (but because of a higher life

Mammography equipment

expectancy among the general population, there has been an increase in the number of women who contract the disease). More than thirty years ago, an American study demonstrated that among women over fifty years of age there was a marked decrease in the death rate from breast cancer for those examined by mammography on a regular basis. These figures have been duplicated in more recent studies in the United States and other countries, and there is increasing evidence that the death rate from breast cancer can be reduced in women who begin regular screening at age forty.

Despite this evidence, most American women do not take advantage of this detection program. A recent survey revealed that only 30 percent are following the recommended guidelines for mammograms beginning at age forty. While this represents an increase from just 10 percent a few years ago, more than two-thirds of American women still do not avail themselves of this important diagnostic test. Regrettably, almost half of the women who never had a mammogram said that their doctors had not recommended it.

The following statements can be made about mammography:

- The only method proven to reduce the death rate from breast cancer is periodic screening with mammography;
- Mammography is the only method of diagnosing malignant breast tumors that are so small that they cannot be felt even by a physician;
- The cure rate is over 90 percent if a tumor can be detected at an early stage;
- Mammography is safe.

The accepted guidelines for use of mammography include:

- Mammograms should be obtained promptly beginning at age forty. They should be performed every other year, but more frequently if there are suspicious findings noted by the patient or on physical examination;
- Beginning at age fifty, mammograms should be obtained every year;
- Patients with a strong family history of breast cancer (mother or sister), particularly

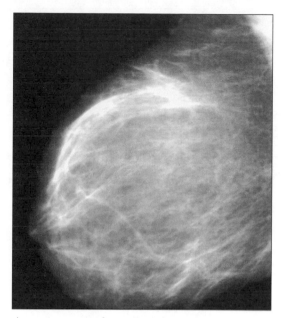

A mammogram of a woman's breast

if the tumor developed before menopause, should have their first mammogram at age thirty-five, or even age thirty, and annually thereafter.

Mammograms can be obtained in a hospital, in a special breast clinic, or in a doctor's office. While there is little doubt about the effectiveness of a properly performed mammogram, the quality of the examination and interpretation of the film must be carefully monitored. The majority of installations now providing mammography are accredited by the American College of Radiology and this information can be readily obtained from the American Cancer Society or the local medical society.

The films are taken in a special room and in the sitting or standing positions. One image provides a side view of the breast and the other a top view: both are necessary. There is occasionally some discomfort because the breasts must be compressed in order to get a clear view of breast tissue. For most patients this is well tolerated and not objectionable. The films are developed and then interpreted by a radiologist skilled in mammography. Occasionally, abnormalities will be noted, such as densities or small areas of calcium. Recommendations include follow-up films in four to six months or, possibly, a biopsy.

Clearly, information that a mammogram is abnormal is unsettling to any patient. It should be noted, however, that 80 percent of the abnormalities revealed by a mammogram are not cancerous. If the mammogram is reported to be abnormal, medical consultation should be sought. If follow-up is recommended, additional films will be taken and further action will depend on these results. If a biopsy is recommended, referral to a surgeon specializing in the procedure is in order (see also BREAST CANCER).

Since abnormal breast areas often cannot be felt by a patient or physician, the biopsy requires a specialized technique. The mammogram is reviewed and a small needle is placed in the area of the abnormality, usually under local anesthesia. The surgeon then follows the needle to the abnormal area. The abnormal tissue is removed and examined. In most cases abnormalities are related to fibrocystic changes and no further treatment is recommended, but if a malignancy is found, additional surgery is likely (see also BREAST SELF-EXAMINATION).

MARITAL RAPE   see CONSENT; POST-TRAU-MATIC STRESS DISORDERS; RAPE.

MARITAL THERAPY Marital therapy is directed at the entire spectrum of relationships and problems likely to emerge between married partners. In contemporary America the term "relationship therapy" may be more appropriate since the techniques and goals of marital therapy are applicable as well to unmarried heterosexuals and to homosexual couples in stable relationships. Marital therapy differs from SEX THERAPY by encompassing much broader areas of the couple's relationship. It covers problems of an interpersonal nature, child rearing, and relationships with the families of origin (both the husband's and wife's parents and siblings) and the extended family. Marital therapy also deals with issues of living arrangements, money matters, goals of the relationship, and emotional satisfactions and dissatisfactions in marriage. While not always the case, many couples with one or more of these problems find that they have an impact on the quality of the sex life in the relationship. Hence,

many sex therapists, it they are not themselves fully qualified, will work closely with a marital therapist to help couples when problems involving sexual dysfunction seem to be interwoven with interpersonal marital problems.

Marital therapy, like psychotherapy, has many different schools and theories on how to best treat couples. It may utilize group therapy as an additional method or by itself. Very often marital therapy is a short-term solution, focusing on immediate problems in the specific relationship rather than on the individual personalities and possible changes.

MARRIAGE   The socially recognized acceptance by a community of the uniting of two individuals in a permanent sexual and family relationship as husband and wife. Their emotions and attentions are focused on each other, but their roles and relationships are expanded if and when children come. Anthropologists and sociologists generally agree that throughout history and in almost all cultures, the main function of the family has been to nurture and socialize offspring in order to ensure the continuity of social institutions from generation to generation. In earlier times, the family was also primarily responsible for physical protection and education of the young and the transmission of religious values, among other functions; to a great extent these have been taken over by such institutions as schools, the police, and organized religion. Meanwhile, an increasingly important function of marriage has been the nurturing, love, and sexual fulfillment that should ideally exist between husband and wife.

Many cultures—throughout history and in many parts of the world—have permitted or preferred polygyny (males having two or more wives at the same time) and some societies have permitted polyandry (women having two or more husbands). Modern societies, particularly those influenced by the Jewish and Christian value systems, almost always limit marriage to monogamy—the union of one man and one woman. (There is, however, some movement in the United States and in parts of Europe toward an acceptance of homosexual marriages.) In

Western culture the concept of monogamy extends to the sexual activity of each partner by limiting sex outside the marriage. (The DOUBLE STANDARD of male and female sexual behavior, has led to greater tolerance for male as contrasted with female sexual freedom.)

In the last few decades, both in Europe and the United States, a small but significant segment of the population has expressed the view that traditional sexual exclusivity may not allow husbands and wives to be as sexually or emotionally satisfied as possible. Some writers have traced this point of view to a post-Freudian idea that individual happiness should be a major goal in life and that marriage should, in large part, focus on the couple's sexual and emotional fulfillment.

Despite high rates of DIVORCE in the United States, a recent national survey done by Drs. Sam and Cynthia Janus indicates that an overwhelming majority of Americans (90 percent of men and 92 percent of women) agree or strongly agree that the family is the most important institution in society. On the other hand, they also note that only 20 percent of the men and 13 percent of the women interviewed believe that to be "truly fulfilled one must be married." This attitude has something to do with the fact that in recent decades it has become more common for couples to live together, sometimes for decades, without getting married. In those cases where they eventually do marry, it is often because a baby is contemplated or expected.

Over the last century marriage rates in the United States have risen and fallen periodically. The low rates (approximately 8 marriages per 1,000 persons per year) occurred around the turn of the century, in 1930, and in 1960. The high rates (12 or so marriages per 1,000 persons per year) were reported in 1920, 1940, and 1990. The age at which people first marry has been climbing steadily—from the mid to late teens early in the century to twenty-six years of age for men and twenty-four for women in the 1990s. In a recent report, the National Center for Health Statistics predicted that about 70 percent of males and females would marry at least once in their lifetimes—an estimate considerably lower than that of the 1970s, when it was esti-

mated that 87 percent of females and 96 percent of males would marry. Several reasons for the decline have been suggested: less social pressure on those who are not emotionally inclined to the intimacy or responsibilities of marriage; large numbers of gay men and lesbian women, who would have been "in the closet" in previous decades and may have married to deny or conceal their HOMOSEXUALITY; increasing economic independence for women; and more social acceptance of single motherhood by choice.

As we move into the twenty-first century, it appears that the definition of marriage as exclusively monogamous and heterosexual will undergo examination and perhaps change. Far from being a cause for worry, this is a healthy reflection of the need for the family as an institution to function harmoniously in a rapidly changing world (see also ADULTERY; AFFAIRS; COMMITMENT; DATING; GAY AND LESBIAN LOVE RELATIONSHIPS; LOVE; MARITAL THERAPY).

MASSAGERS   see VIBRATORS.

MASTECTOMY   see BREAST CANCER.

MASTERS AND JOHNSON   Dr. William H. Masters, a gynecologist, and Dr. Virginia E. Johnson, a psychologist, were the major sex researchers to follow Dr. Alfred Kinsey. In the past forty years they have developed more knowledge of sexual responses than in all previous periods. They also developed all the basic techniques of sex therapy that did not exist before their work became known.

Beginning in the 1950s, in their laboratory in Saint Louis, Missouri, they devised the instruments needed to record the physical responses of their subjects, human males and females, during sexual stimulation. Then, systematically observing their subjects, they amassed information about human sexuality that changed the basic premises about how it worked. They defined four distinct phases of arousal during sexual stimulation (see SEXUAL RESPONSE CYCLE). They showed that female responses to stimulation were the same no matter what manner of stimulation was used, whether friction with a penis, with laboratory recording devices, with fingers, by coitus, or through MASTURBATION. This upset firm beliefs about women's sexuality dating from the time of Sigmund Freud and earlier.

Next, this remarkable pair of colleagues (they married in 1971, but later divorced) identified several distinct types of sexual dysfunction. Until then psychoanalytic treatment, often lasting for years, medication, and surgery had all been based on vague diagnoses of "impotence" in men and "frigidity" in women. This was comparable to doctors treating patients after diagnosing them as "sick." They identified the specific dysfunctions such as erectile difficulty, premature ejaculation, retarded ejaculation, unresponsiveness in women, and vaginismus (the inability to relax the muscles around the vaginal opening to permit a penis to enter). Then, having identified the specific dysfunctions, they devised treatments to overcome them. Finally, Masters and Johnson taught others the practice of SEX THERAPY and trained thousands of therapists.

MASTURBATION The drive to experience sexual pleasure is a very powerful one; nearly everyone stimulates their sexual organs from time to time, probably more often than they care to admit. A natural expression of human sexuality, masturbation may begin in childhood and continue into old age—or it may not. It is popularly believed that masturbation is mainly a teenage phenomenon, but while raging teenage hormones may lead to an increase in masturbation, it occurs at all ages, among married and unmarried people, and among the elderly.

Social and medical attitudes toward masturbation have changed considerably over the last fifty years. They have departed from very negative views of it as "self-abuse" with potentially dire physical or psychological consequences for the individual. Sex educators and therapists now agree that masturbation is normal to the sexual development of the young, it is useful as an aid to sexual interaction between two loving persons, and it is a means of relieving sexual tension when one lacks a partner.

The myths of the recent past about the harmfulness of masturbation seem to have been rooted in medical pronouncements about its ill effects and in religious beliefs that it is immoral. It was believed that excessive masturbation could cause blindness or insanity, that women would grow facial hair and that men would grow hair on the palms of their hands because of it. These myths were reinforced by the common belief that each man had a finite amount of semen; if he lost too much of it from masturbation he risked physical deterioration. Absurd as these myths are, many of them were taught in physical education courses as late as the 1940s.

Persons who based their attitudes on religious belief often cited the biblical story of Onan and his sinful "spilling" of seed (Genesis 38:8-9)—hence the term "onanism," meaning masturbation. However, according to most scholars, the story of Onan's sin probably refers to *coitus interruptus*, not masturbation. Onan withdrew before ejaculation, thereby failing to fulfill his social and religious duty to impregnate his brother's widow.

Today, most people who work professionally in medicine and human sexuality reject these unscientific or pseudoscientific pronouncements about the dangers of masturbation. Contemporary experts caution parents about the potential harm they can cause by too vigorously trying to prevent infants or children from masturbating. They point out that interfering with childhood masturbation—other than communicating proper etiquette (that it should not be done in public)—may actually be interfering with a natural drive that impels children to explore their sexuality. One sex researcher has theorized that masturbation is probably in keeping with the process of growing up. Through it, children learn to respond physiologically, as nature intends them to, in preparation for lives as sexually active adults. Masturbation may help to develop the mechanisms later needed for successful responses and performance in the reproductive cycle.

Studies now report that almost all men and most women have masturbated at some point in their lives and that many masturbate throughout their lives. In *The Janus Report*, a national survey published in the United States in 1993, 55 percent of adult men and 38 percent of adult women reported that they masturbate on a "regular" basis, ranging from daily to monthly. Furthermore, 66 percent of the men and 67 percent of the women said they agreed or strongly agreed with the statement that "masturbation is a natural part of life and continues on in marriage." This view was supported by 63 percent of the Catholics and 73 percent of the Jews who responded to the survey.

Leading sex surveys have indicated that differences do exist between the sexes in the incidence of reported masturbation. The survey results published by Alfred Kinsey in the 1950s reported that 92 percent of his male respondents said they had masturbated to orgasm at least once, compared with 58 percent of the females. The Hunt survey carried out in the mid-1970s reported that 63 percent of the women had masturbated to orgasm at least once, a percentage not much higher than Kinsey's despite the growth of sexual permissiveness during the twenty-year period between the surveys. Both studies observed that women were probably more reluctant than men to admit that they engaged in this sexual behavior, but perhaps more important, that women's masturbation seems to start later than men's. Most of Kinsey's male respondents said they had begun masturbating between the ages of thirteen and fifteen, but many of the women surveyed said they had begun after the age of twenty-five.

In a sex survey sponsored by Consumers Union in the 1980s, 33 percent of the women aged seventy and over reported that they currently masturbated, as did 43 percent of the men. Of these women, 74 percent reported they experienced orgasms every time or nearly every time. Among the men, 73 percent said they experienced orgasms nearly every time. It does seem that masturbation is a lifelong activity in this culture (see also ANORGASMIA; AUTOEROTICISM; DILDOS; ORGASM; VIBRATORS).

Masturbation in Infancy, Childhood, and Adolescence. Handling of the genitals is quite common and normal in infancy and childhood. It is pleasurable for babies and is part of normal curiosity and exploration of the body, in the same way that they explore their fingers and toes. Genital self-stimulation is also very common and normal from ages two to five, when children are discovering the physical differences between boys and girls. The desire to touch themselves and, perhaps, other children in "sex play" partly reflects their natural curiosity about these differences. Children should not be made to feel ashamed about this behavior or to feel that these parts of their bodies are "bad" in any way. There is, of course, absolutely no truth to the myths that masturbation can cause HOMOSEXUALITY, blindness, physical deformity, retardation, hair on the palms, or any physical or mental illness. Parents may want to suggest to their children that it is something which, like toileting, is usually done "in private."

Adolescents have an increased urge to masturbate as a result of the hormonal changes of puberty. Studies indicate that nearly all boys have masturbated to orgasm by eighteen years of age. Masturbation in boys usually consists of rubbing the PENIS with the hand or against a mattress in an up and down motion until ejaculation occurs. The amount of semen and the distance it can spurt from one's penis can vary. Mutual masturbation among two males is believed to occur at least once among 25 percent of heterosexual males and 60 percent of gay males by age fourteen, increasing to 90 percent of gay males by age nineteen.

Girls usually masturbate by rubbing their CLITORIS and the lips of their VULVA, and may become aroused by touching EROGENOUS ZONES such as the BREASTS. Although girls do not ejaculate the way boys do, when a girl is aroused, a clear liquid lubricant is secreted in the vagina. For girls, masturbation may be a way to defer SEXUAL INTERCOURSE. Masturbation seems to be more common among women from lower socioeconomic groups, who also participate more frequently in premarital coitus.

In some instances, the child's or adolescent's masturbation may appear to be excessive or compulsive, or it may continue to occur in public. This may be an indication of excessive tension or worry on the part of the child or adolescent. If there are other indications that the child or adolescent is anxious or preoccupied, if he or she appears to be lonely, or to have few friends or interests, it may be prudent to seek advice from a mental health professional (see also CHILDREN'S SEXUALITY; SEX EDUCATION).

Masturbation in Sex Therapy. Masturbation and other forms of autoeroticism are crucial for sex therapists' treatment of male and female sexual dysfunctions. Because of traditionally negative Jewish and Christian attitudes toward masturbation, as well as old and erroneous popular and medical beliefs that linked "excessive" masturbation with mental illness, therapy for sexual dysfunctions might never have developed as a profession without radical shifts in attitudes toward autoeroticism. Changes in public and medical attitudes toward masturbation stem from the work of Alfred Kinsey, MASTERS AND JOHNSON, and Helen Singer Kaplan. Kinsey's great contribution was in his finding that the vast majority of persons have masturbated—without the terrible consequences some believed would occur. Masters and Johnson reported the significance of masturbation for women, that through manual manipulation of the clitoral area or the use of VIBRATORS they might reach orgasm more reliably than through coitus. Kaplan devised innovative techniques to teach women how to overcome some sexual dysfunctions by becoming orgasmic through self-stimulation.

Since the main reason women seek the advice of sex therapists is orgasmic dysfunction, teaching women how to masturbate and pleasure their own bodies is usually essential before women can fully accept sexual pleasure and stimulation from others. Most sex therapists believe that it is necessary for women with orgasmic dysfunctions to learn to take responsibility for their own orgasms before they can become orgasmic from their partners' stimulations, whether manual, oral, or penile. As a result of the work of Masters and Johnson, sex therapists often recommend the use of vibrators as the most effective means for women to become orgasmic. This does not mean that they will have to continue with or be dependent upon them, however, because success with vibrators is easily transferred to self-stimulation and then to a partner's stimulation. For some women it may be helpful to dis-

cuss their orgasmic difficulties in all-female group therapy settings. Therapists have reported that group support from others discussing a topic not generally discussed in gatherings of women can be a powerful aid in therapy.

Masturbation is rarely used to teach men how to become orgasmic or to ejaculate. It is, however, used in treating the fairly common male sexual dysfunctions of premature ejaculation and anticipatory anxiety (see also KAPLAN, HELEN SINGER; KINSEY, ALFRED; SEXUAL DYSFUNCTION, FEMALE; SEXUAL DYSFUNCTION, MALE).

MATERNAL HEALTH   see PREGNANCY AND DIET; PRENATAL CARE.

MEDICATIONS AND PREGNANCY   see PREGNANCY AND COMMON MEDICATIONS.

MENARCHE   see ADOLESCENCE; CHILDREN'S SEXUALITY; MENSTRUATION; PUBERTY.

MENOPAUSE   The time in a woman's life when her menstrual periods stop. The woman no longer produces an egg each month and therefore no longer sheds the endometrium (uterine lining) through menstrual bleeding. The average age of last MENSTRUATION in American women is fifty-one. A woman, therefore, spends about one-third of her life after menopause.

The time when menopause occurs is also known as the "climacteric." It begins when the ovaries decrease their production of the female HORMONES, ESTROGEN and PROGESTERONE. This may occur one to two years prior to the actual cessation of menstruation. The first signs of menopause are a change (sometimes an irregularity) in the menstrual cycle. A woman's periods may become lighter, she may skip a period, the length of bleeding may be longer or shorter, and the flow may be lighter or heavier.

Another classic symptom of menopause is the HOT FLASH. This is a sudden feeling of heat over the entire body, often accompanied by flushing or sweating. The hot flash may occur at any time of the day or night. When these occur at night, they commonly interrupt a woman's sleep. The amount, frequency, and duration of hot flashes

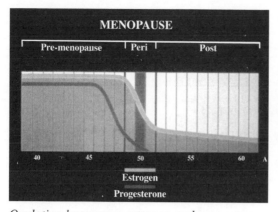

Ovulation hormones: estrogen and progesterone changes during menopause.

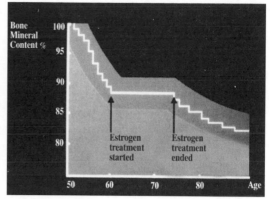

Hormone replacement therapy arrests calcium loss during menopause.

differ in each woman. Some women never experience hot flashes, but 25 percent of women, if untreated, have them beyond two years. A woman has no control over these symptoms, and they often occur at inopportune moments, causing embarrassment.

A decrease in the estrogen level may cause changes in the vagina and the bladder. The lining of the vagina becomes thin or atrophic without the influence of estrogen, causing vaginal dryness, which may, in turn, cause burning, irritation, decreased lubrication, and painful intercourse. The post-menopausal vagina, without HORMONE REPLACEMENT THERAPY, does not always provide sufficient lubrication during lovemaking. This can cause physical discomfort and may lead to a loss of sexual interest. The bladder lining may also become atrophic (thinned out), causing symptoms such as frequency (urinating too often), urgency (difficulty "holding it in"), and burning with urination.

Many postmenopausal women also complain of psychological disturbances. Some of these include depression, anxiety, nervousness, and insomnia. Some women also report sexual dysfunction. This sexual dysfunction may be a result of the vaginal dryness described previously or it may be due to a loss of LIBIDO (sexual interest). The nervousness, anxiety, and insomnia are aggravated by hot flashes, especially when these occur at night. Many women find themselves more emotionally vulnerable and experience frequent crying episodes. The direct re-

lationship of these psychological symptoms to estrogen deficiency is tenuous, however. They are more often a reflection of a woman's situation at that time of her life.

Physical changes that occur with menopause have an important impact on future health. One of these is osteoporosis. Estrogen helps to maintain bone calcium, giving the bone strength. With the loss of estrogen, calcium is taken out of the bone and the bones become more susceptible to fractures. The wrist, hip, and spine are especially vulnerable. Hip fractures are life-threatening occurrences in older patients with serious complications of infection, blood clots, stroke, and pneumonia. A woman is protected from heart and vascular (blood vessel) disease by estrogen. Estrogen helps prevent the build-up of deposits of cholesterol. After menopause the estrogen level drops, decreasing this protective effect and a woman's heart disease risk approaches that of a man.

Hot flashes, vaginal changes, osteoporosis, and heart disease risk can all be addressed by estrogen replacement therapy. Though certain women with specific health problems such as breast cancer, blood clots, abnormal genital bleeding, or clotting disorders should not receive hormones, hormone replacement therapy is very important in maintaining most women's health.

Sexual relations may actually become more enjoyable after menopause. There is no longer fear of unexpected pregnancy; many couples are living alone, their children grown and gone, and there is more opportunity for privacy and intimacy. An older woman and her partner are more experienced in their abilities to please each other. Estrogen helps avoid vaginal dryness, and regular intercourse helps maintain vaginal lubrication and elasticity. Sometimes a woman's sexual interest (libido) decreases after menopuse. Occasionally women may benefit from both male and female hormone replacement, when this loss of libido occurs.

A woman still needs regular gynecological check-ups after menopause. A yearly PAP TEST should be done, as well as a "hands on" yearly breast self-examination and mammogram after age forty. A woman also should do her own monthly breast examination. An annual cholesterol level and a screening test for colon cancer also should be done. If at any point a woman has unexplained vaginal bleeding after menopause, prompt evaluation is mandatory. She should not wait for her routine annual examination.

"Early menopause" is said to occur in women before age forty. This may be due to surgical removal of the ovaries, radiation treatment, chemotherapy, or rarely, from premature failure of the ovaries. The woman who undergoes early menopause is at a higher risk for development of osteoporosis and cardiovascular disease because she will be estrogen-deficient for a longer period of time. It is therefore very important to replace estrogen in cases of early menopause.

Postmenopausal women can lead an active and enjoyable life. Proper diet and exercise are very important. As a woman ages, her metabolism slows and she needs fewer calories, but she also needs sufficient calcium to help prevent osteoporosis. Regular exercise will help retard osteoporosis and give the mature woman a greater sense of well-being. The use of calcium and exercise to help prevent osteoporosis is much more effective if started years before menopause.

The life expectancy of women has increased and, therefore, the number of women in the postmenopausal years is expanding. The physical changes a woman encounters as a result of menopause do not prevent her from enjoying satisfying, productive, and sexually active years, and can be a time of optimism, opportunity, and fulfillment (see also AGING AND SEX; AMENORRHEA; EMPTY NEST SYNDROME; HORMONE REPLACEMENT THERAPY; HOT FLASHES; MAMMOGRAPHY; PAP TEST).

MENSTRUATION A woman's menstrual cycles are the result of an intricately balanced process of communication between the hypothalamus (an area of the brain), the pituitary gland, the OVARIES, and the UTERUS. The messengers for these communications are HORMONES, chemicals produced by the body's glands and transported through the blood to exert their effect at a distant site. Although these processes are obviously interdependent, women's hormone cycles are most easily considered in three subgroupings:

- Hormonal communication between the hypothalamus, the pituitary gland, and the ovaries (hormonal cycle);
- The development of the ovarian follicle containing the egg and the *corpus luteum*, the shell of the follicle after an egg has been released (ovarian cycle);
- The endometrial, or uterine cycle.

Women's cycles will be discussed from these three perspectives, but it is necessary to remember that they are integral parts of the complete female reproductive cycle.

The Hormonal Cycle. The hypothalamus releases one hormone, gonadotropin releasing hormone (GnRH), that causes the pituitary to release the two hormones, follicle stimulating hormone (FSH) and luteinizing hormone (LH), that affect the woman's ovaries. During (or even shortly before) a menstrual period, the levels of FSH start to rise and cause the ovaries to begin development of one or more follicles—fluid-filled cysts in which an egg is developing. The wall of the follicle is made up of cells that, in response to FSH, produce ESTROGEN, the female hormone associated with women's sexual excitement and secondary sex characteristics. In response to the increasing levels of FSH, one follicle becomes dominant and its growth exceeds all the others. This follicle produces increasing amounts of estrogen, and the rising estrogen levels cause the pituitary to decrease the amount of FSH produced.

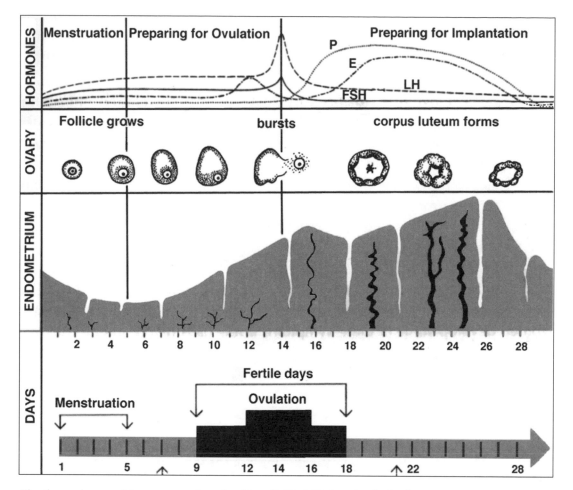

The three phases of the menstrual cycle. Key: FSH: follicle-stimulating hormone; E: estrogen; LH: luteinizing hormone; P: progesterone. Note that the progesterone level rises considerbly within twenty-four hours after ovulation.

When a certain level of estrogen has been produced for a critical period of time, it causes the pituitary to release a large amount of LH (the LH surge). This causes the egg to undergo its final maturation and preparation for fertilization and it initiates the chain of events that results in ovulation (rupture of the follicle and release of the egg) about thirty hours later. The LH surge also transforms what had been the follicle into what is termed the *corpus luteum*. While the follicle's primary hormonal product was estrogen, the *corpus luteum* produces a large amount of PROGESTERONE in addition to estrogen.

The *corpus luteum* has a limited life span unless the woman becomes pregnant. If she does, the *corpus luteum* continues to produce estrogen

and progesterone. Otherwise it stops, and the rapid fall in estrogen and progesterone leads to a rise in FSH, starting the cycle anew.

The Ovarian Cycle. A female infant is born with all the eggs she will ever have. These eggs are surrounded by a layer of granulosa cells and are called follicles. The follicles remain in a resting state until they are selected to begin developing, ten, twenty, thirty, forty, or even fifty years later. It has been estimated that by the time a young girl starts to experience secondary sex development (puberty), she has approximately four hundred thousand developed follicles—each containing an "oocyte" or primitive egg—in her ovaries. Each month, approximately one thousand of these follicles begin development. This

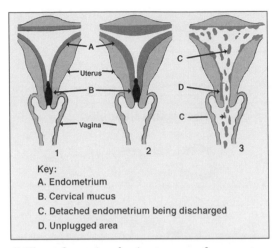

Key:
A. Endometrium
B. Cervical mucus
C. Detached endometrium being discharged
D. Unplugged area

1) The endometrium begins to grow after menstruation. 2) It is now ready for the implantation of an egg. 3) If there is no implantion, the endometrium is discharged during menstruation.

is true regardless of whether she is having menstrual periods, taking birth control pills, attempting pregnancy, pregnant, or breast-feeding. The initial stages of development of these follicles appear to occur without any external hormonal stimulation. Once the follicles reach a certain state, a fluid-filled cavity develops within the granulosa cells. It is approximately at this stage of development that the follicle requires increasing levels of FSH for continued growth and development. The one follicle that is at a perfect state of development when the FSH levels begin rising is able to achieve dominance, and its growth and development will exceed those of all the other follicles. This follicle produces increasing amounts of estrogen and the oocyte within this follicle is destined for ovulation. The other 999 follicles are destined to atrophy, or die, without their egg ever being released.

As noted, when the dominant follicle reaches a certain stage of development, it produces a certain amount of estrogen for a critical period of time, inducing the pituitary to release a surge of LH. The LH causes the final maturation of the egg so that it can be fertilized; it triggers the rupture of the follicle and release of the egg, and transforms the follicle into the *corpus luteum*. The *corpus luteum* has a limited life span of approximately twelve days, during which it pro-

duces both estrogen and progesterone. If pregnancy does not occur, the *corpus luteum* stops producing hormones and fades away. If a pregnancy does result, the early pregnancy produces hCG, another hormone, which stimulates the *corpus luteum* to continue producing the amounts of estrogen and progesterone necessary for its early maintenance. In this situation, the *corpus luteum* continues to be fully functional throughout the first trimester of pregnancy. The first phase of the ovarian cycle during which the follicles are developed until ovulation is termed the follicular phase (referring to what is occurring in the ovary) or the proliferative phase (referring to changes in the lining of the uterus). The second phase of the cycle, from ovulation until menstrual bleeding, is termed the luteal phase. The third phase, during the menstrual cycle, is called the "menstrual" phase.

The Uterine Cycle. The uterine cavity is lined by a tissue called endometrium approximately one quarter of an inch thick. The endometrium exhibits a striking series of changes throughout the menstrual cycle.

During the proliferative stage of the cycle, in response to estrogen the endometrium grows and thickens. With ovulation, and more specifically, the initiation of progesterone production, the endometrium exhibits little additional gain in thickness but a dramatic amount of development in preparation for potential implantation of a fertilized egg. Among the changes is the secretion of fluid from the endometrial glands to nourish the embryo during the three days in which it is floating freely in the uterus, before it attaches to the endometrium. In the absence of successful implantation, the production of estrogen and progesterone ceases about twelve days after ovulation and, without continued hormonal support, the menstrual period begins. The menstrual period actually involves the shedding of the superficial lining of the endometrium. With the initiation of hormone production from the next "crop" of growing follicles, endometrial development begins anew for the next cycle.

In summary, the hormones produced by the hypothalamus, pituitary, and ovaries orchestrate the interrelated development of the ovarian follicles containing a maturing egg and the uterine endometrium into which the egg will implant if fertilized. If there is no pregnancy, the female cycle repeats at about twenty-eight day intervals (see also AMENORRHEA; CLEANLINESS AND SEXUAL ODORS; MENOPAUSE; PREMENSTRUAL SYNDROME (PMS); TAMPONS, PADS, AND SPONGES; TOXIC SHOCK).

Cultural And Psychological Aspects of Menstruation. During ancient times, attitudes about menstruation alternated between repulsion and celebration. Some cultures revered this monthly event as magical and intimately connected with the renewal of life. But it was more common for societies to regard menstruation with disgust. In many places menstruating women were sequestered away from men, sometimes in huts designated for this purpose. In ancient Sumeria women wore a visible towel, a "blood bandage," for the days of their period. During this time they were forbidden to touch plants or crops and were viewed as a source of evil and disease.

Throughout history many have believed that menstrual blood was tainted, and that a man who came into contact with it, as during sex, would be poisoned by it. For that mistaken reason, some societies forbade sex with women during their monthly period. The belief that there is something unholy or unhealthy about menstruation is, of course, pure superstition. Menstruation is a perfectly natural biological process. Yet echoes of these ancient myths still appear in beliefs that forbid women to swim, climb, or follow any of their usual pursuits, including sex, during menstruation.

In fact menstruation is not physically disabling. Exercise, including swimming, is actually beneficial during one's period; women athletes generally report fewer complaints of cramping than their sedentary counterparts. By stimulation of the circulatory system, physical activity helps ease muscle tensions and congested blood vessels. As for sex, while many women experience a loss of interest during their periods, others enjoy it very much. Orgasm may even temporarily relieve mild cramps by accelerating menstrual flow and relieving tensions.

Another false but persistent attitude about menstruation is that it is intellectually or emo-

tionally debilitating. An old wives' tale holds that during menstruation all of the woman's blood rushes out of her brain. While people no longer believe this today, the belief still exists that women are less rational during their periods. Such a belief may, in fact, be a self-fulfilling prophecy. Negative mental attitudes can effect the experience of one's period, making it both physically and psychologically more unpleasant.

Because a good, healthy mindset about one's menstrual period is important, adolescents should be taught about the natural process they are undergoing, one which will someday allow them to choose to have children. Girls should receive specific guidance about bodily changes and hygienic practices. It is most important for parents to demonstrate their pride in their daughters' passage from childhood to sexual maturity, perhaps even celebrating menarche (the first menstruation).

MENTAL HANDICAPS AND SEX   see HANDICAPPED PERSONS AND SEX.

MIDWIVES The midwife is an expert in normal pregnancy and childbirth. The care she gives revolves around supporting BIRTH as a normal physiological process. Midwives offer social, emotional, psychological, and nutritional support during the childbearing year, as well as monitoring physical changes and fetal growth. Midwives guide laboring mothers through the birthing process, and have been defined as "women who help other women empower themselves in birth." In fact, the word midwife means "with women."

While the majority of births in America are attended by physicians, throughout the world the overwhelming majority of births are midwife-attended. This is true in both developed and developing nations. In the United States, approximately 4 percent of births are attended by midwives (1992), as compared to Europe, where more than 75 percent of babies are born into midwives' hands. Nurse-midwives are registered nurses who have completed additional course work in midwifery. Most training occurs within medical institutions, although community-based nurse-midwifery programs are now being offered. Nurse-midwives define themselves as members of the "obstetric team," usually working in conjunction with an OBSTETRICIAN. The vast majority of nurse-midwives attend births in a hospital setting, while the rest work in birthing centers or attend home births. Nurse-midwives are legally permitted to practice in all fifty states, although regulations and scope of practice vary on a state level.

Direct-entry midwives are not nurses but come from a variety of educational backgrounds: Some are trained in midwifery schools in the United States and abroad, while others have learned through apprenticeship. Most have home birth-based practices, with a small number working in birthing centers. Direct-entry midwives are less likely to work directly with an obstetrician, although physicians and hospitals are used for referral. The legal status of direct-entry midwifery varies from state to state. Eleven states have active licensing certification or registration, and direct-entry midwifery is legal in an additional nineteen states (see also HOME BIRTH).

MISCARRIAGE Early spontaneous pregnancy loss—miscarriage—is the most common complication of PREGNANCY. It occurs in approximately 15 percent of clinically confirmed pregnancies, but the very early and often unrecognized pregnancy loss rate is two to three times higher. The incidence increases with the age of the potential mother.

Most miscarriages are due to defects in the developing embryo, such as abnormal cells or chromosomes, defective implantation in the uterus, and perhaps other as yet unrecognized causes. The high proportion of abnormal tissues from miscarried embryos is apparently an indication of a natural selective process that prevents about 95 percent of defective embryos from progressing to birth (see BIRTH DEFECTS).

Miscarriages are usually classified to determine appropriate medical treatment. Physicians have long used the medical term "ABORTION" to describe spontaneous early pregnancy loss, but the word "miscarriage," commonly used by the public and preferred by patients, is gradually re-

placing it. However, medical classifications of miscarriage continue to use the word abortion.

Threatened Abortion. The possibility of miscarriage is usually indicated by a bloody vaginal discharge or uterine bleeding, usually preceding uterine cramping or low backache. On PELVIC EXAMINATION, the cervix is found to be closed and no tissue has passed. Up to 25 percent of pregnant women have some degree of spotting or bleeding during early pregnancy, but about one-half of them continue to progress to normal deliveries. Fetal heart motion, now detectable by ultrasound from six weeks of pregnancy onward, has made the evaluation of threatened miscarriages more precise. Over 95 percent of pregnancies will continue if fetal life is demonstrated by this technique. The prognosis becomes worse if bleeding and cramping is progressive, hCG (human chorionic gonadotropins) pregnancy hormone levels are falling, or the uterus is not growing in size. There is no convincing evidence that any course of treatment, such as bed rest, avoidance of intercourse, or medications, reverses the course of a threatened abortion, but a sympathetic attitude on the part of the physician is important. Initially, it is wise for the woman to remain at home near a telephone until it can be determined whether the symptoms persist or cease. If clinical evaluation indicates that the embryo is no longer alive, evacuation of the uterus by dilation of the cervix and curettage of the inner lining of the uterus ("D & C") is performed, or occasionally, a woman will choose to wait for a spontaneous miscarriage.

Inevitable and Incomplete Abortion. Miscarriage is a process rather than a single event. It is considered inevitable when bleeding or rupture of the membranes is accompanied by pain and dilation of the cervix. The miscarriage is incomplete when the products of conception have only partially passed from the uterine cavity, are protruding from the cervix, or are in the vagina with persistent cramping and bleeding (which can be profuse). A careful vaginal examination can establish the diagnosis. Since no fetal survival is possible with inevitable or incomplete miscarriages, treatment aims at evacuating the uterus to prevent further hemorrhage or infection.

Complete Abortion. Patients being monitored for threatened miscarriage are instructed to save all tissue passed so that it can be inspected. With a complete miscarriage, pain and bleeding cease soon after all the products of conception have passed. If the diagnosis is certain, no further therapy may be necessary. However, in some circumstances, curettage is required to be sure that the uterus is completely emptied.

Missed Abortion. In cases of missed abortion, expulsion of the tissues does not occur for a prolonged period of time after embryonic death. Symptoms of pregnancy regress, pregnancy tests become negative, and no fetal heart motion is detected. Although most patients eventually abort spontaneously, waiting for that to occur may be emotionally trying, and many women prefer to have the tissues removed by "D & C."

Septic Abortion. Infected (septic) abortion, once a leading cause of maternal death because of the poor clinical conditions under which many illegal abortions were performed, has been less frequent in recent years as liberalized abortion laws have made physician-induced abortions available to women with unwanted pregnancies. Women with septic abortion suffer symptoms of fever, abdominal tenderness, and uterine pain, which in severe cases can progress to overwhelming infection and shock. Therapy consists of aggressive use of antibiotics and evacuation of the uterus, often in an intensive care setting.

Recurrent Spontaneous Abortion. Recurrent miscarriage is usually defined as three or more consecutive first trimester spontaneous losses. Such miscarriages have received a great deal of attention in both the media and medical literature during the past few years. Diagnosis and treatment of the woman suffering recurrent miscarriage is still one of the most difficult areas in reproductive medicine. Investigation for chromosome abnormalities, uterine anomalies, hormonal deficiencies, and immunological factors are necessary to rule out potential paternal or maternal factors.

One major specific cause of second-trimester (four to six months) pregnancy loss is premature cervical dilation, known medically as incompe-tent cervix. When this occurs, there is a gradual, painless dilation of the cervix, rupture of membranes, and delivery of a fetus so immature that it almost never survives. Recurrences of incompetent cervix usually can be prevented by a surgical procedure called cerclage, making a purse string-like suture to reinforce the cervix.

Miscarriage is a frustrating problem for both patients and physicians. There is often no good understanding of its causes, and treatment is not always successful. In most cases a miscarriage does not imply that another will occur in the next pregnancy. Nevertheless, the establishment of trust and rapport and appreciation of the distress experienced by these couples permits a thorough discussion between the physician and the couple about treatment of the miscarriage and future pregnancies (see also PREGNANCY; PRENATAL CARE).

MISSIONARY POSITION see COITAL POSITIONS.

MISTRESSES see AFFAIRS.

MOMENT OF INEVITABILITY Just before a male ejaculates, there are premonitory sensations marking a point of no return—when EJACULATION becomes inevitable. Some therapists call this the "moment of inevitability." Once that threshold has passed, it is too late to delay ejaculation; it then occurs beyond the man's control. Many men are bothered by what appears to be a loss of control over when their ORGASM and ejaculation occur. Recognition of the sensations preceding ejaculation is a critical part of sex therapy for men who suffer from PREMATURE EJACULATION. It is necessary that a man learn to recognize the sensations that occur before the moment of inevitability in order to learn how to control the timing of his ejaculation.

Of course, there is a moment of inevitability for women as well, though it occurs much closer to the moment of orgasm than is true for men. However, since early female orgasm is not a common complaint—indeed, it is almost never defined as a complaint—there are few references to it in popular or medical literature.

A common technique recommended by sex therapists is for the male to slowly masturbate a few times while concentrating on the sensations immediately preceding ejaculation, so as to recognize the premonitory sensations that tell him an orgasm is beginning but ejaculation is not yet inevitable. At this moment, he should stop and move his hand away from his penis. He will probably lose part or all of his firm erection. He can then stimulate himself again and stop. On the third time he can bring himself to ejaculation. By this time he will have been able to stop twice and will have learned what he has to do in order not to ejaculate. After several practice sessions, he may ask a partner to help him reach the moment of inevitability by instructing the partner to stop stimulation. When he learns to recognize it in time and have stimulation cease immediately, ejaculation will often not occur.

Some therapists say it is understandable that many men seem unaware of this momentary point between the beginning of the orgasmic sensation and its heightening during ejaculation. They argue that for most men, orgasm is the goal of sexual activity and thus, they are unaware of the continuum of sensations they experience and their physical meaning. Since most men have not been educated about the different sensations, they are unaware that there is time to control the process. As a consequence, premature ejaculation is one of the most frequently reported sexual dysfunctions among males (see also SEXUAL DYSFUNCTION, MALE; SEX THERAPY).

MONS PUBIS   see FEMALE SEX ORGANS; VULVA.

MORALS, SEXUAL   see SEXUAL MORALITY.

MULTIPLE ORGASMS   see ORGASMS, MULTIPLE.

N

NARCOTICS See APHRODISIACS; FETAL AND IN-
FANT SUBSTANCE ABUSE SYNDROMES.

NATURAL CHILDBIRTH What could be
more natural than childbirth? Just as the growth
of the fetus during PREGNANCY occurs at its own
pace, the normal BIRTH process unfolds naturally
and independently of external factors. Labor sets
its own pace and rhythm as the about-to-be-born
baby moves from the environment of the womb
to the world outside. And though a woman can
control the place in which she chooses to give
birth and those who will be present, she cannot
control how the birth itself will unfold.

What is natural childbirth? Some take it to
mean undrugged childbirth or birth without use
of interventions of any kind. Others include any
birth that occurs vaginally while still others
think of prepared childbirth, in which a woman
follows a particular set of rules or guidelines that
take her through labor.

The focus of most prepared childbirth methods
has been twofold: drugless techniques that minimize pain, and education regarding the birth
process. The first such method was introduced
by Dr. Grantly Dick-Read in 1933. He advocated the use of relaxation and deep breathing,
believing pain to be a product of fear and tension. Next came Dr. Fernand Lamaze, with an
entirely different regimen of breathing exercises
used to help women cope with and minimize the
pain of birth. A third method was discussed by
Dr. Robert Bradley, founder of "husband-
coached childbirth." He returned to slower,
deeper breathing, this time with the father as
"coach." Author and surgeon Michel Odent emphasized privacy and darkness to facilitate the
natural process and advocated the use of water
pools in labor.

Today most hospitals offer their own childbirth courses. In addition, independent teachers
are available on referral by a midwife or physician. Such independent courses can offer several
advantages: smaller class size with individual attention, an orientation toward choice in mater-
nity care, the ability to cast a critical eye on
hospital routines, and more innovative information and guidance on working with the female
body's innate birthing knowledge.

None of the methods currently in use offers
"painless childbirth." Why avoid the use of
drugs when they can eliminate pain during birth?
Drugs tend to interfere with the body's natural
processes. For example, anesthesia and sedatives
can slow contractions or render them less efficient; many women then require artificial hormones to augment labor. During the pushing
phase, pain relievers can interfere with a
woman's ability to bear down, increasing the
need for forceps, vacuum extraction, and CE-
SAREAN SECTION. Moreover, many women feel
that being drugged robs them of the full experience of childbirth (see also BIRTH; EPIDURAL PAIN
RELIEF DURING LABOR).

In the end, birth is more than a method. The
essence of "natural childbirth" is respect for the
wisdom of the birthing process, trusting nature
to work in the most efficient way for each particular mother and child. When a woman is taught
to move beyond pain and fear, she can then work
in harmony with her labor, reducing or eliminating the use of interventions. She can be mobile
throughout the labor, choosing positions that allow gravity to assist the birth process, and she

can be fully conscious to appreciate welcoming the baby into her waiting arms (see also LAMAZE METHOD; MIDWIVES).

NATURAL FAMILY PLANNING BIRTH CONTROL based on ABSTINENCE during the time that the woman is supposed to be fertile is commonly known as "natural family planning." There are several ways in which to decide when this time frame is, but none of them is perfectly exact, which is why this type of planning has a failure rate of 20 percent as typically used, meaning that, in the course of a year, 20 women out of 100 will become pregnant using this method of birth control. (Rates are much lower for perfect use, including 9 for the calendar method alone and 3 for the symptothermal method described below.) On the other hand, these same methods can also be used to help plan a pregnancy in cases in which a woman is having difficulty conceiving or in instances when the timing of the arrival of a baby is important.

The first of these is the calendar, or "rhythm," method. The woman must keep track of when she has her periods over a number of months in order to see how regular her periods are. While textbooks may say that a woman ovulates fourteen days after her period ends, there are no absolute rules. Some women are quite regular while others vary greatly. In order to be "safe," a woman must find out what her longest cycle is and what her shortest cycle is, and then work out the mathematics, taking account of the fact that sperm may live some days within her reproductive system, as can the egg (which can survive for twenty-four hours or more), so that there must be a minimal eight-day safety margin. For most couples, what this means is that they must not engage in any unprotected SEXUAL INTERCOURSE for about ten days during the middle of the woman's cycle.

Another way of calculating the safe time is to use the basal body temperature method. The basal body temperature is the body's temperature first thing in the morning before rising. If a woman is ovulating, her basal body temperature will be between 0.4 to 0.8 degrees higher than her normal body temperature. To calculate effec-

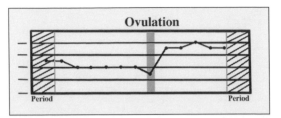

During ovulation, a woman's body temperature rises slightly.

tively the woman must keep a record of her morning temperatures so that she can make a comparison, and she must also use this method in conjunction with the calendar method in order to have an idea of when to expect ovulation, because any sperm already on their way toward the egg could impregnate her. There may also be other factors that can raise a woman's temperature, such as an infection from a cold, so that she must remain in tune with her body's overall health when using this method.

With the cervical mucus method the woman observes the changes in her cervical mucus. Normally the mucus is cloudy and tacky, but a few days before ovulation it will become clear and slippery, stretching between the fingers like raw egg whites, and there will be more of it. When this happens the woman must refrain from intercourse, or use a barrier method. Of the three, this is the least effective method, with pregnancy rates having been shown to be as high as 40 in 100 per year.

A combination of these three methods, called the symptothermal method, is, of course, more effective than any single natural family planning method alone. The last method, called the postovulation method, requires that the woman either abstain from intercourse or use a barrier method from the beginning of her period until the morning of the fourth day after her predicted ovulation, more than half of her menstrual cycle.

Natural family planning methods are safe, do not have any side effects, do not cost very much to implement and are accepted by most religious groups. The more a woman studies how to use natural family planning, the more skilled she will become in using them. Taking a course is highly recommended for anyone thinking of using these methods. However, natural family planning is far from foolproof even if practiced perfectly. There are other factors that can seriously reduce the effectiveness of this method of birth control, such as infections, lack of sleep, or jet lag, which interfere with the basal body temperature, or vaginal secretions which alter the cervical mucus. Finally, natural family planning offers no protection against SEXUALLY TRANSMITTED DISEASES.

NEWBORN INFANTS Immediately after BIRTH the newborn baby is still attached to the PLACENTA by the umbilical cord. The cord is usually tied with two plastic or metal clamps placed about three inches apart, approximately ten inches from the cord's meeting point with the baby's belly. The portion between the clamps is then cut within thirty seconds of the baby's birth.

Many years ago, babies were lifted by the feet by the OBSTETRICIAN and slapped on their back. This practice has been abandoned, largely because lifting a baby by the feet may cause problems to its hip. Instead, the baby is now usually placed with its face up in a warmed-up crib so that it can be examined immediately after birth. If the infant has no problems, the baby may also be placed on the mother's abdomen, usually with its belly down.

Immediately after birth, the baby is still covered with a grayish slippery coating called the "vernix," which represents old skin. It may also be covered with mucus and blood. The baby's head may not yet have its normal round shape and may be pointy and elongated. The skin of the baby should be dried or covered after birth, to prevent loss of energy and to keep its temperature from dropping.

The baby's status is checked right after birth to see if there are any immediate problems. This is done at one minute and five minutes after birth by scoring the baby according to a system called the Apgar score, named after Dr. Virginia Apgar, the doctor who developed it. There are five separate vital signs in the Apgar score, each with an assigned value of 0, 1, and 2. Zero is the worst and 2 is the best. The five scores are then added up for the total. The five characteristics are:

- The baby's heart rate;
- The baby's breathing;
- The baby's muscle tone;
- The baby's reflexes;
- The baby's color.

An Apgar score of between 8 and 10 indicates that the baby needs no additional help, while a baby with an Apgar score below 4 needs more intensive care.

Only a small number of newborns (fewer than 1 out of 100) require intensive care at birth. This is called "newborn resuscitation," and it follows strict guidelines, known as the ABCs:

A Establish the Airway
B Begin Breathing
C Maintain Circulation.

If the baby has problems breathing, fluid and secretions are suctioned out of the mouth, nose, and other airways with a small bulb syringe or a plastic catheter attached to a suction device. A mask is then placed over the baby's nose and mouth, and air and oxygen are pressed into its lungs using a bag connected to the mask. In rare cases, if the baby still does not breathe by itself, a plastic tube is placed into the baby's windpipe to bring a better supply of air to the its lungs.

Most babies are healthy and stay in the newborn nursery. However, if the baby has any problems or if she or he is too small, the baby may be brought to the neonatal intensive care unit for further care. Babies brought there include those who are too small either because they are premature or because they have not grown enough inside the womb, babies with infections, and those with congenital malformations (see also AIDS; BIRTH DEFECTS; FETAL AND INFANT SUBSTANCE ABUSE SYNDROMES; PRENATAL CARE; RH DISEASE).

NOCTURNAL EMISSIONS Soon after puberty begins, both boys and girls may have erotic dreams while sleeping. In boys, this is often accompanied by ORGASM and EJACULATION, an occurrence known as a nocturnal emission or, commonly, as a "wet dream." Teenaged girls who have erotic dreams may also experience an increase in vaginal secretions and orgasm.

Whether the erotic dream precedes sexual arousal and the nocturnal emission during sleep or whether the nocturnal emission during the REM (Rapid Eye Movement) sleep stage precipitates the erotic dream is unknown. The reasons for the nocturnal orgasm and emissions are also not completely known, but researchers have speculated that they may be due to tight, genitally stimulating night wear; sexual activity without a release of tension; sexual desires that one may not be willing or able to fulfill during waking hours; or the need to urinate.

According to Alfred Kinsey, most males have nocturnal emissions at some point in their lives (some for many years) and at least one-third of all women report having experienced erotic dreams leading to orgasm. The content of erotic dreams, as of any dream, may reflect images that would not be ordinarily considered or thought of during waking hours, such as sex with forbidden partners or bizarre sexual acts. While erotic dreams and orgasms may occur at any time in one's life, they are most common during the teens and twenties for males and the forties for females (see also IMPOTENCE; PUBERTY).

NONMARITAL SEX The term premarital sex has been used to describe the range of interpersonal sexual behavior engaged in by young persons up to the point at which they marry. But the word "premarital" is inadequate and often incorrect for the reality of life in the 1990s. It implies that everyone will marry and that all nonmarital sex is merely a prelude to marital sex. For example, can it be said that a fifty-nine-year-old male who has chosen not to marry but has always maintained an active heterosexual life is still engaging in *pre*marital sex? Or a divorced woman of forty-two, who continues to have an active heterosexual life: should her sexual activities to termed *pre*marital or *post*marital? A similar problem arises with homosexual activity since, with few exceptions, homosexuals are not permitted to marry. A more precise term would be nonmarital sex, that is, sexual acts of any sort between two consenting persons, who are not married to one another at the time. If one partner or both are married at the time, this may be termed extramarital sex (see also ADULTERY; AFFAIRS; DOUBLE STANDARD).

NORPLANT A very effective, reversible method of BIRTH CONTROL. Of 10,000 women using Norplant for a year, only 4 will become pregnant. The reason for this very high rate of effectiveness is that, once implanted, it is mistake-free. Like ORAL CONTRACEPTIVES, it prevents pregnancy through the use of hormones, but instead of having to take a pill every day (which some women forget to do every now and then), six thin, rubber-like implants, about the size of a cardboard matchstick, are inserted under the skin of the woman's upper arm and release the hormone continuously. The hormone used is called levonorgestrel. It is similar to PROGESTERONE, a natural hormone manufactured in the ovaries, and keeps the ovaries from releasing eggs. It also thickens a woman's mucus, keeping sperm from being able to reach the egg, and may also prevent a fertilized egg from attaching itself to the uterus. Norplant is effective for five years.

The initial cost of Norplant—currently about $500—is high, but it is a cost efficient method of birth control because it lasts five years. There are some possible side effects:, the most common is irregular menstrual bleeding. After nine months, the pattern of bleeding generally settles down, but some women experience irregular bleeding throughout the five years. Usually women experience less menstrual blood loss with Norplant than they have before receiving the implant. Other possible side effects include headache, weight gain or loss, change in appetite, sore breasts, nausea, acne, gain or loss of facial hair, and enlarged ovaries or fallopian tubes. As with the pill, combining Norplant and smoking greatly increases the risks of heart attacks and stroke in women over thirty-five years old.

In most women the implants are invisible, though in women who are very muscular or thin, they may be noticeable. There may also be some hardening of the skin over the implant site. Any scar that might be left would be almost invisible. One can feel the implant, however, and some women have expressed the view that if a man feels the implant, he might assume that that woman would have sexual relations with him because she cannot become pregnant. That is an issue she will have to be prepared to address.

As with birth control pills, Norplant does not prevent SEXUALLY TRANSMITTED DISEASES. Women with multiple partners should also use a condom.

NURSE MIDWIVES   see MIDWIVES.

NURSING   see BREAST-FEEDING.

NUTRITION AND PREGNANCY   see PREGNANCY AND DIET; PRENATAL CARE.

NYMPHOMANIA   A term once used to describe the behavior of women deemed to have a pathologically high sex drive. The word nymphomaniac was commonly understood to mean a woman whose "abnormal" sexual LIBIDO drove her to constantly seek sexual encounters. The therapeutic community no longer recognizes nymphomania as a real condition, although some men enjoy fantasizing about "nymphos."

Historically, the term made a value judgment—that a woman who seeks many sexual encounters is deviant or "over-sexed." In reality, if a person's sexual activities are genuinely satisfying and have no negative consequences, a high sex drive is neither bad nor unhealthy.

Sex drive can be a problem, however, if it seriously interferes with one's work, health, or other relationships, or if it compels one to routinely search for risky sexual situations or have many sexual encounters, none of which is truly satisfying. But the underlying reason for such compulsive behavior is not so-called nymphomania. A woman may be trying to use sexual encounters to fulfill other emotional needs. If a person senses her sexual habits may be becoming compulsive, psychological counseling may help (see also HYPERSEXUALITY; SATYRIASIS).

O

OBSCENITY By strict definition, obscenity is language, material, or behavior that is socially or legally considered obscene—lewd, disgusting or intended to incite sexual excitement in an offensive way. But the term obscenity is not always used in a sexual context. In fact, many people consider excessive violence on television to be more obscene than explicit sexual materials. For the purposes of this encyclopedia, obscenity will be considered in its sexual context.

PORNOGRAPHY is literature or art that is regarded as obscene. But the terms are not entirely interchangeable. Obscenity may, and often does, refer to spoken language, gestures, movements, and actions, as well as to literature and art. The problem with the label obscenity is that it is subjective. What one person objects to as obscene may be perfectly acceptable and pleasure-giving to another. Individuals within the same community may have very different tastes and feelings about what is indecent or disgusting.

Many people greatly enjoy the use of obscene language or visual materials. For many couples, sexual excitement is enhanced by "talking dirty" to one another or viewing X-rated videos. A problem emerges only if the couple differs on what is acceptable. No one should ever try to force an unwilling partner to participate in something that disgusts him or her. Between consenting adults in the privacy of the bedroom, if no one is hurt and both receive pleasure, whatever "turns you on" is perfectly acceptable.

OBSTETRICIAN An obstetrician is a physician who has been specifically trained to care for pregnant women throughout their PREGNANCY and during labor and delivery. The training of an obstetrician involves a four-year residency after graduation from medical school. The doctor is also trained as a gynecologist (a specialist in women's reproductive health).

Women see an obstetrician either because they are planning to become pregnant or they already are pregnant. It is usually recommended that they see an obstetrician when pregnancy is planned, because if there are any health problems, they should be addressed well before the onset of pregnancy.

OEDIPUS COMPLEX One of the cornerstones of psychoanalytic theory is the Oedipus complex, the name given by Sigmund Freud to one of the key PSYCHOSEXUAL STAGES OF DEVELOPMENT in boys. According to Freud, the oedipal stage of development is characterized by intense attachment to the mother and rivalry with the father. It is accompanied by feelings of guilt over these incestuous desires and a fear of castration as retribution at the hands of the father. Freud also formulated the more complicated ELECTRA COMPLEX in girls, in which love of the mother, the initial love object, dramatically shifts to love of the father. In girls the Electra complex is accompanied by the same feelings of guilt and fears of retribution.

The name Oedipus refers to the classical Greek legend in which Laius, king of Thebes, was warned that an as yet unborn son would kill him. When, Jocasta, the queen, gave birth to a son, the king ordered the infant to be left exposed to die on the side of a mountain. The infant was found and adopted by King Polybus, who raised him as his own son. As a grown man, Oedipus met Laius and slew him during a quarrel. As Oedipus traveled on, he came upon the Sphinx, who asked him to solve the "riddle of life." As a reward for solving the riddle, Oedipus was made king of Thebes and married his mother, Jocasta. But the gods punished him for this incestuous relationship; in the tragic ending Jocasta hangs herself and Oedipus blinds himself with the brooch used to hold together her queenly robes (see also FREUD, SIGMUND).

OLDER PEOPLE AND SEX see AGING AND SEX.

OOCTYTES see MENSTRUATION; OVARIES.

ORAL CONTRACEPTIVES Often referred to as "The Pill," oral contraceptives are a BIRTH CONTROL method in which a woman takes a daily dose of HORMONE which keeps her OVARIES from releasing eggs. A convenient, safe method of birth control, oral contraceptives can be considered one of the major causes of the SEXUAL REVOLUTION that began in the 1960s, because with their high rate of effectiveness they freed women from the risk of unwanted pregnancies. In typical use, the pill has a failure rate of only 3 per 100 women per year of average use, and with perfect use that drops to a fraction of a percent.

There are two kinds of oral contraceptives—combination pills, which contain two hormones, ESTROGEN and progestin, and the mini-pill which contains only progestin. The pill works by preventing the woman's ovaries from releasing eggs. The mini-pill can also prevent ovulation but it also works by thickening the cervical mucus, keeping sperm from joining with an egg. Mini-pills may also prevent a fertilized egg from implanting itself in the uterus.

In the early days of the pill those in common use contained stronger doses of hormones, which did raise fears about side effects, including an increased risk of breast cancer and lowered libido. Because the dosages have been lowered, these risks have been greatly reduced, though the pill is not recommended for women over thirty-five years of age who smoke. The pill has also been found to reduce the risk of certain other cancers, such as OVARIAN CANCER and UTER-INE CANCER. Because of the dangers associated with complications from pregnancy, most women are safer taking the pill, which is a very effective form of birth control, than not taking it.

There are also some minor side effects that women experience, including bleeding between periods, weight gain or loss, breast tenderness, nausea, and vomiting. These difficulties often disappear after the first three months of use.

The one important danger that must be mentioned is that the pill does not prevent SEXUALLY TRANSMITTED DISEASES and unless a woman is in a stable, monogamous relationship, a condom should be used for prophylactic purposes. The other caution for women taking the pill is that they must remember to take it every day. Even if a woman is not engaging in SEXUAL INTERCOURSE very often, if she skips taking the pill and then resumes doing so later, it may not be effective.

Oral contraceptives must be prescribed by a physician after an examination which can cost between $35 and $125 for a private doctor in the United States (less at a clinic). A monthly supply of birth control pills costs between $15 and $25, but again, lower costs can be expected from a clinic (see also VASECTOMY AND THE MALE PILL).

ORAL SEX A commonly used term that usually refers to mouth-genital contacts. When the stimulation is to a woman's CLITORIS or labia from her partner's mouth or tongue it is called CUNNILINGUS. Sexual stimulation to a man's PENIS by his partner's mouth or tongue is known as FELLATIO. The pleasuring of both partners simultaneously through oral sex is colloquially known as SIXTY-NINE. These sexual acts for women and men may involve either heterosexual or homosexual partners. While oral sex was, until very recently, frequently deemed by Western culture a perversion, there is evidence from artifacts and artistic works that it seems to have been much more acceptable in antiquity. Artistic representations from Asia and other parts of the globe tend to support the view that oral sex is not an uncommon sexual act. Statues and carvings within a religious context in India and represented in the KAMASUTRA have depicted oral sex along with many other variants of sexual activity.

Earlier sex manuals viewed oral sex as essentially a part of FOREPLAY before penetration leading to climax and EJACULATION. Today, there appears to be greater interest in the use of oral sex as a more reliable method than coitus for a man to bring a woman to ORGASM. For many couples, oral sex represents just another method for sexual pleasure and the act can climax in orgasm and ejaculation without moving on to penetration of the woman by the man.

In the absence of adequate sexual education programs, most people in the past had to learn about oral sex from others, who may have been just as unknowledgeable. Urologists have reported that some women, possibly influenced by the street term for oral sex—a "blow job"—have inadvertently injured their male partners by blowing air into the urethra.

Recently, the slang expression "giving head" appears to be gaining in popularity in common parlance rather than the more formal expression, "oral sex." The limitation of these terms to oral-genital contact appears to reflect the historical view that the norm for sex should focus on the genitals, while other forms of sexual stimulation involving the tongue or mouth and areas of the body other than genitals were not and are not considered as variants of oral sex (for example, the oral stimulation of the anal area or breast).

Most people use their mouth and tongue to kiss and lick their partner in nongenital areas. While there is no generally used term for this form of oral sex, there is an old term for KISSING and licking the entire body including the genital areas: "going around the world." The subject of oral sex is a good example of how our languages have not developed adequate and correct terminology for all aspects of human sexual behavior (see also HOMOSEXUALITY; LESBIAN SEX TECHNIQUES; SAFER SEX).

ORGASM The intense feeling of physical pleasure that human beings experience at the climax of sexual stimulation. In the male, orgasm is almost always accompanied by EJACULATION, the spurting from the PENIS of a fluid called semen, which contains spermatozoa, the mobile male seed that, when united with the female egg,

begins the process of CONCEPTION. When the man's penis is inside the woman's VAGINA, the forceful action of orgasm helps push the SPERM toward the CERVIX, the opening to the womb, and to their intended goal, fertilizing the egg. Therefore, the pleasure of male orgasm is directly related to continuation of the species (see also CONCEPTION; SEXUAL INTERCOURSE).

Women also experience orgasm, but the female orgasm is not required for procreation to occur. A woman need not enjoy a sexual episode to become impregnated. In fact, in Victorian times some mothers told their daughters that sex was something only to be endured for the pleasure of the male. On the other hand, the pleasure of the female orgasm, together with the desire to have children, is one of the reasons that women, like men, seek INTIMACY and fulfilment—so it does play a role in procreation.

The pleasure and sensation of climax that a man feels from orgasm is centered on the male sexual organ. Women report a wider range of orgasmic sensations; many experience an intense climax which may be centered on the CLITORIS while some report more diffused sensations. In years past, before the development of modern sex research, uncertainty about the nature of women's orgasms encouraged controversy, instigated in great part by Sigmund Freud, over whether women could experience two different types of orgasm—one clitoral and the other vaginal. Freud postulated that a woman had a clitoral orgasm when her clitoris was directly stimulated and a vaginal orgasm without any stimulation to the clitoris, and that the so-called "vaginal" orgasm was the more intense and more "mature" of the two. Many people today continue to believe that if a woman does not have an orgasm during intercourse brought about by the movement of the penis inside her vagina, she is somehow lacking. We now know that this is not true.

All female orgasms are clitoral orgasms, meaning that it is always the stimulation of the clitoris that triggers the orgasm. For most women the clitoris must come into direct contact with something—a finger, tongue, or vibrator—in order for her to have an orgasm. For about one-third of all women, the movement of the penis inside the vagina creates enough stimulation on the clitoris and the adjacent area to produce an orgasm from intercourse alone. For many other women, prior direct clitoral stimulation can bring orgasm close enough so that the movement of the penis inside the vagina during intercourse then becomes a strong enough trigger. Others can only reach orgasm from direct stimulation, which can take place prior to, during, after, or without intercourse.

Literature and the media have helped spread the idea that there is an "ideal" orgasm, which both partners reach together during intercourse and during which "the earth moves" (actually, it was the writer Ernest Hemingway who coined the phrase in his 1940 novel, *For Whom the Bell Tolls*). Many couples become frustrated with their sex lives because they cannot attain this goal. While such simultaneous intensity is not a myth, it is a rare enough occurrence to be something that should not be sought directly, but instead enjoyed if it happens. Instead, couples should learn to appreciate sexual satisfaction by whatever means it takes them to achieve it. Orgasms are not all alike, but each is pleasurable in its own way.

The male orgasm is usually strongest in younger men. As a man grows older, the strength at which the semen is ejaculated diminishes, as does the intensity of the orgasmic experience. (As they grow older, men also require a longer time to obtain an erection after an orgasm.) This time necessary for orgasmic response to occur in a man can be very short. Sometimes this time period is too short, a condition called premature ejaculation. This condition is not physical; it is often a conditioned or psychological disability that can be changed so that the man can, to a greater extent, gain control over the timing of his orgasm. Either because of a physical problem or because of intense training, a man's orgasms may appear not to be accompanied by ejaculation.

The SEXUAL RESPONSE CYCLE is similar in men and women, though women differ in their capacities to have multiple orgasms and their overall response time is usually slower than that of males. There are four stages to the cycle. The first is called the *excitement stage*, in which the body begins to react to sexual stimuli. These can be anything: a sight, a sound, an odor, a touch, or just a memory of a past experience. In the male it begins with an ERECTION, while in females the first reaction is LUBRICATION of the vagina, which results from engorgement of the vaginal blood vessels.

If the stimuli continue, excitement increases and the next stage, called the *plateau stage*, is reached. The name comes from the fact that this stage can continue for a long or short time, depending on the desire of the people involved. During this stage, blood trapped in the sex organs of both sexes causes a pleasurable swelling.

The *orgasmic stage* is reached when the male or female has reached a high degree of sexual tension, triggering an orgasm and a series of muscular contractions in or near the sex organs. According to research done by MASTERS AND JOHNSON, there may be from six to fifteen contractions, each lasting for about a second in the male and occurring more rapidly—often as a "fluttering"—in the female. In the male the mind perceives the orgasm as taking place in the penis, the prostate gland, and the seminal vesicles, while in the female the mind perceives it as taking place in the muscles and tissues around the clitoris and in the vagina and UTERUS. In both sexes, though it is often more pronounced in the female, the whole body can also be involved, often with spasmodic contractions of the limbs, fingers, toes, or face. Some women are multi-orgasmic and may experience many orgasms before achieving complete satisfaction.

In males, the RESOLUTION PHASE comes immediately after orgasm, as the body relaxes and breathing and blood pressure return to normal. There follows a *refractory period*, during which a man cannot have a new erection. In young men this period can be only a few minutes, while in older men it can last for several days. The resolution phase is longer in women, who bask in what is called the AFTERGLOW. During this period they seek continued physical INTIMACY to fully experience sexual satisfaction. However, women's refractory periods are shorter than men's, permitting some of them to experience multiple orgasms some of the time.

While most men do not have any difficulties experiencing orgasms, the same is not true of all women. For many years the term frigid was applied to women who were not orgasmic, but that has been replaced with the word preorgasmic, because in most cases these women can be taught how to have orgasms, usually by teaching them to masturbate (see also AGING AND SEX; FAKING ORGASM; EJACULATION; FREUD, SIGMUND; MASTURBATION; MOMENT OF INEVITABILITY; PARAPLEGICS AND SEX; SEXUAL INTERCOURSE; VIBRATORS).

ORGASMS, MULTIPLE William H. Masters and Virginia Johnson, the pioneering American sex researchers (see MASTERS AND JOHNSON) reported in *Human Sexual Response* (1966) that most women participating in their study felt that mechanical automanipulation to the mons area with the aid of a vibrator produced the kind of stimulation that resulted not only in the fastest and the most intense orgasms but also in multiple orgasms during a single sexual episode. Masters and Johnson reported to a colleague:

> *The average female with optimal arousal will usually be satisfied with three to five manually induced orgasms; whereas mechanical stimulation, as with the electric vibrator, is less tiring and induces her to go on to long stimulative sessions of an hour or more during which she may have twenty to fifty consecutive orgasms.*

At about the same time Mary Sherfey, a psychoanalyst, reported in an article in the *Journal of the American Psychoanalytic Association* (and repeated later in her book, *The Nature and Evolution of Female Sexuality*) that:

> *In clinical practice, a number of married and single women using the electric vibrator to achieve up to fifty orgasms in a single session have come to my attention in the past few years. ... From the standpoint of normal physiological functioning, these women exhibit a healthy, uninhibited sexuality—and the number of orgasms attained, [are] a measure of the human female's orgasmic potentiality. .*

Multiple orgasms during a single sexual episode, that is, before loss of sexual excitement sets in, appears almost exclusively in women. Although there have been some reports of multiple orgasms in males, there is some question as to whether or not they are complete orgasms or a resumption of an interrupted orgasm just before the MOMENT OF INEVITABILITY.

The main reason for the discrepancy between men and women is that while both go through a RESOLUTION PHASE, during which the body returns to the presexual excitement state, only males go through an automatic refractory period, when they experience the ejaculation that accompanies their orgasm. During this period, men quickly lose their sexual excitement and require renewed stimulation to rejuvenate their sexual desires before another orgasm and ejaculation can occur. For men this may take from a few minutes to a few hours to a few days, depending on age, physical condition, and strength of libido. Women, however, do not go through such a refractory period immediately after reaching orgasm. Instead, they remain at a high level of excitement that only slowly—for some women, very slowly—subsides. During this time, if the woman is properly stimulated, she may achieve orgasm again and again.

Some women report that their orgasms may increase in intensity during these multiple orgasm sessions to a level in which they appear to faint from pleasure. Even among males who claim to have had multiple orgasms, none approaches the number of orgasms reported by women.

Compared with the intensity of sexual excitation in women produced by CUNNILINGUS, manual stimulation, and the use of VIBRATORS, rarely are there reports of multiple orgasms occurring from coitus alone. While many women are desirous of multiple orgasms once they become aware that they are capable of them, others are content with one orgasm and still others find the attempt at continuing stimulation after orgasm either unpleasant or even painful. Multiple orgasms should not be a goal imposed upon a woman, and the inability to have multiple orgasms does not constitute sexual dysfunction.

OSTEOPOROSIS   see HORMONE REPLACEMENT THERAPY; MENOPAUSE.

OVARIAN CANCER   Ovarian carcinoma is the third most common gynecological cancer (following BREAST CANCER and UTERINE CANCER), but is the major cause of death from cancer of the female genital tract. Ovarian cancer is a disease of aging: its incidence rises with age up to age seventy-seven. Despite numerous investigations, the precise cause of ovarian cancer has not been determined, but it is thought to be linked to frequent ovulation. Therefore, the protective effect of several pregnancies or the use of ORAL CONTRACEPTIVES is noteworthy. On the other hand, women who experience late MENOPAUSE or late childbearing are at increased risk. Ovarian cancer has also been associated with a diet high in animal fat and is more common among women with a family history of cancer, especially of the ovary or breast.

Screening and Early Diagnosis. There are no satisfying screening procedures for ovarian cancer. Nevertheless, attempts should be made to recognize the cancer as soon as possible. Symptoms in the early stages of the cancer, such as abdominal distention, pain, or discomfort are important, although they usually indicate that the cancer has spread. Enlargement of the ovary beyond 2 1/2 inches is considered abnormal. Usually an ovarian mass in a menstruating woman is a functional cyst, which will disappear spontaneously. Beyond age forty the risk of malignancy rises and the mass must be carefully evaluated. An ultrasound examination helps to evaluate the size of the ovarian mass and to differentiate between functional ovarian cysts and tumors.

Treatment. If a diagnosis of ovarian cancer is made, the surgeon will remove both OVARIES and the UTERUS, FALLOPIAN TUBES, and any other cancerous mass within the abdominal cavity. When the cancer has spread, as is the case in most patients, chemotherapy will be needed as well. It is important to discuss and realize the consequences of such treatment. Following surgery, the woman will be unable to become pregnant and will have an artificial MENOPAUSE.

Not all ovarian tumors are malignant. This is especially true in young women in their reproductive years. An experienced pathologist can determine the exact pathology of the tumor and a conservative treatment will suffice. In this way young women during their reproductive years will be able to conserve their fertility potential.

OVARIES   A woman's internal organs, located on either side of the UTERUS. They are responsible for the monthly release of oocytes (ova) and the production of the female sex HORMONES, ESTROGEN and PROGESTERONE. The ovaries are small, the size and shape of a large almond, but they determine much of a woman's physiology. At puberty hormones from the ovaries stimulate the growth of secondary sexual characteristics, body hair, and the distribution of soft, fatty tissue in the body. Most important, the ovaries give a woman the ability to reproduce.

The ovaries respond to stimulation by "gonadotropins"—luteinizing hormone (LH) and follicle stimulating hormone (FSH)—secreted by the pituitary gland. Gonadotropins stimulate cells in the ovary to produce the sex hormones, control maturation of the follicle that contains the developing egg, and stimulate ovulation. These pituitary hormones also cause the ovary to initiate the female menstrual cycle, preparing the uterus each month to receive a fertilized egg.

The ovaries consist of two basic components; stroma, or cells that make up the bulk of the ovary, and follicles. The stroma contains blood vessels and nerves and helps support and encapsulate the ovary. The follicles are the structures that develop around the oocytes (eggs), providing nourishment and support to them. The follicle cells also secrete the female sex hormones.

The number of oocytes per ovary is determined during fetal development and does not change over the life of the woman. About 200,000 ova are present in each ovary when a female infant is born.

Hormonal changes during puberty stimulate the follicles that contain each egg to begin developing. The egg itself does not undergo any changes during follicular development, but the follicle surrounding the egg changes both in size

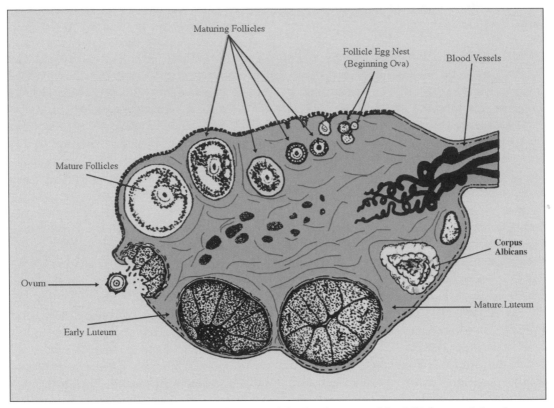

The anatomy of an ovary, showing several stages of the development of the follicle containing the ovum and the breakdown of the corpus luteum after ovulation.

and function (see also CONCEPTION; FEMALE SEX ORGANS; HYSTERECTOMY; MENSTRUATION).

OVULATION see CONCEPTION; MENSTRUATION; PREMENSTRUAL SYNDROME (PMS).

P-Q

PAP TEST   A simple but important procedure designed to detect abnormal cells in the cervix — a condition physicians call dysplasia or cervical intraepithelial neoplasia (CIN) — which can indicate the presence of or potential for CERVICAL CANCER.

The Pap test, or smear, is usually performed once a year — but it may be performed more or less often, depending on a doctor's advice. The Pap test is named after Dr. George Papanicolaou, who developed the technique of swabbing or scraping the cervix and surrounding areas to collect samples of cells, which are then "smeared" on a slide and sprayed with a fixing solution to preserve them. The procedure is generally done to supplement a routine pelvic ("internal") examination in the gynecologist's office. It is almost always painless and has no side effects. The smear is then sent to a pathologist, a doctor specially trained to analyze cell structure. A woman should not douche for at least twenty-four hours before having the test, as douching reduces the number of cells available for analysis.

If all cells appear normal, the tissue of the cervix is presumed to be healthy and the results are termed "negative." The appearance of abnormal cells in the sample may signal that further tests are necessary to determine the cause.

In addition to its use in detecting early stages of cervical cancer, the Pap test is used in diagnosing infections and in determining a woman's estrogen level. This is important in determining whether a woman experiencing menopause needs estrogen replacement therapy.

PARAPLEGICS AND SEX   The spinal cord functions like a telephone cable, linking the brain with the body's other organs. When the spinal cord is injured, many neurological impairments result, including sexual dysfunction. When the cord is severely injured quadriplegia (paralysis of all four extremities) results; if the lower half is interrupted, the lower half of the body is paralyzed (paraplegia).

In women with paraplegia or quadriplegia, transient AMENORRHEA (no menstrual periods) lasts for approximately six months from the time of spinal cord injury (SCI). Their ability to be pregnant is restored with the return of menstruation. Although women with complete SCI are not able to feel sensations in the genital area, they may have orgasms if other sensitive areas in the rest of the body, above the level of the neurologic damage, are stimulated — the ears, neck, nipples, etc. However, spasticity (involuntary muscle spasms) of the legs and poor vaginal secretion may be problematic during sexual intercourse. Under such circumstances, the use of antispastic medication, gentle leg muscle stretching, and lubrication of the genital area are useful prior to physical intimacy. During pregnancy, SCI women are prone to developing urinary tract infections. While in labor, women with quadriplegia or high paraplegia may experience various symptoms, including headaches, excessive sweating, high blood pressure, and changes in the heart rate. The development of this clinical syndrome, known medically as automatic hyperreflexia (overactivity of the physiological reflexes), should be closely watched until the baby is delivered. After delivery, women in this category are considered to be at high risk for thrombophlebitis (blood clots forming in veins) in the pelvis or lower extremities.

Males with quadriplegia or paraplegia commonly experience erections of the penis induced by spasticity. However, such erections are frequently of short duration and do not usually last long enough to enable them to engage a female partner satisfactorily. Male patients who have suffered damage in the lower end of the spinal cord or in the bundle of nerves exiting the lower end of the cord may experience IMPOTENCE. However, male patients lacking adequate erections may be assisted through the use of an external mechanical device such as a vacuum pump with a proximal penile ring. Also, intrapenile injections of papaverine (a blood vessel dilator) just before intercourse may cause erections. For selected cases, penile prostheses are available and can be implanted surgically (see also IMPOTENCE).

When psychologically excited during sexual activity, SCI males may fall out of bed due to heightened muscle spasticity in their bodies. Unfortunately, the majority of male quadriplegics and paraplegics do not experience orgasm or ejaculation. To assist ejaculation when fertility is desired, the injection of prostigmin (a muscle stimulant) into the spinal fluid was tried in the past. However, if prostigmin is used, caution should be taken because it can be accompanied by serious side effects such as high blood pressure and even cerebral hemorrhage. Intrarectal electrical stimulation and penile electrovibration are the two most commonly used methods today and reasonably good results have been obtained. However, there is also a possibility of developing autonomic hyperreflexia during electrical stimulation for ejaculation. Further research is required to improve the quality of sperm in quadriplegic and paraplegic males in order to make successful fertilization possible (see also HANDICAPPED PERSONS AND SEX).

PEDOPHILIA   see CHILD ABUSE; CHILD MOLESTATION LAWS; PROSTITUTION: MALE.

PEEPING TOMS   see VOYEURISM.

PELVIC EXAMINATION   The pelvic examination is that part of the medical examination of a woman in which the physician or other practitioner, by inspection (seeing) and palpation (feeling) of the reproductive organs, can deter-

mine the condition of the external and internal reproductive structures. During the pelvic examination, other procedures such as obtaining a Pap smear or a culture of the cervix can also be performed.

The pelvic examination is performed with the patient lying on her back on an examining table equipped with supports for the woman's legs. The patient places her heels or legs in the leg supports, slides down to the edge of the table, and separates her knees. The practitioner generally covers the woman's legs and abdomen with a drape for reasons of modesty and to decrease the patient's feeling of vulnerability. An examining lamp is utilized to allow better viewing by the practitioner.

The initial step of the pelvic examination is inspection and palpation of the external genitalia. The practitioner examines the mons, clitoris, labia majora and minora, perineum, and perianal area. Evidence of irritation, growths, or infections can be seen at this point. The examiner may palpate the Bartholin glands at the side of the vaginal opening and the urethra. The vaginal walls are inspected and their supporting structures observed. Prolapse of the walls of the vagina is noted at this stage and the hymen's condition is observed.

The next part of the examination is with the speculum, an instrument made of either metal or plastic with two rounded blades that can be separated. The speculum is designed to separate the top and bottom walls of the vagina so that the cervix can be seen. After inserting the speculum into the vagina and opening the blades, one can observe the walls of the vagina and see the cervix between the blades of the speculum. The blades of the speculum come in many sizes, designed to fit all vaginal sizes. With a speculum in place, a Pap smear or cultures can be obtained (see PAP TEST).

The speculum examination, like other parts of the pelvic examination, should not produce pain unless there is a condition present that results in pain. This part of the examination can be made more comfortable by coating the blades of the speculum with either a lubricant or water, selecting a blade appropriate to the size of the woman, and warming the otherwise cold metal speculum to body temperature before use.

The next part of the pelvic examination is the bimanual examination, in which both of the practitioner's hands are used. Two fingers are inserted into the vagina and the opposite hand is placed on the woman's abdomen so that the uterus and ovaries can be felt through the abdominal wall. During the bimanual examination, the examiner can palpate the cervix to determine its shape, size, and position and can evaluate the uterus for size, shape, position and consistency. The adnexa (tissues next to the uterus, including the fallopian tubes and ovaries) are also palpated. These can usually not be distinguished one from the other during a pelvic examination because the fallopian tubes are usually of the same consistency as surrounding tissues. The ovaries can usually be felt and their size, shape, and consistency determined. Ovaries of postmenopausal women are usually too small to feel on examination.

The final step in a pelvic examination is a recto-vaginal examination. This is to determine if there are abnormalities in the rectum and on the uterosacral ligament, one of the supporting structures of the uterus. Frequently, a recto-vaginal examination will improve palpation of the ovaries as well. During a recto-vaginal examination, a finger is inserted into the rectum and an adjacent finger into the vagina. Abnormalities in the septum between the vagina and rectum can also be felt at this time. When the examining finger is removed from the rectum, it can be observed for the presence of blood, which would signify the need for further evaluation, since finding blood in the rectum may be a sign of a disease of the gastrointestinal tract. The recto-vaginal examination is the most uncomfortable part of the procedure and is not always done at every pelvic examination.

Although there is no general agreement on the age at which a young woman should have her first pelvic examination, whenever there is a problem involving lower abdominal or pelvic pain, discharge, or abnormal bleeding, an examination should be performed. If the young woman has no symptoms, it is usually suggested that a pelvic examination be done before becoming sexually active or when obtaining contraception. The examination can be done without affecting the hymen if there is an ample opening in the center of the tissue. If not, much information can be gleaned by inspection and a rectal examination. A pelvic examination should be performed when obtaining a Pap smear, usually annually in young, sexually active women. While there is no agreed upon frequency for routine pelvic examinations, annual examinations are usual for young, sexually active women (see also GENITO-UROLOGICAL EXAMINATION; GYNECOLOGICAL EXAMINATION—THE FIRST VISIT).

PELVIC INFLAMMATORY DISEASE (PID) The term pelvic inflammatory disease (PID) describes all pelvic infections, including those resulting from an infected appendix, diverticuli, or fistula. More commonly it results from an ascending infection of pathogenic bacteria from the lower genital tract. It is estimated that in developed countries, 20 out of 100 women between fifteen and twenty-four years of age acquire PID each year. PID accounts for 25 percent of all admissions to gynecological services.

The major risk factors for PID are having multiple sexual partners, low socioeconomic status, previous episodes of PID, using an intrauterine contraceptive device (IUD), and young age. On the other hand several factors are known to provide some protection against PID:

- Pregnancy, especially after eight to ten weeks of gestation, protects from ascending infection and PID. After this stage PID is very uncommon.
- Women over forty-five years of age rarely develop PID.
- Using a condom as a contraceptive may protect against the spread of venereal diseases in general and have a special implication in preventing PID.
- Oral contraceptive pills offer some protection against ascending infections because of their negative influence on the receptivity of the cervical mucus.

Several sexually transmitted mircroorgisms such as *Neisseria gonorrhea* (gonococcus) and

Chlamydia trachomatis are responsible for most PID infections. If a woman is culture-positive for gonococcus, her male partner has a positive urethral culture about 86 percent of the time. However, only half of these men will have any symptoms. The clinical picture of gonococcal PID is lower abdominal pain, beginning several days after sexual intercourse, accompanied by fever and vaginal discharge.

In the industrialized nations, *Chlamydia trachomatis* may be cultured from the cervix of 5 to 15 percent of asymptomatic women of reproductive age. About one-fourth of women who are cervical culture-positive for gonococcus are also culture-positive for chlamydia. The clinical picture of PID associated with chlamydia is less severe and sometimes asymptomatic. However, both organisms may result in late complications of tubal and pelvic adhesions that may impair future fertility in 20 to 30 percent of the patients.

Other pathogens have been cultured from the fallopian tubes of patients with PID. These included mycoplasma, pneumococci, campylobacter, tuberculosis, and anaerobic bacteria.

The inflammatory process in PID usually begins in the cervical epithelium as cervicitis, followed by uterine infection (endometritis), tubal infection (salpingitis), and eventually abdominal cavity infection (peritonitis). As the infection proceeds, fibrin deposits, along with other inflammatory cells, may damage the tubes, distorting their delicate structure.

Both asymptomatic carriers of *Neisseria gonorrhea* (gonococcus) and *Chlamydia trachomatis* and symptomatic patients need antibiotic treatment to prevent complications. Penicillins, tetracycline, or sulfonamides are usually used, but other equally effective regimens are also available. LAPAROSCOPY is sometimes used to confirm the diagnosis and to obtain cultures in order to give specific antibiotic treatment according to the specific microorganism.

Complications of PID are:
- Tubal and ovarian abscesses: these may require laparotomy and often adnexectomy;
- Recurrence and reinfection: these may require hospitalization and intravenous antibiotic treatment;
- Intrauterine, tubal, peritubal, and pelvic adhesions: these may cause infertility;
- Tubal infections: sactosalpinx, hydrosalpinx, pyosalpinx, or hematosalpinx;
- Peritonitis: a general infection of the abdominal cavity;
- Douglas's abscess: an abscess located between the uterus and the rectum.

Early recognition and treatment of PID will, in most cases, prevent complications. Using a condom and treatment for the sexual partners of a woman with PID will protect against the spread of venereal disease (see also CONDOMS; GONORRHEA AND CHLAMYDIA; SAFER SEX).

PENILE PROSTHESIS   see IMPOTENCE.

PENIS   The male's sexual and reproduction organ. In sexual intercourse, the erect penis (see ERECTION) is inserted in the female partner's vagina and remains there until ORGASM and EJACULATION of seminal fluid, which may or may not impregnate the female.

The human penis has a soft bulge at the tip called the "glans," a body, or "shaft," and a root, called the "crus" of the penis, buried in the pubic area. In uncircumcised males the glans is covered by loose skin called the foreskin. Many, if not most, males in the industrialized West are circumcised; their foreskins have been surgically removed shortly after birth for hygienic or religious reasons (see CIRCUMCISION).

Three elongated structures, the two *corpora cavernosa* and the urethra, constitute the body of the penis. Within the penis, but located closer to the top or the back of the penis's body, are the *corpora cavernosa*, two cylindrical tubes, usually flattened, placed side by side. Each is composed of inner sponge-like tissue surrounded by a very dense fascia, a band-like lining, called the *tunica albuginea*. (This is the densest fascia in humans, much thicker than the dura mater, the fascia that surrounds the brain.) This lining does not totally separate the two *corpora cavernosa*, and several passages allow blood to circulate from one to the other. The sponge-like tissue inside them is best described as a mesh of spaces and cavities separated and surrounded by thick

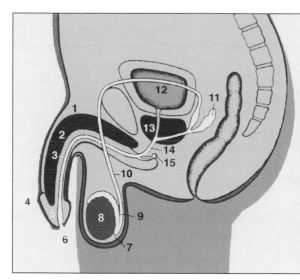

THE MALE SEX ORGANS
1. Penis
2. Corpus cavernosum (one of a pair)
3. Corpus spongiosum
4. Foreskin
5. Glans
6. Opening of urethra
7. Scrotum
8. Testicle (one of a pair)
9. Epididymis (one of a pair)
10. Vas deferens (one of a pair)
11. Seminal vesticle (one of a pair)
12. Urinary bladder
13. Prostate gland
14. Urethra
15. Bulbourethral (Cowper's) gland (one of a pair)

layers of muscle tissue. In the center of each *corpus cavernosum* is an artery with corkscrew-shaped branches that supply blood to each of the tiny cavities.

Underneath the two *corpora cavernosa*, on the penis's midline, lies the third tubular structure, the urethra. The urethra serves as the conduit for urine or semen to the opening at the tip of the glans, called the meatus. The urethra is surrounded by the *corpus spongiosum*, sponge-like tissue that is also capable of engorgement and erection. The *corpus spongiosum* also forms the glans. Unlike the *corpora cavernosa*, the erectile tissue of the *corpus spongiosum* and glans is not contained in a thick fascia like the *tunica albuginea*. No vascular communication exists between the *corpus cavernosum* and the *corpus spongiosum*.

The *corpora cavernosa* separate near the root, or base, of the penis like two branches of the letter "Y." At the point of bifurcation, a ligament links the *corpora* to the pubic bone. Furthermore, each branch of the "Y" is attached to a region of the pelvic bone known as the ischium. This buttressing of the *corpora* to the bone accounts for the change of angulation that occurs when a flaccid penis becomes erect. As a man ages, the suspensory ligament of the penis stretches, explaining why in a man of seventy the erect penis may be pointing downward. The urethra curves upward, passes between the separated *corpora*, and connects to the bladder.

The head of the penis—known medically as the glans—has a conical shape, with the meatus (penis's opening) at its tip and a corona (crown or cornice) at its base. The glans is the external extension of the *corpus spongiosum*, and as noted, in the uncircumcised male it is covered by the foreskin. During erection, blood pressure in the glans is about half the pressure in the *corpus cavernosum*, enabling blood to drain freely into the penis's shaft. One function of the glans is to act as a shock absorber and protect the woman's cervix from the man's thrusting during intercourse. Vaginal pressure keeps the glans full and improves the seal with the corona; this increases friction and promotes ejaculation and the retention of semen near the cervix, where sperm enter to impregnate the woman.

The foreskin covers the glans almost completely at birth. Its opening is tight and the infant's foreskin usually cannot be retracted from the glans. Unless it is removed by circumcision shortly after birth, the foreskin usually loosens and retraction becomes possible as the infant matures. (It is an unresolved question whether the presence of a foreskin increases the sexual pleasure experienced by both partners). The foreskin's function is to protect the sensitive skin of the glans, and some have postulated that it may play a role in the development of the glans during gestation. Removal of the foreskin after birth is a religious practice of Jews and Muslims and has become common even among the general population in some Western societies because it makes it easier to clean the area around the glans. In recent years objections have been raised by by some parents and physicians that male circumcision is unnecessary, and some parents refuse it for newborn sons. Male circumcision is totally unlike female circumcision in its objectives and effects (see CLITORIDECTOMY).

There is a great variation in penis size and in the change in penis size from the flaccid, or soft, state to partial or full erection. This is true both when different persons are compared and for any single individual over his lifetime and even in the course of a single day. Sex therapists and researchers have established that size variations of the penis have little to do with the ability to please a partner or to father children. Variations in penis size are due, in part, to differences in the proportion of the penis that is buried (the crus) and exposed (the body) Individuals with a short crus have larger penises, but during erection the penis may point downward. Those with a larger

Sperm produced in the testicles travel through the epididymis and vas deferens. The seminal vesicles and prostate add their fluids to the sperm to create semen, which is ejaculated through the urethra and out the tip of the penis.

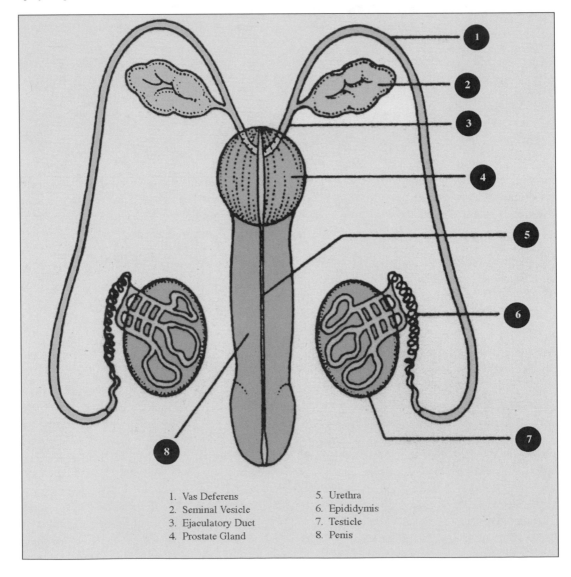

1. Vas Deferens
2. Seminal Vesicle
3. Ejaculatory Duct
4. Prostate Gland
5. Urethra
6. Epididymis
7. Testicle
8. Penis

crus may have penises with shorter bodies and erections that point outward or upward. Variation in the change of size of the penis from the flaccid to the erect state means that men with penises of similar size when flaccid will have erect penises of very different sizes. Individuals will also have erections of different sizes and firmness depending on their physical and emotional state and their state of arousal.

There is no correlation between body size and penis length. Evidence exists that penis size and length decrease with age, but this occurs gradually and most often is not noticed. Penis length can be altered by weight loss: this diminishes the thickness of fat in the pubic area. A good rule of thumb is, "one inch gained in penis length for every thirty pounds of weight loss" (see also CLEANLINESS AND SEXUAL ODORS; EJACULATION; ERECTION; IMPOTENCE; PSYCHOGENIC ERECTION).

PERFORMANCE ANXIETY   see ANTICIPA-TORY ANXIETY.

PITUITARY GLAND AND HORMONE SE-CRETION   A small endocrine gland located at the base of the brain that functions as the regulator of the endocrine system, responding to sig-nals from the central nervous system and passing them on to the rest of the endocrine glands. The endocrine gland secretes HORMONES, the molecules that regulate growth, development, and reproduction and help maintain many metabolic functions of the body.

The central nervous system (CNS) and the endocrine system cooperate in controlling the internal environment of the body in a process known as homeostasis. The CNS receives information about the external environment, such as changes in temperature or day length, and is aware of conditions within the body, such as how the respiratory or digestive system are functioning, and changes in metabolic activity. This information is previewed and relayed to the pituitary through the hypothalamus, a small area of the brain near the pituitary. The messages are changed to chemical, or hormonal, messages. The pituitary then sends out these hormonal messages, and they stimulate other endocrine glands or somatic cells to regulate their activity. Each hormone stimulates a specific endocrine gland, called the target organ, and a specific response within the target organ.

The pituitary has two lobes: the anterior (front) lobe and the posterior (rear) one. The an-

In the female (left), two hormones, FSH and LH, are released from the pituitary gland throughout the month. The ovarian hormones, estrogen and progesterone, help prepare the cervix and uterus for conception. In the male (right), LH and FSH, also released from the pituitary glands, stimulate the testes to produce testosterone and stimulate the production of sperm. Testosterone influences fat and hair distribution.

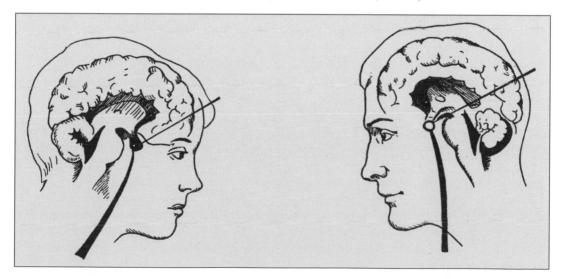

terior pituitary produces trophic hormones. The response may be secretion of hormones, or increased protein production or metabolic activity. The reproductive trophic hormones are called gonadotropins; they control activity of the gonads (ovaries or testicles) and stimulate gamete (egg or sperm) production. There are two gonadotropins, luteinizing hormone (LH) and follicle stimulating hormone (FSH). LH stimulates hormone-producing cells in both the female ovaries and male testes; FSH stimulates development of the sperm cells, or gametes. Other trophic hormones are thyroid stimulating hormone (TSH), which stimulates the thyroid, and adrenocorticotropin (ACTH), which acts on the adrenal gland. Growth hormone, secreted especially during childhood, regulates the ultimate height of an individual. Prolactin, which stimulates milk production, is also produced by the anterior pituitary.

The trophic hormones and other hormones from the pituitary are secreted in response to changing concentrations in the blood of hormones produced by target organs. For instance, hormones from the gonads—testosterone from the male and estrogens from the female—inhibit secretion of the gonadotropins, maintaining homeostasis. Estrogen and testosterone levels are detected by the hypothalamus of the brain. It then signals the pituitary to increase or decrease gonadotropin secretion, depending on the needs of the system. This control mechanism is known as negative feedback. In this way the endocrine system maintains a balance in body functions and systems. In the reproductive system, it helps to regulate the menstrual cycle in the female and sperm production in the male (see also MENSTRUATION; TESTICLES).

The posterior lobe of the pituitary produces hormones that regulate water retention and uterine contractions at the time of birth.

PLACENTA The placenta is the envelope within which a fetus grows and develops in the mother's uterus (womb) during the nine months of a normal pregnancy. It is in the placenta that the blood supply of the future baby and the mother come into intimate contact, allowing the transfer between mother and fetus of the nutritional and other chemical substances essential to the fetus's growth and development. Thus, the placenta serves as the organ of respiration, nutrition, and excretion for the future baby while it is developing within the mother.

The placenta is formed early in the pregnancy when finger-like projections called trophoblasts enter the lining of the mother's uterus. Blood from the mother reaches the placenta through blood vessels in the uterus, and blood from the fetus reaches the placenta through two umbilical arteries located in the umbilical cord, which extends from the fetus's navel to the placenta.

The mother's blood never circulates inside the fetus, nor does the fetus's blood circulate inside the mother. The nutrition and substances needed by the fetus can cross the "placental barrier," while many organisms cannot. Thus, the mother may be suffering from a bad cold and the fetus will remain healthy. However, many viruses and disease organisms can pass through the placental barrier, among them the AIDS virus, syphilis, and German measles. Some drugs taken by the mother can also pass through the barrier.

The placenta itself produces many of the hormones necessary for proper regulation of the pregnancy. For example, it makes human chorionic gonadotropin (hCG), which is the hormone measured by pregnancy tests. Hormones from the placenta help alter the mother's body to accept and adjust to pregnancy and to help her develop the ability to nurse the newly born child. The placenta makes several steroid hormones as well and is capable of producing progesterone from substances obtained from the mother. The progesterone in turn helps to maintain the developing pregnancy. Using hormones produced by the fetus, the placenta can also produce high levels of estriol, the estrogen most plentiful during pregnancy.

During the pregnancy, all the nutrients required for sustenance and development of the future baby are transferred to the fetus through the placenta from the mother's blood supply. The oxygen needed by the fetus to live is transferred through the placenta to the fetal blood stream from the mother's blood supply. Similarly, the waste products from the fetus are excreted by the mother after they have been transferred to her through the placenta.

A healthy placenta is critical to survival of the future baby. If anything happened to separate the placenta from the mother's uterus, such as an abdominal injury from an automobile accident, the fetus would immediately suffocate and die. After the new baby is delivered, the placenta usually separates from the mother's uterus spontaneously and is also delivered (it is then called the "afterbirth"; see also BIRTH).

Usually the placenta is discarded with other biological wastes after birth, but under special circumstances the placenta and its products may be salvaged after birth of the baby. The hCG hormone can be extracted from the placenta, and steroids and protein hormones can be and have been extracted from it for experimental use. Placenta collection is limited to a fairly small number of hospitals. Obviously, the mother has a say in what happens to the placenta, although the issue is rarely raised.

Interestingly, humans are the only known mammals that do not eat the placenta after birth of their young. Other primates do eat it after delivery. In some primitive human cultures the placenta is given a ceremonial burial (see also HIGH-RISK PREGNANCY).

PLANNED PARENTHOOD AND MARGARET SANGER Planned Parenthood of America is a voluntary reproductive health organization with nearly 900 clinics across the country organized under an umbrella of 170 nonprofit corporations. Its roots lie in a clinic formed by a nurse, Margaret Sanger (1879–1966), who in 1916 defied then-current laws by opening a clinic that offered information about contraception. This was illegal because in the 1870s antiobscenity laws had been adopted in the United States which forbade the importing or mailing of contraceptives and contraceptive information. These laws were passed at the instigation of New York Congressman Anthony Comstock and were known as the Comstock Laws.

As a maternity nurse, Sanger knew that many of the women she helped did not want to have any more children but did not know what to do to prevent becoming pregnant. Even doctors were forbidden from disseminating such information. Sanger vowed to fight these laws after witnessing the death from an illegal abortion of a woman whom Sanger had treated once before because of the effects of another illegal abortion.

Sanger traveled to Europe to learn the methods of preventing pregnancy that existed there, and returned to the United States to publish a newspaper called *The Woman Rebel*, in which she coined the term "birth control." Sanger was indicted by the federal government in 1914 and fled back to Europe to avoid trial. During her second stay in Europe she learned more about a method of birth control called the diaphragm. She returned to the United States in 1915 to face trial, but growing support in America for her cause forced the government to drop the indictment. She began to travel around the country starting advocacy organizations for birth control, several of which eventually became the predecessors of today's Planned Parenthood affiliates.

On 16 October 1916 Sanger opened a storefront office in the Brownsville neighborhood of Brooklyn, New York, where she began to provide contraceptive advice. The clinic attracted hundreds of people, but was closed after ten days by the police and Sanger was sentenced to a thirty-day jail term. It only spurred Sanger on.

The 1920s brought women the right to vote and the movement for birth control pushed forward. Though the Comstock Laws remained in effect, in 1921 Sanger launched the American Birth Control League (ABCL), which received more than a million letters from women asking for information during its first four years of existence. Sanger left the ABCL to open an actual birth control clinic under the supervision of a physician who was able to prescribe contraception under a loophole in the Comstock Laws which allowed the use of condoms to "prevent the spread of disease." Although the law permitting condoms was officially intended to protect men from venereal disease, Sanger's center was able to broaden the definition of disease to include the ill health and economic stress brought on by unwanted childbearing.

Bit by bit, under the prodding of Sanger and others in the birth control movement, larger holes were made in the Comstock Laws, and the movement spread to localities across the country. In 1937, the leaders of the ABCL and the nation's hundreds of clinics decided to find a way of joining together, and in 1939 they announced the formation of the Birth Control Federation of America, with Margaret Sanger as honorary president. In 1942 the name was changed to the Planned Parenthood Federation of America.

The 1940s were years of intense struggle for the organization, both on the national and local levels, with clinics opening and being shut down by the authorities all over the country. In 1952, the International Planned Parenthood Federation was founded at a conference in Bombay to deal with the concerns of worldwide population growth. But the biggest development to come out of the 1950s was the invention of oral contraceptives, know as "the pill." Research money, funded by Katherine Dexter McCormick, heir to the International Harvester fortune, and funneled through Planned Parenthood, helped in the creation of this new method of birth control which would revolutionize family planning.

While family planning became more integrated into American life, there were still laws against it. Finally in 1965, in *Griswold v. Connecticut*, the Supreme Court ruled the Constitution barred states from interfering with a married couple's decisions about childbearing. (Unmarried people were not give the right to get contraceptive services until the Supreme Court's 1972 decision in *Eisenstadt v. Baird*.)

In 1970, President Richard Nixon signed into law the first federal legislation specifically designed to expand access to family planning services: Title X of the Public Health Service Act. This fueled an impressive expansion of services offered by Planned Parenthood, especially for low-income women and teenagers.

1970 was also the year that Planned Parenthood began providing abortion in New York State following legislation which gave the state the most progressive abortion law in the nation. Those opposed to abortion fought back, but in 1973, in *Roe v. Wade*, the Supreme Court ruled

that states could no longer interfere with a woman's decision, in consultation with her doctor, to have an abortion in the first three months of pregnancy.

Today Planned Parenthood offers both clinical services—including birth control and instruction and prescription, cancer screening, pregnancy testing, abortion, prenatal care, genetic counseling, infertility testing, HIV testing, adoption screening, and child care—and educational programs on such topics as family planning, sexually transmitted disease, pregnancy prevention, women's health, and parenting skills (see also ABORTION).

PMS   see BIRTH CONTROL; PREMENSTRUAL SYNDROME.

PORNOGRAPHY   Pornography is defined by the law and society as materials or performances that portray a humiliating, cruel, demeaning, or exploitative view of sex, without artistic content or merit. The courts have always had difficulties defining precisely what constitutes pornography; one member of the United States Supreme Court observed that, while he could not give an exact definition of pornography, he knew it when he saw it.

On the other hand, sex therapists sometimes want one or both partners to be highly aroused when beginning a sexual encounter. They may, therefore, recommend reading pornographic stories, looking at pornographic pictures, or watching a pornographic video. Such material is usually called "sexually explicit" or "erotic": pornography is a pejorative term and a nonjudgmental one is preferred. To therapists, an arousing story or picture is neither filthy nor damaging. It is simply an aid to arousal.

This casual attitude toward pornography can put sex therapists at odds with certain politicians and religious leaders. In fact, if it ever became difficult for clients to buy pornography, a system of "prescription porn" might be necessary. It is unfortunate that the creators of pornographic material are not always admirable citizens who just want to promote good sex. Some films involve forced performances, genuine cruelty in rough sex sequences, and worst of all, the exploitation of children as participants in sex scenes. Of course, this should be eliminated and existing laws against such activities must be strictly enforced. No one should be exploited in that way merely to help suburban couples improve their sex lives.

Furthermore, young children and developing adolescents might derive poor images of sex from watching and reading pornography. However, since such materials are widespread and easily available, it is up to parents to keep their children otherwise occupied (see also EROTICA; OBSCENITY; SEX IN THE MEDIA; TELEPHONE SEX).

POSITIONS IN INTERCOURSE   see COITAL POSITIONS; SEX IN PREGNANCY.

POST-PARTUM DEPRESSION   A term "that is commonly used to describe an emotional depression suffered by many women immediately after childbirth. Although it is not a diagnostic term in the medical community, it is frequently used by both medical professionals and the general public to describe a broad range of emotional responses following the birth of a child, ranging from an apparent euphoria to "the blues" and, rarely, to full psychosis.

There are several possible causes for post-partum depression. They include the stress of childbirth itself, the rapid hormonal changes that occur at the end of pregnancy, and perhaps a sudden realization of the new or added responsibilities of motherhood. The degree of the depression's severity may also depend on one's prior emotional strength and stability and the emotional history of the family.

In fact, cases of the "blues" occur after half of all normal deliveries—they are so common that they are considered part of a woman's normal emotional response to childbirth. The "blues" usually start within hours or a few days after delivery and gradually fade away after one or two weeks.

Post-partum depression is marked by sadness, frequent episodes of tearfulness, fatigue and lack of energy, generalized anxiety, and sometimes extreme irritability. Treatment consists of reassurance, emotional support, and, if it seems necessary and the new mother is not breast-feeding, the use of mild, mood-enhancing medications and/or sleeping pills.

Post-partum psychosis, however, can be life-threatening and a true medical emergency. Though classified as an unusual psychosis, it includes all the typical psychotic symptoms: delusions, hallucinations, and greatly disorganized behavioral and thought patterns. It is sometimes accompanied by major depression and weight loss—occasionally to the point of anorexia.

This extreme condition usually occurs in only one or two deliveries per thousand, though it is more likely to occur if the new mother or the family has a history of emotional instability. (In very rare instances it can occur among new fathers.) Cases usually appear within days or at most a month after the delivery. It may evolve from the blues but usually occurs on its own. Early symptoms include those of the blues but also include lack of interest in the baby, fears of wanting to hurt the baby, or obsessive concern with the baby's health. There may be delusions that the baby is dead or was born defective. There may also be paranoid suspicion, and thoughts of killing the infant or of suicide.

The psychotic mother is a danger to herself and to the infant and must be hospitalized. Treatment includes the use of antidepressants and often antipsychotic and sedative medications. During acute phases of the illness, visits with the baby, though usually helpful, must be supervised. As the psychosis subsides, the mother will show increasingly appropriate interest in the child and should be allowed more prolonged childcare visitation.

After discharge from the hospital, when the woman has returned to a more normal emotional state, individual psychotherapy is in order. It will usually help the mother come to an understanding of what has happened and help her deal with the feelings raised by her illness. The father's involvement in some form of counseling is also important. Once a woman has experienced post-partum psychosis, future pregnancies bring an increased risk of recurrence, and counseling is appropriate (see also BIRTH).

POST-TRAUMATIC STRESS DISORDER

When someone is the helpless victim of an extraordinarily distressful event such as war, an earthquake, or intense physical or sexual abuse, they may develop a psychological disorder known as post-traumatic stress disorder. It is characteristically marked by recurrent, intrusive, and disturbing memories of the event, an exaggerated response, and a number of other behavioral changes that signify victims' feelings that their world no longer feels safe.

Rape Trauma Syndrome. Since 1980 the American Psychiatric Association has recognized rape trauma syndrome as an authentic post-traumatic stress disorder. Given the characteristics of rape—physical violation of the victim, the psychological shock, the sexual invasiveness, and society's mixed messages about blame and shame, it is not surprising that many rape victims suffer consequent emotional trauma. The amount of time needed to resolve the trauma depends on the victim and her access to emotional support from professionals and loved ones.

The acute phase of rape trauma begins immediately after the rape and may continue for days or, often, several weeks. A victim may experience sleeplessness, nightmares, nervousness, and/or fear of strangers. She may try to blame herself, become depressed, or turn completely away from sex, even with a trusted partner. It is important during this time for the victim to talk about what has happened. It is equally important for family and friends to provide support and for any special man in the victim's life to be understanding and patient about any sexual fears the victim may have. It is also critical that the victim seek professional help from a rape counselor or psychologist.

Before facing and resolving her trauma, the victim may go through what is called the outward adjustment stage. During this period she may outwardly resume her normal life and appear to be "over" the experience, but she is, in fact, suppressing her disturbing feelings. Once she begins to truly face what has happened to her, however, she may begin the final phase of her recovery. Then she can accept and resolve

her rape, put it behind her, and go on with her life (see also DATE RAPE; RAPE).

Family Rape or Molestation. A woman raped by her husband or a child molested by a family member faces very special problems. The victim of family sexual violence may not be believed by other family members or the authorities and may be especially reluctant to talk about it. In the case of a child, the situation is especially problematic. A child completely dependent on an adult who touches him or her in inappropriate ways is often extremely fearful of revealing this terrible secret. In all cases it is important for victims who experience post-traumatic stress to get professional help—even if it is years after the event (see also CHILD ABUSE; INCEST).

PREGNANCY

Pregnancy is the period beginning at CONCEPTION and lasting until the delivery, during which the fetus develops in the womb into a viable infant (although some pregnancies may end in miscarriage). Pregnancy is generally divided into three stages, or trimesters.

The First Trimester. The first trimester is counted from the first day of the last menstrual period through the twelfth week of pregnancy. Approximately seven days after the egg is fertilized and implants itself in the uterus, it continues to divide and multiply to form the placenta and embryo. Most organs of the embryo are formed in the fourth to eighth week after conception. The heartbeat can ordinarily be detected by ultrasound in the eighth or ninth week; the limb buds appear and orbits of the eyes and the eyelids are formed then too. The spinal canal forms as a groove in the back, which closes by the fifth week. The genitalia are differentiated between the eleventh and fourteenth weeks. By the end of the twelfth week, the fetus has a human shape and, because all its organ systems are now formed, the living organism is referred to as a fetus rather than an embryo.

It is the differentiation of the cells of the body into organ systems during the first trimester that makes this time so critical. It is very important for the mother to maintain a healthy diet and avoid drugs such as tobacco and alcohol, which can be potentially harmful to the growing em-

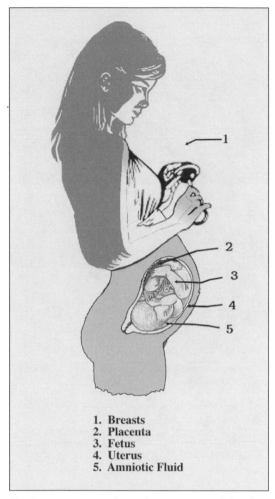

1. Breasts
2. Placenta
3. Fetus
4. Uterus
5. Amniotic Fluid

During pregnancy, the embryo grows and develops in the mother's uterus.

bryo. Tobacco use can result in low birth-weight infants, and alcohol abuse can result in fetal alcohol syndrome, in which the baby grows poorly in utero, and, after birth, has a wide variety of disorders including mental retardation, behavioral disabilities, and abnormal facial characteristics (see FETAL AND INFANT SUSTANCE ABUSE SYNDROMES).

During the first trimester maternal symptoms such as fatigue, nausea, vomiting, and increased frequency of urination are common and represent normal adaptation to the body changes occurring as a result of the pregnancy. There is an enlargement and tenderness of the breasts, increased pigmentation, particularly about the breast and abdomen, and occasionally men-

strual-like cramps, which are normal if not accompanied by bleeding. Most of these symptoms are resolved by the twelfth to fourteenth week of pregnancy and they generally impose no limitation on the mother's physical activity.

Spontaneous abortion (or miscarriage) occurs in nearly 20 percent of all pregnancies. It is most often the result of fetal chromosomal abnormalities that are incompatible with life. More than 80 percent of miscarriages occur during the first twelve weeks of pregnancy and, when due to developmental or chromosomal abnormalities, no preventive treatment is warranted, useful, or beneficial. A miscarriage is more apt to occur in a first pregnancy.

The Second Trimester. The second trimester continues from the thirteenth gestational week until the twenty-fourth or twenty-fifth week. This is a period of continuing development of the organ systems formed during the first trimester and is the period of the most rapid growth of the fetus. The fetus will increase its weight from 14 grams (the weight of a penny) to 820 grams (1 1/2 pounds) in a matter of three months. During this time the fetal bones become increasingly calcified and the nervous system and intestinal tract become more mature.

In the second trimester the mother will begin to feel fetal movement (quickening) at about twenty weeks of pregnancy. The occurrence of leg cramps and increasing maternal weight-gain and increase in abdominal girth occur, especially toward the end of this trimester. Other common symptoms include heartburn, back pain, and occasional lower abdominal cramping from stretching of the ligaments supporting the uterus. These symptoms are all normal and generally minimal. They serve only to remind the woman of the changes her body is undergoing.

The Third Trimester. The third trimester is characterized by marked fetal growth and maturation. Fat is deposited under the skin and the pulmonary system begins to mature in preparation for its breathing functions ouside of the uterus. The fingernails and hair grow, eyelids develop, and the eyes open. By the thirty-seventh completed week of gestation the fetus is considered mature. If born any time after this period, it should survive and do well with no special care in the newborn nursery; fetuses born early in the third trimester of pregnancy now have good chances of survival with modern perinatal and neonatal therapy, but obviously the earlier in the third trimester a baby is delivered, the more medical care will be required.

The average pregnancy lasts 266 days from conception to delivery in humans. There is a remarkable consistency to this length of gestation. What initiates labor at the end of pregnancy still remains one of the true mysteries of life. The uterus begins contracting in a regular fashion and these contractions increase in frequency and intensity as labor progresses. Most often labor begins before the membranes, or "bag of waters," rupture, but occasionally these membranes rupture prior to the onset of labor. When this loss of fluid occurs at term, spontaneous labor nearly always ensues within twenty-four hours. Passage of a bloody mucus plug may be a sign of impending labor, but it is an unreliable signal, particularly after the first pregnancy.

Pregnancy Symtoms and Tests. Pregnancy is usually suspected when a sexually active woman has an abrupt cessation of menstruation. She may experience nausea and vomiting, an increased frequency of urination, fatigue, and often an increased size and tenderness of her breasts. However, these symptoms can be vague, and many pregnancies advance to eight weeks or more before suspicion increases and a pregnancy test is obtained. Fetal movement is a later symptom of pregnancy and can be detected by the woman as early as sixteen weeks after conception. Known as "quickening," it is frequently described as a "flutter" in the abdomen.

Most home pregnancy tests performed on a urine specimen purport to detect a pregnancy within a week of the missed menstrual period; but these tests can have incorrect results reaching above 10 percent, and a diagnosis of pregnancy should be confirmed by pelvic examination or, if necessary, a serum pregnancy test. This sensitive blood test can identify the hormone produced by the fertilized egg and placenta in as little as six days after fertilization, the day the egg is implanted in the uterus.

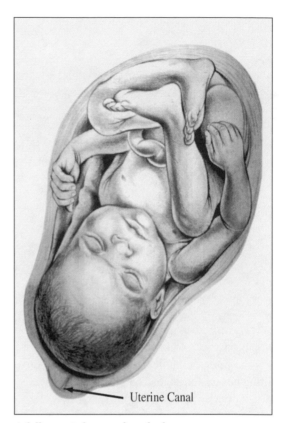

A full term infant ready to be born.

Physical and pelvic examinations give other clues to the presence of pregnancy. An enlarged uterus, a darkening of the areolar part of the breast around the nipple, and increased pigmentation of the abdomen, as well as softening and a bluish hue of the cervix, are all suggestive of pregnancy.

Pregnancy is confirmed by the definition of a fetal heart beat or by visualization of the gestational sac containing a fetus during an ultrasound examination. The fetal heart beat can be heard as early as eight weeks after conception by a specialized microphone known as a Doppler, but in most women the heartbeat is detected between ten and fourteen weeks of gestation by Doppler and at twenty weeks with a fetoscope, a specialized stethoscope. A transvaginal ultrasound examination can be diagnostic as early as the middle of the fourth week of gestation: an intrauterine gestational sac can be seen and fetal cardiac activity can be detected by the end of the sixth week (see also ABORTION; AMNIOCENTESIS;

CONCEPTION; ECTOPIC PREGNANCY; IN VITRO FERTIL-
IZATION; MISCARRIAGE; PLACENTA).

PREGNANCY AND COMMON MEDICA-
TIONS AND SUBSTANCES
In the United
States the average pregnant woman may ingest
from three to seven different drugs in the course
of her pregnancy. Many common drugs can
cross the placenta and enter the circulation of the
developing baby. While only a few have been
shown to directly cause birth defects, very little
information is available on the effects of most
drugs on the fetus and even less is available on
the potential long-term effects of these drugs.
Given the large number of over-the-counter
drugs currently available, it becomes the responsibility of every pregnant woman to consider her
own use of drugs.

The best rule of thumb is that a woman who
suspects she is pregnant use no prescription or
over-the-counter medications without first consulting her obstetrician. The potential for severe
birth defects tends to be higher the earlier during
pregnancy that a drug is used (see also FETAL AND
INFANT SUBSTANCE ABUSE SYNDROMES).

A short list of commonly used drugs is discussed below. This list employs generic names.
In some cases, these drugs may be more popularly known by a brand name.

Acetaminophen. Acetaminophen is commonly
used during each trimester of a pregnancy to
control pain and lower fevers. Appropriate usage, as recommended on the label, is apparently
safe. Acetaminophen does cross the placenta,
but no birth defects have been associated with
this drug. However, continuous high doses cause
fetal liver and kidney problems.

Aspirin. Aspirin is probably the most commonly used over-the-counter drug during pregnancy. Some studies have shown adverse effects
including maternal anemia, prolonged pregnancy, prolonged labor, and excessive bleeding
at delivery. Fetal effects may include impaired
blood clotting ability and hemorrhage into the
brain in a preterm infant. Aspirin should be
avoided during pregnancy.

Caffeine. Caffeine does cross the placental barriers but no evidence establishing a relationship

of caffeine use to birth defects has been found.
Some studies have shown an association between high caffeine consumption (six to eight
cups of coffee per day) and miscarriage as well
as low birth weight infants, but these studies are
not well supported.

Ibuprofen. No reports have associated ibuprofen use with congenital defects. However, use of
this drug has been shown to prolong pregnancy.
In addition, a theoretical risk of ibuprofen includes a change in fetal heart circulation. Therefore, the manufacturer does not recommend
usage during pregnancy.

Antacids. Many different antacid preparations
are currently available, These include buffered
calcium carbonate, magnesium, and aluminum
hydroxide. These have not shown any harmful
effects to the fetus. However, care should be
taken because many of these preparations are
high in salt. Furthermore, use of them may lead
to diarrhea or constipation.

Cold Medicines. There are many over-the-
counter cold medications that contain an antihis-
tamine and/or a decongestant. Two such drugs,
Cyclizine and Pseudoephedrin, are commonly
used during pregnancy. Studies have linked both
drugs to congenital defects, including cleft lip
and club foot; however, those studies are not
well supported. Therefore, it is prudent to avoid
these drugs during the first trimester of pregnancy when possible. Furthermore, continuous
high doses should be discouraged.

Artificial Sweeteners. Questions often arise regarding the safety of artificial sweeteners used
during pregnancy. No congenital defects have
been linked to the usage of these products; however, moderation is certainly advisable.

Antifungal Medications. Yeast infections are
extremely common throughout pregnancy. Medications commonly taken to control them have
not been found to cause birth defects. Care,
however, should be taken when applying these
medications into the vagina.

PREGNANCY AND DIET
Maternal nutrition
can profoundly affect the welfare of the future
baby as well as the health and well-being of the
pregnant woman. Under ordinary circumstances

a maternal weight gain of 25 to 30 pounds is expected during the course of a normal pregnancy. An underweight woman may need to gain more, and an obese woman may be advised to gain less weight during pregnancy, so long as she receives adequate nutrition.

For the average healthy woman, an intake of 2,200 to 2,400 calories per day is appropriate, but in addition to proper caloric intake during pregnancy, the quality of nutrition is equally critical. This should include an increase in protein intake to 80 grams (about 3 ounces) a day, necessary for fetal development. If eaten in sufficient quantities, meat, fowl, fish, dairy products, eggs, and legumes provide reliable protein sources during pregnancy.

Calcium intake should also be increased: it is more effectively absorbed from food than from pills. Green leafy vegetables and dairy products supply most nutritional calcium. Almost all the increased vitamin and mineral needs during pregnancy can be met by a nutritious diet, with a daily "prenatal" vitamin pill representing just an "insurance policy." Only iron supplementation is necessary during pregnancy because of the doubled demand for iron, both for the developing fetus and the expanded maternal red blood cell volume; a supplement of 30 to 60 mg. per day is usually recommended.

Alcohol, tobacco, and recreational drugs should definitely be avoided. In general, it is best to check with an obstetrician before taking any over-the-counter or prescription medications (see also FETAL AND INFANT SUBSTANCE ABUSE SYNDROMES; PREGNANCY AND COMMON MEDICATIONS AND SUBSTANCES).

PREGNANCY AND SEX Sexual intercourse is the primary road to pregnancy, but once there, couples find there is little discussion of sex during pregnancy in the public or scientific media. While no two couples react in the same way, most note a change in their sexual activity during pregnancy. In general a decrease in frequency of intercourse is reported. Pregnancy is a time of many dramatic changes — in hormone level, appearance, and mood — all of which can affect one's sexual feelings or libido.

There are many important changes in a woman's physiology that may influence her sexual activity. Early in pregnancy, she may experience nausea, breast tenderness, and fatigue. There is an increased blood flow through many parts of the woman's body due to hormonal changes. Breasts are vascular tissues and become engorged and tender, making breast stimulation more painful. The increased flow in the pelvic area, especially the vagina and outer genitalia, may lead to a swollen and uncomfortable state. There is also an increase in vaginal secretions. These secretions improve vaginal lubrication, but they also may have odors that may make oral sex unpleasant for the partner. Many women find that as the uterus increases in size as pregnancy progresses, sex in the usual position becomes uncomfortable.

The frequency of intercourse during pregnancy varies from one couple to another. Patterns of sex during pregnancy have been reported differently by several studies. One study showed a steady decline in sex throughout pregnancy. Another showed an increase in sex during the first two trimesters and a decrease in the last trimester. Yet another study showed a decrease of sexual interest during the first trimester, followed by an increase of interest in the second trimester and a decrease in the last trimester. However, nearly all studies agree that there is a decrease in coital frequency during the last months of pregnancy.

Many couples fear that they may harm the fetus or cause a miscarriage by making love during pregnancy. Late in the pregnancy there may be fear of delivering prematurely or of breaking the amniotic sac.

Doctors advise women to abstain from sex early in pregnancy, if they experience vaginal spotting or bleeding. However, most miscarriages occur not because of sex, but because there is something wrong with the fetus. No study has shown conclusively that sex early in pregnancy contributes to miscarriage.

Most doctors agree that vaginal intercourse in the latter part of pregnancy in low-risk women does not seem to lead to any significant problems. Intercourse should be avoided, however, in the latter part of pregnancy by women with poor reproductive histories, such as those who have experienced *placenta previa*, prior premature deliveries, premature ripening of the cervix, ruptured fetal membranes, and those women who have experienced contractions. There is a strong feeling that women should not have any objects placed inside the vagina during pregnancy for fear of injuring the vagina, cervix, or fetus.

Little information is available about ANAL INTERCOURSE during pregnancy. Some studies, however, have suggested that rectal examinations during pregnancy may lead to an increased transmission of potentially harmful organisms from the rectum to the vagina, and this can, theoretically, lead to an amniotic fluid infection. The same would be true of anal intercourse

Oral sex during pregnancy is safe as long as no air is blown into the vagina. Forceful blowing into the vagina during oral sex has been proven harmful to the mother. It may lead to forced air entry into the mother's vaginal blood vessels, which are dilated during pregnancy.

Orgasm during pregnancy may lead to contractions of the uterus. These contractions may be stronger with masturbation than with vaginal intercourse and are sometimes felt very strongly. Most physicians are not concerned about these contractions, unless they last for longer than thirty minutes. Women at risk for premature delivery should discuss this with their practitioner.

Nipple stimulation during pregnancy may release a hormone called oxytocin. This hormone is known to lead to uterine contractions, sometimes leading to hyperstimulation of the uterus and fetal heart rate abnormalities. Some studies have shown that nipple stimulation can be used to induce labor. Most physicians therefore suggest that the nipples should not be rubbed or stimulated during pregnancy.

To avoid infections to the fetus during pregnancy, as well as exposure to potentially harmful prostaglandins (hormone-like substances that can cause uterine contractions) in the semen, some physicians advise the use of condoms during intercourse in pregnancy.

The weeks after birth are a very sensitive time for women. Doctors usually advise against vaginal intercourse for several weeks. The cervix remains open for several weeks after either vaginal delivery or cesarean section, and this open cervix may increase the chance of infection from the vagina into the uterus. If there was a vaginal delivery, a cut may have been made in the area between the vagina and the rectum (EPISIOTOMY) to facilitate delivery. The episiotomy is usually sewn up right after birth, and it requires many weeks for healing. Vaginal or anal intercourse during the postpartum period may injure the episiotomy site and tear the sutures.

PREGNANCY-RELATED DISEASES Over 95 percent of pregnant women will experience a totally normal pregnancy, ending with labor and delivery that have an excellent outcome for both mother and baby. All such women, however, will experience symptoms associated with pregnancy that sometimes bring feelings of illness. The myriad of symptoms accompanying pregnancy—everything from morning sickness in the early stages to backache in the later course of pregnancy—are not diseases; nor are they responses to the physical and hormonal changes associated with pregnancy. There are, however, several diseases that are specific and unique to pregnancy.

Diabetes Mellitus. While 3 in 1,000 pregnant women have diabetes before pregnancy, 30 more will develop gestational diabetes (or diabetes limited to pregnancy). Pregnancy causes a decrease in fasting blood glucose (sugar) and a rise in postprandial (postmeal) glucose because of the body's decreased ability to use insulin. In a gestational diabetic this results in prolonged periods of elevated glucose in maternal blood, which is transmitted to the fetus across the placenta. The higher glucose levels can cause the fetal pancreas to secrete very high levels of insulin which, in turn, can result in complications for the fetus and, later, the newborn infant.

Stillbirth rates and pregnancy losses are therefore higher in diabetic pregnancies. Infants of diabetic mothers are also more likely to have spinal and/or heart defects and/or skeletal abnormalities. There is a relationship between high maternal glucose levels and the frequency of these birth defects, emphasizing the importance of seeking prenatal care early in pregnancy.

Another problem encountered in babies of diabetic mothers is "macrosomia," or excessively large infants. This condition can cause difficulty with labor and vaginal delivery. Macrosomia appears to be a result of high fetal insulin levels. Respiratory distress syndrome and low blood sugar in the newborn period can also be problems in infants of diabetic mothers, particularly when control of diabetes during pregnancy has been less than optimal.

Diabetes in pregnancy imposes additional risks to the mother as well. If a woman is overtly diabetic prior to pregnancy, prepregnancy counseling is essential. Poor control of diabetes during pregnancy can result in accelerated damage to the kidneys, nerves, retina, and other blood vessels in the mother. Special attention to these potential problems is an essential component of good prenatal care.

Hypertension. Pregnancy-induced hypertension (elevated blood pressure) is another disease specific to pregnancy. This illness, also know as toxemia or preeclampsia, occurs in about 7 percent of women, and usually occurs during the second half of a first pregnancy. Symptoms of high blood pressure, protein spillage in the urine, and edema (swelling) are classic. Other less specific symptoms include headaches, nausea, vomiting, visual disturbances, and hyperactive reflexes. Its cause is unknown.

Pregnancy-induced hypertension (PIH) is usually classified as mild or severe. Whereas for mild PIH the treatment prescribed is bed rest and ultimate delivery, in cases of severe PIH, treatment involves prevention of serious complications and prompt delivery. The goal in the management of preeclampsia is prevention of convulsions or coma, control of maternal blood pressure, and preparation for delivery.

Magnesium sulfate is commonly administered to decrease the possibility of epileptic seizures. While the mother's blood pressure, urinary protein, and kidney function are carefully monitored, the fetus is also monitored for signs of distress. If pre-eclampsia worsens in spite of adequate medical therapy, if induction of labor is unsuccessful, or if the fetus shows signs of not tolerating the maternal disease, a cesarean section can be performed. Most women with pregnancy-induced hypertension, however, safely deliver vaginally, and most women who experience the disease with a first pregnancy have no recurrence in future pregnancies.

Blood Type Incompatibility. Rh disease ("isoimmune hemolytic disease of the newborn") can occur when an Rh-negative mother is carrying an Rh-positive fetus. The combination of an Rh-negative mother and Rh-positive father gives a 50 percent chance of the fetus being Rh-positive. When this situation occurs, the potential exists for some of the fetus's Rh-positive blood to get into the mother's circulation; in turn, the Rh-negative mother forms antibodies to the Rh-positive red blood cells, and these antibodies go back across the placenta and destroy the fetus's red blood cells, causing anemia.

This is rare, because nearly 90 percent of the population is Rh-positive, and Rh sensitization can be largely prevented by appropriate administration of Rh immune globulin, which prevents sensitization of the mother to Rh-positive cells. Good prenatal care involves recognition of Rh-negativity in the mother.

Anemia and Urinary Infection. Two other diseases worthy of mention, anemia and urinary tract infection, while not unique to pregnancy, are certainly more common during this time. The most common form of anemia during pregnancy is iron-deficiency anemia, resulting from the increased iron demands of pregnancy. A pregnant woman's blood cell volume increases by nearly 50 percent during a normal pregnancy and these additional red blood cells require iron; the fetus has approximately two pints of blood near the end of pregnancy and these fetal red cells require iron too. Iron-deficiency anemia during pregnancy can be prevented by good nutritional practices prior to and during pregnancy and iron supplementation during the course of pregnancy (see PREGNANCY AND DIET).

Urinary tract infection occurs in about 8 percent of all pregnant women. This increased susceptibility is thought to be due to a variety of mechanical and hormonal factors—pressure on the bladder from the developing pregnancy and dilation of the uterers (the tubes leading from the kidney to the bladder), which occur as normal consequences of pregnancy. Urinary tract infection during pregnancy is nearly always successfully and easily treated, but prompt recognition during prenatal care is important (see also HIGH-RISK PREGNANCY; RH DISEASE).

PREMARITAL SEX   see NONMARITAL SEX.

PREMATURE BIRTH   The classic term "prematurity" refers to a birth weight of less than 2,500 grams. The more correct term is "preterm" for any infant born before thirty-seven weeks of gestation (266 days from the first day of the mother's last menstrual period). Low birth weight (LBW) includes infants who weigh less than 2,500 grams at birth and very low birth weight (VLBW) refers to infants weighing less than 1,500 grams at birth (regardless of gestational age).

Preterm infants are at risk for specific diseases relating to the immaturity of various organ systems. The frequency of these complications varies with gestational age: the earlier the infant is born, the greater the risk. The risk decreases with a gestational age greater than twenty-eight weeks.

Preterm infants are at increased risk for serious neurodevelopmental handicaps such as cerebral palsy, mental retardation, and seizure disorders. They may also be at risk of experiencing chronic pulmonary disease or severe illness in general. Besides prolonged hospitalization at birth, a substantial portion of VLBW infants are rehospitalized during the first year of life. There is also concern that preterm birth disrupts maternal-infant bonding, which can have a major impact on the family function. With advances in medical and nursing care and technology, more premature infants of a younger gestational age are surviving, and the number of healthy survivors is rising.

Studies of neurological outcome are, of necessity, reviews of prior neonatal practices. In general, one to two years of careful follow-up examinations are sufficient to detect major hand-icaps. Longer studies are needed to identify problems with school performance or behavior.

Various factors are associated with increased preterm delivery. Socioeconomic status, race, maternal age (eighteen years or less or forty years or more), low prepregnancy weight, and smoking are major risk factors. Maternal smoking level correlates with perinatal mortality, preterm delivery, premature rupture of membranes, and bleeding during pregnancy. Women who work during pregnancy do not deliver more preterm infants as a whole than nonworking women. Women with a history of poor pregnancy outcomes who work long hours or who work in occupations associated with fatigue may be predisposed to preterm delivery. Coitus and/or orgasm during pregnancy have not been linked to preterm delivery.

Women with poor prenatal care are more likely to deliver before term regardless of their social class. Socially disadvantaged women appear to gain the most from prenatal care. Maternal nutritional status and weight gain in pregnancy are commonly assumed to relate to neonatal birth weight and preterm delivery. Certainly, extremes of malnutrition and starvation lead to a decrease in birth weight.

The incidence of preterm birth correlates strongly with prior obstetric outcome. The history of one previous preterm birth is associated with a recurrence risk of 17 to 40 percent, with the risk factor increasing with the number of preterm births and decreasing with the number of term deliveries. Women with uterine malformations are also at greater risk of preterm delivery. The risk varies with the abnormality. Cervical incompetence often leads to painless second trimester cervical dilation and miscarriage. Once dilation has occurred, preterm labor and/or rupture of membranes can occur, making it difficult to establish the etiology of the preterm birth.

Identifying women at high risk of experiencing preterm labor is a necessary first step in preventing preterm births. Identification permits the physician to monitor the selected patients more carefully and to intervene should problems arise during pregnancy. Once identified, the question arises if there are additional approaches above routine prenatal care that can prevent preterm labor and birth in these high-risk patients. A number of treatment regimes have been proposed, including the use of progesterone supplementation, tocolytic agents (medications that suppress uterine contractions), cerclage (stitching of the cervix during pregnancy), and bed rest. Most high-risk women are usually treated with a combination of two or more of these regimes.

No other fetus benefits more from fetal monitoring than the very premature. Careful and intensive surveillance of these fetuses has been found to result in significantly improved outcomes (see also HIGH-RISK PREGNANCY).

PREMATURE EJACULATION see MOMENT OF INEVITABILITY; SEX THERAPY; SEXUAL DYSFUNCTION, MALE.

PREMENSTRUAL SYNDROME (PMS)
The cyclic appearance of psychological irritation, depression, and other symptoms during the luteal phase (after ovulation) of the menstrual cycle. This is the phase seven to fourteen days prior to menstruation. More than 150 symptoms have been associated with PMS, and many normal women who menstruate regularly have some of these symptoms to a greater or lesser degree.

The term PMS should be reserved for symptoms that are incapacitating enough to interfere with performance of daily activities. More common symptoms include severe mood swings, irritability, hostility, abdominal bloating, breast tenderness, changes in appetite, insomnia, headache, poor concentration, anxiety, crying spells, and edema (swelling) of the extremities. Preexisting conditions such as epilepsy and migraines can also be aggravated during the luteal phase of the menstrual cycle. Spontaneous ovulatory menstrual cycles must be present to diagnose PMS and the symptoms must occur during the luteal, or premenstrual, phase of the cycle.

Many causes of PMS have been suggested, including progesterone deficiency, fluid balance abnormalities, and nutritional deficiencies. However, there is no scientific evidence to unequivo-

cally support any of these as the sole cause of PMS. Hormonal imbalance does not seem to play a role; actually the converse is true—a woman must have ovulatory cycles and therefore correct hormone levels to be diagnosed with PMS.

In order to determine whether she is experiencing PMS, a woman must keep a menstrual calendar with a record of her symptoms, correlating them with menstrual cycle phases. What is seen in PMS is an interval without symptoms during the follicular phase (preovulation), then symptoms, starting with ovulation. These continue until menstruation, when they disappear. If symptoms persist beyond menstruation, other disturbances must be considered, such as depression or anxiety disorders.

Many therapies have been proposed for PMS. No single treatment has been shown to be universally effective. Oral contraceptives eliminate the cyclic hormonal pattern and this improves some symptoms in some women; however, others experience PMS-like symptoms throughout the entire cycle when taking birth control pills. Vitamins and supplements of calcium and magnesium have been investigated, but their benefit is inconsistent and transient.

Some research has focused on the use of psychiatric medications in treating PMS, when mood and behavioral symptoms predominate. There are medications which can lessen irritability, anxiety, and depression, but the difficulty lies in the correct diagnosis. Are such women truly suffering from PMS, or do they have an underlying emotional disorder? Those with symptoms

The emotional symptoms of premenstrual syndrome

The behavioral symptoms of premenstrual syndrome

that are not cyclic should be referred for appropriate counseling and psychological evaluation. Alleviating some of the physical symptoms of PMS can also improve the quality of life for many sufferers. A mild diuretic can be used to reduce fluid retention and bloating, and anti-inflammatory agents can relieve pelvic and back pain. Stress reduction strategies are important in diminishing the symptoms of PMS. Exercise contributes to a sense of well-being which can lessen overall symptoms. Limiting salt and eliminating caffeine seem to lessen irritability and fluid retention.

Premenstrual syndrome remains a frustrating entity for both the health-seeker and the provider. Neither cause nor cure has been found; however, a combination of appropriate alterations in life-style and sympathetically addressing specific complaints will benefit the woman suffering from these symptoms (see also MENSTRUATION).

PRENATAL CARE The aims of prenatal care are to maintain or improve the health of the mother, reduce the potential complications of pregnancy, and obtain optimum health and safety for the newborn infant. Significant improvements in pregnancy outcome and a reduced incidence in the occurrence of prematurity, stillbirths, and pregnancy losses can be achieved with appropriate prenatal care.

One may consider the concept of a "twelve month" pregnancy. This incorporates preconceptional planning, in which the prospective mother seeks care even prior to attempting to become pregnant. A full and detailed medical history is obtained. When factors that might adversely affect pregnancy are discovered, they are corrected prior to pregnancy.

Work and home histories can often give clues of the presence or absence of dangerous exposure to chemicals or other substances, as an example. A physical examination may bring to light a previously unknown condition or verify a healthy status. Prepregnancy counseling encourages cessation of detrimental habits (e.g., tobacco or drug use), that can lead to pregnancy difficulties or even birth defects. Laboratory testing can discover nutritional problems, such as iron deficiency anemia, or lack of immunity to various diseases, such as rubella (German measles). Other prepregnancy testing that may be appropriate include a cervical cancer screening with a Pap smear and hepatitis screening. When maternal health is found to be optimal, pregnancy is then attempted. Most couples successfully achieve pregnancy within the first year. After conception, the first sign is often a missed menstrual period. Susbsequent visits will again include a history to update events bearing on the conduct of pregnancy, and a repeat physical examination to assure that maternal health and fetal anatomy are normal.

At the time of the first visit following conception, appropriate laboratory studies are performed. These include a complete blood count, a serology test to exclude syphilis (often required by state law), a test for immunity to rubella and a blood type and Rh type. A blood test for exposure to hepatitis and vaginal cultures for infection are commonly performed too. A Pap smear is also obtained for cervical cancer screening if this had not been obtained earlier. During the initial pelvic examination the obstetrician assesses the architecture and the adequacy of the bony pelvis for any potential problems that may arise at the time of vaginal delivery. The estimated due date will be calculated utilizing Naegle's rule—adding nine months and one week to the first day of the last menstrual period.

By the tenth to twelfth week of pregnancy, counting from the first day of the last menstrual period, the fetal heart beat can usually be detected with a specialized microphone known as a Doppler. At this time the uterus is the size of a medium grapefruit and the fetus can be easily visualized by ultrasound techniques.

For the first six months of an uncomplicated pregnancy, monthly examinations are adequate. At these visits the mother's weight is recorded, along with her blood pressure and the presence or absence of protein or glucose in the urine. Fetal heart tones are noted. The normal rate is 120–160 beats per minute (the rate is *not* indicative of the fetus's sex). The size of the uterus is approximated by abdominal examination to document growth of the fetus during pregnancy.

Between fifteen and twenty-four weeks of pregnancy, a maternal serum alpha feto-protein test is offered. This is a screening blood test for neural tube defects in the infant, such as spina bifida, or open spine. If this screening test indicates possible problems, further testing, such as ultrasound to visualize the defect, is appropriate.

Another special study that can be performed in the middle trimester of pregnancy is AMNIOCENTESIS, the removal by a syringe and needle of a sample of amniotic fluid surrounding the fetus to determine if the fetal chromosomes are normal. Amniocentesis is generally offered between fourteen and twenty-two weeks of pregnancy to women with a strong family history of genetic disorders, to women thirty-five years of age or older at the time of delivery, and to women in whom some prenatal exam or test suggests a possibility of chromosomal abnormality. This is a low-risk procedure if performed by an experienced obstetrician.

Examination of the fetus by ultrasound is often performed at sixteen to twenty weeks of pregnancy. At this time the fetal anatomy can be examined and sex can be determined in most cases. The volume of amniotic fluid (an index of fetal wellbeing) can be measured, the location of the placenta determined, and the movement and anatomy of the fetus observed.

At the beginning of the third trimester, at approximately seven months of pregnancy, a screening test for diabetes mellitus is commonly performed. This is a blood sugar determination

obtained after a glucose-laden beverage is ingested. In some women, glucose intolerance develops during pregnancy due, in part, to hormones manufactured by the placenta. This condition is known as gestational diabetes and is easily managed but important to detect.

After the second trimester, prenatal visits usually increase in frequency; they commonly occur at weekly intervals during the last month of pregnancy. During this time a pelvic examination is usually repeated to check for dilatation and effacement of the cervix, and to document the presenting fetal part—head or feet. If the pregnancy extends beyond forty weeks, prenatal visits may include more in-depth tracing of the fetal heart rate over a period of approximately thirty minutes, sometimes in conjunction with ultrasound testing. The participation and active cooperation of the woman with her doctor will most often result in a comfortable, healthy pregnancy and a healthy baby approximately 266 days after conception (see also AMNIOCENTESIS; BIRTH DEFECTS; FETAL AND INFANT SUBSTANCE ABUSE SYNDROME; PREGNANCY-RELATED DISEASES).

PREPARED CHILDBIRTH   see LAMAZE METHOD; NATURAL CHILDBIRTH.

PROGESTERONE   One of the major female sex hormones, progesterone serves to prepare the uterus for the reception of a fertilized ovum. Progesterone is regularly produced in the ovaries by the *corpus luteum*. After ovulation, the endometrium is kept in a receptive state for the possible implantation of a fertilized ovum by increased levels of progesterone and ESTROGEN. Production continues if the woman becomes pregnant. If not, the *corpus luteum* ceases to produce progesterone and estrogen, resulting in a rise in FSH (follicle stimulating hormone). The woman menstruates, and the cycle begins anew.

As a woman ages, the amount of progesterone she produces begins to decrease. A drop in progesterone levels is also believed to result in PREMENSTRUAL SYNDROME, although no scientific evidence proves that this is the sole cause (see also AMENORRHEA; HORMONE REPLACEMENT THERAPY; MENOPAUSE).

PROMISCUITY The dictionary definition of promiscuity is the casual or thoughtless joining of individuals without regard to reason. In sexual terms, a man or woman who is promiscuous is someone who is non-discriminating in his or her sexual partners; that is, someone who engages in a great deal of sex with many different partners. In colloquial terms, it is someone who, by their actions, is sexually "easy" to a wide variety of people.

It is important to remember that the concept of promiscuity is a relative one. The question of how much sex with how many different partners one has to have in order to be considered promiscuous is, in reality, a judgment call, and will depend on a person's religious, moral, or ethical values. However, generally speaking, promiscuity does imply that one's attitude toward sex is casual; one seeks a quantity of different sexual partners rather than the intimacy and quality implicit in one or a few sexual relationships.

In some cultural settings, promiscuity is admired. In ancient Rome, where orgies were commonplace, the desire to have sex with many different partners was more than accepted: it was celebrated. Even today, in America, there are individuals who regard sexual conquest as an achievement; they will brag about the "scores" they have made. However, most Americans today regard promiscuous behavior as both destructive and dangerous.

The drive to seek sexual opportunities outside a marriage can be particularly destructive, making trust impossible between a husband and wife. Promiscuous exploits have broken up many families, hurting children in the process as well. Habitual promiscuity can have negative consequences even if one is single. The relentless pursuit of new and different sexual partners may make the forming of a single, solid, reliable relationship very difficult. Promiscuity almost always brings with it problems of jealousy and mistrust. For most relationships to be stable, monogamy is preferred.

Today there is also a very real health risk associated with promiscuous behavior. The more sexual partners one has, the greater the chance of contracting AIDS or other SEXUALLY TRANSMITTED DISEASES (STDs). This holds true for everyone—boys, girls, men, women, heterosexuals and homosexuals of all ages. With AIDS and other STDs at epidemic levels today, indiscriminate sex partnering is highly risky behavior (see also HYPERSEXUALITY; SAFER SEX).

PROPHYLACTICS see CONDOMS.

PROSTATE A walnut-shaped organ found beneath the man's bladder. (Women do not have a prostate gland.) The prostate gland is essentially a sexual organ that produces some of the fluid that makes up a man's ejaculate. The gland surrounds the urine passage (the urethra) as it travels out of the bladder down to the penis. As men age, the prostate tends to enlarge (usually a benign process) and may partially block the flow of the urine. The bladder can overcome this partial blockage at an early stage since the bladder is composed of muscle that can squeeze harder to push urine out. This urinary blockage becomes noticeable by about one-third of all men as they reach their fifties, sixties, or seventies. Benign prostate enlargement does not affect sexual function.

Diseases and abnormalities of the prostate include PROSTATE CANCER, prostatitis, and prostatodynia. Prostatitis, an inflammation of the prostate gland, may be caused by a bacterial or other organic infection. It usually results in an increased frequency of urination, pain or burning during urination, and/or a feeling of pain deep in the pelvis or lower back. If recognized promptly, it can be treated with antibiotics.

Prostatodynia is pain traceable to the prostate without the presence of inflammation or infection. Prostatodynia causes pain similar to prostatitis, but since it is not an infection, treatment is very different. Only a doctor can evaluate whether symptoms are caused by prostatitis, prostatodynia, or another process affecting the urinary tract.

While many men wonder whether frequency of sexual intercourse may cause or alleviate problems associated with the prostate gland, in fact there are no prostate problems caused by too frequent or infrequent sexual intercourse (see also AGING AND SEX; COITAL FREQUENCY).

PROSTATE CANCER Cancer of the prostate is the most common cancer affecting men. Approximately 10 percent of all men develop prostate cancer during their lifetime. While advanced prostate cancer may diminish urinary flow and sexual function, unfortunately there are no symptoms in its early and curable stages.

Prostate cancer is usually a slow-growing tumor that arises within the prostate gland. It is more common in men who have had a brother, father, or son affected by prostate cancer. It is also more common in African-American men and men from societies with a diet high in fats, such as the United States.

Early and potentially curable prostate cancer can be detected with a digital (finger) rectal examination or a blood test referred to as PSA (prostate specific antigen). The PSA blood test detects a protein made in the prostate gland and normally secreted out of the body in seminal fluid. When PSA "leaks" into the blood stream, it signals an abnormal condition, such as a benign growth, infection, or cancer, but does not

During a digital rectal examination, the physician inserts a lubricated, gloved finger inside the rectum to examine the prostate.

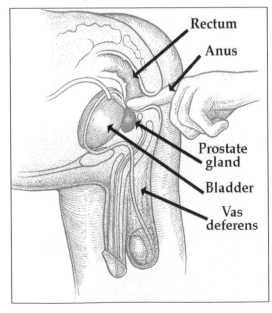

Rectum

Anus

Prostate gland

Bladder

Vas deferens

specifically indicate the presence of cancer. The discovery of a nodule during a rectal examination of the prostate or elevated PSA levels in the blood may lead a urologist to perform a biopsy of the prostate. It is only with a biopsy that the presence of prostate cancer can be confirmed. If prostate cancer is present, additional tests are needed to evaluate the extent, if any, of its spread. If the cancer has not spread beyond the prostate gland, surgical removal or radiation may cure the patient. To maximize the potential for a cure, a digital examination and PSA test should be done during routine health maintenance examinations, before symptoms begin.

Pain from the spread of prostate cancer to the bones or the obstruction of urinary flow from prostate cancer may be treated with male hormones. This may be achieved by surgical castration or medications. This type of hormonal treatment often results in a decrease in libido, or sexual drive, and may also result in difficulties in having erections.

Since prostate cancer can be a slow-growing disease and it often affects very elderly men, its progression may take six to ten years or more to be fatal for patients diagnosed too late for cure. Therefore, not all men who have prostate cancer require aggressive treatment. New approaches to the surgical treatment of prostate cancer have allowed for good cure rates, with the preservation of normal sexual and urinary function in most men. Each year medical research brings new potential for more effective treatment of even advanced prostate cancer (see also PROSTATE).

PROSTITUTION Prostitution is the exchange of sexual services for money or other rewards. The word derives from the Latin *prostituere*, meaning to offer for sale. Most people think only of women as prostitutes, but male prostitution also exists. Prostitution was known in antiquity, sometimes as part of temple worship rites. Over two thousand years ago, in ancient Greece, there were prostitutes known as *hetaerae*. Prostitution is mentioned in the Bible and has existed in Western culture ever since. Prostitutes have at times been limited to working in brothels — houses or apartments inhabited by prostitutes and located in quasi-legal "red light districts" (these are areas, tolerated by the authorities in many countries, in which prostitution and other illicit sexual activities take place). In the United States, prostitution is illegal except in a few counties in Nevada.

Some of the types of people involved in the world of prostitution include the "panderer," who recruits women for prostitution; the "pimp," who sometimes protects but more often lives off the earnings of the prostitutes; and "madams," who manage the brothels.

Female Prostitution. There is a hierarchy of female prostitution, with the "call girl"—who is contacted by a client seeking her company and sex—considered to be the most elite and best paid, while "streetwalkers," who solicit their contacts on the streets or in bars, are often the most likely to be arrested. Streetwalkers are frequently in the grip of a drug or alcohol dependency and are often abused by pimps. Compared to streetwalkers, call girls are rarely arrested or subjected to abuse from pimps, but some have met violence and even death at the hands of their customers.

Call girls often work as individual entrepreneurs, making their own contacts with clients through social connections. Clients usually reach call girls by phone when they want their services and establish on the telephone where and when the sex is to take place—it may be at a hotel or at either of their homes. They are sometimes middle class and college-educated women. Many call girls work as part of an organization headed by a madam, who collects a large percentage of their sexual fees in return for providing initial contacts with affluent customers. Some of the most famous madams of recent time (and the titles of their memoirs) have been: Xaviera Hollander (*The Happy Hooker*), Sydney Biddle Barrows (*The Mayflower Madam*), and most recently Heidi Fleiss, charged with procuring for a Hollywood clientele.

Between call girls and streetwalkers are the women who work in brothels and "massage parlors." These massage parlors are not operated by legitimate and licensed therapeutic professionals, but rather are staffed by untrained and scant-

ily clad young women, who provide a cursory rubdown and often masturbation or oral sex.

The reasons for women going into "the life" vary considerably and by social class. Many women involved in prostitution report experiencing abuse during childhood. Streetwalkers and massage parlor workers usually come from the lowest socioeconomic classes and are women who feel they have no reasonable alternative for making enough money, particularly when they have drug dependencies. Some women in brothels, and particularly independent and educated call girls, believe this is a way to make a great deal of money in a short period of time (see also BROTHEL).

Male Prostitution. Male prostitutes fall into two main categories depending upon whether their customer is heterosexual or homosexual. These do not necessarily reflect the sexual preferences or orientation of the male prostitute but only the nature of the sexual act he is paid to perform. The heterosexual male prostitute, historically known by the French term "gigolo," has to some extent been glorified in literature and movies as a suave, handsome, Continental type, who escorts rich and unattractive widows. Although some are connected with escort services in the larger cities—usually advertised in the Yellow Pages—most heterosexual male prostitutes meet their clientele more informally in resorts, spas, vacation areas, and other locations, where they may prey on lonely older women. Those who work for escort services may or may not have sex with their female clients; there are escort services that are strictly legitimate and will not permit their employees to engage in prostitution.

It appears, however, that many more male prostitutes engage in homosexual activities than in heterosexual ones. Their advertisements appear in specialized magazines and newspapers that cater to the sexual underground in the United States. Many of these male homosexual prostitutes—often referred to as "hustlers"—do not consider themselves homosexuals because even though they may enjoy the sexual contacts, they limit the activity to being fellated rather than performing fellatio on a customer or engaging in anal intercourse. Male homosexual prostitutes tend to be young, usually between the ages of eighteen and twenty-five, but they are not as young as another category of male prostitute—"chickens," or young boys or teenagers preferred by older men—"chickenhawks." While the number of teen and preteen boy prostitutes is unknown, authorities believe that there may be tens of thousands in the United States.

PROSTITUTION LAWS   In ancient times, prostitution was generally accepted; in some cultures it was even linked with religion, as "temple" or "sacred" prostitution. Cultures in which prostitution flourished included those of ancient Greece and Rome, Persia, China, and Japan. But while prostitution is legal today in many European countries, in the United States it is outlawed in all states but Nevada.

Those in favor of legalizing prostitution have tried to challenge the laws against "the oldest profession" by arguing that it should be protected under the right of sexual privacy. However, in 1973, in *Paris Adult Theater I v. Slaton* (an obscenity case), the Supreme Court ruled that the states' legal right to regulate commercial activities superseded the right to privacy. Based on this case, other courts have repeatedly ruled that activities occurring between prostitutes and their clients are not protected by any constitutional rights to privacy because, although these acts are performed by consenting adults, money is exchanged, making them commercial transactions and under the states' jurisdiction.

Another argument against existing prostitution laws is that prostitutes are discriminated against because only they, not their customers, are prosecuted. Courts have responded that the states do have the right to tackle prostitution from one side—not prosecuting customers is, they say, similar to not prosecuting purchasers of obscene material while prosecuting its sellers.

One argument for keeping prostitution illegal is that its legalization would increase the spread of SEXUALLY TRANSMITTED DISEASES—although studies have shown that prostitutes contribute to only a small percentage of the spread of these diseases. Contrary arguments claim that the legalization of prostitution, accompanied by regulation of the prostitutes' health, would actually decrease the spread of STDs by prostitutes. This is backed by studies done in Europe, in which the rates of venereal diseases have been shown to drop after the legalization of prostitution. Nevertheless, with state legislators and courts in the hands of persons who consider any legalization of prostitution to be a sign of the country's moral decline, there is little chance that other states will be joining Nevada in legalizing prostitution in the near future.

PSYCHOGENIC ERECTION   During most of his life a man's penis is limp. For most men this limpness is interrupted periodically with periods of stiffness and hardness—"erectness." Through childhood, youth, and vigorous manhood, a signal from the brain can cause the penis to become erect: a sexy thought can trigger an erection. A boy in bed thinks of women taking off their clothing: his penis hardens. A man riding home on the commuter train thinks of his lover (or perhaps of an attractive coworker): he has an erection. A man in bed with his wife has a problem raising an erection: he thinks of someone more exciting to produce an erection. This successful signalling from the brain to the penis is called a psychogenic erection. In later life the penis may need more direct stimulation; stroking by the partner can be effective. The thought-induced, mental image-induced, or situationally-induced erection may not be attainable in later years, but many middle-aged or older couples are still sexually active and gratified without it (see also ERECTION; PENIS).

PSYCHOSEXUAL STAGES OF DEVELOPMENT   Toward the end of the nineteenth century and with the waning of the Victorian era, new ideas about the mind began to appear and take currency. These focused on people's emotional states, inner feelings, and somewhat daringly, the relationship of sexual drives to one's overall well-being. The greatest contribution to this innovative way of thinking was made by Sigmund Freud (1856–1939), the founder of psychoanalysis. His discoveries of the unconscious and of infantile sexuality led to the development of important new ideas in the field of general psychology.

Before Freud, little thought was given to the mental life of children; they were to be "civilized" by training and discipline (and undoubtedly by a good thrashing when appropriate). The mind was seen as a *tabula rasa*, a "clean state," that accumulated stimuli from the outside world. Freud's revolutionary concept was that the mind is actually composed of innate drives and unconscious fantasies and wishes. According to him, the two most dominant drives are the hunger drive and the sexual drive. Freud called the sexual drive "the sexual instinct of the libido."

All people are born with sexual desires and the wish to fulfill sexual needs. Freud noted that sexuality begins in infancy, and this led him to map out a series of psychosexual stages of development. He came to understand these stages from the psychoanalysis of his adult patients, who, in the course of their treatment, revealed to him their repressed, unconscious sexual fantasies. He saw these fantasies as the keys to their illnesses, emotional difficulties, and neurotic symptomatology. This was an original new "paradigm" of mental life. It made Freud one of the most important figures of the twentieth century and created an extraordinary interest in psychoanalysis. Ernest Jones, the English psychoanalyst, called Freud the "Darwin of the Mind."

The Oral Stage. The first of Freud's psychosexual stages is the oral phase. Freud reconstructed this from his patients' accounts of their early lives and from direct infant observation. He believed that in the earliest stages of infancy the baby receives enormous gratification from being fed by its mother or its mother substitute. Suckling at the breast and being well nourished is the model of ultimate satisfaction. It is at the root of the mother-infant relationship. (That the feeding situation and bonding with the mother is critical to future wellbeing is supported by an enormous body of literature.) Freud saw in this oral phase a generalized sexual state, not sexual in the reproductive sense of intercourse, but in the sense that it creates excitation, a building up of tension, and a release in intense pleasure. It is the residue of this state that we find in the adult pleasures of kissing and in the many forms of oral sexual gratification.

The Anal Stage. As the baby becomes a toddler, biological maturation and psychological development come together around control of the sphincter muscle and the beginning of toilet training. This is when the baby becomes more independent, being able to control its own needs and bodily functions. Of course, the proper age for toilet training varies with each child, and the proper negotiation of toilet training needs considerable care and balance to prevent forcing a toddler to be independent too early or, on the other hand, to not allowing him or her to take control into his or her own hands. Freud called this stage of development the anal stage. It usually occurs around the second year of life, and like the oral stage, was described by Freud as a psychosexual stage. It is also a critical phase in the relationship between the baby and its parents. The child becomes proud of its independence in caring for its bodily functions. Freud gave the famous example of the child who sees his feces as a "gift" to his parents and will often not feel ashamed at presenting them with a sample. Parents must be willing to accept their toddlers' feelings of accomplishment and encourage their newly won victories in motor control and psychological maturity.

The Phallic Stage. Roughly between their third and fifth years children begin to focus on their genitals. They begin to derive pleasure from touching the penis and the vagina—much like the feelings that come with early states of arousal. It is at this stage that children become intensely curious about the genitals of their parents and of other children, in particular their siblings. They like to examine and touch each other's genitals. Boys feel it is important that their penis can grow and become big and hard. At this time children also discover the pleasures of masturbatory activity. According to Freud, they also discover the anatomical differences between the sexes. Girls discover that they are without a penis, which can make them envious of boys and lower their self-esteem. Boys, on the other hand, believe that they can lose their penis (which is what they sometimes think happened to girls) and become filled with "castration anxiety." According to Freud, castration anxiety and penis envy play significant roles in the character development of children. They also become central to the development of the oedipal constellation that overlaps with and then develops separately from the phallic stage.

The Oedipal Stage. Perhaps the most important of all of Freud's psychosexual stages of development, the oedipal stage stands at the center of all future personality development. It is at the foundation of our character traits, our identification, and our mature sexuality. During the oedipal stage children become attached to what Freud called the "family romance." Boys become possessive of their mothers and sees them as their most important love objects. The attachment also makes them fearful of their fathers, who, they believe, become their rivals in love for their mothers. They develop aggressive feelings towards their fathers and would like to replace them as their mothers' loved ones. This can lead to unbearable anxiety and strong fears of castration. Girls, on the other hand, begins to fall in love with their fathers and wants to replace their mothers as their fathers' love objects. They develop tremendous rivalry with their mothers (whom they also love), and become convinced that this aggression toward their mothers is what resulted in them not having a penis, or in having "lost" their penises.

It was this development that Freud called the Oedipus complex, and it is in living through and successfully negotiating the oedipal drama that children learn to overcome the frustration of the incest taboo, the urge to play an adult sexual role and to tame their instinctual drives, making use of them to develop the ego skills, their sense of themselves as children of worth. Freud took the idea of the Oedipus complex from Greek mythology, in particular from the play *Oedipus Rex* by Sophocles. In this play a baby, abandoned at birth, returns to his native Thebes as King Oedipus and unknowingly falls in love with his mother. He has sex with her and is punished—blinded and sent into the wilderness to die—by the wrath of the gods. Freud believed that the reason *Oedipus Rex* has maintained its

power over audiences for thousands of years is that it touches our own inner unconscious oedipal drives. He also felt that the power of William Shakespeare's *Hamlet* rests in the young Danish prince's oedipal love for his mother.

The oedipal period is one of tremendous volatility. Parents must be able to help their children renounce their oedipal wishes without feeling that they are unloved or unsupported in their struggle. Parents who exploit the oedipal stage, either by overstimulation or actual sexual seduction, can cause lasting damage to their children. It is difficult enough, even in healthy environments, for children to come to terms with their oedipal feelings, and it often takes many years to work these feelings through and resolve them (see ELECTRA COMPLEX; OEDIPUS COMPLEX).

The Latency Stage. Freud believed that following the stormy oedipal stage a period of biological and psychological quiescence occurs. He called this period, which usually starts when the child is around seven, the latency stage. There is less focus on inner drives and sexual energy. The emphasis is on the ego and cognitive development. It is a period of great intellectual development in children and the beginning of their ability and efforts to relate to others in the world. It is a period in which children normally focus on their education and on team sports. Children experiencing the latency stage are also noted for their shyness and asceticism and their first interest in moral, spiritual, or religious feelings. They often become detached from the family drama of earlier years and can find comfort in isolation and introspection. The Freudian theory of the latency stage has been greeted with considerable controversy because there is evidence to show that by no means do all children give up their inner sexual drive, their tempestuousness, or become generally pacific and malleable in the years between seven and the onset of puberty.

Puberty. Adolescence and puberty bring together the onset of reproductive sexuality and a reawakening of psychic drives from early childhood. The residues of the oral, anal, phallic, and oedipal stages all find new outlets in the formation of adolescent sexuality and identity. Puberty is often a turbulent phase, with bodily and hormonal changes meeting head on with sexual appetites and sexual fantasies. Adolescents who, in the course of the latency period, have resolved their pregenital and oedipal strivings, will find themselves able to transfer childhood sexual feelings toward parents and siblings to suitable members of the opposite sex. This is the time when dating begins and "falling in love" is common. It is also the period when sexual life can become quite active in teenagers. The strains of these sudden developments can also cause promiscuous behavior on the one hand or isolation and withdrawal on the other. This is also the phase when identification with parents, if not adequately transferred to relevant partners, can lead to a variety of sexual preferences. In some cases, guilt and anxiety affect teenagers so severely that they are unable to find themselves, suffer from mood swings, rebelliousness, and even asocial and delinquent behavior. The adolescent stage is for many a time of confusion; the young person is being bombarded by inner drives, outside cultural forces, and the technological world of television and movies. It is also when teenagers will often experiment with alcohol and drugs and develop odd eating habits. The adolescent is, at the same time, trying to forge ahead with educational and career plans. In order to win this struggle for maturity and independence, teenagers must seek ways to overcome the internal and external pressures that surround and often overwhelm them.

The Final Stage. The final stage is the person's gradual movement from adolescence to mature adulthood. It is the stage that involves the stabilizing of one's sense of identity, the resolution of educational and career decisions, and the ultimate choice of a sex partner and a life partner, which usually leads to marriage and reproduction. In this way new families are started and the life cycle begins anew. There is no specific timetable for the entering and resolving of the final stage. Individuals vary tremendously in their ability to find themselves, to feel comfortable in committing themselves to a partner, and in their ability to take on the responsibility of having a family. In modern times, cultural pressures, economic needs, and sexual behaviors shift rapidly and widely. There are fewer traditional solutions or answers to the urgent issue of finding oneself at ease with oneself and happy in the company of others (see also FREUD, SIGMUND).

PUBERTY   see ADOLESCENCE.

PURITANISM   In the context of a sexual discussion, puritanism means sexually repressive and inhibited behavior inherited from past times. Puritan religion and ethics combined to teach that sexual and related pleasures such as the decorative and entertaining arts, dancing, theater, and non-sacred music, were no more than temptations offered to men and women by the devil in his effort to lead them away from the path of decency and heaven. Carryovers of these attitudes are labeled "puritanism."

QUICKENING   see PREGNANCY STAGES.

R

RAPE Unlawful sexual intercourse, by force or threat of force, without the woman's CONSENT. While it is possible for men to be raped, nearly all reported rape cases involve men raping women. Sexual assault is a broad term that covers a variety of sex offenses including rape, child molestation, and spousal rape. These definitions are accepted generally in Western societies; in the United States, however, each state has its own laws defining the precise elements of rape and sexual assault in that state.

In recent years many states have reformed their rape laws to reflect more enlightened attitudes. Before this, many states imposed rules of corroboration that essentially precluded successful prosecution in cases in which the only evidence was the woman's testimony against the man. Another aspect of rape reform addressed the definition of rape as sexual intercourse between persons not married to one another; it is now accepted in most states that rape can occur within a marriage. Also, before rape reform, much discussion centered on how much force was necessary for a sexual act to be considered rape. It is now understood that a person can be raped without suffering a severe beating.

Perhaps the most decisive turn in rape reform came with the key phrase, "No means No." In the past it was assumed that a woman also said "no" to a man when in fact she meant "yes." This was based on two outmoded premises: that women neither knew what they meant or meant what they said, and that since women were under pressure to protect their virtue, they had to appear disinterested in sex. The current consensus is that not only do women know that they mean, but that men must listen to them.

This change in attitude about a woman's words opened the way for date rape to be accepted as real rape. It is no longer assumed that a woman can only be raped by a stranger, or that she provoked being raped by wearing sexy attire or going to a man's apartment. The accepted view now is that DATE RAPE is real rape. Men are not expected to be mind readers, and a woman's regrets the next morning do not make sex into rape. But men are expected to take no for an answer: if they refuse to and overpower the woman, the claim that she was asking for sex by going on a date or coming to the man's room for a drink is no longer a valid defense (although, unfortunately, it continues to influence juries in rape cases).

Rape law no longer focuses as much on what counts as force or what is required to prove nonconsent. Instead, today's debate is about credibility; when should a woman be believed, and what does a jury need to know about a woman before it can decide whether to believe her? This move, from issues of culpability (blame) to issues of credibility, has consequences for tactics of rape defense. An accused man cannot argue that no means yes, so the best strategy is to present the woman as either a "nut or a slut" in order to discredit her. No study has ever found that women lie about rape more often than men lie about other crimes. Even so, women are still forced to challenge the myth of the lying woman, the spurned lover who seeks revenge, or the deflowered virgin, who refuses to assume responsibility for her sexual activities.

Another issue prevalent in rape law today is whether evidence of prior sexual experience by the woman or prior sexual abuse by the man should be presented in a rape trial. Many states have rape shield laws that prevent the intimate details of a woman's sexual past from being paraded before the court as evidence of her consent. Rape shield laws were enacted to prevent women from being harassed by defense attorneys and to undermine the view that if a woman has had intercourse in the past, in the future she is somehow unable to say "no" to any man, including one with whom she has previously had consensual sex.

Many judges now opt for a symmetrical approach, whereby evidence about prior sexual acts by either the man or woman are excluded from a trial. On the surface this seems like a fair approach, but many observers believe it is more damaging to women than to men. Evidence that a man has abused other women is much more suggestive of rape than evidence that a woman has had consensual sex with other men is suggestive of consent.

Today most people agree that no means no, and that force can be established if a man pushes a woman down in order to have sex with her. However, there is very little agreement about what information is needed about the woman or man before deciding whether she actually said yes or no. The challenge facing rape laws will be to resolve the issues of credibility, so as to maintain a balance that will protect both the innocent woman and the innocent man.

RAPE TRAUMA SYNDROME see POST-TRAUMATIC STRESS DISORDER.

RELIGION AND SEX see ABORTION; ADULTERY; CELIBACY; CHILDREN'S SEXUALITY; SEX EDUCATION; SEXUAL MORALITY.

RESOLUTION PHASE After experiencing orgasm, both women and men enter a resolution phase that returns them to a sexually unexcited state and blood leaves the tissues engorged during sexual excitement. The resolution phase may last from a few minutes to an hour or more. For men, there is also a refractory period during which, almost immediately after ejaculation, they lose not only their erection, but usually also the desire to have more sex. This period is defined by the time it takes for men to have a new erection. The length of this period is usually a function of the man's age and whether the sexual encounter continues or not. But for women, the resolution phase is much slower than for men because women do not have a refractory period or experience a sudden loss of desire. Thus, some women complain that their partners want to go to sleep right after ejaculation, while men may complain that their wives want to continue being held and caressed long after they have their orgasms. Even though a man does become greatly relaxed following ejaculation due to the sudden release of sexual tension built up before his orgasm, he can keep himself from falling asleep immediately. Knowledge on the part of the couple of the length and nature of the refractory period may avoid some misinterpretations of male behavior following ejaculation.

This lack of a refractory period during the resolution phase for women helps explain why women are so much more likely to have multiple orgasms than men. While some women do not want clitoral stimulation during the resolution phase, others do. If a woman who desires additional stimulation and orgasm during the resolution phase does not have her needs met, the resolution will not be satisfactory. Males must learn not to impose their own model of resolution—their refractory period and a desire to sleep—upon their female partners. Thus, a successful outcome to the resolution phase often depends on both partners understanding and being willing to work with the other's needs or limitations (see also SEXUAL RESPONSE CYCLE).

RETARDED EJACULATION see SEXUAL DYSFUNCTION, MALE.

RH DISEASE A complication of pregnancy in which the red blood cell types of the pregnant woman are incompatible with the fetus she is carrying. On their surface red blood cells are covered by antigens, structural markers that give the cells a distinct immunological identity. All the red blood cells in a person's body have the same surface antigens, but these surface markers differ from person to person. When a woman is exposed to blood that is unlike her own (most commonly as a result of the passage of fetal red blood cells across the placenta or from a blood transfusion), she develops antibodies to destroy the foreign blood in her circulation as part of a normal immune response.

Called Rh disease because it was first studied in rhesus monkeys, this incompatibility most commonly occurs when a woman lacks the D antigen in her red blood cells ("Rh negative") and carries a fetus with the D antigen ("Rh positive"). However, there are dozens of other, less common blood cell antigens that can cause the same clinical problems.

The antibodies produced persist for life and, during pregnancy, can cross the placenta and destroy fetal red blood cells if they are positive for the antigen that caused the original immune reaction. This results in fetal anemia, ranging from only mild to severe anemia, in which hydrops fetalis (an accumulation of fluids throughout the fetal body) or even fetal death occurs.

Woman who are Rh sensitized are usually identified by routine testing for red blood cell antibodies during early pregnancy. If it is present, the amount of antibody is determined; if it is below a certain level (usually 1 to 8), then it is not likely that the fetus is severely anemic. If the level of antibody is above this threshold, the severity of fetal anemia must be more closely evaluated. Usually, the extent of the anemia is indirectly estimated by analyzing amniotic fluid obtained by amniocentesis. In some cases, the fetal red blood cell count is measured directly by drawing blood from the umbilical cord in a procedure like amniocentesis known as umbilical cord blood sampling.

If testing indicates that the fetus is severely anemic and if the pregnancy is not close enough to term to permit a safe delivery, a transfusion is performed. Transfusion is done by injecting Rh negative red blood cells into the fetal abdomen or directly into the fetus's blood stream by way of the umbilical cord. The procedure is repeated at regular intervals until delivery.

Fortunately, Rh disease can largely be prevented by giving Rh negative pregnant women an injection of Rh immune globulin at about twenty-eight weeks of gestation and at any time during pregnancy or after delivery (if their baby is Rh positive). No such protective treatment is available for the minor antigens (see also HIGH-RISK PREGNANCY; PREGNANCY-RELATED DISEASES).

RHEUMATISM AND SEX   see ARTHRITIS AND SEX.

RHYTHM METHOD   see BIRTH CONTROL; NATURAL FAMILY PLANNING.

ROMANCE   The idea of romantic love developed in Europe during the Middle Ages. It was a very idealized concept of love — courtly love, celebrated by troubadours — one that put a very high value on feelings and emotions. In fact, those who accepted the romantic ideal believed that sexual relations were dishonorable and obscene if they occurred without love. Today some people today still share this notion. But many feel that we are living in unromantic times.

What exactly is romance? Is it walking in the moonlight with someone you love? Is it candlelight and roses? Is it the belief that there is only one true love, a perfect mate that each person is fated to meet? Romance is best described as a state of mind, an attitude toward sex that celebrates love and works to keep it alive.

Romance really belongs to all lovers: both sexes must cultivate and nourish it. Send your lover roses. Send yourself roses. Share a bubble-bath. Take time to say, "I love you." Even after fifty years of marriage, you can have romance without sex, and sex without romance. Still, the combination of sex and romance is unbeatable (see also COURTSHIP; LOVE).

RU–486   Seen popularly as a BIRTH CONTROL method, RU–486 is a drug developed in France that induces abortion when administered in early pregnancy. RU–486 is an antiprogesterone that blocks corticoid receptors of progesterone, a key hormone in the establishment and maintenance of pregnancy. The effect is that it can either be used in the early weeks of pregnancy to induce an abortion without the need for aspiration (suction), or if administered within seventy-two hours of intercourse it will act as a "morning-after" pill, with contraceptive effect. This is especially useful to women who have been raped or had a contraceptive failure. RU–486 can also prevent implantation of a fertilized egg and induce menstruation when given in the last half of the menstrual cycle.

RU–486 is given orally; after two days prostaglandin is administered. Most women experience bleeding and the passage of the pregnancy within four hours of receiving the prostaglandin. Through the end of the eighth week of pregnancy, RU–486 in combination with prostaglandin has been found to induce a complete abortion in 96 percent of women to whom it has been given. As a "morning-after" pill, RU–486 has been found to be 97 percent effective. This compares to the effectiveness of other "morning-after" pills, but the side effects of RU–486 are much less severe.

So far the only side effects reported are those that usually occur during a spontaneous miscarriage—uterine cramps, bleeding, nausea, or fatigue. Since RU–486 does not require anesthesia and is a noninvasive method of performing abortions, it may prove to be safer than the usual abortion done by aspiration. This might spell the end of the standard abortion, except that political pressure has been brought to bear on its manufacturer, Roussel-Uclaf of France, not to sell the pill in certain countries, including the United States. The drug has been approved in Great Britain and Sweden, as well as in France, and it remains to be seen whether the anti-abortion movement can stop the drug from being widely used in the United States, although this seems unlikely in the long run.

S

SADISM/MASOCHISM (S & M) There are people who find cruelty and humiliation very stimulating sexually. The act of whipping another person can stimulate certain people to high arousal—ERECTION or LUBRICATION—and even to EJACULATION and ORGASM. To some, giving pain is FOREPLAY that will lead to coitus or direct stimulation of the genitals; to others, the punishment is the main event of the encounter.. Orgasm is reached while whipping, spanking, or inflicting other types of pain. This is apparently related to childhood experiences of punishment—possibly for masturbating or for bedwetting. Whatever the cause, sadomasochistic behavior is beyond the range of normal behavior.

Children who feel neglected may learn to seek punishment so as to receive attention. They misbehave and are rewarded with physical and emotional punishment. Abused children often grow up to be child abusers. Though not all children who get spanked turn out to be sadists (pain-givers) or masochists (pain-receivers), sadists and masochists usually seem to have become so early in life.

The sexual transaction between partners in this kind of sexual ritual is called sadomasochism. One partner is by custom and desire the pain-giver and the other the receiver, but either one may want to switch roles occasionally. For some sadomasochists the actual pain involved may be light and bearable for the average grown-up. But others who engage in this kind of sexual behavior can be quite dangerous, give great pain, and lose control. Some can even kill a partner.

While some "normal" lovers do engage in a mild form of sadomasochism, a kind of bedroom play-acting, to get and give pleasure, it is best if lovers do not become dependent on this one kind of arousal. They must agree to stop whenever one of them wants to.

Sadism is named after the Marquis de Sade (1740–1814), a French nobleman and soldier, who spent many years in prisons and asylums, much of it for sexual behavior that was considered abhorrent. He also wrote novels describing scenes of sexual cruelty. Leopold von Sacher-Masoch (1836–1895), a German novelist whose characters took pleasure in receiving pain, lent his name to masochism (see also DOMINANCE AND SUBMISSION; HYPERSEXUALITY).

SAFER SEX While the term "safe sex" is sometimes used to denote sexual activity between two people that will never lead to the transference of SEXUALLY TRANSMITTED DISEASES (STDs), the sad truth is that there is no such thing. Precautions can be taken which greatly reduce the risks, but no one can say with absolute certainty that any safe sex practices guarantee risk-free sex. The only perfectly safe form of sexual release is MASTURBATION. This can be a shared experience by watching a partner masturbate, but if there is any physical contact between the partners, the possibility, no matter how slim, exists that something might be transmitted between them. That is why the applicable term is "safer sex," not safe sex. Having thus qualified the term, words like "prevent" and "protect" will be used because, for the most part, the spread of these diseases can be successfully prevented through safer sex—although not with 100 percent certainty.

Many people practice safer sex because they are afraid of catching AIDS: this dreadful disease is a killer, and they are right to do so. But there are many other sexually transmitted diseases, including SYPHILIS, GONORRHEA AND CHLAMYDIA, HEPATITIS, and HERPES, whose transmission can also be prevented by practicing safer sex, and that provide an added reason for doing so.

There are many levels to the practice of safer sex. As mentioned, the only one to guarantee absolute safety is masturbation. Two virgins who enter into a monogamous relationship are also safe, assuming both partners are telling the truth and remain monogamous. Love and trust, therefore, become important aspects of safer sex in sexual relationships, which is why a strong commitment should be encouraged if safer sex practices are ever abandoned.

In recent decades, monogamous marriages between two virgins have become less common. Young people are willing to delay getting married in order to further their education and their careers. It is more rare, however, for them to be willing to delay forming sexual relationships, which is why they must become informed about safer sex practices.

Many people ask if a specific activity, like French, or deep, KISSING, is safe. They want to know what the risks of catching a communicable disease from kissing might be. Actually, the risks of transmitting AIDS through kissing are low. While we do know that the HIV virus is present in the saliva of infected persons, we do not know of any cases where HIV has been transmitted solely through kissing—even deep kissing. Does that mean that such practices are entirely safe? As with so many issues involving AIDS, the answer must be vague: you must use your own judgment. Again, the best way to practice safer sex is to only have sexual contact—even contact short of intercourse—with someone who has tested negative for STDs and with whom you have a relationship built on trust.

Let us say that you have met someone with whom you want to enter a relationship. Assuming that neither of you are virgins, you might decide that each person goes for an HIV test prior to having sexual relations. This practice is becoming more and more common. Going for such

a test is part of the practice of safer sex but, sadly, it does not mean that the couple can engage in sex without practicing safer sex. The blood test does not detect the HIV virus itself, but only the body's reaction against it. This reaction can take six months or longer to show up on a test, so an infected person could transmit the HIV virus and still pass the test. Although it is rare, the test can also give a false-negative result, so that a person may be told that he or she is disease-free when, in fact, they are not. Life was certainly easier before AIDS.

Of course, some practices are riskier than others. HIV is spread through the passing of bodily fluids—blood, semen, and possibly secretions of the cervix and vagina. These fluids may be exchanged in a limited number of ways: by anal or genital sexual intercourse or ORAL SEX; by receiving contaminated blood; or by using a contaminated hypodermic needle. If contaminated blood or semen comes in contact with an open sore or wound in the mouth, vagina, or rectum, or through the mucous membranes that line the vagina, rectum, urethra, and possibly the mouth, the virus can be transmitted. ANAL INTERCOURSE, particularly for the recipient, is considered the riskiest practice by many experts because there is a greater possibility that blood or an open wound will be present in the ANUS or rectum.

Many people inquire about the risks involved in oral sex. FELLATIO is considered to be a high-risk sexual activity if the man ejaculates into his partner's mouth. The HIV virus is present in semen and can be absorbed through the mucous membranes or through any small tears or cuts in the lining of the mouth, stomach, or intestinal tract. But even if the penis is withdrawn prior to ejaculation, there is always a small amount of pre-ejaculatory fluid that can also contain the virus. In terms of safer sex, using a condom when performing fellatio is important (be sure that it is of the nonlubricated variety).

Oral sex performed upon a woman becomes high-risk during MENSTRUATION because of the possible presence of the virus in menstrual blood. Even when a woman is not menstruating, the vaginal and cervical secretions of the woman can contain some concentrations of the virus.

Obviously, the greater the number of sexual partners, the greater the risk of the disease being transmitted. But in the same way that a woman can become pregnant the first time she has intercourse, HIV can be transmitted through a single sexual episode. When you have sex with someone, you are having sex with all of that person's past and present partners, as far as risks are concerned. If you slept with ten partners in the past year, and each of them, before sleeping with you, slept with ten others, who in turn had slept with ten others, you have basically come into sexual contact with one thousand people and have raised your chances of catching AIDS or some other STD tremendously. (And this only considers everyone's partners for one year!)

Some people wrongly consider HIV to be a disease limited to homosexuals: this piece of misinformation could have deadly consequences. In parts of Africa where AIDS is widespread, it is primarily a heterosexual disease, and the rate of infection among heterosexuals in the Western nations is growing rapidly. Both women and men can get the disease through heterosexual intercourse, though women seem to be at significantly greater risk. One study showed that women who were long-term partners of infected men were almost twenty times more likely to be infected with HIV than were men who were long-term partners of infected women.

But whether an individual is involved in male-to-male, male-to-female or female-to-female sex, because HIV and all other STDs are passed on through the transmission of bodily fluids, the best way to lower the odds of getting STDs is to use a barrier method to block the exchange of fluids. Since the most highly-infected fluid that is exchanged during sexual acts is semen, CONDOMS are the most popular barrier method.

Do condoms work? Very effectively, provided that they are used. Some people say they use condoms, but not every time, or only prior to ejaculation. A condom that remains in your pocket or on the nightstand is useless. Sometimes condoms fail, in other words they break open during the sexual act and the semen spills out. Condoms were originally made to prevent both pregnancy and STDs, but now that a broken condom can result in death, the manufacturers of condoms are making them stronger than ever. However, nonlatex condoms, usually made out of a natural substance such as sheeps' intestines (called "lambskin" by the manufacturers), provide good protection against pregnancy but much less protection against STDs. They contain microscopic holes large enough for a virus, such as HIV or hepatitis B, to pass through and are not recommended as part of a safer sex protection system.

Another difficulty in effective condom use is that of slippage, that is, the condom coming off the penis within the partner's vagina or rectum during intercourse. There is a brand of condom that includes an adhesive that helps it stick to the penis for those concerned about this danger. A spermicide, such as nonoxynol-9 has also been shown in laboratory tests to have the ability to kill the HIV virus, and condoms that are coated with such a substance offer some protection from STDs even if there is slippage or breakage. However, nonoxynol-9 has not been proven 100 percent effective in protecting against HIV outside the laboratory, so it should never be used alone as a method of safer sex.

Some condoms come prelubricated, which is fine, but if an external lubricant is applied, always make sure that it is not oil-based: oil can break down the latex in the condom so that it is no longer as effective against disease transmission. Vaseline should be avoided, as should any other oil-based products. Always remember to use a new condom for each act of intercourse or oral sex.

When a condom is put on is also important. Some people wait until just before the actual act of penetration, but that can be too late. Before ejaculation small droplets of fluid appear at the opening of the penis. These droplets contains thousands of spermatozoa (which is why the withdrawal method is ineffectual for birth control) and in an HIV-infected person they also contain viruses. Penetration is not necessary for the virus to be passed to a partner if the penis comes into contact with vaginal fluids. The solution to this problem is simple; the condom should be placed on the erect penis before things get too hot and heavy. If both partners share in the experience, this does not have to be an interruption of foreplay—it can be part of the fun leading up to intercourse. (It would help if the condom was kept nearby, rather than in the glove compartment of your car!)

While a nonlubricated condom can be used during fellatio, condoms are inappropriate for CUNNILINGUS. However, another product, the dental dam, can take its place. This is a piece of rubber that can be stretched to cover the entrance of the vagina or the anus. One problem with these dams is that during the movements that naturally occur during sex, they might slip. Special products to hold them in place with elastic can be found in specialty stores.

While these safer sex practices all apply to AIDS, some other safer sex practices, while not applicable to AIDS, can be effective to some degree against other STDs. CONTRACEPTIVE CREAMS FOAMS AND GELS can help kill STD bacteria and viruses. Washing the genitals before intercourse can help remove bacteria. Urinating before and after intercourse can help keep bacteria out of the urethra. And finally, unlike HIV, many other STDs have visible signs. If you see a chancre, wart, herpes blister, or any discharge in or around the genitals of a potential partner, do not have sex with that person.

Until medical science finds a cure or vaccine for AIDS, the practice of safer sex is a must for *any* person having sex outside a long-term monogamous relationship—heterosexuals and homosexuals, men and women, non-intravenous drug users and those who do use such drugs. No matter how low you and your partner are in the risk pool, accidents do happen. With AIDS that accident could very well be fatal.

SATYRIASIS   An uncontrollable, obsessive craving among men for sex. Satyriasis derives its name from the satyr—the riotous and lascivious half man, half goat creature of Greek mythology. This mythical creature, with the torso, head, and arms of a man, and the loins and lower body of a goat, loved to drink wine, carouse, play the reed pipe, and, most importantly, chase nymphs. The human victim may seek sex with women, other

men, children, or animals. Satyriasis is the male counterpart to NYMPHOMANIA.

This pathological behavior appears to be rooted in anxieties about the sufferer's masculinity or sexual adequacy. In some cases a man's promiscuity with women may be a defense against homosexual thoughts or fears of HOMOSEXUALITY. This sexual behavior is believed to be aimed at continual reduction of anxiety and reinforcement of the person's self-esteem.

Fortunately, cases of true satyriasis are rare. They have been treated successfully with intense psychotherapy (see also HYPERSEXUALITY).

SCROTUM   see TESTICLES.

SEMEN AND SEMINAL FLUID   Semen is composed of seminal fluid (the material produced by the internal male sexual organs) and SPERM (produced by the TESTICLES). It is released during EJACULATION. The volume of semen normally ranges up to a full teaspoon and is affected by the degree of sexual arousal and the frequency of ejaculation. In general, the volume of semen does not correlate with fertility or virility.

Semen is whitish in color and opaque. It usually has a distinctive odor, sometimes described as somewhat like that of chlorine bleach. It is usually ejaculated in a viscous state that thins as it liquifies over a period of twenty to thirty minutes. Most of the seminal volume comes from the seminal vesicles, which produce a gel-like coagulum. This coagulum is liquified by fluid produced by the PROSTATE, that makes up the next largest component of seminal fluid. Together, these organs provide a number of chemicals and nutrients that support the function and motility of sperm. The smallest volume of fluid (about 3 to 5 percent of the total) provided to the ejaculate comes from the testicles themselves. This fluid is highly concentrated with sperm.

After a vasectomy (see VASECTOMY AND THE MALE PILL), when sperm from the testicles no longer reach the semen, there is no detectable difference in semen volume. Men who have had a vasectomy also have no change in the odor or color of semen, and ejaculation is unaffected by the procedure. The presence of sperm can only be evaluated by examining the semen microscopically. A small part of the seminal volume is also produced by the periurethral and bulbourethral glands. Some of this fluid may be released prior to ejaculation and is noticeable as a drop of fluid at the end of the penis during sexual arousal. Bulbourethral secretions are thought to cleanse and lubricate the urethra, the urine and semen passage, prior to ejaculation.

In men who are HIV-positive, preejaculatory fluid contains detectable levels of the HIV virus. Semen contains high levels of fructose and other substances necessary to nourish sperm, but it has no properties other than its ability to help support sperm function. It does not contain any proteins beneficial to the health or beauty of skin, nor is there any evidence that infrequent ejaculation has any adverse effects on a man.

Although sperm are highly concentrated in the first spurt of ejaculated seminal fluid, they may be found throughout the ejaculate and even in the pre-ejaculatory fluid. It is for this reason that withdrawal of the PENIS from the VAGINA just before ejaculation is not a reliable method of BIRTH CONTROL (see also SAFER SEX).

Some of the components of semen act on the female reproductive tract to "signal" to the vagina and UTERUS that it is time to transport sperm up into the female reproductive tract after intercourse (see also ORGASM; PROSTATE).

SEX AFTER HEART ATTACK see HEART CONDITIONS AND SEX.

SEX AND HEADACHE Sexual headache is relatively rare but often is extremely painful. In one recent survey, it was found in approximately 1 out of 360 headache patients seen at a general neurology clinic. Men are affected four times more frequently than women. The second through sixth decades (teens through fifty-nine) are the usual ages of onset. The headache is unpredictable, occurring at one time and not another. This variability makes it difficult to evaluate the effectiveness of therapy.

There are three general types of sexual headaches: the dull type, the explosive type, and the postural type. Twenty-four per cent of pa-

tients with sexual headache have the dull or muscle contraction type, also known as type I. Patients often complain of a tightness or dull pain over all or just the back of the head. This pain may last from hours to days and usually starts early during SEXUAL INTERCOURSE, intensifying at ORGASM. The headache seems to correlate to the amount of sexual excitement experienced and the contraction of facial and neck muscles. Some patients have found that deliberate relaxation of these muscles during sex sometimes results in moderate relief.

The explosive type headache is the most common subtype. It occurs in 69 percent of patients with sex-related headaches. The pain is described as "explosive" and "throbbing," usually over the back or frontal areas of the head, on both sides. The headache is often severe enough to interrupt sexual activity. Approximately one-quarter of these patients have a personal or family history of migraine.

Seven per cent have the postural type headache. This headache is felt over the upper neck and base of the head and is accompanied by nausea and vomiting. It may last two to three weeks and then disappear spontaneously.

According to criteria of the International Headache Society (IHS), a professional group devoted to the study and treatment of the symptom, serious brain disorders must be excluded to make a valid diagnosis. A patient who complains of headache during sexual activity needs medical evaluation to exclude the possible presence of brain disease. The sudden onset of severe pain in the explosive type headache is suggestive of bleeding inside the head. It is very important that such patients be evaluated by their physician immediately. Certain strokes may have sexual headaches as the initial symptom; meningitis, an inflammation or infection of the membranes surrounding the brain, may cause sexual headache; and hydrocephalus, or the abnormal enlargement of the normal fluid-filled spaces in the brain, may cause it. Sexual headache may also be the result of a bleeding brain tumor. The sudden onset of an explosive headache may be triggered by a "pheochromocytoma," a rare, non-malignant tumor that does not occur inside the head and can cause headaches associated with exertion by secreting a chemical with significant effects on blood pressure, the heart, and the blood vessels of the brain. "Recreational" drugs such as amyl nitrate, or birth control pills may contribute to sexual headache too.

The Causes of Sexual Headache. There are a number of speculative theories as to why such headaches occur. It is not known whether the dull (muscle contraction) and explosive subtypes of sexual headache have a common basis. Some believe there are distinct mechanisms, while other authors suggest that various types of headaches are on a continuum and have similar causes. In the 1970s J. W. Lance treated ten patients with tension headache unrelated to sexual activity. Seven of his patients experienced pain in a similar site and with a similar quality during sex, leading to his theory that muscle contractions account for the dull type sexual headache. Some of Lance's patients did not meet IHS criteria for headache associated with sexual activity because their headaches did not occur only with sexual activity.

The precise cause of the explosive headache is equally unclear. One might invoke the body's changes with sexual climax to explain this headache's origin. An increase in blood pressure with simultaneous acute dilation of the blood vessels and an augmentation in the heart's output occurs as ORGASM approaches. Somehow these changes may lead to a transient increase of pressure in the head.

Treatment with propranolol has been successful in some cases (propranolol is effective in treating migraines). A personal history of migraine was found in 23 percent of patients with the explosive type of sexual headache. Eleven percent had a family history and 28 percent had either a personal or family history of migraines.

Treatment. Propranolol has been the most successful treatment, in doses of 40 to 200 mg per day. Bellergal S and ergotamine tartrate have also been used. The headache may be avoided or significantly decreased by taking either oral or rectal ergotamine approximately thirty minutes before orgasm. Indomethacin (50 mg) given af-

ter dinner, as needed, achieved "clear cut success" in 80 percent of patients with headaches associated with sexual activity. Indomethacin has also been recommended.

Sex in the Relief of Migraine Headache. James Couch and Candice Bears studied the possible relief of intermittent migraine by sexual intercourse in fifty-seven of their married patients. Twenty-seven (47 percent) of this group achieved some relief of their migraine with sexual intercourse. Ten patients had complete relief and five had moderate relief. Some patients had only transient relief, with freedom from pain for one hour or less. Five percent of these patients reported that sexual intercourse made their headaches worse.

SEX CHANGE SURGERY see HERMAPHRODITE; TRANSSEXUALITY.

SEX DISCRIMINATION see SEXISM; SEXUAL HARASSMENT.

SEX DURING PREGNANCY see PREGNANCY AND SEX.

SEX EDUCATION Modern sex education embraces the entire spectrum of scientific information and cultural attitudes and learning that are implicit in being male and female and becoming a man or a woman. It includes both the information expected today on human sexual physiology and reproduction, and all of the sexual learning—formal, verbal and even non-verbal—acquired in experiences from birth onward through the life cycle.

Sex education was once seen primarily as education for eventual heterosexual intercourse and childbearing, although in some high schools and in the military it was primarily aimed at curbing venereal disease. The focus was on the female and male bodies and genitals, brief or vague information on how sperm and egg come to be in the right place at the right time, and on how the resulting embryo grows through the stages of pregnancy to produce a new life nine months later. Many early sex "manuals" had titles that were variants on the words "sex without fear," referring to the very real fears that result from ignorance of sex, especially women's ignorance—though men were often just as likely to be ignorant of sexual matters.

While many parents hope that sex education classes in schools will remove the burden of an embarrassing task for which they may feel ill-equipped, they should accept the fact that, in one way or another, all parents are sex educators. Sex education clearly begins in infancy as a product of parental emotions and attitudes communicated by interactions with the new infant. Reinforcing scientific knowledge are the observations of those who have younger brothers and sisters or who take responsibility for changing a baby's diaper—even infants seem to love playing with their genitals. Judging from the smiles and cooing sounds many infants make while touching themselves, they appear to be obtaining a great deal of pleasure.

Despite the pleasure that their child may be having, many parents seem bothered by this behavior and try to make the baby stop. Very likely, the first moral teaching and education about sexual behaviors we experience has to do with this infant and childhood MASTURBATION. Some parents will slap the infant's hand and firmly say: "No! That's bad for you !" Others will try to divert the infant's attention to something else by offering a toy or food. Some parents may carry this to an extreme by fastening the blankets with diaper pins in such a manner that the infant cannot touch this source of pleasure. In all cases these are impressions and associations that may have a lasting effect on the emotional development of the child, and may even carry through to their adult years. Thus, the first and one of the most important aspect of sexual education that the infant should learn is that it is not wrong or unhealthy to touch or explore the genitals or any other parts of the body. Later the infant can be taught cultural norms, among them the need for privacy in sexual matters.

As the child becomes a social being and relates to peers, sex education will continue, whether taught by parents, educators, or other children. Because children of all ages are naturally curious about sex, there is no easy way for parents to avoid sex education. Parents must decide whether they wish to abrogate their responsibility and leave the teaching to strangers or whether to learn how to meet their children's needs in this matter. Most parents realize that some form of education will fall on their shoulders and that they cannot leave all instruction to schools, because most school systems studiously avoid going beyond the biomechanics of reproduction, disease transmission, and other acceptable "social hygiene" facts into the more controversial areas of SEXUAL MORALITY and responsible decision making.

The content of sex education, as well as the specific goals, are necessarily age-related. What a six-year-old needs for adequate sex information is obviously not what a prepubescent child needs or wants. At all age levels, however, parental (as well as school) education of children must consider not only the facts concerning reproduction, but also decision-making skills appropriate to their age level to help them make moral and responsible decisions and deal with the emotional content and consequences of encounters that may be sexual in nature. Well intentioned, but misguided, efforts of parents to equate sex education with a litany of prohibitions probably do not equip children or teenagers for responsible sexual decision-making and are certainly not going to enhance a young person's self-esteem or belief that he or she is a trusted and loved child.

At the earliest level of infancy (from birth to two years), there is very little a parent can teach a child about sex. The task is rather one of not teaching the child to associate the penis or vagina with something "bad" or "dirty." It is even too early to teach the child that masturbation may be acceptable if carried out in the privacy of the child's bedroom. In early childhood (three to seven years), there is great interest in sex and children ask many questions about it. Parents have the opportunity to help the young child begin to build sexual knowledge and confidence by providing him or her with clear and appropriate answers, using correct terminology rather than euphemisms that often distort information and confuse children. Questions should be answered literally and at a level that the child is capable of comprehending without making the subject so complicated that an air of mystery or forbiddance is evoked. Children's curiosity about sex play is normal and common at this stage, and their sex education should reflect the questions brought up by the child.

Preadolescent children (eight to twelve years) are usually much more shy about asking parents sexual questions and often will turn to their peers for information. Rather than permitting erroneous and possibly harmful information to be gathered by the child, parents of preadolescents should be assertive in ensuring that the child receives information that is age-appropriate and correct. For parents who are uncertain about the information preadolescents need and how to provide it, pediatricians and librarians may suggest a number of current books.

Changes in the bodies of both boys and girls near the end of this period—girl's developing breasts and the growth of pubic hair on both boys and girls—may cause them to be unduly self-conscious and may create problems in the development of healthy sexuality. This is especially true because these changes are usually accompanied by the beginnings of strong sexual urges. This is an important time for parents to help their children begin the development of notions of healthy sexuality and acceptance of one's body. The beginning of or an increase in masturbation during this period among both boys and girls may result in questions about what is "normal," and this should be addressed by the parents. Questions about the appropriateness of various degrees of sexual activity and how far children should go on a "date" may begin to emerge during this period, with the peer group emerging as an important reference group for the child. Parents of emerging adolescents should, therefore, address values and moral issues and their relationships to behavior. This is an important time to begin this aspect of sexual decision-making because during the adolescent period (roughly thirteen to nineteen) sexual activity in varying degrees, from petting to intercourse, can be assumed among most teenagers. By the early or middle adolescent period, if a child neither knows the "facts of life" and the importance of BIRTH CONTROL, nor possesses the moral, responsible decision-making standards best learned before puberty, it may be too late for the child to avoid making a serious mistake.

Many parents, however, make the common mistake of believing that they are helping their child get a good sex education coupled with strong moral values and a sense of responsibility by teaching the child to "say 'No.'" Voiced prohibitions (and it is difficult to make such prohibitions more than voiced) are no substitute for helping a child develop a strong moral sense to help him or her make wise and responsible choices in sexual matters throughout life. If parents want to assume the role of formal sex educators for their children, they should become more knowledgeable about sexuality in general, and not rely only on personal experiences.

It is a continuing problem for sex education in American schools that local school authorities often fail to press for its inclusion in school curricula, usually in the belief that a political storm will result. Sex education for school children has been favored by most of the organizations of professional educators as well as the American Medical Association, the National Council of Churches, the Synagogue Council of America, and the United States Catholic Conference. On the other hand, there is a small but well-organized minority opposed to sex education in the schools. While their belief that sex education should be a product of the home and religious institutions may sound laudable, studies have shown that neither families nor religious institutions are always equipped or willing to take on this role. Generally, the courts have ruled that sex education is a legitimate part of the curricula of public schools and does not infringe upon the freedom of religion of parents any more than teaching about natural selection and evolution violates the rights of religious conservatives who believe in the biblical account of creation. In spite of these court rulings, religious objections have been the most intractable barrier to sex education in public schools. This has meant that, even in states permitting or mandating sex education classes, there is often an absence of discussion of the relationship between sexual behavior and morality and values. In some other states sex education classes have been prohibited from any discussion of morality on the ground that moral matters and values are the responsibility of parents. Most educators believe, however, that to ignore values and morality in sex education classes may confuse children and create the impression that sex can and should be separated from morality and values. In light of the strong sentiments of many religious and ethnic groups in American communities, this controversy has become very complex for educators and school boards, but it cannot be ignored (see also CHILDREN'S SEXUALITY; TEENAGERS AND SEX).

SEX IN THE MEDIA Sex and erotica have been part of the arts and media from their earliest beginnings, and many examples exist of ice age pornography and of nude and erotic paintings and objects from ancient Greece and Rome. Erotic art is found across the globe, from pre-Columbian artifacts to statues and paintings decorating temples in India (see also EROTICA).

However, it was only with the invention of photography in the nineteenth century that sexual depictions of the human body spread through Western societies. The potential grew for widespread access to subjects with a sexual core in the first years of this century with the development of motion pictures. As erotic as a statue, a painting, or even a photograph may be, they cannot compare with what became possible with the birth of motion pictures. Sexual intercourse is not a sedentary act, but full of movement; from a first caress to the throes of passion, sex is the union of two moving bodies. The motion picture camera was quickly put to use to demonstrate the possibilities.

Just as the world of painting has long been divided into legitimate and underground markets, this has been the case with films. As quickly as cinematographers developed new techniques for films intended to be shown to wide audiences, those whose business it was to sell sexually explicit material followed suit. The very first movies were very short affairs and were available only in the nickelodeons, where they were hand cranked by individual viewers. These private viewing machines cost only a nickel, but one coin allowed the viewer to see only part of the reel. A viewer who wished to see the climactic scenes at his local peep show had to keep feeding nickels into the slot.

As films got longer and the projector was invented, sexually explicit films moved into the smoke-filled back rooms of bars and private clubs. Called "stag" films, they were shot in a hurried style, with the men often wearing masks and usually keeping their socks on. Viewers often felt that the police were going to break in at any second.

As the years went by, pornographic films improved in quality but the genre remained short on plot, dialogue, and decent acting. The industry did have a sort of Renaissance period in 1973. In that year three pivotal films were released: *Behind The Green Door* and *The Devil in Miss Jones*, starring Marilyn Chambers; and *Deep Throat*, starring Linda Lovelace. (In later years, Linda Lovelace recanted her enthusiasm for *Deep Throat* and claimed that she had been forced to make it.) These films did not take themselves as seriously as was the norm and it suddenly became popular for couples to go to see them. This was the first time that women were seen in pornographic film audiences in any numbers. But because of a 1973 United States Supreme Court ruling, such films were shown only in communities with liberal standards, like New York City, and were banned in more conservative areas. What really brought erotica to the masses was the invention of the VCR.

With VCRs anyone can watch sexually explicit films in the privacy of their living rooms. In addition to making MASTURBATION easier to integrate into the viewing process, it also vastly increased the number of women who watched these films. Despite the small statistical blip that occurred when *Deep Throat* was released, most women would not be seen going into a movie theater that showed X-rated films. But watching in the privacy of their own home is another matter; video store owners report that women are not shy about renting such films. Indeed, some have probably discovered that watching these films together with spouses may bring a night of intense love-making. While most pornographic films being made have stayed with the old formulas, new producers, including some women, have tried to broaden the plots of their films to bring more ROMANCE, a change most women find to be more appealing than straight sex.

As popular as watching pornographic movies has become, it is still something done by only a minority of the population. What has changed significantly is the integration of sex into mainstream movies and television programs, leading many people to wonder whether there will come a day when the distinction will blur altogether.

The world of silent films may look prim and proper to today's audiences, but because movies were also new once, even the commonplace was daring. One of the earliest shorts (1896) was entitled *The Kiss*, and that is all it was: a kiss between two fully dressed, ordinary-looking people. It started rather tentatively and lasted only a few minutes, but to audiences then it was quite daring. Here was a private act being shown to anyone with a nickel for the nickelodeon.

Actors and actresses in silent films communicated with exaggerated facial expressions and body language. Despite the need to abide by community standards that demanded that in a bedroom scene one of the partners keep at least one foot on the floor, vamps like Mae West and Theda Bara, male lotharios led by Rudolph Valentino, and even their more "innocent" compatriots like the Mack Sennett Bathing Beauties conveyed a sensuousness that drew wide audiences. As with Renaissance painters, one excuse for showing a sexual scene was to portray an event from the past. D.W. Griffith did this in *Intolerance* (1916), featuring an orgy scene from the days of Sodom and Gomorrah.

The late 1920s and the 1930s brought in a new era, and as the flappers changed society at large, the "talkies" brought a real blast of sexuality to the motion picture industry. In the early 1930s many films had overtly sexual themes: if there was no actual nudity, there was plenty of skin. Directors used any ploy they could to get such stars as Jean Harlow, Joan Crawford, Greta Garbo, Marlene Dietrich, Bette Davis, and Barbara Stanwyck out of their clothes. The themes of these films included child prostitution, sexual bondage, and women sleeping their way to the top, along with murder, mayhem, drinking, smoking and skullduggery of all kinds.

This alarming trend led to the Hollywood Production Code, or Hayes Code, an industry-wide self-censorship plan, that was the forerunner of today's MPAA codes. The code warned against showing too much skin and especially suggestive acts such as "excessive and lustful kissing, lustful embracing, suggestive postures and gestures." Not only did everyone have to stay properly dressed, but when the plot caused the characters to engage in forbidden activities such as premarital sex or adultery, the last reel had to show that in the end the just are rewarded and the wicked are punished.

Because Europe did not have the same restrictions, the first nude scenes in a commercial film were shot on the other side of the Atlantic. The most famous of these is probably the 1933 Czechoslovakian film, *Ecstasy*, which featured a nude Hedy Lamarr. While filmmakers in the United States were not allowed the same freedoms for some time, there was one exception—the breasts of black women portraying native Africans. Just as *National Geographic* published photographs showing nudity long before any other magazine, movie "documentaries" that showed bare-breasted native women were never censored, although both sexes were always shown wearing loin cloths.

Europeans kept pressing the limits and one of the films that caused a breakthrough was Roger Vadim's *And God Created Woman*, starring a new ingenue, Brigitte Bardot. European audiences flocked to see Brigitte's amorous adventures. But even though she bared her body (seen from the front in the French version but not in the version released generally in the United States) and embraced her lovers, Vadim still had to make sure that she kept her legs together.

The courts made sure that all of this European flesh did not show up on American screens, ruling that such films as Max Ophuls's *La Ronde* and Louis Malle's *Les Amants* were obscene and banning them from being imported into the country. However, while nudity was banned, sex was certainly an important part of the American movie scene, especially in the years of Marilyn Monroe, Sean Connery's James Bond, and the beach blanket movies. Only in 1966, however, when the Hayes Code was finally abolished, did actual nudity return to the American mainstream cinema, copying what had been going on in magazines under the lead of Hugh Hefner's *Playboy* magazine.

In 1957 the Supreme Court rejected the idea that obscenity should be protected under the First Amendment. According to Justice William Brennan, it was "utterly without redeeming social importance." Only nine years later the Court reversed its position, stating that unless certain elements were proved, among them that the dominant theme of the material catered to prurient interest and it was utterly without redeeming social value, material could not be judged obscene. In 1973 the Supreme Court added that the determination of obscenity was also provable if "the work, taken as a whole lacks serious literary, artistic, political or scientific value." Nevertheless, the barn door had already been pushed wide open.

In line with what was going on in the courts and in society, the movie industry made its own changes. The Hayes Code was replaced by the MPAA rating system. Rather than banning nudity and sexual activities, they were merely categorized. The most explicit films were given an X, now replaced by NC–17. Some movie exhibitors quickly converted into specialty houses showing nothing but sexually explicit films. Many actually used the rating system to advertise the erotic content of what they were showing by making up their own label, Triple X.

Movie companies looking to make the most money have always considered an X or NC–17 rating to be the kiss of death, so the R-rating has been the category that really brought sex to mainstream American audiences. *Midnight Cowboy* was the first major film to be given an X rating, but it was quickly edited so that it could earn the respectability of an R, and it went on to become one of the top films of the year, winning an Academy Award. *I am Curious Yel-*

low/Blue (1967) were really the first widely shown films in America to show male and female genitalia. The films' main message, an attack on the values of the Swedish welfare state, was probably lost on American audiences, who went mostly to see something that they had never seen on screen before. Bernardo Bertolucci's 1973 film, *Last Tango In Paris*, was the first X-rated film with a major star, Marlon Brando, though in order to reach a wider audience it was later released in a cut, R version. It also had the distinction of being the most explicit film to be released by a major Hollywood studio, United Artists.

Each year a new film would break one more taboo. There was the casual sex romp in *Blow Up* (1966), Raquel Welch as a transsexual in *Myra Breckinridge* (1970), the bedroom foursome of *Bob and Carol and Ted and Alice* (1970), the violent sex of *A Clockwork Orange* (1971), the gentle sex of *The Summer of '42* (1971), George Segal's bare bottom in *Harold and Maude* (1971), the animated sex in *Fritz the Cat* (1972), the adulterous cousins in *Cousin Cousine* (1975), Brook Shields as a child prostitute in *Pretty Baby* (1978), and the outrageous homosexuals in *La Cage Aux Folles* (1979).

While the barriers tumbled in the field of motion pictures, television remained rather tame. As a medium that was beamed into everyone's home, it was available to adults and children alike. Even married couples, like Mary Tyler Moore and Dick Van Dyke in the *Dick Van Dyke Show*, slept in separate beds. If one genre should be given credit for breaking out of this mind set, it was the soap operas, especially in their nighttime versions like *Dallas* and *Falcon's Crest*. But television would have advanced only so far and no further as long as it remained a broadcast medium. The advent of the VCR and cable were its instruments of change.

As already noted, the VCR allowed even pornography to be viewed on the home screen, as well as the tamer R-rated features that could not be shown by the networks in their uncut versions. Then cable came along, and while the X-rated feature was usually trimmed to an R, adult films were one of the main reasons that people subscribed to movie channels like HBO and Cinemax, even though viewers had to pay additional fees to receive them (some larger American cities have also had to deal with nudity broadcast on public access channels, although it has not been a widespread phenomenon).

With video sex so available in people's living rooms, it was only natural that broadcasters were going to fight back to reclaim some of their lost viewers. *N.Y.P.D. Blue* is the first network series to show nude male and female bodies and to use words never heard before on television. It is undoubtedly only the first of many.

Another medium where sex is fast on the rise is computers. As soon as modems enabled people to communicate through their computers and telephone lines, part of the communication was devoted to sex. Some of the sexy communications between people at their keyboards is strictly amateur, but others are professional, with names like EROSLink. People type fantasies into their keyboards that those on the other end want and pay for.

With the advent of color screens, computers have become another way to show sexy pictures. Discs are easily available from smaller firms as well as from long-time players in the field of sex such as *Penthouse*. With the advent of the CD ROM devices, much more information could be put on one disk, including both still and video pictures: this became one reason some people added CD ROM drives to their personal computers. Those interested in computer sex have their own world, complete with bulletin boards, magazines and even their own lingo, which includes terms like "cybersex." A few years ago, the idea that so many people would be searching for fantasy sex instead of the real thing would have been unthinkable, but because of AIDS—or for other reasons—many people too frightened to find real partners prefer the safety of electronic companionship (see also CHILDREN'S SEXUALITY; EROTICA; OBSCENITY; PORNOGRAPHY).

SEX ROLES   The prescribed social roles—the things people are expected to do and the ways they are expected to behave—that are believed to be appropriate for men and women, based on

their sex, are called sex roles. The culture of each society typically defines women's and men's roles and regards them as "natural." They are communicated informally but forcefully from one generation to another through family and media and institutions such as schools and churches; often they are embodied in the country's laws. (In the recent past, for example, American laws prohibited women from working in occupations such as mining on the grounds that such work was too dangerous for them.)

Yet, although some roles are nearly universal—such as the mothering role for women and the soldiering role for men—other roles associated with women and men may vary in different societies or change over time. Thus, in the United States certain occupational roles such as secretary or primary school teacher, which today are commonly regarded as women's roles, were once considered to be men's occupational roles.

Today a distinction is made between *sex roles*, which refer to biologically determined activities (such as a nursing mother or a sperm donor), and *gender roles*, which are socially constructed (such as those defining an attorney's work or a plumber's work as male and a nurse's work or a kindergarten teacher's work as female).

It is often difficult for people living in one society to believe the differences that exist in the assignment of gender roles in other societies. Thus, dentists, nearly always male in America, are nearly always female in Denmark and other countries. Similarly, a majority of lawyers and accountants are female in many Eastern European countries and over 75 percent of the physicians in the former Soviet Union are women.

Typically, additional expectations are attached to sex roles or gender roles specifying the preferred behavior the person in the role is expected to exhibit, as well as the behavior considered inappropriate. When an individual exhibits preferred behavior, he or she is rewarded and given social approval; when an individual defies social convention and behaves in a way considered deviant or inappropriate, the behavior is disapproved and he or she is punished in some way.

Thus, a woman who becomes an engineer may be regarded as someone taking on a role deviant to her sex, and if in addition she acts domineering and aggressive she is seen as violating the rules for behavior expected of a woman. (Trying to explain such a case, some might say she is "trying to be like a man.") Men, too, face social disapproval if they take an occupational role regarded as female (perhaps as a nurse or a telephone operator) or if they play their roles in a way regarded as feminine.

All societies impose general behavior norms (meaning what is regarded as normal behavior) for men and women and specific norms for their roles in different social spheres such as occupations or the family. Gender role behavior is specified in all spheres of life, even in the most private sexual activities. But in spite of traditional expectations, we are finding more and more that all men and women are capable of a wide range of behavior, both in the bedroom and the world outside (see also ANDROGYNY; GENDER).

SEX SURROGATES Persons, both male and female, who serve as sex partners as part of sex therapy under the supervision of a sex therapist. Their function is to teach and aid a client with no partner to work with and carry out exercises in body sensitivity. They also help males to control ejaculation timing and women to achieve orgasmic functioning. Some therapists have discontinued the use of sex surrogates because clients have become emotionally involved with them. In addition, in many states and countries the use of sex surrogates may be considered illegal because of laws banning PROSTITUTION: surrogates usually have some degree of physical sex with their clients and are paid for it. However, a small number of reputable and highly qualified sex therapists maintain that there is value in using sex surrogates for some single clients and continue with them.

SEX THERAPY Although we are certainly more open about sex than our Victorian great-great grandparents, and studies have shown we probably experience sex earlier, in more ways, and with more partners than preceding generations, it seems certain that we are not totally free of sexual illiteracy or sexual problems. Studies

have shown that a majority of adults, when interviewed, claim to have experienced periods when they had difficulties with their sexual desires, performance, or response (see SEXUAL DYSFUNCTION, FEMALE; SEXUAL DYSFUNCTION, MALE). Dr. William Masters, the great pioneer of modern sex therapy in the United States, believed that as many as 50 percent of all Americans—single or married—have developed or will develop sexual difficulties at some point in their lives.

Modern sex therapies are based on the scientific information that came out of the first large-scale research into sexual behavior and practices of Americans, carried out by Dr. Alfred C. Kinsey in the 1940s, Masters and Dr. Virginia E. Johnson, beginning in the 1950s, and Dr. Helen S. Kaplan, beginning in the 1960s. Earlier sex research and theorizing by Dr. Sigmund Freud and others had centered on middle class groups in prewar Germany and France and much of it was rooted in the rigid biases of the time. For example, Freud and many of his colleagues believed that women were and should be sexually passive and should be brought to orgasm primarily by the efforts of the man. They also thought that women who showed too lively an interest in sex should be classified as deviates or even as nymphomaniacs—a term that has since fallen into disuse because of its pejorative implications. We see things very differently today.

The key breakthrough in modern sexual science was the work of MASTERS AND JOHNSON (as they came to be known), who gave us the first information on human sexual behavior and responses under truly laboratory conditions. They studied nearly seven hundred men and women for more than ten years, observing and analyzing more than ten thousand sexual episodes. The subjects, who were paid for their participation in the research, were filmed and monitored by sensitive medical instruments during their experiences. Some of the women were even filmed internally before and during ORGASM by tiny cameras contained in clear plastic DILDOS inserted in their vaginas. This gave us the first—and very vivid—pictures of what really happens inside a woman during sex. The pictures were linked to precise medical data on heartbeat rates, blood pressure, and other important measures at each moment of the experience. The Masters and Johnson research, published in 1966, provided the scientific basis for much of the development in sex therapy that came in later years.

Sex therapists today have built upon these and other findings to develop an effective treatment method that focuses on helping persons or couples to overcome their problems and attain sexual fulfillment in a nonjudgmental framework. Although some of their early work—including some of Masters and Johnson' s therapy—involved the use of SEX SURROGATES, i.e., trained sex partners, their use has largely been abandoned for legal and ethical reasons. Sex therapists now focus on helping single and married persons work out their sexual problems and overcome them by themselves or together with their partners. Theirs is largely a "talking cure."

The most common sexual problem reported by Americans—but not necessarily the one for which help is most likely to be sought—appears to be a LACK OF SEXUAL INTEREST. Sexual, that is, performance problems are much more disturbing to individuals—particularly persons involved in ongoing relationships—and are more likely to be thought of as problems justifying discussion with a sexual therapist. Fortunately these performance problems are easily diagnosed and can be as successfully treated as problems of inhibited desire. In men, the most common problems of sexual response include ANTICIPATORY ANXIETY, premature ejaculation, and ERECTILE DIFFICULTIES. Among women, the problems most commonly reported include ANORGASMIA, orgasm difficulties, and painful intercourse.

How does someone who wants help find a reliable sex therapist? There are three main ways: choosing a therapist certified by the American Association of Sex Educators, Counselors, and Therapists at 11 Dupont Circle, NW, Suite 220, Washington DC, 20036; contacting the nearest teaching hospital and asking for a recommendation; and asking a family physician or other helping professional, whose competence you respect, for a referral source. Modern sex therapists will most often be professionally trained and licensed individuals with backgrounds in psychology, education, medicine, psychotherapy, social work, or nursing.

Most sex therapists work on a sliding fee scale. That means that what they charge will depend on your ability to pay. On average, fees for sex therapy are usually somewhat lower than those charged by a clinical psychologist. However, sex therapy, as other behavior therapies, is usually short-term and generally does not go beyond ten to twelve one-hour sessions. It is best suited for persons who are highly motivated to help themselves to change and are partners in a good stable relationship. The age of the client is not a factor because people of all ages can be successfully treated.

While most sexual dysfunctions can be successfully treated, some persons may want a homosexual or bisexual partner or loved one to be "treated" so that they may become exclusively heterosexual. However, there is no evidence that a bisexual or homosexual orientation can be altered through sex therapy or any other known traditional therapeutic modality. But if a person has doubts and anxieties about their own sexual identity and orientation, a sex therapist may help him or her understand and accept what they are rather than remain torn by inner conflict.

In short, almost any sex difficulty that does not have a physiological or pathogenic basis can be treated and usually can be helped, resulting in a more confident sexual person. Successful sex therapy may even help one in the search for a romantic partner by reducing anxiety about one's sexual performance.

A basic principle underlying sex therapy holds that sexual responses of males and females are natural, not learned, functions, in the same sense that a sneeze is produced by inborn physiological processes. However, the inhibition of these natural sexual responses may be learned through behaviors that negatively alter or inhibit the conditions that precede these natural responses. Therefore, a main goal of sex therapy is to remove these conditions and allow natural sexual functioning to continue.

What does a sex therapist do with clients during these therapeutic interviews? In order for a therapist to understand the full nature and depth of the client's problem(s), a sexual history must be taken. This is known as a "sexual status examination." However, if the sex therapist is a physician and the nature of the complaint might be physical rather than behavioral, a physical examination may be given. If there is a physical complaint (e.g., pain or an apparent physical irregularity) the nonmedical sex therapist will invariably refer the client to a physician and will be informed of the results of the physical examination and any treatment by that physician.

During the sexual status examination, the therapist will try to determine the client's specific sexual dysfunctions, the causes of these problems, the presence of other problems that may affect the main sex problems, the objectives of the therapy and the client's relationships, and his or her level of sexual literacy.

Sessions with sex therapists are essentially "talk therapy" accompanied by specific sex exercises conducted by the clients in the privacy of their own homes to teach them skills in coping with those parts of their lives that may be affecting their sexual performance. After practicing the recommended exercises at home, clients report results to their therapist, who may suggest modification of the exercises or suggest moving to a more advanced stage of exercise pertinent to the specific problem of the client. Most sex therapists do not use trained sex partners to assist in the exercises. They believe that a partner is more effective for exercises involving couples. In addition, as most sex therapists believe it is more efficient for both partners in a stable relationship to be involved in the therapy, they will usually ask to meet with the partner. Some therapists will work with a cotherapist of the opposite sex because they believe that when each partner has a therapist of his or her own sex it may enhance communication between them (see also FREUD, SIGMUND; GAY AND LESBIAN LIFE; HOMOSEXUALITY AND SEX THERAPY; HYPERSEXUALITY; KAPLAN, DR. HELEN SINGER; MARITAL THERAPY; MASTURBATION IN SEX THERAPY; SEX SURROGATES; SEXUAL DYSFUNCTION, FEMALE; SEXUAL DYSFUNCTION, MALE).

SEXISM Discrimination or disapproval directed at people because of their sex is called "sexism," just as discrimination against people because of their race is called "racism." Usually sexism is based on the belief that a person's sex, whether male or female, would interfere with their performance of certain social roles, such as an occupation or a position of importance in a corporation or a profession or a church.

Thus, gatekeepers—the people who hold power in a society or an institution—often believe that women or men cannot and should not do certain work because their sex gives them incapacities that make them unable to perform as expected or because others in the society would be angry or uncomfortable at finding them in certain jobs. Women have encountered sexism when denied jobs as construction workers or stockbrokers or when excluded from military service or promotion to jobs as supervisors or executives. Men have encountered sexism when school directors refused to hire them as nursery school teachers or airlines excluded them from jobs as flight attendants (see also SEX ROLES; SEXUAL HARASSMENT; SEXUAL STEREOTYPES).

SEXUAL ANXIETY see ANTICIPATORY ANXIETY.

SEXUAL CLIMAX see ORGASM.

SEXUAL DEVELOPMENT see ADOLESCENCE.

SEXUAL DYSFUNCTIONS, FEMALE Sexual problems are not always easy to define. How do you know if you have a sexual problem? If you want to have sex but cannot find a safe and conveniently available partner, it is cetainly a problem but not one usually considered a sexual problem. If you have lost most or all sexual desire for your mate, it is more likely to be an emotional or relationship problem than a sexual problem. Perhaps the clearest definition of a sexual problem is: dissatisfaction with any persistent aspect of your sexual performance, sensation, or satisfaction at any stage during the sex act (assuming you really care for your partner). Such problems are called "sexual dysfunctions," a term meaning that something is interfering with one's desired sexual performance or feelings. What are the most common sexual problems of women who come to sex therapists for help? The most common of these sexual dysfunctions are: orgasm difficulties; painful intercourse; and LACK OF SEXUAL INTEREST.

Other problems, such as boredom with sexual routine and worries about the content of sexual fantasies are not sexual dysfunction problems at all. These require a little more sexual literacy rather than sexual treatment.

There are other kinds of sex problems that are more complicated and are really psychological problems requiring the services of a psychotherapist before any significant sexual behavior changes may take place. For example, there are women (and men) who do not permit themselves to have any pleasure—sexual or otherwise. For other problems one may have to go to a physician. If there is pain or discomfort during intercourse, this may indicate a medical problem. The causes of this problem could be in the penis or in the vagina (or for some, in the head), or in the way the partners are having intercourse. In all cases, these problems are real and must be dealt with if one is to enjoy his or her sex life. They must be diagnosed and treated quickly.

If you think you have a sexual problem or dysfunction, it is probably wise to see a sex therapist or physician about it. Today most sexual dysfunctions are relatively easy to treat and correct (see also ANORGASMIA; EATING DISORDERS AND SEXUAL DYSFUNCTION; MARITAL THERAPY; MASTERS AND JOHNSON; MASTURBATION IN SEX THERAPY; PREMENSTRUAL SYNDROME (PMS); SEX AND HEADACHE; SEX THERAPY; SEXUAL RESPONSE CYCLE).

Orgasmic Difficulties in Women. Much of the contemporary writing on sex might be entitled *In Search of the Female Orgasm*. Perhaps the most common concern about women's sexual performance is related to ORGASM or lack of them. We know that once a woman is sexually aroused, the flow of blood to the labia, clitoris, and other parts of the genitals creates a tension that is best relieved through orgasm. Frequent sexual excitement without orgasmic relief results, for some women, in aches and pains in different parts of the body and in nervous tension.

While it is true that women can conceive without experiencing orgasm, and they may feel much sexual pleasure, excitement, and satisfaction without orgasm, in missing orgasm they clearly miss nature's bonus to the body. Many sex therapists support the view of scientists who point out that the process of evolution (or God) has created magnificent human male and female bodies, whose every part, system, and response exists for a reason. The female, as well as the male, is given the ability to have this marvelous sensual experience we call an orgasm.

Some professionals and lay persons unfairly label women who fail to experience orgasm as suffering from an affliction. Whether it is due to a medical problem, or whether the woman has not learned how to create conditions for orgasm or has not been given stimulation sufficient to allow the orgasm reflex to occur, she might be labeled "frigid" (see ANORGASMIA). Some husbands and partners put counterproductive pressure on women, even out of loving consideration, to try to have orgasms every time they make love. The reality and complexities of female physiology and factors such as stress work against the likelihood of orgasm under such conditions.

Some women are not certain whether they are having orgasms or just "good sensations." Orgasmic responses are subjective—they may be consistently mild for some women, while other women may feel overpowering orgasms. If a woman's partner gives her or if she gives herself sufficient stimulation, she will be quite aware of the sensation of reaching orgasm—usually a sense that she is still sexually aroused. She may still want to continue, but she will usually know that she has had an orgasm. Women who are concerned about experiencing only mild sensations should speak to a sex therapist.

A woman who knows that she consistently does not have any orgasms may be considered to be, at *present*, nonorgasmic. But this is not a permanent condition and is certainly not a sickness. It simply means that the right conditions or stimulation have not occurred to create the optimal sexual response we call orgasm.

When a woman is with a partner whom she very much likes, in an environment she enjoys (not in the back seat of a car or any other place where she may worry or feel uncomfortable), feeling no legal, religious, or other restraints, and is experiencing sufficient sexual stimulation—if all these conditions are right and she still cannot reach her peak, then she represents a classic case of a nonorgasmic woman.

Orgasmic difficulties may be broadly classified in two types. One is when the "problem" is due to the inability of a partner to bring a woman to orgasm, and the other when, no matter how sexually skilled her partner, the woman cannot reach orgasm. The conditions under which orgasms may or may not occur are very varied. A woman may be orgasmic with self-stimulation but not with her partner, she may be orgasmic with one partner but not another, or she may not achieve orgasm either by herself or with a partner. Each situation requires somewhat different approaches by the sex therapist.

Another type of orgasmic problem is sometimes experienced: some women may have a "flat moment" preceding the orgasmic response when it seems as if nothing is going to happen. Many women say they do not experience this at all. But others, when it occurs, sometimes think: "Nothing is going to happen, and I might as well forget about it," creating a self-fulfilling prophecy. However, if a woman who experiences a "flat moment" keeps up stimulation, she may very well have an orgasm.

If a woman is able to reach orgasm through self-stimulation, or if a woman reached orgasm with a previous partner but not with her present mate, it does not mean that she is subconsciously rejecting her present lover. It may indicate an inability to communicate to the man what kinds of physical pressures and movements she needs to reach an orgasm. The problem does not necessarily point to sexual diffidence on the part of the man—he cannot guess what is on her mind.

In order to have a clearer understanding of what is producing an orgasmic problem, a woman must consider the relationship she has with her husband or partner. All the sex therapy and advice in the world will not help women who basically dislike the person they are having sex with or who find their partner unattractive. If they really dislike their partner, they should see a marriage counselor, pastoral counselor, or other professional to explore their interpersonal problems and find means of dealing with the unsatisfactory relationship.

One type of orgasmic difficulty, caused mainly by the mass media and folk myths, is the idea that only young women are sexually attractive and that when a woman gets older she loses her attractiveness to men and her interest in sex. These are merely cultural stereotypes; not even HYSTERECTOMY, MENOPAUSE, or the EMPTY NEST SYNDROME results in significant decreases in sexual desire (or in attractiveness to men). You have to will yourself to lose interest by believing in these myths. A "HOT FLASH" that often accompanies menopause is sometimes used as an excuse by women who do not want to have sex with their husbands for other reasons. It is as if they are saying to themselves: "See, my body is now telling me that my sexual life is over." Hot flashes do signal hormonal changes during menopause, but they definitely do not mean the end of sexuality. On the contrary, many women find that, freed of worry about pregnancy and with children gone from the house, menopause is a time to celebrate a rediscovered privacy and intimacy that may have been buried for decades. Husband and wife can now have a renewed opportunity to behave as two newlyweds, if they so desire. Sexiness is mainly in the head, and often a change in attitude is needed before there can be a desired change in orgasmic response. For some women sex can be better than ever when they get older. Although the orgasmic response may be a little weaker, it can still be very enjoyable and satisfying for women into their seventies and eighties (see also AGING AND SEX).

SEXUAL DYSFUNCTION, MALE Prior to the rise of modern SEX THERAPY research, the sex life of the male of our species was often mythologized as that of a "sexual beast" or "great lover," always ready to woo, seduce, and conquer women and gifted with the *a priori* knowledge of how to accomplish all this. Women, of course, often knew the truth. Rarely did male sexual problems of obtaining and maintaining an

ERECTION and performing as lovers appear in medical literature—and certainly not in the literature of the popular culture. Within recent decades much of the veil of secrecy and shame has been lifted, and sex therapists are now learning that a considerable number of men—the true percentage has still to be researched—suffer from some form of sexual dysfunction either on a temporary or chronic basis.

We can classify male sexual dysfunction difficulties into four main categories:
- Premature ejaculation;
- Retarded ejaculation;
- Erectile difficulties;
- Lack of sexual interest.

Premature Ejaculation. Premature ejaculation means different things to different people. Essentially, it is any situation in which a male believes his EJACULATION occurs too soon. However, "too soon" can have a variety of meanings:
- The man may be so excited by FOREPLAY and the thought of making love that he ejaculates before he can penetrate his partner;
- The man ejaculates just as he is attempting penetration;
- The man ejaculates seconds after penetration, even though he does not move;
- The man may penetrates his partner, begins thrusting, and ejaculates after very few movements;
- The man is thrusting in and out and though he does not want to climax yet, his reflex actions produce an ejaculation.

What is common to all of these scenarios is that the man is not in control over the timing of his ejaculation. His body is in control, not his will, and his mistimed ejaculation—and it does not matter whether it occurs before, during, or after penetration—leaves him with feelings of inadequacy or frustration. However, sex therapists have devised fairly simple techniques for the treatment of this problem—with a very high rate of success—by teaching men to recognize the MOMENT OF INEVITABILITY just prior to the beginnings of the ejaculatory response and learning how to delay the orgasm.

Retarded Ejaculation. Retarded ejaculation occurs when a man cannot achieve orgasm within a reasonable time *after* he decides to achieve it. While some may think that prolonged intercourse is always desirable, retarded ejaculation often results in no ejaculation at all.

This is not an enviable condition. It often brings with it physical and emotional frustrations, discomfort, and loss of interest. Men who suffer from it may experience anger, and they may question their masculinity or sexual orientation. What some men do, therefore, is to turn a disturbing problem into a virtue. By bragging about their "staying power," they can more easily avoid facing their problem, while appearing to be experienced lovers. Some men "advertise" to their female acquaintances that they do not climax quickly because they are great lovers. Unfortunately, this may be a cover for a deeply rooted psychological problem.

There are many men who can *choose* to delay their ejaculation until their partner has had an orgasm. This is perfectly normal if that is what both partners want. But the key word here is "choose." Someone experiencing retarded ejaculation is just as sexually out of control as the premature ejaculator. Only honest discussion by males with their partners about when they would like him to climax and the expression of their own honest feelings about when they want to ejaculate will start the partners on a path to fulfillment. Consultation with a sex therapist is in order if a man is often disappointed with the timing of his ejaculation and cannot begin to exercise control over it.

Erectile Difficulties. How long should it take before a man develops a firm erection once he is stimulated by his partner's touch? Should a man always get an erection by just thinking about a sexy person or a sexy scene? How long should a man be able to maintain an erection while he is engaged in foreplay? And, what about maintaining the erection after penetration and movement? Should a man get an erection when kissing his lover? How hard should his erection be? Can a man have an erection while he is asleep but not when awake?

As commonly as these questions are addressed to sex therapists, the answers are necessarily less than specific because, as with premature ejaculation, erectile difficulties may be highly subjective. Basically, as long as a man is concerned about the hardness, frequency, or duration of his erection, he has a problem that is real to him. Whether the problem is due to a physiological problem that affects the erection, to psychological factors, or merely to sexual illiteracy or misinformation, must be determined in each individual case. Since this problem can indicate a medical difficulty, one should rule out physiological problems first. Before even considering possible psychological or situational causes with sex therapists, a man should get a thorough examination from a physician or urologist.

Men are often the victims of a Catch-22 situation when it comes to erectile difficulties. They are worried that they are not performing satisfactorily, and the stress this worry produces may cause them to perform poorly: stress is itself often the cause of erectile problems. In other words, the concern that they *may* have difficulty with erections can actually *cause* the difficulty. This is sometimes called a "self-fulfilling prophecy" or ANTICIPATORY ANXIETY.

Different kinds of situations may lead men to think that they might have a problem with their erections:

- The weakening of visual stimulation—not getting erect from seeing nude women, viewing suggestive photos, or watching erotic movies;
- The weakening of physical stimulation—not obtaining an erection from either self-stimulation or physical stimulation by others;
- A firm erection takes much more time and effort to achieve than it once did;
- An erection requires far more "exotic" kinds of stimulation—either in fantasy or in behavior—than before.

Some men report that they never get an erection and that they must, therefore, be "sexless" or "impotent." These two words are more misleading and frightening than useful. Men who experience great difficulties obtaining an erection—or who cannot experience one—may have a physiological problem requiring treatment by a urologist. In some cases it may be due to med-

ications taken for other health reasons. If a man is taking medications and experiences an erectile difficulty or loss of libido, he should consult his physician as soon as possible.

But in many cases there are nonsexual lifestyle factors that may inhibit an erection, for example, stresses from work or money shortages, problems with a partner's hygiene or weight gain, or just plain boredom with the same partner. Even though these men may have difficulty with an erection when attempting intercourse, they may be perfectly capable of having a full-blown erection while asleep. To argue that an erection while asleep is not real because it is stimulated by bladder pressure or something else is nonsense. As long as the body's apparatus works, a man is probably just as capable of having his erection in a sexual situation. If he wants a simple but not necessarily fool-proof test to see if he does have erections in his sleep, he can try the STAMP TEST.

A second class of erectile difficulties is found in men who are able to obtain erections, but find their erections are not as strong, as rigid, and as long-lasting as they once were. In ways similar to those who cannot obtain an erection, these problems may be due to the natural process of maturation and aging, in which repeated exposures to stimulations seem to weaken the desired response.

A third class of erectile difficulties involves an all-too-brief erection before ejaculation. That is, the man complains that his penis gets soft before he has his climax, and that the orgasm occurs during the period in which his erection is waning. Often such men, though they have achieved an erection, begin to worry that they may lose their "hardness." As with those unable to obtain an erection, therapists surmise that stress and worry are often the real culprits. Learning how to "relax and enjoy it" is of vital importance.

Lack of Sexual Desire. Understanding the role of culture in our lives helps us more clearly understand and define the problems a male might have with sexual desire. For example, a male might reach manhood, get married, father children, and soon find himself having little sexual desire or interest. This does not mean that he does not love his wife, that he is latently homo-sexual, or any other simplistic explanation. This is often a lack of desire that would probably be unaffected by a different partner. Although he may appear to be bored with his wife, he is not ready for an extramarital affair. In some cases, weeks or even months may pass before the husband and wife engage in any sexual activity. The wife may want sex, but she might feel uncomfortable about initiating it due to his apparent loss of interest. The man might even feel that he would have sex, but his desire is too weak to motivate him.

These are not situations in which loss of desire has resulted from a change in the relationship: rather, there still is love but no desire. In some cases, the man may never have experienced much "horniness," or physical desire, while in others there has been a marked loss of desire over the years. There are cases in which an operation or a touch of heart trouble has elicited enough fear to drive a husband's desire away. In one case, a man had one testicle which had not descended and another which did not develop properly. He was perfectly capable of having sex, but he believed that no woman could be interested in him. Shame and self-doubt just pushed sex out of his mind. His case is similar to those of women who have lost sexual interest after a mastectomy or some other such operation. They now feel they could not possibly be attractive to men, so they defensively avoid intimacy and the possibility of rejection.

We know that these men and women are not sexually dead. The same men and women can show an interest in sex—in romantic novels, erotic movies, and in talking or thinking about it—but they have no real desire to initiate and complete a sexual act. They are lacking "horniness"—that sense of urgency to have sex. Their problems can often be helped by sex therapy or even by "self-help" books that offer suggestions for revitalizing sexual relationships.

Sometimes, men (and women) may have such strong negative images or feelings of disgust about the sex organs that they do not want to think about or visualize sex. Others were taught as children, and still believe as adults, that the sex organs are dirty or dangerous, or tools of the devil. Some have an irrational fear that the vagina may injure the penis. These deeply rooted problems are best treated by a psychotherapist, who must try to uncover the patient's unconscious, severe emotional blocks against sex. A sex therapist can only help to suggest if this course of action is needed, but will not usually attempt to directly treat severe psychological blocks without coordinated help from other therapists (see also AGING AND SEX; ANORGASMIA; EATING DISORDERS AND SEXUAL DYSFUNCTION; ERECTION; GENITO-UROLOGICAL EXAMINATION; IMPOTENCE; INFERTILITY; LACK OF SEXUAL INTEREST; LIBIDO; MARITAL THERAPY; MASTERS AND JOHNSON; SEX AND HEADACHE; SEX THERAPY; SEXUAL RESPONSE CYCLE).

SEXUAL HARASSMENT   Sexual harassment is illegal under Title VII of the American Civil Rights Act of 1964, which prohibits discrimination on the basis of sex. While it is possible for both men and women to be victims of sexual harassment, the vast majority of cases involve female victims. The United States Supreme Court has defined two types of sexual harassment: *Quid pro quo* and "hostile environment."

Quid pro quo sexual harassment occurs when a job privilege or promotion is conditioned upon sexual conduct. The prototypical example of *quid pro quo* harassment is a male boss telling a woman employee "if you sleep with me, you'll be promoted; if you don't, you'll be fired."

Two factors are necessary to prove *quid pro quo* harassment: the existence of an actual threat, and proof that the victim's reaction to the threat, rather than some other factor, resulted in firing or demotion. These elements are often quite difficult to prove because threats usually occur when two people are alone, so it becomes a question of the employee's word against the employer's. Also, because very few employees are perfect, an employer can almost always find or construct a legitimate reason to fire someone.

The more difficult case is sexual harassment grounded in a workplace environment. This type of case was only recognized by the Supreme Court in 1986. Hostile environment harassment occurs when conditions at work render it uncomfortable for a person to do her job. For instance, if male employees make sexist remarks, if they refer to women in derogatory ways, or if they are given privileges that female employees at an equal level do not share, this constitutes hostile environment harassment.

A court must look into the entire context of the working environment to determine whether it is in fact "hostile." In *Harris v. Forklift Systems* (1993) the Supreme Court listed the following factors to consider in that evaluation: the frequency and severity of the discriminatory conduct; the type of conduct at issue (whether it was physically threatening, humiliating, or merely offensive); and whether a reasonable person would think that the conduct interfered with the employee's work performance.

The Supreme Court has also ruled that in order to have an actionable claim, a plaintiff (usually a woman suing her employer) need not have suffered serious psychological harm or injury as a result of the harassment. Thus, a woman can sue for sexual harassment even though the uncomfortable situation did not prevent her from adequately doing her job or cause her severe emotional distress.

The key to both types of sexual harassment is the "unwelcomeness" of the sexual attentions. This is problematic for three reasons: it shifts much of the focus to the behavior of the victim, rather than that of the perpetrator; it makes conduct the yardstick with which to measure assent, thus implying that a woman's polite "no" may not suffice; and since the focus of inquiry is on the plaintiff, the door is open to questions about her conduct, including what she wears, how she talks, and even with whom she sleeps. This is troubling, because it brings back outdated notions of women inviting trouble by the sexual image they may portray, and of them being merely potential sexual objects for men.

Making a case of sexual harassment under federal law is not easy. It is not enough to show that one has been harassed at work. *Quid pro quo* must be shown, the existence of a pervasively hostile environment must be established, or arguments that employers had cause to fire or not promote the plaintiff must be defeated. To meet these burdens, the woman must first be believed—no easy task when the rules of credibility are stacked against women (see also CONSENT).

SEXUAL IDENTITY   see ADOLESCENCE; BISEXUALITY; GENDER DYSPHORIA; HOMOSEXUALITY; TRANSSEXULITY.

SEXUAL INTERCOURSE   The song may go, "Birds do it, bees do it," but there is a world of difference between what occurs in the animal and insect kingdoms and sexual intercourse between humans. Sexual intercourse is the act in which a man's PENIS is inserted into a woman's VAGINA and together they begin the rhythmic movement that may lead to male ORGASM and the CONCEPTION of a child. Sexual intercourse is also called coitus, which is drawn from the Latin root *coire*, meaning to go or to come together.

While sexual intercourse is obviously an integral part of the reproductive process and, therefore, basic to the very existence of the species, the solely reproductive aspects of sexual intercourse, as it has evolved among humans, have become only a small, one could almost say vestigial, part of the act. But while humans may have developed ways of reproducing that do not require actual sexual intercourse (see ARTIFICIAL INSEMINATION BY DONOR; IN VITRO FERTILIZATION), the act is no more likely to disappear from human physical activities than walking.

Humans have long faced one problem with reproduction. Having developed from apes, *Homo sapiens* branched off from their ancestors because of their larger brains. With this larger brain, however, the human baby could not pass out of the mother with a fully or even nearly developed brain. Much of the human child's cranial development must take place outside of the womb, meaning that humans are burdened with the full-time care of helpless and fragile babies during the time this development takes place. This turns the relationship between the human male and female into a very complex one with many interactive elements, including a gamut of emotional attachments, many of which come together around the act of sexual intercourse.

One key development that arose over time was that in human beings sexual intercourse occurred throughout the year, not just when the female was ready to reproduce. This separated the sexual act from reproduction to such an extent that throughout the ages there have been people who are totally ignorant of the consequences that might arise from engaging in sexual intercourse. Even today this is something that has to be taught to young people, though one would think that something as important to the species as its own reproduction would be inately known. Of course, the safety measure that nature has taken against such ignorance to insure the continuation of the species is to have made the desire for sexual intercourse so strong that it cannot be ignored. That is why humans engage in sexual intercourse many more times than is needed for procreation, and continue to engage in it throughout their lives, long after the ability to reproduce has been lost by the female.

Humans are driven to seek sex by the LIBIDO, the part of the human psyche that creates the desire for sexual intercourse. Animals also share that desire, but we differ in that, intertwined with the desires instigated by our libidos, are the equally strong passions stirred by our hearts. Certainly not all acts of sexual intercourse are connected with the emotions we associate with LOVE (if that were so, the world's oldest profession—PROSTITUTION—would never have existed), but for us and the optimum functioning of our species, love is actually the more important of the two drives.

Humans also differ from other animals in the positions they use for intercourse. While humans have a whole repetoire of sexual positions, the most common one is labeled the "missionary position," in which the man lies on top of the woman with their faces close together (in animals, males mate with females from the rear). This position facilitates communication between the partners, with words, visual stimuli, and KISSING, again showing how important a role the brain plays in the total sexual act.

While technically the act of sexual intercourse can be considered to take place when a male and female human being place their genitals to-gether, in a broader sense that act can be considered to begin much earlier. If a person sends his or her beloved a bouquet of flowers in the morning, it may begin an arousal process that will culminate in sexual intercourse that night. And since many women stay aroused for a long time after intercourse, those same flowers might trigger another episode of sexual intercourse the following morning. The conversation that takes place over a leisurely dinner is another ritual that often becomes part of the process of sexual intercourse. (The restaurant industry recognized this long ago and usually does its part to set the mood for romance and seduction by lowering the lights in the evening.) Other human behavior that is part of the process includes dressing provocatively, wearing certain scents, and dancing together closely.

The act of sexual intercourse has evolved over time, especially as women have been freed from the risk of pregnancy by effective contraceptive methods. Though in the past many women would engage in the act as a duty more than as a source of pleasure, modern women seek sexual gratification as much as their mates do. A woman requires physical stimulation of the CLITORIS in order to reach sexual satisfaction, but because of the location of the clitoris, she does not necessarily receive adequate stimulation from the movement of the penis inside her vagina. This need has resulted in what is now known as FOREPLAY, an integral part of sexual intercourse, in which the woman's clitoris is manipulated by her mate, either manually or orally, until she reaches a high enough state of stimulation to reach orgasm, either prior to the entry of the penis or after penetration (see also AFTERGLOW; BIRTH CONTROL; COITAL FREQUENCY; CONCEPTION; EJACULATION; ERECTION; HETEROSEXUALITY; LUBRICATION; ORGASM; PARAPLEGICS AND SEX; RESOLUTION PHASE; SAFER SEX; SEXUAL RESPONSE CYCLE).

SEXUAL MORALITY Sexual conflict frequently arises from differences among people about what behavior is right, moral, or permissible. There are many opportunities for individuals to confront moral issues that require them to make choices about how they will proceed.

Sometimes choices relate to SEXUAL INTERCOURSE, as when a person wonders whether it is right to have extramarital sex when a spouse is an invalid incapable of sexual activity. Sometimes choices are the consequence of having had sex: for example, can or should an unmarried, young, pregnant woman have an ABORTION? There are also less momentous issues, as when a mother finds her seven-year-old daughter naked with a six-year-old boy, the pair examining each other's genitals. She may react with a great feeling of anxiety and think that her daughter is behaving immorally and should be punished. Whether this is truly a moral issue is less important then parental beliefs that this childish behavior is "sin." Most commonly, young people who have strong feelings for someone and want to express them physically may wonder: "How could something that feels so good and is done by so many peers be so wrong?" If a teenager whose family has just purchased a hot tub invites several friends of both sexes over for a party and they would like her to go skinny-dipping with them in the tub, what should she do—particularly when she, like most people, was brought up to believe that nudity in front of strangers is not only immodest but immoral?

How do people know what is the right choice to make in situations such as these? What is right and what is wrong? What is moral and immoral? These are not always easy decisions to make and, unfortunately, the "wrong" choice may sometimes have long-lasting and tragic repercussions. Many people suffer great emotional pain and social difficulty because of wrong choices they made about sexual behavior. Much of the judgmental criticism directed at people who have made "mistakes" is based on the assumption that they "knew better" and nevertheless chose to do the wrong thing. But studies of teenage pregnancy, for example, do not indicate that many individuals rationally choose to engage in sexual behavior that will cause them harm, but rather that they act spontaneously and in a state of passion.

It is true that people are different when it comes to various aspects of moral decision making, but they are alike in the sense that all humans need guidelines, particularly in the years during which they develop what they believe to be their own personal value systems. However, without personal values that are consistent with accepted moral beliefs, their choices may be confused and their responsibility for the consequences may be unclear to them.

Why can't everyone do things the way their parents did? Because no society in history has provided a milieu in which people grow up with as many alternatives for social behavior as we find in today's Western societies, and in the United States in particular. Why is this so? Freedom of choice and variations in social behavior depend upon awareness and available alternatives. Why are there so many alternative behaviors from which to choose? For one thing, Americans are among the best educated peoples in the world. Young persons are not only aware of the behaviors of their own ethnic and religious groups but also of the ways and beliefs of others.

Although some groups choose not to expose their children to the values, belief systems, and lifestyles of people who are different, most Americans seem to feel that it is good and valuable for young people to see and learn how different groups vary, with their different foods, languages, customs, and religious expressions. Parents have learned that it is difficult to prevent their children from learning about these differences. Consequently, most children grow up knowing that other people—good and well-intentioned individuals—may have sexual values and attitudes, for example, that are quite different from those of one's own ethnic group.

In America there are more television sets per capita than in any other nation in the world. Television has an immense impact on learning and conveys an awareness of a vast range of human behavior to its viewers. This appears to have a liberalizing and educational impact rivaling that of the printed page. In addition, people travel a lot, not only on this continent but to Europe, Asia, the Middle East, and elsewhere. This too has a liberalizing effect and increases awareness of different values and moral attitudes about sexual behavior.

Finally, during the past century, migrations to the cities have resulted in social environments that are less controlling and less supervised, with a consequent weakening of ties to parental value systems. This is very different from the worlds of our parents, grandparents, and great-grandparents, who usually lived in smaller communities in which it was easier to reinforce the values shared by everyone in the community and easier to pass these values on to their children.

What is meant by morals, ethics, and values? Where do they come from and how are they changing in contemporary society? In a world of ever-increasing and ever-changing choices, what role do they play in shaping attitudes and guiding behaviors?

By morals we mean a set of principles, usually given form through the ages by great religious leaders and philosophers, that have withstood the test of time. These are guidelines that serve as the bases for determining right or wrong conduct in situations that are not always clear to us. Sociologists call these moral norms, that is, rules for moral behavior that have been with us for a long time and often have their roots in religion. Some moral norms are embodied in secular laws, such as in the criminal codes of each state. Also, some moral norms that at one time reflected only religious views have been modified by civil laws because they conflict with civil rights embodied in American and other Western civil codes and constitutions. Abortion and adultery laws are just two examples.

Ethics are the practical ways of making decisions so that we can determine if a particular behavior we are uncertain about is right or wrong according to a moral code. Ethical considerations are necessary because the morality of a specific social behavior often cannot be judged as an isolated act; we must also consider the social context in which it occurs. Ethics help us evaluate the morality of social behaviors by taking other information into consideration. For example, the Bible includes a commandment not to kill. If one person takes the life of another, it may be difficult to judge the morality or immorality of the act unless we know the ethical and situational context within which it is done. If a man cold-bloodedly takes the life of a shopkeeper during a robbery because he does not want the shopkeeper to identify him later, we can easily determine that this is murder and therefore an immoral act. On the other hand, consider a police officer confronting a robber who has just killed two innocent people. The robber refuses to surrender his gun and even shoots at the officer. Almost everyone would agree that it is ethical for this police officer to then draw his own gun and shoot the robber in order to protect innocent bystanders and himself, even if he kills the robber. In this case, he might even be considered a hero because he endangered his own life in the line of duty.

Values are another essential element in the determination of sexually moral conduct. Values are related to, but not the same as morals or ethics. By values is meant the desirability, worth, emphasis, or "value" placed by society or the individual on a particular behavior, symbol, or material thing relative to other things. Thus, we may know that having sex with someone we are attracted to is immoral according to our religious beliefs, but we may place a greater value on expressing love for this person physically and choose to engage in sex, even thought it violates what we were raised to believe is right.

Values influence nearly every aspect of our social behavior—from the very mundane to the most far-reaching. The career we choose, the kind of car we drive, the people with whom we associate, the kinds of food we eat, and certainly our sexual behaviors—all are reflections of our values. In studying social behavior, social scientists tell us that values are often more influential than morals or ethics in shaping of day-to-day behavior. This is true even when we are aware that our values may be in conflict with the moral standards to which we are supposed to subscribe by virtue of our religious upbringing. The images that we project to others (reflections of our values)—idealistic, materialistic, aesthetic, intellectual, sexy, and others—are often the bases for how we want them to think of us. In this way values are very active in our daily lives, while moral codes may remain dormant in the absence of continuous social reinforcement by the people around us—our peers and significant others. Thus values, which are often very changeable, can have more of a day-to-day influence over us than our moral and ethical beliefs.

While there is no simple or single answer to what is moral and ethical, it is clear that since sexual behaviors have consequences for one's self and others, principles and guidelines cannot be lightly derived to conveniently suit one's needs and desires. Everyone needs to consider the moral and ethical considerations implicit in sexual activity, as in all other areas of life. Perhaps an examination of the historical and traditional perspectives may provide a beginning, if not the complete answer (see also ABORTION; ADULTERY; AFFAIRS; NONMARITAL SEX).

SEXUAL ORIENTATION   see ADOLESCENCE; BISEXUALITY; HOMOSEXUALITY.

SEXUAL POSITIONS   see COITAL POSITIONS.

SEXUAL RESPONSE CYCLE   By the time they reach adulthood, almost all persons are aware that their bodies go through a series of changes when they become sexually aroused and proceed to MASTURBATION or SEXUAL INTERCOURSE. The most obvious changes for the males are erections and EJACULATION, and for females increased vaginal LUBRICATION and enlargement of the CLITORIS and the external fold of the VAGINA. A systematic study of this sexual response cycle was first carried out by Dr. William Masters and Dr. Virginia Johnson, who studied over 10,000 response cycles in 694 men and women during the late 1950s and early 1960s. Masters and Johnson described the sexual response cycle as having four stages, or phases, that blend into one another: excitement, plateau, ORGASM, and resolution. As they reported in their scholarly publications, however, there is a wide variety of individual variation in each of these stages with respect to their duration and intensity. Furthermore, for any given individual, the perception of the intensity of the excitement and response to stimulation may vary with the type of stimulation: oral, manual, penile, or vibrator (see MASTERS AND JOHNSON).

Helen Singer Kaplan modified the Masters and Johnson sexual response cycle based on her work treating sexual dysfunction problems in men and women. Dr. Kaplan added a prior stage of sexual desire (its absence is a common sexual dysfunction treated by Kaplan and other sex therapists), while eliminating the RESOLUTION PHASE that she believes to be an absence of sexual response rather than part of the cycle itself. In addition, Kaplan eliminated the plateau phase as defined by Masters and Johnson because she believed that it is essentially a continuation of the excitement phase and because it is of little value in sex therapy, due to the virtual impossibility of a patient distinguishing it from the excitement phase. Therefore, her model has only three phases: sexual desire, excitement, and orgasm (see KAPLAN, DR. HELEN SINGER).

Sexual Desire Phase. (Kaplan model only.) Sexual desire, sometimes termed LIBIDO, is the interest or sexual energy that precedes physical or psychological stimulation. Kaplan described the physiology of sexual desire as originating in the "sex circuits of the brain—mediated by TESTOSTERONE." She pointed out that while all the mechanisms involved in sexual desire are not known, "adequate levels of testosterone and a proper balance of the neurotransmitters serotonin and dopamine and the catecholamines are necessary for the normal functioning of the brain's sex circuits, both in male and females." This inner sexual feeling needs no erotic stimulation and is the basic sensation that may initiate sexual activity and upon which sexual stimulation then builds. When sexual desire is low or absent, sexual functioning may be inadequate, unsatisfying, or absent (see SEXUAL DYSFUNCTION, FEMALE; SEXUAL DYSFUNCTION, MALE).

Excitement Phase. (Kaplan and Masters and Johnson.) This stage is marked by vasocongestion (in this instance, a swelling of the genitalia due to more blood coming into the tissues than can be quickly drained away) leading to an ERECTION of the penis in males, and for females a swelling of the clitoris and vaginal lips, increased vaginal lubrication, an increase in breast size, and erection of the nipples. These are usually precipitated by physical, visual, or psycho-

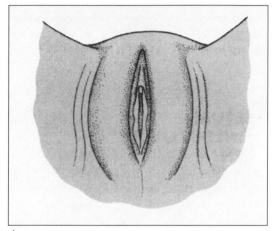

At rest

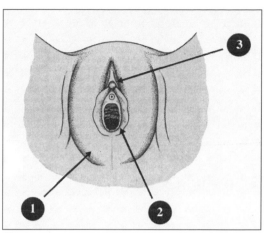

Excitement

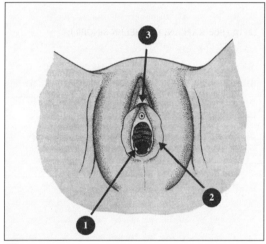

Plateau

In the excitement stage: 1) the labia majora become separated and elevated; 2)the labia minora
increase in size and become elevated; and 3) The
clitoris grows two to three times longer.

In the plateau stage: 1) the Bartholin gland ex-
cretes a few drops of fluid; 2) the labia minora redden and increase in size; and 3) the clitoris retracts
under the clitoral hood.

In the orgasm stage: there is no specific response
from 1) the labia majora, and 2) the labia minora;
the clitoris is retracted under the clitoral hood.

In the resolution stage: 1) the labia majora, 2) the
labia minora, and 3) the clitoris return to their normal size.

Orgasm

Resolution

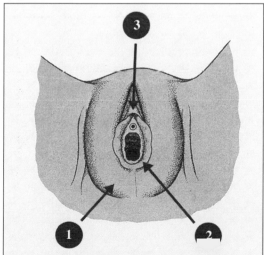

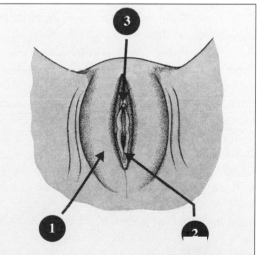

logical stimulation by one's self or a partner. In many men and women a "sex flush" appears on the upper abdomen and may spread to the chest. Arm and leg muscles, among others, begin to tense and there is an increase in heartbeat, breathing rate, and blood pressure.

Plateau Phase. (Masters and Johnson only.) This is a continuation of the excitement phase, with tensions building in all the processes cited above until an orgasm is triggered. For the male, an indication of reaching this phase is the presence of two or three "love drops," called Cowper's fluid, at the tip of the penis, composed of the preejaculatory fluid (these drops may contain sperm, thereby making withdrawal before ejaculation an ineffective form of contraception). The testes of the male are enlarged and are pulled closer to the body. (Kaplan incorporates these aspects of the plateau phase in her description of the excitement phase.)

Orgasm Phase. (Kaplan and Masters and Johnson.) For both men and women there are strong contractions in the penis and vagina at 0.8–second intervals, with the male ejaculation occurring in two stages: the feeling of inevitability (see MOMENT OF INEVITABILITY) and the actual ejaculation of semen. (Some authors have written about female ejaculation, but there is no scientific evidence that it exists.) Muscular contractions and spasms, including contortions of facial expression, appear for both sexes as does an increase in the respiratory rate to about 40 breaths per minute, in heart beat to as high as 180 beats per minute, and a further increase in blood pressure.

Resolution Phase. (Masters and Johnson only.) In this last stage of the sexual response cycle, the body slowly returns to the conditions that existed before the onset of the excitement phase. However, the rate of return appears to be much faster for males than for females. In addition, Masters and Johnson claim that males have a refractory period almost immediately after ejaculation, during which the body does not respond to further sexual stimulation for lengths of time varying from a few minutes (usually only in adolescents) to several hours or days depending upon one's age and physical condition. For the female, however, the length of the resolution phase may be considerably longer.

SEXUAL REVOLUTION A rapid change in sexual mores took hold in Western societies during the 1960s and 1970s. Often described by the media as "the sexual revolution," it reflected an increase in sexual activity among unmarried persons and changes in the traditional moral standards of marriage. For some people, what had once been secretive and marriage-threatening — cheating on one's spouse — became more open and even justifiable. Social commentators have attributed most of the changes in sexual behavior to the widespread use of ORAL CONTRACEPTIVES, eliminating fear of PREGNANCY; the growing legalization of ABORTION; increased nudity in the arts, particularly the stage and cinema; and much freer availability of sexual materials.

However, when examining data on changes in sexual behavior beginning in the 1960s, it appears that the term sexual revolution is somewhat misleading. It is true that more unmarried young men and women engaged in sex; that college dorms went co-ed; that many young couples lived together instead of dating; that some couples openly advocated what many had formerly done in private; and that women acknowledged their sexuality more openly. But social critics and sociologists today see all this not as a "revolution" but rather as an evolutionary trend that still continues, with the central theme of increasing the individual's freedom and choices and the curtailment of government interference in interpersonal sexual behavior.

It has been argued that radical change did not take place in sexual *behavior* but rather, in sexual *semantics*. Many sexual activities in which people have probably always engaged were now viewed as legitimate and acceptable, rather than as immoral and perverted. Indeed, if there is any sense to be made out of this period, it is that it reflected people's wishes to be seen as moral in the physical expression of their love and biological urges. That is, the traditional moral code condemning sexual expression outside of heterosexual, monogamous, marital relationships was being challenged.

The trend toward curtailing repression of human sexuality continues with the gay rights movement, the women's movement, the pro-choice movement, and many other struggles for respect of individual choice in sexuality. This evolutionary process is still going on.

SEXUAL STATUS EXAMINATION see SEX THERAPY.

SEXUAL STEREOTYPES The traits men and women are believed to possess because of their sex—whether or not they really are related to their sex—are called sexual stereotypes. Like assumptions about the qualities or characteristics of members of other groups (for example, racial or ethnic groups that often are regarded as being more or less violent than others, or more or less trustworthy or athletic or intelligent than others), stereotypes about men and women and the differences between them tend to stem from personal observations or old conventions.

Stereotypes of women usually focus on their presumed personality traits and intellectual abilities, so that they often are seen as more caring and nurturing and more emotional, less analytic, and less sexual than men (although some women may be stereotyped as insatiably sexual if their libidos are freed from restraint). The stereotypes associated with men characterize them as emotionally detached, aggressive, ambitious, and less concerned with relationships.

Stereotypes assume that any member of a group will possess the traits associated with it. They do not recognize the range of variation of personality traits and abilities among individuals in all groups (see also SEX ROLES).

SEXUALLY TRANSMITTED DISEASE (STD) More than twenty different microbes can be transmitted by sexual contact. These include bacteria, viruses (including the HIV viruses that cause the autoimmune deficiency syndrome [AIDS]), parasites, lice, and scabies. Several of these microbes can infect more than one anatomical site and many invade the blood stream, where they can spread to all organs and tissues of the body. It is also common for more than one STD microbe to infect the same anatomical site simultaneously, especially the urethra, the opening of the cervix, and the rectum (see specific sexually transmitted diseases, e.g.: AIDS; CHANCROID; CRABS AND SCABIES; GENITAL WARTS; GONORRHEA AND CHLAMYDIA; HEPATITIS; HERPES; SYPHILIS; VAGINITIS; YEAST VAGINITIS).

In any community there are persons whose sexual orientation or life-style puts them at high risk of acquiring an STD. Successful treatment and control of STDs, therefore, requires treatment of not only those who seek medical care because of their symptoms, but also their sexual partners, whether or not they have symptoms of infection. Treatment must be given simultaneously to sexual partners to avoid one or the other being re-exposed and infected (see also ANUS; PROMISCUITY; SAFER SEX).

SIXTY-NINE A form of ORAL SEX that two persons engage in simultaneously. The term, also known by the French words for sixty-nine, *soixante-neuf*, derives from a graphic representation of the number sixty-nine that, with a little imagination, can be visualized as two bodies entwined, with each person's head facing toward the other's feet. Sixty-nine may be engaged in by two women who perform CUNNILINGUS on each other, by two men who engage in FELLATIO with each other, or by a man and a woman—one performing cunnilingus and the other fellatio. This sexual variant has been known throughout history and is even depicted on ancient temple walls in India.

Although most people visualize sixty-nine with one partner on his or her back and the other on top, it may also be engaged in with both partners lying on their sides. While there are many jokes about sixty-nine and much speculation by young persons concerning its imagined virtues, writers on the subject of oral sex—including sex therapists—believe that, because of the acrobatics involved, it is not always a suitable method for providing stimulation to the CLITORIS or PENIS. In particular, it is very awkward for a person in this position to utilize any sophisticated techniques involving fellatio. For many people, sixty-nine is tiring and may inhibit the ability of each to stimulate the other. Sequential oral sex, rather than sixty-nine, probably offers greater latitude for sexual skills.

One problem, although not exclusive to sixty-nine, is the possibility that the male will have an ORGASM more quickly than his female partner and will be unable to continue the stimulation to bring her to orgasm for at least a few minutes, during which time her passion may wane. Other difficulties reported are a function of the many activities and sensations occurring simultaneously, resulting in each partner not fully enjoying the sensations being produced in them because they are concentrating on pleasuring their partner. Also, some women report that they feel uncomfortable when their male partner is on top and thrusting with his penis in their mouth if they are then unable to move their head back. For couples who find sixty-nine stimulating but arduous, the decision to use it during an early stage of lovemaking and then switch to a more comfortable position may be more sensible.

SODOMY A term that refers to "unnatural sex acts," usually defined legally as ANAL INTERCOURSE, FELLATIO, or ZOOPHILIA (see also RAPE LAWS).

SPANISH FLY see APHRODISIACS.

SPERM Microscopic cells produced in the testicles that carry a man's genetic potential. When sperm meet and combine with a woman's egg, together they begin the process leading to pregnancy and the creation of a new life. In the head of the sperm are chromosomes containing one half the genetic content of all other body cells (the other half of the genetic material in the cells of the fetus will come from the mother's egg). Half of a man's sperm cells contains the Y chromosome, which will produce a male child when combined with the X chromosome from the egg, and half carry the X chromosome, which specifies femaleness.

The sperm is the only cell in the human body that has a tail, enabling it to swim from the vagina, through the CERVIX and UTERUS, and to the FALLOPIAN TUBES, where it will meet the woman's egg. Each sperm has a cap (acrosome) containing powerful enzymes that enable the sperm to penetrate the protective coating around a woman's egg. A single sperm is a bit longer than one-thousandth of an inch and can swim one to two inches an hour.

A man's TESTICLES begin to manufacture sperm at the time of puberty and produce 50,000 sperm per minute, every minute of every hour, well into old age. Sperm production inside the testicles takes about seventy-seven days. It then takes another four to five days for the sperm to learn how to swim, in the duct called the epididymis. The vas deferens is the powerful muscular tube that propels the sperm from the epididymis to the PENIS. A man will normally

Left: The anatomy of a sperm cell: 1) head; 2) tail; 3) midpeice; and 4) acrosome. Right: Sperm cells are only one one-thousandth of an inch long. Each ejaculation contains several hundred million sperm cells

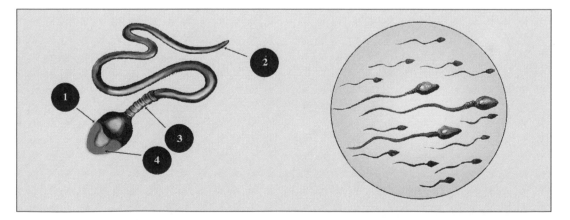

ejaculate 80 million to 300 million sperm at the time of ORGASM. Only a few of the millions of sperm deposited in the female vagina will survive the arduous journey to the fallopian tube, where one may meet and fertilize the woman's egg. Sperm can live from two to seventy-two hours inside the female reproductive tract.

Because sperm cells are so tiny, all 80 to 300 million can fit inside a space the size of a pinhead. Most of what comes out when a man ejaculates is the fluid that nourishes the sperm, not the sperm itself. The sperm and fluid from the testicles make up only 3 to 5 percent of the ejaculate. The rest is nourishing fluid made in the seminal vesicles (65 percent) and prostate (30 percent; see also CONCEPTION; IN VITRO FERTILIZATION; HEREDITY; INFERTILITY; ORGASM; SEMEN AND SEMINAL FLUID; SEXUAL DYSFUNCTION, MALE; SPERM BANKS; VASECTOMY AND THE MALE PILL).

SPERM BANKS For approximately forty years it has been known that human sperm can be frozen at very low temperatures (minus 196 degrees Celsius) and stored indefinitely. Facilities in which sperm are stored are known as "sperm banks."

Sperm can be stored for two reasons. The first is to be used by the man producing the sperm himself, as, for instance, someone who is facing potential chemotherapy for cancer, surgical loss of one or both testicles, or someone who is contemplating a vasectomy but wants to preserve the potential for creating a pregnancy in the future. In these situations, a man can make arrangements with a sperm bank for storage of his own sperm. Sperm samples are collected and are frozen in liquid nitrogen; they can be stored indefinitely until their use is desired to establish a pregnancy. Generally, the man storing the sperm does not need to undergo special testing.

The second, and more common use of sperm banks is for the storage of anonymously donated sperm. A major cause of infertility in couples is the male partner's low sperm count or low sperm motility (mobility). Although many of these men are helped with current medical and surgical treatments, there are many others for

whom these treatments are unsuccessful or who are completely lacking in the ability to produce sperm. In general, anonymously donated sperm is used in these cases. The physical characteristics of the donor are matched by the physician to the physical characteristics of the man so that the resulting child will resemble his or her parents as much as possible.

Since it is possible to transmit SEXUALLY TRANSMITTED DISEASES (including AIDS) through donated sperm, donors are carefully selected and screened, and semen samples are checked for the presence of diseases. At present, all semen used for anonymous donor insemination in this country is frozen and quarantined for a least six months before use. After the quarantine period, but before the sperm is released for insemination, the donor is called back and retested for sexually transmitted diseases, specifically AIDS, before the sample is released.

Donors are typically college students, medical students, or young professionals, who are paid for several sperm samples that will be used for artificial insemination to produce pregnancies in women unknown to them (see also ARTIFICIAL INSEMINATION BY DONOR).

SPERMICIDES see CONTRACEPTION; CONTRACEPTIVE FOAMS, CREAMS, AND GELS; SAFER SEX.

SPONTANEOUS ABORTION see MISCARRIAGE.

SPOTTING see HIGH-RISK PREGNANCY.

STAMP TEST Many men are troubled from time to time by bouts of impotence—the inability to obtain an erection when attempting to have sex—or some other form of erectile difficulty. Although a urologist should be consulted to ensure that there is no organic problem, some men can reassure themselves that they do not have a physical problem by taking the "stamp test." Simply buy a roll of postage stamps (the least expensive, of course). When you are ready to retire for the night, take five to eight stamps in a continuous strip and run them snugly around the base of your penis. Place a little moisture on the end of the last stamp so that the "ring" of stamps will stay in place during the night. If the strip of stamps is torn or split when you wake in the morning, you have probably had a good, stiff erection. If it is not, try again the next night, but make the stamps a little tighter.

Most men, even though they think that they do not have erections during sleep, do indeed have them. If your sexual apparatus is working (verify this with your physician if you wish), you will have to determine what kinds of psychogenic or situational factors may be causing you to have temporary impotence. If you cannot correct the problem quickly on your own, consult with a psychologist or a sex therapist (see also IMPOTENCE; SEXUAL DYSFUNCTION, MALE).

STERILIZATION   A surgical procedure performed on men or women to cut the path taken by the SPERM or ova to the point in the woman's body where fertilization would normally take place. Intended to be permanent, it is the most common form of BIRTH CONTROL used by married couples in the United States. The procedure performed on women is known as tubal sterilization; on men it is known as vasectomy (see also VASECTOMY AND THE MALE PILL).

Sterilization seals off a woman's FALLOPIAN TUBES, where eggs are normally fertilized by the sperm. By closing off these tubes, sperm cannot reach the eggs and the woman cannot be impregnated. This method of BIRTH CONTROL is very effective, though in rare cases the tubes may reconnect on their own and the woman might become pregnant. When this happens, a fertilized egg may develop outside the UTERUS, and such pregnancies will have to be ended with a surgical procedure.

Except for those rare instances, tubal sterilization—also known as tubal ligation—is a permanent procedure, so that if at a later time the woman decides that she does want to have children, she will not be able to do so. This would be so even if her current partner passed away and she married someone else and wanted to start a new family. Therefore, the decision to have tubal sterilization must be carefully consid-

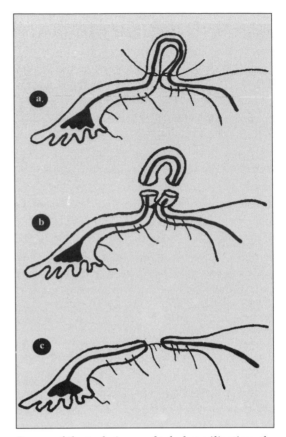

In one of the techniques of tubal sterilization, the tube is a) ligated (tied) and b) cut. After healing, the two ends are disconnected

ered. Among the reasons that some women undergo the procedure is that they might face serious health risks were they to become pregnant or if there are risks that they would pass on a hereditary disease to any offspring.

There are several different ways that sterilization can be performed. The two most common are laparoscopy and mini-laparotomy. In laparoscopy, the woman's abdomen is inflated with a harmless gas, the surgeon makes a small incision into the navel and inserts a laparoscope (a rod-like instrument with a light and viewing lens) with which to guide instruments used to close the tubes.

Laparotomy is usually performed on an outpatient basis and takes less than half an hour. In mini-laparotomy no gas is used and the surgery often takes place right after childbirth. Laparotomy, which involves more invasive surgery, and two vaginal procedures, culdoscopy and colpotomy, are more rarely used today because of the increased risks they pose.

The two most common forms of sterilization are low-risk procedures with minimal aftereffects, though with any surgical procedure there is always the chance of infection developing, internal bleeding, or a reaction to the anesthetic used. Because it does not interfere with the OVARIES or the normal production and cycle of sex HORMONES, sterilization does not affect the woman's sex drive and she will still have her normal periods.

The cost for tubal sterilization ranges from $1,000 to $2,500 in the United States, though some doctors are willing to adjust their fees in cases of need and some insurance policies may pay all or part of the cost.

SURGICAL MENOPAUSE see HORMONE REPLACEMENT THERAPY; HYSTERECTOMY.

SURROGATE MOTHERS Until recently this term was used to describe anyone standing in for a mother, such as an elder sister who really raised a child, or a house mother at school. Today, however, "surrogate mother" means just one thing—a woman who has had another woman's fertilized ovum implanted in her womb and who carries the PREGNANCY until delivery of the infant. In cases when a woman cannot carry a child to term but can persuade another woman to do so, this is now medically possible. A middle-aged woman of child-bearing age recently bore her daughter's child in this way; when the baby was born, she held her own grandchild.

A woman who obliges a childless couple by letting her own egg be fertilized by artificial insemination, contracting in advance to give up the child when it is born, is not a surrogate mother. She is that baby's own mother and the other woman's husband is its father.

The woman who bears a child for others provides a great service to the couple that want it. It is often heart-wrenching to give up the child, and counseling about what to expect at the end of the pregnancy is necessary (see also ARTIFICIAL INSEMINATION BY DONOR).

SURVEYS OF SEXUAL BEHAVIOR see KINSEY AND THE INSTITUTE FOR SEX RESEARCH; MASTERS AND JOHNSON.

SWINGERS The term "swinger" has evolved during the past thirty years. Before the 1960s it connoted a carefree, premarital, and youthful sexual lifestyle. During the 1960s and 1970s it applied, more specifically, to persons, usually married, who engaged in sexual activity involving three or more persons with all parties consenting. This included: mate swapping, troilism (threesomes), GROUP SEX (four or more persons), and open marriage. "Swinger" now carries both meanings and must be understood in context.

There are three main reasons given by swingers for their involvement in nonconventional sexual activities: sexual incompatibility with their partner or spouse, whom they otherwise love; a very high degree of libidinal energy, causing the swinger to get bored by only one partner; and feelings of insatiability, reported by some women—the Sherfey syndrome. A common view expressed by swingers is that there is a psychological difference between sexual variety with one person and a variety of sexual partners. The explanation for the difference is often based upon the view that sexual intimacy has a unique and unduplicable effect on each person for each unique combination of persons.

Earliest public attention to swinging occurred in the mass media in 1957. Social scientists began research on swinging during the early 1960s on both coasts and in the Midwest and Southwest. One of the researchers, Carolyn Symonds, noted a difference between "utopian swingers" and "recreational swingers." Utopian swingers were ideologically oriented persons who placed sex in the context of a philosophical system. They believed that war, violence, ecological destruction, wildlife extinction, and materialism were social evils—along with possessiveness, jealousy, and sexual exclusiveness. Many of them were attracted to the communes of the 1960s and 1970s or were in group living arrangements. They believed in love as a motivating and civilizing force, with the physical expression of that love being sex. They were in the tradition of American nineteenth century utopian groups such as the Oneida community. While some swingers today might still be considered "utopian," they seem to have been replaced by the second type: the recreational swingers. These were, and are, men and women, often married, who believe that it is more fun to have sex with friends and acquaintances than to play bridge or go bowling. Today the term "swinging" usually refers only to the "recreational" type.

Swingers today tend to be over the age of forty, middle class, politically conservative, and from a very restrictive sexual background and childhood. Most married swingers report that engaging in swinging was due to a deteriorating marriage, where dissatisfaction with sex was a major source of the marital discord. While many swingers report that their impending marital dissolution was temporarily avoided, very often one of the partners became bored or began to feel threatened when the other partner became more deeply involved in swinging, precipitating another marital crisis (see also PROMISCUITY).

SYPHILIS Syphilis was first recognized in the late fifteenth century in Europe, coinciding with the return of Christopher Columbus from the New World. Debate continues over the origin of syphilis: was it brought to Europe from the Americas, or did it arrive in Europe with West African slaves who were being imported by the Portuguese and Spanish at this time? At first, syphilis caused a massive European epidemic with a high fatality rate; the infection has become less virulent over the ensuing centuries.

Syphilis is caused by *Treponema pallidum*, a spiral-shaped, snake-like microscopic organism, and one of the few bacteria that cannot be artificially grown in a test tube. Syphilis is known as the "great imitator" because it can clinically resemble so many other diseases. It causes a disease that progresses over time by stages (primary, secondary, and tertiary), with each stage separated by intervals ranging from months to years, during which no signs of infection are evident.

The primary syphilitic lesion is the chancre, a circular, painless, and firm lesion that appears at the site of the invasion. A chancre may appear anywhere on the lips, mouth, tongue, nipples, rectum, or genitalia, from nine to ninety days after infection. Lymph nodes near the chancre are usually enlarged but not painful. The chancre heals spontaneously in six to ten weeks, and a quiescent period of time, lasting from six weeks to six months, passes before the symptoms and signs of secondary syphilis appear. These result from spread of the microbes by blood and the lymphatics from the infection site to every organ and tissue of the body. The most visible lesions are nonpainful skin rashes of various types: these often appear on the palms and the soles, do not itch, and heal without scars. Soon after secondary lesions heal, another quiescent period ensues. This period can last a lifetime, but late, tertiary lesions can also appear after a period of years. Late syphilitic lesions can destroy normal skin, bone, and joints by ulceration and scarification. Tertiary syphilis attacks the nervous system by interrupting the blood supply to the brain and nervous tissue or by replacing normal tissue with tumor-like masses. Treatment with a long-acting, injectable form of penicillin is curative when given to patients with primary, secondary, and latent syphilis. However, the nervous tissue, heart, skin, and bone damage of tertiary syphilis cannot be reversed by penicillin therapy (see also SAFER SEX; SEXUALLY TRANSMITTED DISEASES).

T

TAMPONS, PADS, SPONGES During MEN-STRUATION, women need to wear some form of absorbent material to collect their menstrual flow. Women in different cultures have handled their menstrual flow in many ways. From the earliest times, women have made tampons and pads from available materials, often washing and reusing special cloths or rags. In America today most women wear tampons or pads (pads are also referred to as sanitary napkins). A few women use menstrual sponges.

Commercially sold tampons are made from soft pieces of cotton compressed into the size and shape of a long lipstick tube. A tampon is worn inside the vagina and is inserted by pushing it up into the vagina with one's fingers. Some brands of tampons come in a cardboard tube or on a stick. These devices help the woman guide the tampon into place. A tampon also has a piece of string attached to one end. This string does not get inserted into the vagina and is used to pull the tampon out for disposal. One important advantage of tampons is that they prevent any external flow of blood. Because they are inside the vagina, they can be worn while swimming or with tight-fitting clothes. In the late 1970s an extremely rare but serious disease was associated with tampon use—TOXIC SHOCK syndrome (TSS). The disease occurred when bacteria multiplied in the vagina during use of certain types of tampons. It is important to remember that TSS is extremely rare and appears to be preventable if tampons are not left inside the vagina beyond the recommended period.

Menstrual pads or napkins are made of a soft, absorbent material and are shaped and sized to fit inside the bottom of a woman's panties. They usually attach to the underwear by means of a sticky backing. The first successful disposable sanitary napkin was marketed in 1921. They now come in a variety of thicknesses to handle different levels of menstrual flow—from light to heavy.

Some women have discovered that natural sponges (not artificial cellulose sponges) have many advantages for menstrual use. A sponge is soft and comfortable and when damp it conforms to the shape of a woman's vagina, eliminating the irritation of dryness common with tampons during a light flow. A sponge is also reusable. A woman can cut one to size with a pair of scissors, dampen it with water, and insert it gently into her vagina with her fingers. When she senses it is full, she can then remove it with her fingers, rinse it out in cool water, and reinsert it. Nevertheless, anyone contemplating the use of a sponge should consider that the United States Food and Drug Administration does not approve of them for menstrual use. Although they were used by some women in the 1970s, they are rarely encountered today.

TEENAGERS AND SEX Whether American society approves of it or not, sexual activity is common among adolescents. Teenagers are at a biological apex of energy, enthusiasm, and sexuality, and stern adult warnings to control their behavior do not often succeed. Physically, teenagers are biologically ready for sex. This does not mean that teenagers must engage in intercourse or that they cannot learn to approach sex responsibly or practice abstinence until they are married. It simply means that sexuality is a force that must be considered.

The number of adolescents having intercourse has steadily increased during the second half of this century. A generation ago, fewer than half of young Americans had sexual intercourse before marriage. Today, one-third of all adolescents have had intercourse by age fifteen. By age twenty, nearly 80 percent have experienced sex.

Adults must recognize that sexual feelings are a natural part of growing up and sexual curiosity and exploration are natural results of maturation. Yet, however natural sex may be for teenagers, there is good reason for adults to be concerned. More than one million teenage girls become pregnant each year in the United States, and 84 percent of these pregnancies are unintentional. The Center for Population Options estimates that 41 percent of these pregnancies could be avoided if all sexually active teenagers used contraception, but only one-third of all sexually active teenagers say that they always use contraceptives.

There is also a growing problem of SEXUALLY TRANSMITTED DISEASES (STDs). Every year, 2.5 million teenagers are infected with a sexually transmitted disease—approximately one out of every six sexually active teenagers. Young people may believe they are invulnerable, but the fact is that when they engage in sex they are at risk. AIDS, too, is on the rise within the teenage population.

It is not a good idea for teenagers to deny their sexuality—sex, after all, is a natural part of life—but they must understand that a sexual relationship can have consequences and must, therefore, be approached in a responsible manner. There are plenty of ways to be sexual without endangering oneself or becoming pregnant.

Teenagers who have made the decision to have intercourse must use contraception. The most common methods of BIRTH CONTROL for teenagers are ORAL CONTRACEPTIVES and CONDOMS. Of sexually active teenage girls who practice contraception, 64 percent rely on the pill, while 21 percent rely on condoms. Both methods are easily available: condoms can be purchased in any drug store and, in most cases, girls can get prescription contraceptives at Planned Parenthood without the clinic notifying their parents.

Teenagers must never feel obligated to engage in intercourse. If a teenager has doubts or thinks that he or she might later regret having sex, it is probably a good idea to wait. The decision to become sexually active must not be based on what others think. After all, there are always other sexual options.

MASTURBATION is an acceptable way of releasing sexual tension. About 80 percent of adolescent girls and 90 percent of boys masturbate with frequencies ranging from once a day to once a week. Masturbation is a normal, safe, and readily-available sexual experience (although some religions forbid it). For most teenagers, masturbation is the most frequent sexual outlet. It is also a good way for a young person to discover the kinds of touching that bring him or her the most pleasure.

Some adolescents, especially boys, masturbate together or masturbate each other. This kind of experimentation is normal and does not mean they are gay. Girls may also touch or rub each other and it does not mean they are lesbians. Sexual curiosity is very intense during adolescence, and can naturally lead to different types of exploration. Of course, if a teenager is certain that he or she is gay, it is probably a good idea to find someone with whom he or she can talk about it. Many cities have support groups for young people who think they might be gay. But it is also important for teenagers to know that many heterosexual adolescents experience crushes on a person of the same sex.

While teenagers often rush headlong into SEXUAL INTERCOURSE, sometimes before they are really ready to handle it, this is often because there is not a lot of good information available on SAFER SEX. Teenagers are often pressured by peers or influenced by the media to think that intercourse is the only way to have sex. For many teenagers "outercourse" (bringing a partner to ORGASM without intercourse) is actually a better option. Outercourse can involve an entire range of sexual activity—playing with a partner's genitals, exploring their whole body, KISSING, or ORAL SEX. It reduces the chances of STDs and can be extremely pleasurable. Girls consistently have more orgasms and boys have the opportunity to learn better love-making techniques. Outercourse compels a couple to slow down and explore the kinds of touching that give the most pleasure, and it teaches sensitivity to a partner's needs. Outercourse is a wonderful way for teenagers to enjoy their sexuality.

If teenagers do decide to engage in intercourse, they must recognize some important ground rules. If they think they are old enough to have sex, then they must be adult enough to do it with respect—for themselves and their partner. They must respect their partner's tastes, and never do things just for their own pleasure. They must not pressure their lovers into doing something they do not want to do. They must not lie to get what they want. They must protect their partners against PREGNANCY and STDs. Sex should never become just "scoring."

Sometimes, even when acting responsibly, a teenage girl becomes pregnant. An unwanted pregnancy can be a frightening experience. When a boy makes a girl pregnant, he is likely to be anxious or even terrified by the situation and ignorant about where to turn for help. The first thing he should do is talk things over with the girl. The pregnancy is taking place in her body, and ultimately she is the one who will have to decide what to do, hopefully with his agreement and support. For the girl, pregnancy can cause fear and guilt. She must not waste a lot of time trying to deny it. If a teenage girl thinks she may be pregnant, the first thing she must do is find out whether she really is pregnant. If she feels she cannot discuss this with her parents, she should talk to a counselor or other health professional. Counselors at Planned Parenthood will keep their meetings with a girl confidential. If a girl discovers that she is pregnant, she should ideally discuss her options with her parents. Sometimes, however, there are compelling reasons why she cannot, and Planned Parenthood's counselors can offer further help.

There are generally four options available to a teenage girl if she becomes pregnant:

- Have an abortion;
- Keep the baby and raise it by herself;
- Keep the baby and marry the father;
- Have the baby and give it up for adoption.

The girl should consider her options carefully, weighing all the pros and cons. She may be pressured by her parents, boyfriend, girlfriends, and others, but the decision is hers alone. She must live with whatever follows her decision.

Abortion. Four out of ten teenagers with unwanted pregnancies have abortions. The decision to have an abortion is never easy, and many girls feel sadness or guilt over it. But the overwhelming emotion most teenagers feel is relief. They can choose to have babies later in their lives, when they are able to provide them with lots of love and care.

Keeping and Raising the Baby. Each year more than half a million teenagers decide to keep their babies. Some of them end up feeling trapped, resentful, and cheated of their childhood. It is not easy to raise a baby even under the best of circumstances. A teenage girl must ask herself is she is prepared for the responsibility of motherhood. For some, however, this is the best choice, and a very rewarding decision.

Marrying the Father and Raising the Child Together. For older teenager girls, and especially ones who are already engaged, the chances of feeling good about keeping the baby are better than if they are young and alienated from the baby's father. Many couples who marry because a baby is on the way end up in miserable or broken marriages. Marrying for the sake of a baby is very risky.

Giving the Baby up for Adoption. Each year thousands of teenagers choose this option. They realize they are too young or too alone to be the kind of mother they would like to be. Some may ask how they can give their baby away. But for girls with religious or other objections to abortion, it is, in fact, very courageous to offer their baby to a couple that desperately wants a child and is able to give one the future it deserves.

None of these choices is easy. Certainly the best situation for a teenage girl is to never be forced to make such a decision. But pregnancy is a real possibility if one is having sexual intercourse, and contraception must always be used. If a teenager is not ready to deal with that fact responsibly, then he or she is not ready for intercourse (see also CHASTITY; VIRGINITY).

TESTICLES (TESTES) The main organs of the male reproductive system. They are egg-shaped and paired and reside in a sac outside of the male body called the scrotum. In this location, they are kept about 4 degrees Celsius cooler than the rest of the body's organs because they function better at the lower temperature.

The testicles have two separate but related main functions. Most of the testicle is devoted to production of SPERM, the microscopic cells with tails that carry the man's genetic potential to a woman's egg. The other important function of the testicle (testis) is to manufacture the male sex hormones, primarily TESTOSTERONE. At the time of puberty, the testicles receive a hormonal signal from the pituitary gland of the brain that tells them to start making testosterone. These hormones trigger the growth of a man's pubic hair, beard, muscles, and PENIS, along with voice change and sex drive. Together with the brain's hormone signal, the testosterone made by hor-mone-producing cells in the man's testicles stimulates the reproductive cells (spermatogonia) to start dividing and producing sperm. In normal men sperm is produced at the rate of 50,000 sperm per minute, every minute of every day, from puberty until old age. The sperm manufacturing process takes about seventy-seven days, after which the sperm leave the testicles through a series of tiny ducts at the top and enter the epididymis, a 15–foot-long coiled duct, where they acquire the ability to swim and fertilize an egg. The sperm are then propelled from the epididymis to the penis by the vas deferens, a muscle-clad tube about fifteen inches long.

The testicles are very sensitive to heat, drugs, alcohol, radiation, and environmental toxins. Exposure to any of these can impair the ability of testicles to manufacture healthy sperm and hormones. About 15 percent of men have varicose veins called a varicocele surrounding their testes. These overheat the testicles and, over time, decrease a man's fertility. Varicoceles can be safely repaired by an operation called varicocelectomy to prevent or treat male infertility. If one or both testicles do not descend into the scrotal sac by infancy (a condition called cryptorchidism, or an undescended testicle) it must be brought down with hormone shots or surgery. Men with this condition may have reduced fertility and have a higher risk of developing cancer in the affected testicle (see also TESTICULAR CANCER; VASECTOMY AND THE MALE PILL).

The anatomy of the testicle

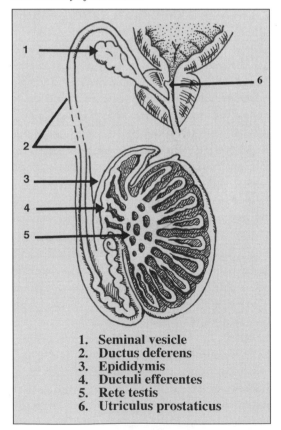

1. **Seminal vesicle**
2. **Ductus deferens**
3. **Epididymis**
4. **Ductuli efferentes**
5. **Rete testis**
6. **Utriculus prostaticus**

TESTICULAR CANCER A relatively rare disease that usually causes no symptoms in its earliest stages. It normally occurs in men between the ages of fifteen and thirty-five, although in one form or another it may affect men of any age. It is a young man's disease and is actually the most common form of cancer among men in their late twenties and early thirties. Fortunately, it is also one of the most curable of all cancers if caught early, and since the TESTICLES are outside the body, they are easy to examine.

Cancer of the testicle usually begins as a painless lump or mass in one testicle. It is often noted after minor trauma or injury to the scrotum and its presence is often missed because of

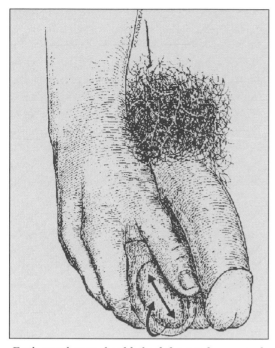

Each month men should check for any lumps or abnormal growths on their testicles by gently rolling them between their thumb and forefingers.

the presumed injury to the testicle. The best method for early detection of the cancer is to perform a monthly examination of the testicles, most conveniently while taking a shower or bath. (Men who are reluctant to perform the recommended examination could urge sexual partners to do it.) A testicle should be smooth and firm with slight softness. Hardness to the testicle, a lump, or any difference between one testicle and the other should result in prompt examination by a qualified doctor. Further examination may include an ultrasound examination of the testicle, which uses sonar and is painless.

Injury to the testicle does not cause testicular cancer. Testicular cancer is more common in men whose testis was not descended at birth (cryptorchidism). Treatment for cryptorchidism does not affect the chance of testicular cancer occurring, however, and testicular self-examination is critically important for men with a history of undescended testicles.

Treatment of testicular cancer involves removal of the testicle and evaluation for spread of the cancer with a CAT scan, blood tests, and possibly other tests. If the cancer has spread beyond the testicle itself, surgery on the abdomen or chemotherapy may be needed. The vast majority of cases of testicular cancer are now curable either with surgery or a combination of surgery and chemotherapy or radiation. Early diagnosis and initiation of treatment is critical to allow the best possible cure rates. Any man who notices a difference in his testicles or a hard area in one testicle should promptly see a urologist or other qualified physician.

If a testicle is removed during treatment, the remaining one takes over to produce the normal amount of TESTOSTERONE and sperm. Only one testicle is necessary for normal sexuality and fertility (see also CASTRATION).

TESTOSTERONE The reproductive HORMONES are classified into three major categories: progestins, estrogens, and androgens. These three types of hormones are found in both males and females, but the amount of each is determined by the individual's sex. The progestins and estrogens are female hormones, and the androgens are male hormones. The androgen produced in the highest concentration in the male is testosterone.

Testosterone has a complex role in the determination of secondary sexual characteristics. At puberty, testosterone production begins and affects growth, bone structure, and muscle size and tone. The male pattern of hair distribution of the body and face are also determined by testosterone and it affects the distribution of hair on the head as the man ages.

Testosterone also affects LIBIDO and, to some extent, sexuality. Its effect on the brain accounts for some male-associated behavior characteristics, such as aggression. FSH (follicle stimulating hormone), produced by the pituitary gland, stimulates the testes to produce sperm cells. A second pituitary hormone, LH (luteinizing hormone), acts on the testes to stimulate the production of testosterone which, in turn, helps maintain the production of sperm cells. The concentration of testosterone in the male remains at a fairly constant level thoughout life once past puberty (see also AGING AND SEX; TESTICLES).

TOBACCO see FETAL AND INFANT SUBSANCE ABUSE SYNDROMES.

TOXIC SHOCK In the early 1980s the emergence of a virulent type of infection, sometimes fatal, was associated with women's use of tampons. Labelled toxic shock syndrome, the illness, which attacked many vital organs, resulted from the release of a toxin in infections caused by a strain of bacteria called the coagulase positive staphylococcus.

The disease was distinctive, with fever, low blood pressure, and involvement of the skin (initial reddening and later peeling), particularly of the palms of the hand and soles of the feet. There was a multisystem involvement that sometimes included three or more of the following: gastrointestinal, muscular, mucous membranes, kidney, liver, blood (decreased platelet counts), and the central nervous system. In these patients the coagulase positive staphylococcus could frequently be isolated from the primary site of infection, usually the vagina, but the organism did not invade the blood stream.

As the disease reached epidemic proportions in the early 1980s, some distinctive characteristics were noted. Ninety percent of toxic shock syndrome (TSS) victims were women, most under the age of thirty-four, and the onset of their symptoms occurred either during the menstrual period or immediately afterward. TSS was also four times more common in North Central and Mountain States than in Mid- or South Atlantic States. The association of TSS with tampon use was noted from the earliest reports and users of super-absorbent tampons that remain in the vagina for the longest period of time were at the greatest risk.

The removal of super-absorbent tampons from the market markedly reduced, but did not totally eliminate, TSS. Any body infection with this strain of bacteria, for example an abdominal wound infection after an operation, can result in toxic shock syndrome.

Antibiotics such as penicillin and cephalosporin are effective against this organism and corticosteroids help obviate the effects of the toxin on body organ systems. Recently, a syndrome identical to TSS in clinical presentation and laboratory abnormalities has been reported in patients with an infection from another form of bacteria called the group A beta hemolytic streptococcus. A review of case reports of infections caused by this bacteria in the 1960s and 1970s suggests this syndrome was already noted then although not recognized as such. These infections, however, are very rare. The group A beta hemolytic streptococcus can be killed by a variety of antibiotics, and organ system changes can be obviated by medical care.

TSS is a serious problem for the patient involved, but fortunately it is a rare event in the 1990s (see also TAMPONS, PADS, AND SPONGES).

TRANSSEXUALITY Transsexuals are biologically normal persons whose core gender identity is the opposite of their anatomic sex. They share three common characteristics: dislike of their own sexual anatomy; determination to become a member of the opposite sex; and an urge to cross-dress, although little sexual arousal accompanies the act. Transsexuals feel that they are emotionally and psychologically of the opposite gender and that a biological error has occurred that traps them in the wrong-gender body. Most transsexuals are born biological males.

Transsexuality is frequently equated in the popular press with "sex change" surgery, but the term actually refers to the condition, not the treatment. Another area of confusion arises from popular usage of the terms "transsexual," "transvestite," and "homosexual." These terms describe separate conditions but are frequently used interchangeably. Homosexuals are persons who prefer relations with a member of their own gender. Genital orgasm is important to homosexuals, and they have no true urge to rid themselves of their genitals. Most prefer to wear clothing specific to their own gender. A transvestite is a man who finds sexual arousal in wearing women's clothing. An important difference between a transvestite and a male transsexual lies in the transvestite's feelings toward the PENIS. For the transsexual his penis, especially when erect, is disgusting, while the transvestite may have satisfying heterosexual relationships.

Transsexuals are more intense in their cross-gender identity and are interested in male sex partners. Transsexuals are more likely to dress continuously as women.

The modern treatment of transsexuality began with the first successful "sex change" operation performed in Denmark in 1952. References to transsexuals exist throughout history, beginning with Greek mythology and extending through ancient Rome to the seventeenth and eighteenth centuries, when several prominent transsexuals wrote their autobiographies.

Male-to-Female Sex Change Treatment and Surgery. Arndt describes five steps in the evaluation and treatment of transsexual patients. The first is to determine whether the patient is appropriate for gender reassignment. This is done to exclude homosexuals, transvestites, and patients who appear to be psychologically unstable, such as gender-confused schizophrenics. Also excluded are those who have a transient or situational motivation for sex change, for example, a homosexual who views gender reassignment as a way to escape anxiety and guilt over his homosexuality. This type of patient responds well to psychotherapy and would adapt poorly to gender reassignment. The second step is counseling to explore the stability of the patient's gender identity and any misconceptions or extravagant expectations.

In the third step, nonsurgical alteration of secondary sex characteristics is attempted. Estrogen treatment to reduce libido produces testicle atrophy, re-distributes body fat, and augments breast tissue. The voice is most difficult to alter and, although its pitch can be raised with estrogen, a fundamental male quality usually remains.

The fourth stage is to test the patient's ability to live as a female for a year or more at work, socially, and at home. During this time the patient should achieve gender reorientation by assuming the status of the opposite sex.

The fifth step is reconstructive surgery to remove the male organs and construct female genitalia. This involves amputation of the penis, removal of the TESTICLES, and construction of a VAGINA. The vagina must be adequate for intercourse and should retain erectile tissue for in-creased sensation during sexual arousal. It is also important to locate the urethral opening in a normal female position. Parts of the male organs are used to create the new female genitalia. Further cosmetic surgery is sometimes performed to augment the BREASTS, feminize facial features, and reduce the Adam's apple. Sex reassignment surgery is associated with more complications than many other surgical procedures. One-half to two-thirds of patients may experience loss of the new vaginal lining, vaginal stenosis, infections, bleeding, or loss of skin grafts.

Female-to-Male Gender Reassignment. Male transsexuals outnumber female transsexuals by a ratio of approximately four to one. The female applicant to a reputable gender identity program is required to pass through the same initial steps as the male. Many urologists believe that long-term psychotherapy, not surgery, is the treatment of choice in these cases. There have been few reports of successful gender identity changes involving biological females. The failure of sex reassignment surgery in the female is related to the difficulty of creating an adequate length of urethra and a functional penis for intercourse.

Transsexualism is a mind-versus-body gender contradiction that can often be treated surgically and hormonally. It is very important that the diagnosis of transsexualism be firmly established and a deliberate step-by-step treatment plan be followed. Hasty diagnosis and failure to follow the step-by-step method risks performance of mutilating surgery on homosexuals, transvestites, and schizophrenics, who will adapt poorly to their new gender. Good social and sexual adaptation can be expected from gender reassignment surgery on properly selected transsexuals (see also GENDER DYSPHORIA).

TRANSVESTISM Transvestites, or "cross-dressers," are people who derive sexual pleasure from dressing as a member of the opposite sex. Transvestites are not necessarily homosexuals, and many have satisfying heterosexual relationships. Transvestism is actually an extreme form of FETISHISM (see also TRANSSEXUALITY).

TUBAL PREGNANCY see ECTOPIC PREGNANCY.

U

URETHRITIS An inflammation or infection of the urethra (urine passage) common to either sex. In men there is usually a sensation of burning on urination or a discharge from the PENIS. The discharge may be white or yellow and may be noticed by the man on his underwear.

In addition to being caused by infection, urethritis can also be caused by chemical or mechanical irritation. Chemical irritation of the urethra can occur from spermicides or other vaginal lubricants. Mechanical irritation of the urethra can occur during sexual intercourse, especially if inadequate lubrication is present.

Symptoms of urethritis may also be caused by infectious or other problems arising elsewhere in the urinary or genital tract. For example, men with early prostatitis (inflammation of the prostate gland) may initially develop symptoms of urethritis. In women, the symptoms of urethritis can also be caused by a severe episode of VAGINITIS. Distinguishing between these two problems is sometimes difficult and requires an examination of urine and vaginal secretions.

In most cases, infectious urethritis is easily treated with antibiotics. Since urethral infections are commonly transmitted through sexual contact, it is often necessary to treat the sexual partner too.

UROLOGIST'S EXAMINATION see GEN-ITO-UROLOGICAL EXAMINATION.

UTERINE CANCER Cancer of the UTERUS is a disease of advancing age. Most cases occur in women over the age of fifty. It is estimated that 3 percent of women develop carcinoma of the uterine mucosa (endometrium) by age seventy-five. The increasing rate of endometrial cancer during the last decade is partly due to an increasing proportion of older women in the general population. Environmental factors may also play a part in the development of endometrial cancer. In the West there was a rise in the incidence of the disease in the early 1970s and there are substantially lower rates in Asia and South America.

Risk Factors. The incidence of uterine cancer is highest among women who have no children—with impaired fertility due to lack of ovulation; with few or no pregnancies; with impaired menstrual patterns, especially with long intervals between periods; obese women who suffer from diabetes mellitus or hypertension; women with a family history of malignancy; and women of higher socioeconomic groups. Continuous estrogen stimulation with hormonal imbalance is associated with the development of endometrial cancer. On the other hand, women taking ORAL CONTRACEPTIVES for more than one year are at lower risk of developing endometrial cancer than other women.

Symptoms. The most common first sign of uterine cancer is abnormal vaginal bleeding: vaginal bleeding in postmenopausal women is abnormal and should be immediately investigated. In premenstrual women symptoms such as spotting, heavy prolonged vaginal bleeding, and intermenstrual bleeding should be investigated. These symptoms usually appear early in the course of the disease. If diagnosis is established then and treatment undertaken immediately, survival rates are above 95 percent. On the other hand, the cure rate for advanced cases is negligible. Other symptoms such as pressure and distension of the pelvis and bladder irritation occur as the disease progresses.

Screening and Early Diagnosis. Any woman who experiences abnormal bleeding should be investigated by a physician and an endometrial sampling should be taken. Other procedures for screening high risk populations include: a PAP TEST; ultrasonography, endometrial samplings, and hysteroscopy.

Treatment. Fortunately, symptoms usually occur at an early stage, before the disease has spread beyond the uterus. With early diagnosis, there is a high cure rate. Both surgery and irradiation have been effectively used to treat carcinoma of the endometrium. For patients in good physical condition, surgery is the main treatment. During surgery the extent of the cancer's spread is evaluated and the uterus and both ovaries are removed. For early stages of uterine carcinoma, this treatment alone provides a five-year survival rate of more than 85 percent. For patients who cannot medically tolerate an operation or for women with cancer that has spread beyond the uterus, irradiation, either locally (vaginal or intrauterine irradiation) or externally is the treatment of choice. There are several combinations of different treatment modalities and any woman with endometrial cancer should be treated at an experienced oncological center where the best treatment routine will be chosen. Treatment should be discussed with the patient, taking into consideration the advantages and disadvantages of each modality.

UTERUS The female uterus, or womb, is the organ within which a newly fertilized egg is implanted to begin its development through successive stages as an embryo, a fetus, and at BIRTH, a newborn infant.

The uterus, an organ with roughly the size and shape of a pear—except during PREGNANCY—is situated in the woman's lower abdomen at the internal and upper end of the vagina. The lower opening of the uterus, the cervix, can be exposed at the time of a physician's PELVIC EXAMINATION with the aid of an instrument called a speculum, which gently separates the walls of the vagina. The opening of the cervix, called the cervical canal, leads to the interior lining of the uterus, the endometrium. Within the uterine cavity are two more openings, the canals of the fallopian tubes, through which the egg or ovum passes after fertilization to reach the uterus.

Pregnancy is considered to begin with implantation of a newly fertilized egg in the endometrium. The uterus will provide the environment and protection necessary as a new pregnancy begins the complex process of growth through the nine months of gestation required by a full-term infant. The blood vessels to the uterus develop to make it possible for the mother's blood supply to provide oxygen and other metabolic and nutritional substances needed for growth and development as the fertilized egg grows into the embryonic and then fetal stages. These life-supporting substances are transmitted to the fetus through the PLACENTA, a fluid-filled sac that forms within the uterus and around the developing embryo and cushions and protects it. The uterus and placenta expand to many times their initial size during the course of pregnancy.

In what may seem a contradiction to its ability to stretch to many times its usual size during pregnancy, the uterus is primarily a muscular organ. The muscular component surrounding the endometrium is called the myometrium. During labor, the myometrial contractions force the emerging baby down through the dilated cervix and vagina toward delivery. In the nonpregnant woman, myometrial contractions are the cause of menstrual cramps (dysmenorrhea). Prostaglandins, natural hormones, initiate myometrial contractions, and pitocin, a pituitary hormone, also causes uterine contractions.

When a sexually mature woman is not pregnant, her uterus responds to the cyclic hormonal secretions of her ovaries, almond-sized organs on either side of the uterus that contain her ova. Once each month an ovary releases one ovum (egg) into a fallopian tube for potential fertilization. Prior to ovulation, the point in the menstrual cycle when the ovum is released by the ovary, the lining of the uterus is built up in response to increasing levels of the hormone estrogen. After ovulation, the endometrium is kept in a receptive state for the possible implantation of a fertilized ovum by increased levels of progesterone and estrogen. If an ovum does not implant, there is an abrupt drop in these hormone levels, the small arteries supplying the uterine lining (the endometrium) constrict, and the lining disintegrates and is shed with the bleeding we call "MENSTRUATION." Women usually begin having menstrual periods sometime after the age of ten and continue to have them at regular intervals until middle age. The time when menstrual periods cease is called menopause.

V

VAGINA One of the woman's principal FEMALE SEX ORGANS, the vagina is a hollow muscular tube extending from the CERVIX at the entrance to the UTERUS to the external opening between the woman's labia (lips). It is the organ into which the erect male PENIS is inserted during SEXUAL INTERCOURSE and it receives the sperm ejaculated by the male's ORGASM. Unless a barrier such as a condom or diaphragm prevents sperm from reaching the inner vagina, it is there they begin their voyage into the woman's body—from the vagina into the uterus and one of the FALLOPIAN TUBES, where fertilization of the woman's egg may take place.

An adult woman's vagina is about 3 to 4 inches (8 to 10 centimeters) long when it is at rest. Its walls lie against each other but it is extremely flexible. During intercourse the vagina expands to receive the male's penis and during childbirth it expands to many times its normal size, becoming the birth canal through which the child about to be born passes from the uterus to the world outside.

The walls of the vagina have three layers: the vaginal lining (or mucosa), the muscular layer, and a layer of connective tissue (the advunticia). The mucosa is very thick and forms several longitudinal and circular folds. Its tissue changes in response to hormonal changes in the menstrual cycle, due primarily to estrogen levels. Under the stimulus of estrogen, glycogen (a storage form of carbohydrates) synthesis and accumulation take place. The bacteria normally present in the vagina metabolize the glycogen and form lactic acid, responsible for the vagina's usually acidic environment. During medical treatment involving antibiotics, these bacteria are suppressed and the acidic vaginal environment is lost, allowing fungal or bacterial growth.

The vaginal mucosa is lubricated by the transudation (passage) of fluids through the vagina's walls, especially during sexual excitation. Mucus from the cervix lubricates the vagina as well.

The muscular layer contains muscle bundles running longitudinally and circumferentially. These muscles are rich in blood and during sexual arousal vasocongestion of the vaginal wall occurs. Muscles of the pelvic floor blend with the vaginal wall at the middle (mid-length) of the vagina. These muscles are responsible for keeping the vagina elevated, tight, and firm. Repeated exercise of these muscles prevents their loosening (see KEGEL EXERCISES).

In prepubertal girls who lack adult hormonal development, the vaginal wall is thin, glycogen deficient, and predisposed to bacterial infections. During the reproductive years, poor hygiene, contraceptive agents, sexual intercourse, and use of tight, nonabsorbent underwear may cause vulvo-vaginal infections.

In postmenopausal women, due to low estrogen levels, the cells of the vaginal mucosa lose glycogen and vaginal acidity declines, resulting in vaginal tissue that is fragile and susceptible to trauma and infection. The hormone replacement therapy taken by many women after menopause reverses the thinning of the vaginal mucosa and restores the acidic environment of the vagina.

The lack of estrogen common in postmenopausal women affects the pelvic blood supply and soft tissue of the vagina, compromises the elasticity of pelvic structures, and may result in internal slippage of the uterus, bladder, rectum, and intestine. The most common symptom of vulvo-vaginal disease is an intense itching, which can be caused by either infection, or rarely, by precancerous or cancerous diseases. Any such complaint should be carefully investigated by a physician (see also CLEANLINESS AND SEXUAL ODORS; EPISIOTOMY; LUBRICATION).

VAGINAL HYSTERECTOMY see HYSTERECTOMY.

VAGINAL LUBRICATION see LUBRICATION.

VAGINITIS A woman suffering from vaginitis experiences either an increased vaginal discharge or burning or itching in the vaginal area. This is not a trivial problem for women. For one thing, it occurs frequently, accounting for an estimated one-third of women's out-patient visits to a gynecologist. Patients with these symptoms are hindered in their normal business and social activities. It can also be a sign of more serious disease in some cases, such as genital tract cancer or GONORRHEA AND CHLAMYDIA. Because of this, it is important that women with persistent or recurrent vaginal symptoms seek a medical evaluation and not rely on over-the-counter medications.

There are a wide variety of infectious agents that can cause vaginitis. The three most common are *Bacterial vaginosis*, *Candida vaginitis*, and *Trichomonas vaginitis*. Although the three have some similar symptoms, there are some characteristic clinical findings for each. Patients with *Bacterial vaginosis* have a persistent, often malodorous discharge that is often most pronounced when they have had intercourse and the VAGINA has been exposed to the male ejaculate. This overgrowth of a group of bacteria in the vagina calls for treatment with either systemic or local antibiotics. Patients with *Candida vaginitis* often display increased vaginal discharge and itching after receiving systemic antibiotics for another reason, such as an abscessed tooth or a sore throat. Since the symptoms are caused by an overgrowth of yeast (*Candida*) in the vagina, treatment is with a topical antifungal preparation. Patients with *Trichomonas vaginitis* usually have a persistent and uncomfortable vaginal discharge. The symptoms are cause by an overgrowth of the protozoa *Trichomonas vaginalis* in the vagina, and the antiprotozoal medication, oral metronizadole, is given for cure. Male sexual partners can be asymptomatic carriers of the organism and should be treated as well.

There are other causes of vaginitis. Postmenopausal women can have vaginal discomfort and burning from a lack of ESTROGEN. These symptoms can be alleviated by the use of systemic or vaginal estrogens. Obviously, their use should be preceded by a thorough physical and pelvic examination to be sure that there is no other pelvic pathology. In sexually active young women, an abnormal discharge may be due to an infection of the cervix caused by *Neisseria gonorrhea*, *Chlamydia trachomatis*, or the Human Papilloma Virus (HPV). The presence of the first two can be determined by laboratory cultures and all three can be detected by DNA probe techniques. The first two organisms are bacteria and, when present, should be treated with antibiotics. Male sexual partners should be treated as well. HPV is treated with local laser ablation of abnormal tissue, or with trichloracetic acid or 5 fluorouracil.

Another common cause of vaginitis is allergy. The most common sources are vaginal contraceptive gels, vaginal anti-fungal creams, suppositories, and the male ejaculate. In most cases, the cause of the allergic reaction is not determined. For many of these women, antihistamines are quite helpful.

Vaginitis remains a complex medical problem. It requires a physician's evaluation to insure an accurate diagnosis and appropriate treatment (see also YEAST VAGINITIS).

VAN DE VELDE, DR. THEODOOR HENDRYK The name Van de Velde was made famous by no fewer than three painters of the Netherlands' artistically glorious seventeenth century. A later Van de Velde, Theodoor Hendryk (1873–1937) painted an inspiring picture of marital sex in a book entitled *Ideal Marriage*. This early sex manual was a highly regarded authority for brides and bridegrooms, long before such books were sold openly by reputable booksellers. It was specific and helpful to those young persons who had no idea of what sex was. It approached the subject of sexual functioning in a very tactful way that was reassuring to young women, who were nervous about what would happen to them and afraid to do anything "not nice." From a modern perspective the book is too solemn (but it had to be then); it makes no mention of what new sex partners need most—permission to smile, giggle, or laugh out loud about their mutual mistakes and clumsiness. It put responsibility for conducting the first sexual encounter entirely on the man: he had to run the whole show and any failures were his. In modern sexual counseling both partners are responsible for mutual gratification. In its time, however, *Ideal Marriage* was important. It put in print that mutual pleasure in marital sex was good and desirable, and it taught that the man did have a role to play in giving as well as taking pleasure.

Engaged couples were still reading *Ideal Marriage* in the 1940s and 1950s, steered to it by loving elders. Van de Velde deserves a place of honor in the history of sexual enlightenment.

VASECTOMY AND THE MALE PILL   Two important approaches to male contraception, or BIRTH CONTROL, center on blockage of the passage of SPERM from the TESTICLES to the ejaculatory area, or medical treatment to prevent production of sperm. The surgical blockage of sperm flow from the testicles to the ejaculatory area is easily performed in the minor surgical procedure called vasectomy. With this approach, the vas deferens, the strong muscular tube that carries sperm from the testicles to the ejaculatory area, is divided and tied off with sutures or metal clips. This is a simple and highly effective surgical procedure, that has only minimal side-effects. However, many men are concerned about the potential effects on their testicles and sexual function after vasectomy. These fears are generally ungrounded, because vasectomy does not affect the functioning of the testicles or hormonal levels that affect sexual desire and function. Some men are concerned about the reversibility of vasectomy should they later desire to father children.

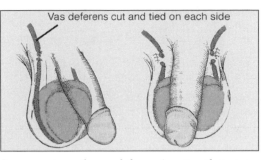

In a vasectomy the vas deferens is cut so that sperm cannot reach the ejaculatory area.

Because of these fears, alternatives have been attempted. These include the "no-scalpel vasectomy," a surgical procedure that also divides the vas deferens and ties off the ends, but does this through a smaller incision than a standard vasectomy. In addition, a number of techniques to place obstructing substances, such as plastics or an "on-off valve" into the vas deferens have been attempted. These attempts are more reversible but have higher failure rates because sperm can squeeze around the blockage.

Because there is some sperm still stored beyond where the blockage is formed, other methods of birth control must still be employed by a man who has had a vasectomy until up to fifteen ejaculations have occurred subsequent to the surgery. A simple test can be administered to insure that no sperm are present in the ejaculate.

Because it is a minor operation (with some new methods of microsurgery, the "operation" really amounts to little more than a puncture in the scrotum) there are rarely complications, though some pain is normal, and swelling and bruising are possibilities, as is risk of infection. Most men lose no time from work after having the procedure, though some do take a few days to recover. Strenuous exercise must be avoided for a time.

Having a vasectomy does not affect a man's "maleness" in any way. He continues to produce all of the male hormones. The amount of a man's ejaculate decreases by only about 5 percent, which is not noticeable. Sperm (they are microscopic in size) are still created, but they are not ejaculated and instead are dissolved and absorbed by the body, a harmless process, which takes place within the body all the time with other dead or unused cells.

There are no known health problems resulting from vasectomy. However, it was reported in 1978 that laboratory monkeys that had undergone the operation were at increased risk of arteriosclerosis, especially when fed a high cholesterol diet. But more than twelve studies carried out on men have failed to find any excess cardiovascular disease, hospitalization, or illness in men who have had vasectomies. Similarly, many studies have examined the incidence of PROSTATE CANCER in men with vasectomies. A 1993 study indicated there may be an increased risk of such cancer after the operation, but the study has not been duplicated or substantiated and no other studies or reports have found an association between the disease and vasectomies.

Although most vasectomy procedures can be reversed with careful microsurgery to reattach the two ends of the vas deferens, vasectomies are not 100 percent reversible. Therefore, this should be considered a permanent procedure (see also STERILIZATION).

An alternative, non-surgical approach to male contraception is aimed at decreasing the production of sperm by the testicles or causing sperm to become nonfunctional through medication. The most common approach in the past has been with HORMONES, since there is a delicate hormonal control of sperm production in the testicle. Unfortunately, to completely block sperm production by hormonal means has meant removing all effects of male hormones in the body. This "medical castration" results in changes in libido (sex drive) in the man as well as other possible changes in secondary sexual characteristics, such as beard growth. New, alternative approaches to a male pill, with lower doses of hormones, different hormones, or hormone-like drugs with less pronounced effects on the LIBIDO are currently being tested and evaluated.

Given the many millions of sperm produced in a man every day and the need to achieve zero sperm production to absolutely assure contraception, it is difficult to perfect a drug that will work effectively as a male contraceptive pill. Long-term effects of suppression of sperm production

and its subsequent recoverability are unknown. Certainly, the ideal male pill would act promptly, not affect libido or other hormonal action, and be completely reversible.

The Chinese drug gossypol has been applied in an attempt to affect sperm function without necessarily stopping sperm production. Gossypol, a derivative of cottonseed oil, blocks the motility of sperm and therefore renders the sperm nonfunctional. This drug has been used extensively in China with good results. Unfortunately gossypol appears to affect kidney function and the processing of fluids within the body, and its long-term use has not been proven safe. Therefore, gossypol is unlikely to be widely accepted as a male contraceptive, or "male pill." Derivatives similar to gossypol hold some promise of providing an ideal male pill.

One problem that limits all attempts to affect male fertility is the fact that sperm production and maturation in the testicle takes approximately seventy-seven days. Therefore, any drug that affects sperm production or function may take up to three months to achieve its full effects or to have those effects wear off. Development of a successful male contraceptive pill is one of the more challenging areas of medical research.

VIBRATORS Also known as massagers, vibrators are mechanical devices used for erotic stimulation leading to and including ORGASM. While some vibrators may be used on males as well as females, they are primarily designed for the stimulation of the female genitalia. Some manufacturers have attempted to develop vibrators to bring the male to climax, but these have not proved satisfactory. The appearance on the market of vibrators or massagers designed specifically for sexual stimulation is of recent vintage—dating from the 1940s. However, massagers for muscle relaxation and skin toning go as far back as the early 1900s. These may also have been used for sexual stimulation, but it was not the intent of the manufacturers. Almost all vibrators and massagers used for sexual stimulation may be classified into five types: 1) "Swedish massagers," 2) phallic shaped, 3) pistol grip, 4) wand, and 5) oscillators.

Swedish Massagers. One of the oldest of these devices to have made the transition from being used solely for muscle relaxation to now being used also for sexual stimulation was one that men and women were exposed to through professional massaging sessions and in barber shops. This is the "Swedish" type massager (one that is strapped to the back of the hand) and originally used for neck and facial massage, as well as muscle relaxation. These are not easy to use on oneself, except on the front of the body. Because they are heavy and strapped on over the hand, they are too awkward to use anywhere on one's back and are best used on another person. Their greatest value lies in that the vibrations of the motor are transferred to the user's fingertips. The vibrating effect of the fingers magnifies the sensitivity that the massaged skin feels, and most people prefer to be massaged by human fingertips rather than something artificial, especially in the genital area.

Phallic Shaped. Phallic-shaped plastic cylinders, about 6 inches long and battery powered, appeared in the 1940s. They seem to have been designed for insertion into the vagina as a penis substitute. This association left little doubt as to the primary function of this "spot massager," as it was sometimes advertised. Some sex educators and therapists have claimed that phallic-shaped vibrators seem to be more the product of male fantasy than designed for effective use by women. While some women use them as dildos, they are not generally considered to be as effective as other types of vibrators for stimulation and reaching orgasm.

Pistol Grip. In the early 1960s another type of massager became more readily available for sexual stimulation. These were usually called spot, scalp, or skin massagers (or just plain "massagers"), since they included attachments and instructions for massaging various parts of the body but no mention of sexual stimulation. However, the advertisements for them placed in sex magazines and sex newspapers defined their more pertinent usage.

The pistol grip massager looks something like a hand-held electric mixer. Instead of mixing attachments, however, there are small, non-revolving attachments, or adapters, good for massaging the scalp, face, or small areas of the body and for sexual stimulation. According to the description in the booklet *Good Vibrations*, a pistol grip massager is "shaped somewhat like a hairbrush [or small hair blow dryer] … with [a] vibrating head. … The metal vibrating shank is mounted on a piece of flat metal at the end of [the] coil so that, when the switch is on, it vibrates at … [about 30 cycles per second]. The coil-operated vibrators come with four to six plastic attachments of varying flexibility which slide or snap onto the shank."

These vibrators can often be found in drug or department stores and in the mail order catalogs of the larger department store chains. Some brands also provide deep heat, but some women find that this may become a distraction when using it for erotic stimulation. The most useful ones have an attachment that is about 1 to 1 1/2 inches in diameter with a convex surface for broader areas of skin, or an attachment that is about 3/4 inch long and shaped like a skinny egg for more precise stimulation of the genitalia. Some massagers have both attachments.

Wand. The wand vibrator has a long cylindrical body, or handle, about 12–14 inches long, with a vibrating head on the end (about 3 inches in diameter) that looks like a door knob or a slightly flattened tennis ball. The vibrating head is attached to the body by a short flexible neck. It can be used in a number of ways for erotic arousal, and is probably the best type for a relaxing self-massage as well. The wand is designed to self-massage parts of one's back. There are also attachments available that can enhance its use for sexual excitation through insertion into the vagina, but the wand massager itself is not designed for penetration. These massagers are used all over the world and are manufactured by major international companies and readily available in most large department stores. Some models have rechargeable batteries rather than electric cords, allowing for greater flexibility of use. The wand has been reported to be especially useful by couples during coitus by placing it between the two bodies, close to the genitals, and allowing the vibrations to enhance stimulation.

Oscillator. The oscillator is technically not a vibrator, since the stimulation it provides comes from the oscillating motion of the head from side to side—up to 3,600 movements per minute—rather than the up and down vibrations of other types of vibrators. Three heads are usually provided: a 3–inch finger-like head, a 1–inch diameter "grape cluster," and a 1–inch cup. The oscillator, because it is the first vibrator designed exclusively for sexual excitation of the female genitalia, is more highly specialized and, many sex therapists believe, is the best for stimulation of the labia and clitoris. The oscillator is small—only 7 inches long—and shaped like an electric toothbrush, with an oscillating head and a variable speed motor. It cannot be used for wider massaging and muscle relaxation.

A Note of Caution. If you buy a massager from a reputable store or mail order service, there will probably be a paragraph in the instruction booklet that will warn you not to use the vibrator or massager on areas of the body that are swollen. This applies to all vibrators. You also should not use it on the calf of a leg if there is any pain there. These are wise precautions to maintain because sometimes these pains or unknown swellings may conceal a blood clot which could break loose and cause harm. If you have any questions about massaging any pains or swellings, consult a physician. The use of massagers to relax muscles is so common that there is no oddity concerning someone who uses one.

During the past three decades, the use of vibrators has played an important role in the treatment of sexual dysfunctions. In sex manuals as early as 1949 it was recommended for the treatment of nonorgasmic women.

It was not until twenty-five years ago that the use of vibrators moved out of the underground press and the "do-it-yourself" sex manuals to become an instrument of SEX THERAPY. In the late 1960s it became associated with the scientific study of sexual functioning carried out by MASTERS AND JOHNSON and reported in their book *Human Sexual Response*. There was much reaction and controversy concerning findings by Masters and Johnson that most women in the study felt that automanipulation of the mons area with the aid of a vibrator produced the kind of stimulation that resulted in the fastest and the most intense orgasms.

Although Masters and Johnson did not discuss the use of vibrators in the treatment of nonorgasmic females, the work of the sex therapist and educator Helen Singer Kaplan did. In her book, *The New Sex Therapy: Active Treatment of Sexual Dysfunctions*, Dr. Kaplan notes several ways in which a vibrator may be used as an aid in the treatment of orgasm dysfunction. For one, she suggests a combined penis insertion and vibrator-assisted clitoral stimulation for those women who have difficulty reaching orgasm during coitus. For those women who have never had an orgasm, she suggests that if MASTURBATION with fingers is not intense enough to bring on an orgasm, a vibrator will usually provide a much stronger and more intense form of stimulation. Also at later stages, when a person is learning how to transfer orgasm to the heterosexual situation, she suggests that the husband may use a vibrator, guided by his wife's hand, to bring her to orgasm, without the pressure for her "to perform" during coitus.

Vibrators may also be used as a learning tool to discover the most sensitive areas of the body. This is not the use of a vibrator to excite the clitoris and bring on an orgasm, but rather to become more aware of how skin sensitivity varies in each part of the body. The use of a vibrator in this manner applies equally to both men and women. In this manner the use of a vibrator merely multiplies the effect of touching lightly in each area. As an illustration, if you touch the area just below your armpit with your fingers and gently rub in a circular motion, you will probably experience a pleasant, somewhat erotic sensation. If you try the same thing with a vibrator, you will notice how much more you will feel the sensation.

Now that the value of vibrators to produce fast and intense orgasms for women has become widely known, more creative uses by individuals and couples are written about and discussed. The fear that because they are so efficient some women would become dependent upon them does not seem to be borne out by the experiences of users or sex therapists. In turn, wider acceptance is leading to an increase of convenient and effective vibrators manufactured for a specifically sexual purpose. These may be found in stores and catalogs specializing in female EROTICA and devices (see also DILDOS).

VIRGINITY The term "virgin" is commonly used to refer to someone who has never had sexual intercourse. For women, according to popular belief, is has also been commonly understood that a virgin is a female who has never had her HYMEN broken by the insertion of a male's PENIS. The hymen is a membrane that partially closes off the entrance to a woman's vagina, and may act as a barrier to insertion until broken by pressure. While an intact hymen has historically been used to verify a woman's virginity, most especially on a "virgin-bride's" wedding night, this is a totally false notion. A woman's hymen, for no known reason, may naturally open, offering no resistance to a first sexual partner's penis. Or it may have been torn for other reasons in the past and may have virtually disappeared.

While the experience of actual SEXUAL INTERCOURSE is the usual way to define the "loss" of one's virginity, there is, in reality, a big gray area in which people may be sexually experienced and yet still "technical virgins." If you have engaged in ORAL SEX or have been brought to ORGASM by a partner's hands stimulating your genitals, you are technically considered a virgin. Yet you may, in fact, have had much more sex than someone whose only experience is a single act of sexual intercourse.

Both sexes can, of course, be virgins, but most cultures view virginity differently for males and females. Traditionally there has been a DOUBLE STANDARD. Women have been expected to be virgins before MARRIAGE, while men have been allowed, sometimes even encouraged, to have many sexual experiences.

While in America today that attitude is changing, the double standard still persists. Girls are still often labelled "easy" if they too readily say yes to boys. And boys are still often encouraged by society to "score" with girls. Teenage boys who are still virgins may actually worry that they will be labelled "losers" by their peers.

Actually, today, in seeming contradiction to the double standard, the pressure to lose one's virginity is now being felt by girls as well as boys as societal attitudes towards teenagers and sex have loosened. Many teenagers of both sexes now feel tremendous pressure from peers to become sexually active. Sex seems to be everywhere one turns—on TV, in the movies, in music videos, in magazines. So it is not surprising that many young people feel an increasing sense of urgency about having their first experience of sexual intercourse, and some of them even feel embarrassment about being a virgin.

It is important to say that no one should ever make the decision to lose one's virginity on the basis of peer pressure, shame, embarrassment, or anyone else's values. A person's first sexual intercourse is something one never forgets. To have that experience at the wrong time, or with the wrong person, or according to anyone else's rulebook, is certainly a big mistake (see also ABSTINENCE; CHASTITY).

VOYEURISM Voyeurism (also known medically as scopophilia) comes from the French verb, *voir*, meaning "to see." It describes a man or woman who looks at a member of the opposite sex (although voyeurs can also be gay or lesbian) in a state of undress, when he or she is not supposed to. A person who enjoys watching strippers or nude performers in a movie is not considered a voyeur; the voyeur obtains his or her primary arousal in looking at a woman or man without her or his knowledge or permission. To some extent, voyeurism is a form of compulsive behavior. The voyeur feels driven, periodically, to seek out situations in which he may, unobtrusively and without consent, observe another person getting dressed or undressed or engaging in a sexual activity. The sexual satisfaction achieved by the voyeur may extend to MASTURBATION, although this is not always the case. Voyeurs may have conventional sex lives but still obtain great satisfaction from their clandestine activities. While most voyeurs look but do not touch, some have assaulted the people spied upon. Because of this, law enforcement personnel view voyeurism as a serious crime.

Voyeurs are found in all age categories from childhood on, although most seem to outgrow the practice in middle age. In most cases in our society, voyeurs are male heterosexuals—the ratio of male to female voyeurs is about nine to one. There is no reason for this discrepancy other than, possibly, the socially learned belief that only the female body is a desirable sex object and is "forbidden fruit" to viewing by strangers (see also HYPERSEXUALITY).

VULVA The visible external parts of the FE-MALE SEX ORGANS. The vulva, consisting of the labia majora, labia minora, CLITORIS, urethra, and vestibule glands, is located between the mons pubis and the ANUS.

The labia majora are composed of two rounded mounds of tissue. They originate in the mons pubis and terminate in the perineum, forming the lateral boundaries of the vulva. After puberty, hair grows on the skin of the labia majora; on their inner sides they have many sweat glands. The male and female genitalia develop from the same embryonic origin, and the labia majora are homologous to the male scrotum.

The labia minora are smaller folds of hairless skin usually hidden between the labia majora. They surround the vestibule—the entry to the opening—of the VAGINA. These folds are smooth and pigmented, and at their upper ends meet to form around the clitoris. The labia minora are equivalent to the skin of the PENIS in males.

The clitoris is the principal organ of female sexual pleasure. It lies beneath the mons pubis at the top of the vaginal vestibule. Similar to a small button or pea in size and shape, it is capable of some enlargement, caused by increased blood supply during sexual excitement or when touched. It is rich with nerve endings and is a very erogenous organ. It is comparable to the penis, developing from the same tissue in the embryo. The urethra is a membranous structure for the passage of urine. It is approximately two inches long. Its opening lies below the clitoris.

The vestibule is the area bordered by the labia minora laterally, the clitoris above, and the fusion of labia minora below. It is the entry into the vaginal canal. In girls and young women prior to SEXUAL INTERCOURSE and PREGNANCY, the junction between the vagina and the vestibule is covered by a membrane called the HYMEN. There are usually one or several orifices in the hymen that allow menstrual blood or other secretions to flow out of the vagina, but in some cases the hymen is imperforated (has no openings) and menstrual blood accumulates in the vagina. A simple procedure called hymenectomy can resolve the problem. After sexual intercourse the hymen tears and only fragments of it remain on the edges of the vaginal opening. In some cases bleeding may occur when the hymen is torn,

The Batholin glands lie at the lateral aspect of the vulva, beneath the labia. These glands' secretions, which lubricate the vulva and vagina, especially during sexual activity, appear through two duct openings that lie on the low lateral position of the vaginal opening. After about age thirty the glands undergo involution and shrink. The Batholin glands tend to form cysts and abscesses. While cysts may not be bothersome, abscesses should be surgically treated.

W-Y-Z

WITHDRAWAL METHOD see BIRTH CONTROL; BIRTH CONTROL MYTHS.

WOMB see UTERUS.

YEAST VAGINITIS A nonmedical term used to describe symptomatic vaginal infections caused by an overgrowth of fungi. This, and bacterial vaginosis, are the two most common fungi found in women seeking medical care for vaginal infections. The most common fungus causing this infection is *Candida albicans*, but infections can also be caused by *Candida tropicalis* and *Torulopsis glabrata*.

The diagnosis of a yeast infection can be confirmed by an examination of vaginal secretions. A woman should suspect this infection if she has an excessive vaginal discharge accompanied by itching, particularly when this begins during or following antibiotic treatment, usually for an unrelated complaint. In these symptomatic women, a microscopic examination of vaginal secretions often reveals yeast forms. A culture can also be obtained for confirmation and is a more sensitive diagnostic test than microscopic examination.

The initial treatment of an acute vaginal yeast infection is with a local agent, available as a cream, suppository, or vaginal tablet. Fortunately, few of these yeast forms are resistant to therapy. In chronic or recurrent cases, oral antifungal medications can be employed if the cultured fungal organism is resistant to the local antifungal medications or if the patient has developed a local sensitivity from repeated use of vaginal creams and suppositories.

There is considerable misunderstanding of the nature of vaginal yeast infections in women. Recurrent yeast infections are not usually caused by a foreign fungal form that must be eliminated by chemotherapy from all sites in the body for a cure. In the normal woman, the number of yeast organisms on the skin or surface of mucous membranes is kept at low or undetectible numbers through the competition of normal surface bacterial flora for a finite amount of nutrients and an efficient local defense mechanism mediated through white cells and their metabolic products of defense, the cytokines. Any change in this complex, competitive environment can tip the balance, allowing yeast overgrowth.

There are many examples of this delicate balance going astray and, if the imbalance is not rectified, repeated use of antifungal agents will not work. Examples include pregnant women, who have an increased amount of sugar in their urine and vaginal secretions, a metabolic environment that favors yeast overgrowth, and women taking antibiotics; the antibiotics kill much of the normal bacterial flora in the VAGINA and allow an overgrowth of yeast forms. Also, intercourse with an infected male, often uncircumcised, may introduce more yeast forms to the vagina, shifting the normal balance. Another example is the lowering of the vaginal cellular response that can occur through diseases like HIV infection, or through treatments such as immunotherapy for cancer.

These can all result in repeated vaginal fungal infections. In recurrent infections, the goal should be to restore the microbiological balance of the vagina. Antifungal agents are only the first step. The key to finding an effective cure is determining what is modifying the local host response. If this can be corrected, a cure can be achieved; without this, antifungal treatment is destined for failure (see also VAGINITIS).

ZOOPHILIA   Also called bestiality, zoophilia means having sex with animals. While some of the stories about such activity are mythical, such as Leda and the Swan, it is an activity that does occur. In fact, Dr. Alfred Kinsey found that a small number of the men he surveyed had sexual contact with animals, although usually only once or twice in their lifetimes. Such practices are not recommended and are often illegal.

GLOSSARY

ADOPTION The legal process by which one person, usually a child, is formally made a member of a family into which he or she is not biologically tied.

ALUM An astringent (a substance that causes the skin cells to contract). Douching with alum was once thought to be a method of birth control, but it is not effective.

ANABOLIC STEROID A hormonal drug prepared from either testosterone or from a synthetic compound. It counters the effect of female hormones and helps growth.

ANDROPAUSE The change of life in males, considered by some to be similar to menopause. It is caused by a lowering of the levels of male hormones.

AXILLARY HAIR Arm pit hair. Its appearance is a signs of puberty.

BASAL BODY TEMPERATURE The temperature of the body, taken early in the morning, after sleep, and before any activity. Because a rise in this temperature may signal that ovulation has taken place, it is used as part of natural family planning.

CALENDAR METHOD A method of natural family planning in which a woman keeps careful record of her periods so as to calculate the time of the month when ovulation occurs.

CARNAL A term derived from the Latin word for fleshy (*carnalis*); when used in the phrase, carnal knowledge, it means sexual intercourse.

CHASTITY Abstention from intercourse, most commonly used for women.

CHROMOSOMES Thread-like structures located in the nucleus of a cell that carries genetic information.

CLIMACTERIC The emotional changes that accompany menopause.

COITUS Sexual intercourse.

COLUSTRUM The yellow fluid released by the breast just prior to milk production.

CONSENT The act of agreeing to a sexual act, including sexual intercourse. The term is also used to describe agreement to other actions such as marriage or divorce.

CONSENTING ADULT A person over the age of eighteen who agrees to have sexual intercourse.

CONTRACEPTION Any of the techniques available to prevent pregnancy.

COPULATION The sexual act, usually used in reference to animals.

COUNSELING The process by which a person attempts to persuade another to love or marry them.

COWPER'S GLAND A gland that secretes a slippery substance prior to ejaculation. This substance may assist the sperm on their journey through the urethra.

CROWNING The moment when the baby's head is first seen through the vaginal opening.

CRUSH A romantic feeling towards another person, often not reciprocated.

CULTURE A way of testing for microorganisms.

CURETTAGE Scraping of material from an inner space in the body to remove a tumor, or when used in the uterus, to scrape away the lining.

CYSTITIS An inflammation of the urinary bladder caused by a bacteria. It is most commonly found among women.

D & C Dilation and curettage—the widening of the opening of the uterus and scraping of the lining.

DELIVERY The act of giving birth.

DES A strong hormone, Diethylstilbestrol, used in the "morning-after" pill.

DEVIATION A sexual act though to be outside the norms of acceptable behavior.

DILATOR A device used to widen an opening, such as speculum, which is used to dilate the vagina during a pelvic examination.

DNA Deoxyribonucleic acid, a large chemical molecule that makes up the chromosomes of a cell and carries the genetic information.

DYSFUNCTION In sexual terms, dysfunctions are either physical or psychological problems which keep a person from enjoying their sexuality fully.

DYSMENORRHEA Pain associated with menstruation, commonly called cramps.

DYSPAREUNIA A condition in which the vaginal muscles contract involuntarily, making sexual intercourse painful.

EFFACEMENT During labor, the shortening of the cervix and thinning of its walls as it is stretched by the fetus.

EGG A female cell produced in the ovaries. When united with a male's sperm, it will grow into an embryo.

ELISA TEST A test to determine whether HIV antibodies are present.

ENDOCRINE SYSTEM The network of glands that secrete hormones directly into the bloodstream. It includes the testicles, which secrete testosterone, and the ovaries, which secrete estrogen.

ENGAGEMENT The time between when a man and woman agree to marry and their actual wedding.

EPIDIDYMIS The long tubes coiled along the surface of the testicles in which sperm are stored.

EPIDIDYMITIS An infection of the epididymis, symptoms of which include severe pain in the testicles as well as swelling and tenderness in the scrotum.

EUNUCH A male whose testicles have been removed.

FANTASY Sexual fantasy is the imagination of scenes or events involving sex or romance that usually are never carried out.

FEMINISM A socio-political philosophy advocating that the legal, social, political, economic, and sexual right of women should be equal to those of men,

FERTILE PERIOD The time in a woman's menstrual cycle when she has the potential to become pregnant.

FERTILIZATION The union of the male and female gametes (the sperm and the ovum). Also known as the moment of conception.

FIMBRIA The fingerlike border of the fallopian tube at the ovarian end. The fimbria helps guide the egg into the tube, where it may be fertilized.

FORESKIN A loose fold of skin that covers the tip of the penis or clitoris, also called the "prepuce."

FRENCH KISS A kiss in which one's partner's tongue penetrates the other's mouth.

FRENULUM The underside of the penis

FRIGIDITY A term once applied to people who exhibit low sexual desire.

GAMETE A cell that functions during fertilization—the egg or the sperm.

GAY Homosexual.

GAY LIBERATION MOVEMENT The political movement fostering equal rights for homosexuals and lesbians.

GENES The physical units that determine an individual's inherited characteristics.

GENETIC COUNSELING Counseling with future parents with regard to any possible diseases or other birth defects that might be inherited by the child.

GENITALS The sex organs.

GERM CELLS An organism's reproductive cells—the ovum and the sperm.

GESTATION The time required between fertilization of the ovum and birth of offspring. In humans, the average length of pregnancy is 266 days.

GLANS The cone-shaped head of the penis in males or the tip of the clitoris in females.

GONAD A gland that release gametes, such as an ovary or testicle.

GROIN The area where the abdomen joins the thighs.

GROUP THERAPY The treatment of psychological or sexual dysfunctions in which a group of people, focusing on a particular problem, meet with a qualified therapist.

GYNECOLOGIST A physician specializing in the branch of medicine that deals with the health care of women's reproductive systems.

GYNECOMASTIA A temporary and abnormal swelling of one or both male breasts. It generally affectsboys entering puberty.

HEAT The period during which a female animal is ovulating. Heat is not found in humans.

HEDONISM A set of values that emphasizes sexual pleasure over moral constraint.

HUMAN PAPILLOMA VIRUS A virus that causes warts, some of which are transmitted through sexual contact.

HYPOXYPHILLIA Sexual arousal caused by oxygen deprivation.

HYSTERECTOMY The surgical removal of the uterus.

HYSTEROTOMY A type of abortion in which the fetus is surgically removed.

ILLEGITIMATE CHILD A child born out of wedlock.

IMPLANTATION The embedding of the fertilized egg into the uterine wall.

INCUBATOR A medical apparatus used to provide a controlled environment for a premature baby.

INDUCED ABORTION An abortion caused by artificial means.

INDUCED LABOR The artificial initiation of labor by an obstetrician through the use of drugs.

INFERTILITY The inability to achieve pregnancy

INTERSEXUALITY An intermediate state in which a person has male and female body features to varying degrees.

KAPOSI'S SARCOMA A type of cancer that often afflicts people with AIDS.

LABIA The two folds of skin that form the outer and inner edges, or lips, of the vagina.

LABOR The process of giving birth.

LEBOYER METHOD A birthing technique that emphasizes a gentle delivery.

LITHOTOMY POSITION The position of a woman during a pelvic examination. Thewoman lies on her back with her knees bent and her feet up in stirrups.

LYMPHOGRANULOM VERNEREUM A sexually transmitted disease caused by chlamydia trachomatis that leads to a swelling of the lymph nodes in the groin.

MADAM A woman who heads a house of prostitution.

MALE CHAUVINISM An attitude held by some men that the male of the species is superior to the female.

MAMMARY GLAND The female breast.

MAMMOPLASTY Surgical reshaping of the breast.

MARRIAGE COUNSELING A type of counseling in which all factors in marriage are considered when giving advice.

MASSAGE The manipulation of tissues for remedial purposes or to cause pleasure.

MENARCHE A woman's first menstruation.

MENSES The normal flow of blood and uterine cells that takes place during menstruation.

MINI-PILL An oral contraceptive containing no estrogen.

MISTRESS A woman who acts as the sexual partner and companion to a married man.

MITTELSCHMERZ Pain felt in the lower abdomen. It is caused by ovulation .

MONITRICE A childbirth coach trained in the Lamaze method.

MONOGAMY The marriage of one man to one woman.

MONS PUBIS In women, the mound of fatty tissue over the pubic bone.

MORNING-AFTER PILL A method of birth control that involves taking a pill containing a large dose of estrogen within seventy-two hours of sexual intercourse. Because of the risks, it is generally given only cases of rape or incest.

MORNING SICKNESS Nausea experienced by women during the first trimester of pregnancy, often in the morning.

NARCISSISM Love or sexual desire for oneself and one's body.

NAVEL The area of the abdomen where the umbilical cord joins the fetus.

NECKING A form of sexual and emotional expression in which the couple mostly kiss and hold each other, often putting their arms around each other's necks.

NECROPHILIA Deriving sexual pleasure from either seeing or having contact with a corpse.

NOCTURNAL EMISSION Ejaculation during sleep.

NONGONOCOCCAL URETHRITIS An infection of the urethra caused by the chlamydia microorganism.

OBSTETRICS The branch of medicine dealing with pregnancy, labor, and delivery.

OLIGOSPERMIA Lack of sperm in the ejaculate.

OPEN MARRIAGE A marriage in which both partners are free to engage in sexual relations with others.

ORGY A scene of sexual interplay between a number of people.

OVULATION The release of an ovum from the ovary.

OVUM A female germ cell, an egg.

PANDERER A pimp.

PEDERASTY Sexual activity with young boys.

PEDOPHILIA Sexual activity with younger persons of either sex.

PEEPING TOM Someone who derives sexual satisfaction from surreptitiously watching others undress or perform sexual acts. A voyeur.

PELVIS The lower part of the trunk of the body, formed by the basin-shaped circle of pelvic bones.

PENILE IMPLANT A prosthesis inserted into the penis of a man who is unable to have erections.

PENIS CAPTIVUS The penis becoming trapped inside the vagina during sexual intercourse. It does not occur in humans.

PERINEUM The area between the anus and the external genitalia—the vagina in women and the scrotum in males.

PERVERSION Sexual behavior or practices that vary from normal behavior.

PERVERT A person who engages in perversion.

PESSARY A device placed inside the vagina. The diaphragm, a barrier method of birth control, is a type of pessary.

PETTING Sexual activity, usually among young people, that includes deep kissing and touching of various erogenous zones, sometimes including the genitals. While it can bring one or both partners to orgasm, it does not include sexual intercourse.

PHALLUS Penis, from the Greek, phallos.

PHIMOSIST A tightness of the foreskin of the penis so that it cannot be pulled back to expose the glans.

PIMP A man who lives off the earnings of one or more prostitutes.

PLATONIC LOVE A bond of friendship between two people who are not related and which does not involve a sexual relationship.

PLEASURING Erotic activities, other than sexual intercourse, that give physical pleasure.

POLYANDRY Marriage between one woman and two or more men.

POLYGAMY Marriage between a partner of one sex and two or more partners of the other. It generally refers to marriages in which the multiple spouses are women.

POLYGYNY Marriage between one man and several women.

POTENCY The ability of a male to have erections and ejaculate.

PREMARITAL COUNSELING Talking about an intended marriage with a trained counselor. Some religions require couples to discuss marriage with a counselor or religious leader.

PREMARITAL SEX Sex between two unmarried people; the phase is sometimes used when the couple intends to be married.

PREMATURE BIRTH The birth of a baby before it has come to full term.

PREMATURE EJACULATION A sexual dysfunction in which the man regularly ejaculates before he would like to, often immediately or shortly after entering the vagina.

PRENATAL CARE Health maintenance techniques followed by a pregnant woman to maximize her health and the well-being of her baby.

PRIAPISM A sexual dysfunction in which the penis remains in a state of erection for too long.

PRIMARY SEX CHARACTERISTICS The male and female sex organs as they appear in children before puberty.

PROMISCUITY Having sexual intercourse with several partners over a short period of time.

PROPHYLACTIC A device that keeps disease from spreading, notably as applied to a condom.

PSYCHOSEXUAL Having to do with the mental and emotional aspects of sex.

PSYCHOSEXUAL DEVELOPMENT The five stages that a person must pass through to achieve sexual maturity according to Freud.

PUBIC HAIR The hair that develops around the genitals during puberty; one of the secondary sexual characteristics.

PUDENDUM The outer genitals.

QUICKENING The first movements of the fetus that can be felt by the mother.

RECTUM The part of the large intestine before the anal opening.

REFRACTORY PERIOD The period after orgasm during which a man does not respond to sexual stimulation.

REPRODUCTIVE SYSTEM The male and female sex glands and organs that are involved in the process of procreation.

RETARDED EJACULATION A condition in which the man is repeatedly unable to ejaculate inside the women's vagina even after and extended period of sexual intercourse.

RETROGRADE EJACULATION An ejaculation in which the semen goes into the bladder rather than out of the body through the urethra.

RHYTHM METHOD A natural method of birth control that relies on the regularity of a women's menstrual cycle to determine on which days she should refrain from unprotected sexual intercourse.

RIGHT TO LIFE The political movement that opposes the legalization of abortion.

SAFE PERIOD The period during a woman's monthly cycle when she may engage in sexual intercourse without birth control and not risk getting pregnant.

SALINE ABORTION A type of induced abortion in which saline is injected into the amniotic fluid, killing the fetus and initiating labor.

SANITARY NAPKIN A disposable pad used by women to absorb menstrual blood during their period.

SCABIES A contagious disease caused by a mite. Scabies can be transferred during sex.

SCROTUM The pouch of loose skin containing the testicles. It is found below the penis.

SECONDARY SEX CHARACTERISTICS The physical characteristics that develop during puberty and which distinguish adults from children, including pubic hair, underarm hair, and breasts.

SEDUCTION The act of persuading or enticing someone into conduct they might not otherwise engage in voluntarily.

SELF-PLEASURING Masturbation.

SEMINAL VESICLES Two small pouches located at the back of the prostate gland. They release seminal fluids upon ejaculation.

SENSUAL Relating to the gratification of the senses, especially sexual pleasure.

SEX CHANGE OPERATION An operation to physically change a transsexual from one sex to the other.

SEX DISCRIMINATION Unequal treatment of a person because of their sex.

SEX FLUSH A vasocongestive response that causes the skin to redden during heightened sexual excitement.

SEX ORGANS The parts of the body that link during sexual intercourse; the penis, in the male, and the vagina, in the female.

SEXUAL DESIRE The urge or need for sexual activity, also called sex drive.

SEXUAL HARASSMENT Any type of unwanted verbal or physical sexual advance that continues after being initially rejected.

SEXUAL HISTORY Information taken down by a sex therapist about a person's sent sex life.

SEXUAL IDENTITY The feeling that a person has that he or she is male or female.

SEXUAL ORIENTATION The personal preference of someone for either heterosexual, homosexual, or bisexual sexual activity.

SEXUAL RESPONSE SYSTEM The parts of the body involved in human sexuality.

SEXUALITY The condition of expressing one's sexual nature. as either male or female.

SMEGMA The cheesy substance that accumulates under the foreskin of an uncircumcised penis or under the hood of the clitoris.

SODOMY A term used to describe "unnatural" sex acts.

SPERMARCHE The first ejaculation of seminal fluid.

SPERMATOGENESIS The process by which sperm is created in the testicles.

SPERMICIDE A substance that kills sperm when placed inside the vagina.

SPONTANEOUS ABORTION A miscarriage.

STATUTORY RAPE Sexual intercourse with a female under the "age of consent." Consent of the female is not relevant to it being a crime.

STERILITY In men, the inability to impregnate a woman, in women, the inability to become pregnant.

STILLBIRTH The birth of a dead child.

STOP-START TECHNIQUE A method recommended by sex therapists to help cure premature ejaculation.

SUCTION METHOD A method of abortion in which suction is used to remove the embryo.

SYMPTOTHERMIC TECHNIQUE A method of birth control that combines several of the methods used in natural family planning.

TABOO Something band, either because of religious belief or taste.

TAMPON A small, absorbent plug inserted into the vagina to absorb the menstrual flow.

TELEPHONE SEX Commmunicating erotic material over the telephone in order to excite and potentially cause an orgasm.

TEST-TUBE BABIES A baby created through in vitro fertilization.

TRANSVESTITE A cross-dresser; someone, generally male, who derives sexual pleasure from dressing as a member of the opposite sex

TRICHOMONIASIS An infection of the vagina. It can be transmitted sexually.

TUBAL LIGATION A method of female sterilization in which the fallopian tubes are cut.

TUBAL PREGNANCY Ectopic pregnancy in which the fertilized eggis implanted in the fallopian tubes.

ULTRASOUND A method of probing within the body without causing any damage, used to determine the health of a fetus.

UMBILICAL CORD A cord that connects the placenta to the baby, supplying nourishment and oxygen and removing wastes.

UNDESCENDED TESTICLES Testicles that have not descended into the scrotum..

UNISEX A manner dressing and style that can be adopted by either sex.

UNNATURAL An unscientific term applied to sexual behavior which does not follow the norm.

URETHRA The tube through which urine passes from the bladder and, in men, which transports semen.

URINARY TRACT The path taken by urine from the kidneys, through the ureters, to the bladder, to the urethra.

UROLOGIST A physician who specializes in the treatment of the urinary tract of both sexes and teh genital tract in males.

UROPHILIA Sexual arousal caused by contact with urine.

VACUUM ASPIRATION The most common method of abortion, in which the contents of the uterus, including the embryo, are suctioned out.

VAGINAL ORGASM An orgasm centered on the vagina. Its existence is a matter of controversy.

VAGINISMUS A condition in which the vaginal muscles constrict involuntarily, making intercourse painful or impossible.

VAS DEFERENS The tubes that transport sperm from the testicles to the urethra.

VASOCONGESTION The increased flow of blood into body tissues, causing them to swell; the cause of erections.

VENEREAL DISEASE Sexually transmitted disease.

VIABILITY The point at which a fetus that has not yet reached full term can survive outside the womb with the proper medical care.

WITHDRAWAL METHOD A method of birth control in which the male withdraws his penis from the vagina before ejaculating.

ZYGOTE The single cell produced from the fertilization of an egg by a sperm.

GLOSSARY OF SEXUAL SLANG

AC/DC	bisexuality
Arse/Ass	buttocks
Asshole/A-hole	anus
Aunt Flo's here	menstruation
B & D	bondage and discipline/sadomasochim
B-girl	a prostitute
Babe	an attractive woman
Bad blood	syphilis
Bag	scrotum
Ball (to)	to have sexual intercourse
Balls	testicles
Bang somebody (to)	vaginal or anal intercourse
Basket	male genitalia
Bazongas	large breasts
Bazookas	large breasts
Bazooms	large breasts
Bearded clam/lady	vulva
Beat off (to)	to masturbate (male)
Beat one's meat (to)	to masturbate (male)
Beaver	vulva
Behind	buttocks
Bitch	lewd or malicious woman
Bleeping	replacement word for a curse
Blow somebody (to)	to fellate somebody
Blow job	fellatio
Blue balls	a term used to signify the feeling a man may have from being aroused and unable to relieve the sexual tension
Boink (to)	to fornicate
Bone	penis
Boner	erection
Boobs	breasts
Bottom man	a man who has a penis inserted into his rectum
Bordello	house of prostitution
Box	vagina
Broad	woman
Buck naked (to be)	to be nude
Bull dyke	a masculine-looking lesbian
Bump (to)	to fornicate
Bump and grind	to have sex; to dance using sexual movements
Buns	buttocks
Butch	masculine-looking
Butt	buttocks
Butt naked	nude
Butt hole	anus
Button	clitoris
Can	buttocks
Cathouse	brothel
Cherry	hymen
Chick	girl
Chicken	a male adolescent
Chicken hawk	a man who prefers male adolescents as sexual partners
Chicken ranch	house of prostitution
Circle jerk	group masturbation
Clap	gonorrhea
Clit	clitoris
Closet queen	a homosexual who does not openly admit to it

Cock	penis	**Fag hag**	a woman who keeps
Cocksucker	a male homosexual		company with male
Come	semen		homosexuals
Come (to)	to have an orgasm	**Fairy**	a male homosexual
Come out	to admit one's	**Family jewels**	testicles
(of the closet) (to)	homosexuality	**Fanny**	buttocks
Comhole (to)	to have anal inter-	**FFA**	Fist Fuckers of
somebody	course		America, men who
Cream (in one's	ejaculate		enjoy certain homo-
pants)**			sexual practices
Cruise (to)	to look for a sexual	**Finger oneself (to)**	to masturbate
	partner		(female)
Cum	semen	**Fistfucking**	inserting the hand or
Cunt	vulva		fist into the rectum
Cunt lapping	cunnilingus	**Flagwaver**	an exhibitionist
Curse (the)	menstruation	**Flog the Bishop (to)**	to masturbate (male)
Daisy chain	group sex	**Fool around (to)**	to have sex
Deep-throat (to)	to perform fellatio	**French active**	a person who sucks
Dick	penis		somebody's sex
Dick (to) someone	to have sexual inter-		organs
	course	**French art**	oral sex
Discipline	sadism	**French kiss**	an open-mouth kiss
Do somebody (to)	to suck somebody's	**French letter**	condom
	sex organs; to have	**French passive**	a person who has his
	sexual intercourse		or her sex organs
Do the nasty (to)	to have sexual inter-		sucked
	course	**French somebody**	to kiss open-
Dong	penis	**(to)**	mouthed; to suck
Dose (a)	gonorrhea		somebody's
Drag	clothing of the other		sex organ
	sex	**Frigging**	a euphemism for
Drag queen	a male homosexual		fucking
	who wears female	**Fruit**	a male homosexual
	clothing	**Fruit fly**	a woman who prefers
Drip (the)	gonorrhea		the company of
Dropping beads	testing if another per-		male homosexuals
	son is gay	**Fuck (to)**	to have sex
Dry hump (to)	to rub up against	**Fur pie**	vulva
	someone to the point	**Furburger**	vulva
	of orgasm with	**Gang bang**	group sex or gang
	clothes on		rape, usually with
Dyke	a lesbian		one woman and
Easy lay (to be an)	to be promiscuous		two or more men
Eat somebody (to)	to have oral sex	**Gay**	homosexual
Eat pussy (to)	to perform cunnilin-	**Get into somebody's**	to have sexual inter-
	gus	**pants (to)**	course
F word	euphemism for fuck	**Get laid (to)**	to have sexual inter-
Fag, faggot	a male homosexual		course

Get off (to)	to have an orgasm
Get a piece of ass (to)	to have sexual intercourse
Get some tail (to)	to have sexual intercourse
Get the curse (to)	to menstruate
Get one's rocks off (to)	to ejaculate
Get to first, second, or third base (to)	to reach a certain point in sexual activity
Give head (to)	to fellate someone
Gleet	gonorrhea
Go all the way (to)	to have sex
Go down on somebody (to)	to suck someone's sex organs
Golden shower	urination on a person's body
Gonads	testicles
Gones	testicles
Greek active	a man who inserts his penis in his partner's rectum
Greek passive	a person who has a penis inserted in his rectum
Greek way (the)	anal intercourse
Grind (to)	to have hard sex
Group grope	group sex
Haircut	syphilis
Hand fuck	masturbation
Hand job	masturbation
Hard-on	an erection
Hardcore	very pornographic
Have the banana peeled (to)	to have sexual intercourse
Have a quickie (to)	to have quick sex
Have a visitor (to)	to menstruate
Have the hots for (to)	to desire sexually
Headlights	breasts
Hole	vagina
Homo	a male homosexual
Honeypot	vagina
Hooker	a female prostitute
Hooters	large breasts
Hop in the saddle (to)	to have sex
Horny	sexually excited
Hot	sexually exciting
House of ill repute	a house of prostitution
Hung (to be)	to have a large penis
Hump somebody (to)	to insert one's penis into either the vagina or rectum of a partner
Hustle (to)	to solicit sex
Hustler	a male prostitute
Jack off, Jerk off	to masturbate (male)
Jerkin' the gherkin	to masturbate (male)
Jerk the joint (to)	to masturbate (male)
Jism	semen
John	a prostitute's customer
Johnson	penis
Joy stick	penis
Jugs	breasts
Juicy	sexually exciting (female)
Jump on one's bones (to)	to fornicate
Junior	penis
Keester	buttocks
Knock up (to)	to make pregnant
Knockers	breasts
Lady of the evening	a female prostitute
Lay somebody (to)	to have sexual intercourse
Lech	a lecherous person
Les, lessie, lez	a lesbian
Load	semen
Loose (to be)	to be promiscuous
Love glove	a condom
Love juice	semen
Love muscle	penis
Mack	pimp
Madam	head of a house of prostitution
Maidenhead	hymen
Make out (to)	to have sexual intercourse or to kiss passionately
Make somebody (to)	to have sexual intercourse
Make whoopie (to)	to have sexual intercourse

Manhole	vagina		homosexual
Meat	penis	Queer	a homosexual
Meat market	brothel, a place to	Quim	vulva
	pick up members	Raincoat	condom
	of the opposite sex	Ram (to)	to fornicate violently
Melons	breasts	Rammer	penis
Moon (to)	to expose one's but-	Raunch	rough sex
	tocks to	Ream somebody	to lick somebody's
Morning drop	gonorrhea	(to)	rectal opening
Mother-fucker	despicable person	Ream job	anilingus
Mr. Happy	penis	Rear	buttocks
M/S	master/slave	Rice queen	a homosexual who
Muff	vulva		prefers Asian part-
Muff diving	cunnilingus		ners
Nellie	an effeminate male	Rim somebody (to)	to lick somebody's
	homosexual		anus
Nookie	sex	Rod	penis
Nuts	testicles	Roll in the hay (to)	to have sexual inter-
O. P. P.	one's sexual organs		course
Old Joe	syphilis	Rub bellies (to)	to have sexual inter-
One-night stand	sex with someone		course
	for just one night	Rub off (to)	to masturbate
On the rag	menstruating		(female)
Organ	penis	Rubber	condom
Out (to)	to reveal someone	Sack	scrotum
	else's sexuality	Safe, safety	condom
Pansy	an effeminate male	Salami, sausage	penis
	homosexual	Score, screw (to)	to have sexual inter-
Pecker	penis		course
Peeping Tom	voyeur	Screw (to), screw	to have vaginal or
Peter	penis	somebody (to)	anal intercourse
Piece of ass, tail	a women, especially	Service station	brothel
	one sexually	Shake hands with	to masturbate (male)
	available	the governor (to)	
Play hide the	to have sexual inter-	Shift gears (to)	to masturbate (male)
salami (to)	course	Shlong	penis
Play with oneself	to masturbate	Shmuck	penis
(to)		Shoot (to)	to ejaculate
Poke (to)	to fornicate	Shoot one's load,	to ejaculate
Pole	penis	or wad (to)	
Prick	penis	Short eyes	a child molester
Privates	genitals (male)	Setup (to)	to fornicate
Pocket pool	masturbation	Siff (or syph)	syphilis
Pox	syphilis	Sissy	effeminate
Pussy	vulva	Sister	a male homosexual
Put out (to)	to give sexual favors	Sixty-nine	simultaneous mutual
Putz	a limp penis		oral intercourse
Queen	an effeminate male	Slut	a prostitute

S / M	sadomasochism		his penis in his part-ner's rectum
Smooch (to)	to kiss		
Snatch	vagina	**Trade**	a bisexual man
Social disease	venereal disease	**Tramp (to be a)**	to be promiscuous
Soul kiss	an open-mouth kiss	**Trick**	a prostitute's cus tomer
Spade queen	a homosexual who prefers black partners	**Truckdriver**	lesbian
Spear	penis	**Trouser trick**	penis
Squeeze box	vagina	**Turn a trick (to)**	to find a customer for prostitution
Steam queen	a homosexual who frequents bath houses	**Turned on**	sexually excited
Strain	gonorrhea	**TV**	a transvestite
Streetwalker	female prostitute	**TS**	a transsexual
Stroke oneself (to)	to masturbate	**Twat**	vulva
Stud	a sexually active man	**Unit**	penis
Suck face (to)	to kiss	**VD**	venereal disease
Suck somebody (to)	to fellate somebody	**Versatile**	willing to engage in all forms of sexual intercourse
Sugar daddy	an older man who rewards his sexual partner financially	**Wang**	penis
Swing (to)	to engage in partner swapping	**Wank (to)**	to masturbate
Swing both ways (to)	to be bisexual	**Water sports**	urination on a person's body
Swinger	a sexually promiscu-ous person	**Watermelons**	large breasts
		Wazoo	buttocks
Swishy	effeminate	**Wearing the rag**	to menstruate
Switch hitter	a bisexual	**Weenie**	penis
T and A	tits and ass, i.e. nudity	**Wet dream**	nocturnal emission
		Whack off (to)	to masturbate
Tail	buttocks	**Wham bam, thank you ma'am**	quick sex
Tea room	a public toilet		
Tea room queen	a male homosexual who seeks partners in public toilets	**Whip the weenie/ worm (to)**	to masturbate (male)
That time of the month (to be)	to menstruate	**Whites (the)**	gonorrhea
		Whore	a prostitute
Thing	penis	**Whorehouse**	a brothel
Tits, titties	breasts	**Wiener**	penis
Tool	penis	**Wild thing (the)**	sexual intercourse
Tool box	vagina	**Woody**	an erection
Top man	a man who inserts	**Working girl**	a female prostitute
		X-rated	pornographic
		Yank the yak (to)	to masturbate (male)

BIBLIOGRAPHY

General Reference:
Bechtel, Stephan, *The Sex Encyclopedia*, Fireside, New York, 1993.
Brecher, Edward M., *The Sex Researchers, Little, Brown and Co., Boston, Mass., 1969.*
Burke, David, Bleep: A Guide to Popular American Obscenities, Optima Books, Los Angeles, Calif., 1993.
Calderone, Mary S., and Eric Johnson, *The Family Book About Sexuality*, Harper Collins Publications, Scranton, Penn., 1989.
Glanze, Walter D., *Mosby Medical Encyclopedia*, Plume, New York, 1985.
Haeberle, Erwin J., *The Sex Atlas*, A Continuum Book, The Seabury Press, New York, 1983.
Macmillan Health Encyclopedia, *Sexuality and Reproduction*, New York, 1993.
McVay, Chester B., *Atlas of Surgical Anatomy*, W. B. Saunders and Co., 1984.

Abortion:
Callahan, Sidney, and Daniel Callahan, *Abortion: Understanding Differences*, Plenum, New York, 1984.
Lader, Lawrence, *Abortion*, Beacon Press, Boston, Mass., 1966.
Weddington, Sarah, *A Question of Choice*, G. P. Putnam and Sons, New York, 1992.

Aging and Sex:
Brecher, Edward M., *Love, Sex and Aging*, Little, Brown and Co., Boston, Mass., 1984.
Butler, R., and M. Lewis, *Sex after Sixty*, Harper and Row, New York, 1976.

Arts and the Media:
Frank, Sam, *Sex in the Movies*, Citadel Press, New York: 1986.
Taylor, Gordon Rattray, *Sex in History*, Vanguard Press, New York, 1970.
Tyler, Parker,. *Sex in Films*, Citadel Press, New York, 1993.
Westheimer, Ruth, *The Art of Arousal*, Abbeville Press, New York, 1993.

Birth:
Balaskas, Janet, *Active Birth: The New Approach to Giving Birth Naturally*, Harvard Common Press, 1992.
Berger Gart. S. Marc Goldstein, and Mark Fuerst, *The Couples' Guide to Fertility*, Doubleday, New York, 1989.
Cohen, Nancy Wainer, *Open Season*, Bergin and Garvey, 1993.
Davis, Elizabeth, *Heart and Hands: A Midwife's Guide to Pregnancy and Birth*, Celestial Arts, 1987.

"Midwifery and the Law", *Mothering Mazagine*, 1990.

Mitford, Jessica, *The American Way of Birth*, Dutton, 1992.

Richards, Lynn Baptisti, *Vaginal Birth after Cesarean*, Bergin and Garvey, 1987.

Tew, Marjorie, *Safer Childbirth*, Chapman and Hall, 1990.

Cancer:

Copeland, Edward M. (ed.), *Surgical Oncology*, John Wiley and Sons, 1983.

Montague, Albert, et al (eds.), *Breast Cancer: Proceedings of the International Breat Cancer Con-ference*, Alan R. Liss, Inc., 1977.

Wyhus, Lloyd M., and Robert J. Baker (eds.), *Master of Surgery*, vol. I, Little Brown and Co., 1984.

Children and Sex:

Erikson, Erik H., *Identity: Youth and Crises*, Norton, New York, 1968.

Furstenberg, Frank F. Jr., and J. Brooks-Gunn, and S. Philip Morgan, *Adolescent Mothers in Later Life*, Cambridge University Press, New York, 1987.

Madaras, L., and D. Saavedra, *What's Happening to My Body? Book for Boys*, Newmarket Press, New York, 1984.

Madaras, L., and D. Saavedra, *What's Happening to My Body? A Growing Up Guide for Mothers and Daughters*, Newmarket Press, New York, 1986.

Westheimer, Ruth, *Dr. Ruth Talks to Kids*, Macmillan Publishing Company, New York, 1993

Westheimer, Ruth, and N. Kravetz, *First Love*, Warner Books, New York, 1985.

Fetal and Infant Abuse Syndromes:

Fried, P. A., "Marijuana Use During Pregnancy: Consequences for the Offspring", *Seminars in Peri-natology*, 1991.

Hogerman, G., and S. Schnoll, *Narcotic Use in Pregnancy*, Clinics in Perinatology, 1991.

Jones, K. L., "Fetal Alcohol Effects", in: *Smith's Recognizable Patterns of Human Malformation*, W. B. Saunders Co., Philadelphia, Penn., 1988.

Pietrantoni, M., and R. A. Knuppel, "Alcohol Use in Pregnancy", *Clinics in Perinatology*, 1988.

Homosexuality:

Bell, Alan P., and Martin S. Weinberg, *Homosexualities: A Study of Diversity Among Men and Women*, Simon and Schuster, New York, 1978.

Brown, Howard, *Familiar Faces, Hidden Lives: The Story of Homosexual Men in America Today*, Harcourt Brace Janovitch, New York, 1978.

Fay, R. E., and C. F. Turner, and A. D. Klassen, and G. H. Glassen, "Prevalence and Patterns of Same-Gender Sexual Contact among Men", *Science*, 1989.

Hunter, Nan D., and Sherryl E. Michaelson, and Thomas B. Stoddard, *The Rights of Lesbians and Gay Men: The Basic ACLU Guide to a Gay Person's Rights*, 3d ed., Southern Illinois University Press, Carbondale and Edwardsville, Ill., 1992.

Masters, William H., and Virginia E. Johnson, *Homosexuality in Perspective*, Little Brown and Co., Boston, 1989.

Spong, John Selby. *Living in Sin? A Bishop Rethinks Human Sexuality*, Harper and Row Publishers, San Francisco, 1988.

Incest:

Brady, Katherine, *Fathers Days*, Seaview, New York, 1979.

Herman, Judith Lewis, *Father-Daughter Incest*, Harvard University Press, Cambridge, Mass., 1981.

Prostitution:

Bess, Barbara E., and Samuel S. Janus, "Prostitution", in B. J. Sadock, et al (eds.), *The Sexual Experience*, Williams and Wilkins, Baltimore, Md., 1976.

Hollander, Xaviera, *The Happy Hooker, My Own Story*, Dell Publishing Co., Inc., New York, 1972.

Lloyd, Robin, *For Money or Love: Boy Prostitution in America*, Vanguard Press, Inc., New York, 1976.

Winick, Charles, and Paul M. Kinsie, *The Lively Commerce: Prostitution in the United States*, Quadrangle Books, Chicago, Ill., 1971.

Sexual Dysfunctions and Impotence:

Kales, J. D., and E. D. Martin, and T. J. Rohner, Jr., "The Role of the Sleep Laboratory in the Evaluation of Impotence", *Psychiatric Medicine*, vol. IV, no. II, 1987.

Kaplan, Helen Singer, *The New Sex Therapy: Active Treatment of Sexual Dysfunctions*, Brunner and Mazel, New York, 1974.

Leiblum, Sandra R. and Raymond C. Rosen (eds.), *Sexual Desire Disorders*, The Guilford Press, New York, 1988.

Lipshultz, L. I., and S. S. Howards (eds.), *Infertility in the Male*, Mosby-Year Book, Saint Louis, Mo., 1991.

Masters, William H., and Virginia E. Johnson, *Human Sexual Inadequacy*, Little Brown and Co., Boston, Mass., 1970.

Meisler, A.W., and M. P. Carey, "A Critical Reevaluation of Nocturnal Penile Tumescence Monitoring in the Diagnosis of Erectile Dysfunction", *The Journal of Nervous and Mental Disease*, vol. CLXXVIII, no. II, 1990.

Sexual Intercourse:

Sadock, B., and V. Sadock, "Techniques of Coitus", in Sadock, B., and H. Kaplan, and A. Freedman (eds.), *The Sexual Experience*, Williams and Wilkins, Baltimore, Md., 1976.

Westheimer, Ruth, *Dr. Ruth's Guide to Safer Sex*, Warner Books, New York, 1992.

Westheimer, Ruth, and Louis Lieberman, *Dr. Ruth's Guide to Erotic and Sensual Pleasures*, Shapolsky Publishers, New York, 1991.

Zilbergeld, Bernie, *Male Sexuality: A Guide to Sexual Fulfillment*, Little, Brown and Co., Boston, Mass., 1978.

Sexually Transmitted Diseases:

Anagnoston T. N. and C. A. Tehachaypi, *Surviving the AIDS Plague*, American West Publishers, 1991.

Brandt, A. M., *No Magic Bullet: A Social History of Venereal Disease in the United States Since 1880*, Oxford University Press, New York, 1985.

Cohen, P. T., and M. A. Sanda, and P. A. Volberding (eds.), *The AIDS Knowledge Base*, Medical Publishing Group, Waltham, Mass., 1990.

Dienstag J. L., and J. R. Wands, and K. J. Isselbacher, "Acute Hepatitis", in: J. D. Wilson, E. Braunwald K. J. Isselbacher, et al (eds.), *Harrison's Principles of Internal Medicine*, 12th edition. McGraw-Hill, 1991.

Hein, Dr. Karen, and Theresa Foy DiGeronimo, *AIDS: Trading Fears for Facts: A Guide for Young People*, Consumer Reports Books, Yonkers, New York, 1991.

Holmes, K. K., and P. A. Marsh, and P. L. Sparling, et al (eds.), *Sexually Transmitted Diseases*, 2d ed., McGraw-Hill, New York, 1990.

Kaslow, R. A. and D. P. Francis (eds.), *The Epidemiology of AIDS: Expression, Occurrence and*

Control of Human Immunodeficiency Virus Type I Infection, Oxford University Press, NewYork, 1989.

Leibowitch, Jacques, A *Strange Virus of Unknown Origin*, Ballantine Books, New York, 1985.

Sex Studies and Surveys:

Hunt, Morton, *Sexual Behavior in the 1970s*, Playboy Press, Chicago, Ill., 1974.

Janus, Samuel, and S. Cynthia L. Janus, *The Janus Report on Sexual Behavior*, John Wiley and Sons, Inc., New York, 1993.

Kinsey, Alfred C., and Wardell B. Pomeroy, and Clyde E. Martin, *Sexual Behavior in the Human Male*, W. B. Saunders Co., Philadelphia and London, 1948.

Kinsey, Alfred C., and Wardell B. Pomeroy, and Clyde E. Martin, and Paul H. Gebhard, et al, *Sexual Behavior in the Human Female*, W. B. Saunders Co., Philadelphia and London, 1953.

Maslow, Abraham, *Motivation and Personality*, Harper and Row Publishers, Inc., New York, 1987.

Masters, William H., and Virginia E. Johnson, *Human Sexual Response*, Little Brown and Co., Boston, Mass., 1966.

Masters, W.H., and V. E. Johnson, and R. C. Kolodny, *Masters and Johnson on Sex and Human Loving*, Little, Brown and Co., Boston, Mass., 1982.

Sternberg, Robert J., *The Triangle of Love*, Basic Books, New York, 1988.

Women's Issues:

Friday, Nancy, *Women on Top: How Real Life has Changed Women's Sexual Fantasies*, Simon and Schuster, New York, 1991.

Heiman, Julia R., and Joseph L. Piccolo, *Becoming Orgasmic: A Sexual and Personal Growth Program for Women*, Prentice Hall Press, New York, 1988.

Rubin, Lillian B., *Women of a Certain Age: The Midlife Search for Self*, Harper and Row, New York, 1979.

Sarrel, P. M., "Sexuality in Menopause", *Menopause Management*, vol. XI, 1989.

Miscellaneous:

A Tradition of Choice, Planned Parenthood, New York, 1991.

Blumstein, Philip, and Pepper Schwartz, *American Couples: Money, Work, Sex*, William Morrow and Co., New York, 1983.

Britton, Bryce, and Belinda Dumont, *The Love Muscle*, New American Library, New York, 1982.

Dodson, Betty, *Sex for One: The Joy of Self-Loving*, Harmony, New York, 1987.

Fromm, Erich, *The Art of Loving*, The Julian Press, Inc., New York, 1956.

Gosselin, Chris, and Glenn Wilson, *Sexual Variations: Fetishism, Sadomasochism, Transvestism*, Simon and Shuster, New York, 1980.

Green, Richard, *Sexual Science and the Law*, Harvard University Press, Cambridge, Mass., 1992.

Hartman, William E., and Marilyn Fithian, and Donald Johnson, *Nudist Society*, Crown Publishers, New York, 1970.

Jones, E., *The Life and Works of Sigmund Freud* (3 vols.), Basic Books, New York, 1953-1957.

Ladas, Alice Kahy, and Beverly Whipple, and Beverly and John D. Perry, *The G Spot*, Holt, Rinehart, and Winston, New York, 1982.

O'Neill, George, and Nena O'Neill, *Open Marriage: A New Life Style for Couples*, M. Evans, New York, 1972.

Pomeroy, Wardell B., *Dr. Kinsey and the Institute for Sex Research*, Harper and Row Publishers, New York, 1972.

INDEX

This index contains a thorough listing of the many topics covered in this book and where the reader can find more information about them. Bold highlighting indicates that the topic appears as a separate entry in this encyclopedia.

doms; Contraceptive Foams, Creams, and Gels; Safer Sex
NORPLANT → Birth Control
NUDITY → Breasts as Sex Objects; Exhibitionism; Sexual Morality
NURSEMIDWIVES → Midwives
NURSING → Breasts; Induced Labor
NURSING BRASSIERE → Breast-Feeding
NURSING FACILITIES → Aging and Sex
NUTRITION → Pregnancy and Diet
NYMPHOMANIA → Hypersexuality; Nymphomania; Satyriasis

OBESITY → Breast Cancer
OBSCENITY
OBSTETRIC TEAM → Midwives; Sex and the Media
OBSTETRICAN → Birth; Midwives; Newborn Infants; Pregnancy and Diet; Prenatal Care
OCCUPATIONAL ROLES → Sex Roles
ODENT, MICHEL → Natural Childbirth
OEDIPAL STAGE → Oedipus Complex; Psychosexual Stages of Development
OEDIPUS COMPLEX → Electra Complex; Freud, Sigmund
OIL GLANDS → Acne
OILS → Erogenous Zones
ONOFF VALVE → Vasectomy and the Male Pill
ONANISM → Masturbation
ONE-NIGHT STANDS → Affairs
ONEIDA COMMUNITY → Swingers
OOCYTE → Menstruation; Ovaries
OPPORTUNISTIC PATHOGEN → AIDS
OPTHALMIA NEONATORUM → Gonorrhea and Chlamydia
ORAL CONTRACEPTIVES → Birth Control; Condoms; Endometriosis; Norplant; Oral Contraceptives; Ovarian Cancer; Pelvic Inflammatory Disease; Planned Parenhood and Margaret Sanger; Premenstrual Syndrome; Sexual Revolution; Teenagers and Sex; Uterine Cancer
ORAL SEX → Cunnilingus; Fellatio; Gonorrhea and Chlamydia; Herpes; Incest; Lesbian Sexual

Techniques; Pregnancy and Sex; Safer Sex; Sixty-Nine; Teenagers and Sex; Virginity
ORAL STAGE → Freud, Sigmund; Psychosexual Stages of Development
ORAL TRACT INFECTION → Herpes
ORCHITIS → Gonorrhea and Chlamydia
ORGASM → Afterglow; Anorgasmia; Autoeroticism; Birth Control Myths; Children Sexuality; Clitoris; Cunnilingus; Ejaculation; Faking Orgasm; Foreplay; Freud, Sigmund; Kegel Exercises; Lesbian Sexual Techniques; Masturbation; Menstruation; Moment of Inevitability; Nocturnal Emissions; Oral Sex; Orgasm, Multiple; Penis; Pregnancy and Sex; Resolution Phase; Sadism/Masochism; Sex and Headache; Sex Therapy; Sexual Dysfunction Female; Sexual Dysfunction Male; Sexual Intercourse; Sixty-Nine; Sperm; Teenagers and Sex; Transsexuality; Vibrators
ORGASM DIFFICULTIES → Sex Therapy; Sexual Dysfunction Female
ORGASM DYSFUNCTION → Vibrators
ORGASM, MULTIPLE
ORGASM PHASE → Sexual Response Cycle
ORGASMIC DIFFICULTIES → Masturbation
ORGASMIC FUNCTIONING → Sex Surrogates
ORGASMIC RESPONSE → Lack of Sexual Interest
ORGASMIC STAGE → Orgasm
OSCILLATORS → Vibrators
OSTEOPOROSIS → Castration; Estrogen; Hormone Replacement Therapy; Hysterectomy; Menopause
OUTERCOURSE → Teenagers and Sex
OUTING → Coming Out
OVA (EGGS) → Adolescence; Sterilization
OVARIAN CANCER → Breast Cancer; Oral Contraceptives; Ovarian Cancer
OVARIAN CYCLE → Menstruation
OVARIAN FOLLICLE → Menstruation

OVARIES → Castration; Ectopic Pregnancy; Endometriosis; Estrogen; Fallopian Tubes; Female Sex Organs; Hysterectomy; In Vitro Fertilization; Menopause; Menstruation; Oral Contraceptives; Ovarian Cancer; Pelvic Examination; Pituitary Gland and Hormone Secretion; Progesterone; Sterilization; Uterus
OVERSEXED → Nymphomania
OVULATION → Artifical Insemination by Donor; Conception; Embryo/Fetus And Development; Endometriosis; Female Sex Organs; Natural Family Planning; Oral Contraceptives; Ovarian Cancer; Premenstrual Syndrome; Uterus
OVULATION DISORDERS → Infertility
OXYTOCIN → Abortion; Induced Labor; Pregnancy and Sex
OYSTERS → Aphrodisiacs

PADS → Tampons, Pads, and Sponges
PAIN → Sadism/Masochism
PAIN CONTROL → Birth
PAIN RELIEF → Epidual Pain Relief During Labor
PAINFUL INTERCOURSE → Sex Therapy; Sexual Dysfunction Female
PAINLESS CHILDBIRTH → Natural Childbirth
PAIRBONDING → Heterosexuality
PALPATION → Breast Self Examination; Pelvic Examination
PANCREAS → Hormones
PANDERERS → Prostitution
PAP SMEAR → Pap Test
PAP TEST → Bisexuality; Cervical Cancer; Cervix; Estrogen; Genital Warts; High Risk Pregnancy; Menopause; Pap Test; Pelvic Examination; Prenatal Care; Uterine Cancer
PAPANICOLAOU, DR. GEORGE → Pap Test
PAPAVERINE → Paraplegics and Sex
PARAPHILIA → Dominance and Submission; Hypersexuality
PARAPLEGIA → Paraplegics and Sex
PARAPLEGICS AND SEX → Handicapped Persons and Sex
PARASITES → Sexually Transmitted Diseases